RED LIGHT LABOUR

SEX WORK REGULATION, AGENCY, AND RESISTANCE

Edited by Elya M. Durisin,
Emily van der Meulen, and
Chris Bruckert

UBCPress · Vancouver · Toronto

27 26 25 24 23 22 21   5 4

Printed in Canada on FSC-certified ancient-forest-free paper (100% post-consumer recycled) that is processed chlorine- and acid-free.

978-0-7748-3823-8 (hardcover)
978-0-7748-3824-5 (pbk.)
978-0-7748-3825-2 (PDF)
978-0-7748-3826-9 (EPUB)
978-0-7748-3827-6 (mobi)

Cataloguing-in-publication data for this book is available from Library and Archives Canada.

Canada

UBC Press gratefully acknowledges the financial support for our publishing program of the Government of Canada (through the Canada Book Fund), the Canada Council for the Arts, and the British Columbia Arts Council.

This book has been published with the help of a grant from the Canadian Federation for the Humanities and Social Sciences, through the Awards to Scholarly Publications Program, using funds provided by the Social Sciences and Humanities Research Council of Canada.

Printed and bound in Canada by Friesens
Set in Segoe and Warnock by Apex CoVantage, LLC
Copy editor: Robert Lewis
Proofreader: Kristy Lynn Hankewitz
Indexer: Susan Brown
Cover designer: Will Brown

UBC Press
The University of British Columbia
2029 West Mall
Vancouver, BC V6T 1Z2
www.ubcpress.ca

This book is dedicated to the generations of sex workers who have fought for sex worker rights. The conversations we have today are their legacy.

Contents

Foreword

Knowing that I am a long-time sex worker and advocate for sex worker rights, people often tell me they would not want their daughter to work in the sex industry, and they ask me how I would feel if a daughter of mine decided to. My reply is that perhaps your daughter (or son) already is a sex worker and you just don't know it. And if so, do you want her to work in dangerous conditions and to be stigmatized and deprived of basic rights because you disagree with or are ashamed of her choice? Instead, I think you would want her to have a safe work environment with access to legal and labour protections, free from discrimination. This is what the sex worker rights movement has been fighting for.

As one of the three plaintiffs in the constitutional challenge to Canada's prostitution laws in *Canada (Attorney General) v. Bedford, Lebovitch and Scott,* I thought sex workers were getting close to realizing our human and labour rights when the Supreme Court unanimously ruled in our favour on December 20, 2013. The court effectively declared sex workers to be persons deserving of the same rights and protections as all other Canadians. But it was not to be; the problem was the timing. When we launched the challenge on March 20, 2007, we thought it would take the usual nine to ten years to wind its way through the three levels of courts. Instead, for reasons outside of our control, the case "raced" through in just under seven years. After the ruling, the federal Conservative government under Prime Minister Steven Harper had just enough time before the next election to play political football with our lives. The Harper government introduced and passed a regressive, multilayered anti-prostitution act less than one year after the Supreme Court's landmark decision.

Despite this major legislative setback, *Canada (Attorney General) v. Bedford* (2013) changed and emboldened our community. We now know that freedom is a real possibility, and we are not letting that go. Instead of admitting defeat and accepting this new form of criminalization, sex workers in Canada are organizing like never before. Many more of us are speaking out and writing about our work and lives. We are fed up with prohibitionists, religious fundamentalists, and politicians using our lives for political gain.

The sex worker rights movement is not limited to Canada. There are now at least 237 sex worker rights organizations in over seventy countries worldwide.[1] This is a first in history. Importantly, even with our different social and geographic contexts, we all oppose the criminalization and legal oppression of sex work. It is unusual to have hundreds of thousands of independently minded people of differing cultures, languages, and religions agree on anything. This growing global movement demonstrates sex workers' commitment and resilience in the face of adversity. Together, we fight against police raids, the violence of the rescue industry, and predators who take advantage of the prohibitionist laws against us. With new and ever-changing technology, we communicate with each other on a regular basis. As I have been a sex worker and rights activist for the past thirty-two years, it is a joy to see and hear so many more sex worker voices locally and around the globe.

The laws regulating sex work are important, not just in an obvious way for what they prohibit but also for the conditions they create and their influence on how sex workers are perceived. When discussing any group other than sex workers, people intuitively understand that there is a direct connection between what the law says about a group of people and how individuals of that group are treated. Canada did not go to hell in a handbasket when the homophobic gross indecency law was removed, when abortion was decriminalized, or when spousal rape was recognized as a criminal offence; our society is better for having taken these steps. This country would likewise be a better place if we decriminalized sex work. Decriminalization views sex work as the legitimate occupation that it is and argues that sex workers' legal, civil, and occupational rights should be entrenched in law. New Zealand decriminalized sex work in 2003, and there is ample evidence that this system works best for everyone. Decriminalization also includes quite a number of responsibilities for sex workers, and we have no issue honouring obligations based on fairness and logic.

Red Light Labour: Sex Work Regulation, Agency, and Resistance comprises twenty-six intelligent and passionate chapters from different experiences and perspectives. This book will put to rest any misconceptions that sex workers do not have the capacity to make their own choices. It documents the harms that shame-based laws can cause as well as sex workers' efforts to resist and challenge the anti-prostitution regime that has developed in Canada. You will learn of the resilience and determination of female, male, and trans sex workers as they lay bare prohibitionists' tactics in the war against us. You will learn why it is important that we gain our legal, civil, and occupational rights: the right to work in safe and clean environments; the right to share information with one another and, if we want, the right to work together; the right to be free of discrimination in housing, by financial institutions, and at border crossings; and the right not to lose our children because of our occupation. We long for the day when we are casually asked, "What do you do?" and we can say, "sex work," without being ridiculed or, worse, pitied.

After reading the following pages, you will be far better informed on sex work than most people in Canada. If you wish to help us, I ask you to stand with us. When you hear misinformation about our work and lives and when you hear insulting comments, speak out and defend us. As comprehensive as this book is, no book can cover everything. If you need help understanding a point, find other resources written by sex workers or search for information on the website of your local sex worker rights organization. There is a wealth of information at your fingertips that is produced by sex workers, both in this book and online. Listening to and learning from those of us with experience is the best way to support us.

Wishing you an arrest-free day,

Valerie Scott

Note

1 See, for example, the list of organizations led by sex workers that are signatories of the Global Network of Sex Work Projects' "Statement of Support for Amnesty International," which regards its policy on decriminalization, dated July 29, 2015, at http://www.nswp.org/resource/nswp-statement-support-amnesty-international.

Acknowledgments

In what follows, we build on the lengthy history of sex workers' struggle for human and labour rights in Canada and around the world. In particular, we would like to acknowledge the contributions of Terri-Jean Bedford, Amy Lebovitch, and Valerie Scott. These courageous activists spent years in the courts challenging unjust and harmful laws in an effort to improve sex workers' lives. That the government introduced the repressive Protection of Communities and Exploited Persons Act in response to their historic Supreme Court of Canada win of 2013 does not diminish their contribution. Also important are the hundreds of sex worker activists and allies who work tirelessly for sex worker rights and agitate for systemic improvements. As editors, we are proud to consider ourselves members of a dynamic, creative, and courageous community fighting for social and economic justice.

We are similarly proud to be part of a vibrant network of scholars conducting research that challenges dominant discourses and examines the laws, policies, and practices that condition the personal and professional lives of sex workers. We follow in the footsteps of John Lowman and Frances Shaver, researchers we deeply respect and admire, who laid the groundwork for critical sex work studies in Canada. In this book, we endeavour to pay homage to the important contributions of scholars and sex work activists, as well as the many scholar-activists who straddle both roles. Chapter authors are themselves members of diverse activist and scholarly communities, and we are extremely grateful to them for generously sharing their knowledge and wisdom – and for their patience during the editing process!

We are also grateful to those who helped as we developed the book, including the anonymous reviewers, who provided knowledgeable commentary and feedback; the staff at UBC Press who supported and guided us through the process; and to both Ryerson University and the University of Ottawa for providing financial support for the index. More specifically, Elya would like to thank Benson and Lucy for their unconditional support and enduring patience. Emily is indebted to Rob for the decade of hilarity and solidarity; long may it continue. And Chris thanks Sasha, Odin, and "Frosty" for their innumerable acts of encouragement – both small and large.

RED LIGHT LABOUR

1

Contextualizing Sex Work

————— Challenging Discourses and Confronting
Narratives

ELYA M. DURISIN, EMILY VAN DER MEULEN, AND CHRIS BRUCKERT

In recent years, we have witnessed major and unanticipated changes in the criminal regulation of prostitution in Canada, most notably the introduction of Bill C-36, the Protection of Communities and Exploited Persons Act (PCEPA), in 2014, which specifically criminalized the purchase of sexual services for the first time in Canadian history. This shift occurred within a broader context characterized by prostitution law reform in numerous countries over the past two decades, with the criminalization of those who obtain sexual services emerging as the new regulatory framework governing prostitution transnationally. Against this backdrop, discourses that frame sex work as violence against women and that locate state actors and police as agents of protection or salvation contradict sex workers' own narratives and analyses that centre human rights violations as rooted in social stigma, discrimination, and the criminalization of their lives and work.

Alongside these developments, we have also seen the continued mobilization of the global sex worker rights movement and the expansion of research on the sex industry that is rights-based, driven by sex workers, and challenges not only the legal regime but also popular understandings of sex work victimization (recent publications from the Canadian context include Benoit et al., 2014, 2016; Bowen, Bungay, and Zangger, 2015; Bruckert and Law, 2013; Bruckert and Parent, 2018; Ferris, 2015; Hannem and Tigchelaar, 2016; Krüsi et al., 2014; Lyons et al., 2017; Parent et al., 2013; Shannon et al., 2015; van der Meulen, Durisin, and Love, 2013). Situated within the emerging and evolving field of sex work studies, this edited collection contributes to the scholarly literature that critiques conventional discourses on sex work and is a reflection of the rapid growth of a robust global movement actively advancing sex worker rights and justice. The chapters that comprise the collection highlight the range of actors, approaches, and perspectives found within the movement today. They showcase cross-disciplinary research from diverse contributors, including established scholars, student researchers, community activists, and sex workers; many of the authors occupy more than one of these positionalities, illustrating a fluidity between advocate, researcher, and researched.

An important factor in theorizations on sex work is the words used to describe it. For the purposes of this collection, we use the language of "sex work" and "sex worker" to connote a demand for social and economic justice for some of the world's most marginalized and stigmatized workers. As Kempadoo (1998) explains, "The idea of the sex worker is inextricably related to struggles for the recognition of women's work, for basic human rights and for decent working conditions" (p. 3). As we will explore further below, framing sex work as work broadens the conversation to include dancers in strip clubs, porn actors, phone sex operators, webcam workers, erotic massage providers, street-based sex workers, and in-call and out-call escorts, among many others. Reflecting the subject position of industry workers, the "sex-work-is-work" paradigm gained purchase as sex workers organized in what has become an international sex worker rights movement (see NSWP, 2013).

Despite its undeniable importance for both advocacy efforts and redefining commercial sexual labour as legitimate work, we recognize that "sex work" also has practical and theoretical limitations. The emergence of "sex worker" as an identity category may exclude those who do not consider what they do to be a form of labour. As many aspects of sex work are criminalized and profoundly stigmatized, often falling outside of dominant norms surrounding respectable feminine sexual behaviour, there are incentives to distance one's activities from the category of work. Framing sex work as work may also serve to elide the experiences of those for whom the sale or exchange of sex is not experienced as a labour activity or is perhaps experienced as a form of harm. It thus risks glossing over the wide diversity of sexual and economic relationships that exist within commercial and/or personal contexts. Although we acknowledge these limitations, "sex work" remains a central conceptual framework unifying this collection. The term "prostitution," however, is also used when particular policies, such as specific case law or sections of the Criminal Code, are being analyzed or when it is historically relevant. Further, some sex workers employ the words "prostitution" or "prostitute" to describe their labour activities. Thus the use of "prostitute" and "prostitution" in this collection signals the ongoing relevance of these terms for legal, policy, and personal matters.

With the significance of language in mind, we begin this chapter with a brief introduction to the common legislative frameworks, each with particular goals and objectives, that govern and regulate sex work in most international contexts: criminalization, which includes both full and asymmetrical criminalization, and regulation through legalization or decriminalization. Through an exploration of these frameworks and their objectives, we can better understand how and why the Canadian policy context developed the way that it did. Next, we engage in a more fulsome discussion of sexual labour, locating it within a "sex-work-is-work" paradigm, which acknowledges both the range of experiences of people in the industry and the diverse activities in which they engage. We then examine some of the challenges of the sexual labour framework, especially when conditions of coercion or duplicity are involved. Here, we advocate for social and economic justice for sex workers, regardless of occupational activity, social positioning, or geographic location. Finally, we introduce the collection itself, highlighting its tripartite structure – law and policy contexts, diverse experiences, and sex workers' resistance – and the various chapters that explore sex work in Canada, each contributing unique scholarly and/or experiential knowledge.

Legislative Frameworks and Objectives

The ways that sex work is conceptualized have a direct impact on how it is governed. In international contexts, policy approaches to sex work have tended either to criminalize sex industry activities and the people involved through various criminal law provisions or to regulate it through labour, public health, or other policies. Of course, there is also significant variability within criminalized and regulated contexts. For example, although all criminalized regimes are inherently prohibitionist (i.e., they endeavour to eradicate the industry through the application of punitive criminal laws), the term can apply to jurisdictions where only some aspects of sex work are criminalized as well as jurisdictions where virtually all are. Previous to the Supreme Court's decision in *Canada (Attorney General) v. Bedford* (2013),[1] which is discussed throughout the collection, Canadian criminal laws on sex

work were aimed at virtually all of the parties involved in the sale and purchase of sexual services (e.g., sex workers, clients, drivers, third-party managers, and establishment owners/operators), as well as the locations where
the sale and purchase occurred. While some politicians and others have
suggested that the implementation of PCEPA in 2014 alleviated the criminal
sanctions aimed at sex workers, who were described in many instances as
victims of the commercial sexual exchange, the present legal framework is
still one where criminalization reigns supreme.

Currently, the Criminal Code prohibits sex workers from communicating in specified public spaces, as well as stopping, or attempting to stop, a
motor vehicle or impeding the free flow of pedestrians or traffic for the purposes of offering sexual services (s. 213). Purchasing sex is against the law,
no matter whether it occurs in public or private locations (s. 286.1), and
receiving material benefit in the context of a "commercial enterprise that
offers sexual services for consideration" (s. 286.2) is criminalized. The laws
against procuring a person to offer or provide sexual services (s. 286.3) make
it illegal to have a manager or employer arrange a sex worker's appointments
with clients. Further, web hosts and others who advertise sexual services can
face stiff penalties (s. 286.4); sex workers, however, are indemnified from
prosecution in advertising their own services (s. 286.5). This framework of
criminalization thus positions sex workers and the sex industry as both a
public threat and a public nuisance, with the laws used to penalize perceived
disturbances to social order (see the Appendix for text of the key anti-
prostitution sections of the Criminal Code). The current legal context is not
an improvement to the pre-*Bedford* era; indeed, beause of the layers of additional Criminal Code provisions, it may be worse.

In many ways, Canada has followed other criminalized jurisdictions that
have targeted their criminal laws most directly at certain parties and activities. In Sweden, for example, clients and managers are criminalized, but in
most instances sex workers are not. Some have referred to this as asymmetrical criminalization to connote both the philosophy and the specific legal
characteristics and asymmetrical application of the regime. In the Swedish
context, sex workers are understood to be the victims of male sexual exploitation (Ekberg, 2004; Scibelli, 1987). Thus, in an effort to protect them from
the perceived harms of the sex industry, this prohibitionist approach targets
those who purchase sexual services as well as the third parties who are
involved in managerial and other facilitative roles. Implemented in 1999,
Sweden's law is aimed at eradicating the sex industry by penalizing those
who are seen to benefit from it (e.g., "johns," "pimps," and "traffickers"),

while "saving" the sex-working victims through exiting strategies. We saw this rhetoric advanced in Canada when PCEPA was being introduced. Yet, as noted above, the Canadian government has continued to maintain aspects of criminalization aimed at sex workers.

The Swedish model has been strongly advocated for by anti-prostitution and radical feminist groupings, often referring to themselves as "abolitionists" in their efforts to liken sex work to sexual slavery. In this collection, however, we avoid the term "abolitionist" and are judicious in our use of the term "feminist," radical or otherwise, in reference to this legislative framework and those who support it. As editors, we perceive it to be an irreconcilable contradiction to advocate for policy approaches in the name of feminism that have been empirically proven to cause harm to sex-working women and that current sex workers – the population most affected by such policies – have vocally opposed. In our view, although there are numerous branches, traditions, and ideological positions within feminist theory and politics, some of which espouse conflicting views, it is untenable to support the criminalization of aspects of sex work when it is known to result in serious harms and violations of human rights.

As chapters in this collection show, by declaring themselves to be abolitionists and by mobilizing the affective language of the movement to end chattel slavery, prohibitionists have drawn on highly emotive and controversial language to describe the commercial sex industry and those who work within it (for example, as prostituted women who are bought and sold as sexual slaves and who suffer from post-traumatic stress disorder). This strategy has been highly successful in shifting both the public perception of sex work and the legislative and policy objectives surrounding it. Intended to evoke sympathy for victims of abuse and to prompt anger toward male perpetrators of violence, the terminology is not only misleading but often also makes "sweeping claims not supported by empirical studies" (Weitzer, 2005b, p. 212) and "is designed for maximum shock value" (Weitzer, 2005a, p. 935). Yet prohibitionists' passionate zeal for the topic has influenced a growing number of countries to incorporate their perspectives into legislation, including Finland, Iceland, Ireland, Norway, Scotland, and Sweden.

Such legislative approaches rely on carceral systems, policing efforts, and criminal justice intervention to criminalize sex workers' labour relationships and clients. Internationally, these prohibitionists tend to be highly politically organized and are often aligned with conservative religious ideologies and institutions (Bernstein, 2001). In their arguments in support of criminalizing the "demand side" of prostitution, however, they have neglected nuanced analyses and disregarded discussions of sex worker agency and self-determination (see Barry, 1979, 1995; Dworkin, 2004; Farley, 2004; Farley and Barkan, 1998). Interestingly, proponents of asymmetrical criminalization sometimes refer to it as decriminalization, as they suggest that sex workers are decriminalized (e.g., Baptie, Falle, Perrier, and Walker, 2014, p. 2). We contend that this likely intentional misuse of the term "decriminalization" not only obscures the ways that sex workers continue to be criminalized in these regimes (e.g., cited for contempt when they refuse to provide evidence in court or charged as third parties when they assist a colleague) but also obfuscates the harms that result from criminalizing clients. As a result, this policy approach fits squarely within a criminalization framework (see Amnesty International, 2016b).

True decriminalization can be found in New Zealand, which opted for a regulatory approach that upholds and advances the rights and dignity of sex workers. New Zealand introduced the Prostitution Reform Act in 2003, with the explicit goal to "safeguard the human rights of sex workers and protect them from exploitation" (s. 3a, 3b), relying on labour and public health policies, among others, to regulate the sex industry (Abel, 2014; Abel, Fitzgerald, Healy, and Taylor, 2010). Like the variability within criminalized systems, however, regulatory approaches are also not homogenous. Whereas decriminalization, discussed in further detail below, is the preferred framework of sex workers and their allies, other regulatory models, such as legalization, have been deemed problematic. The key differentiation is how sex workers and the sex industry are conceptualized.

In a legalized context, sex work is simultaneously understood to be a necessary, if unfortunate, reality and a public nuisance. Unlike criminalization, where sex work – and sometimes workers as well – is seen as a social evil or social ill that needs to be eradicated by punishing third parties and those seeking services, and unlike decriminalization, where sex work is a form of labour and sex worker rights are central, the legalization framework perceives sex work as a necessary evil that requires strict rules to keep it under control (Shaver, 1985; Wijers, 2001). In this way, sex work is conceptualized as an intractable problem that warrants often excessive regulation to reduce the most undesirable effects. The best-known examples of regulation through legalization include the Netherlands, Germany, and Nevada in the United States.

In legalized systems, discussions of prostitution are often underscored by a distinction between forced and voluntary sex work: forced workers are generally understood to be victims of trafficking or of exploitative third parties, whereas voluntary workers are those who willingly choose the work. Some have argued that this characterization is imbued with gendered and racialized assumptions of guilt and innocence, such that the sex work of middle-class, white women is much more likely than that of working-class and/or racialized women to be deemed voluntary rather than forced (Ditmore, 2005; Doezema, 1998). Others have drawn attention to the strict penalties that are applied to those who violate various laws and bylaws, and they have critiqued legalized contexts as being overly onerous (Scibelli, 1987; Wijers, 2001). Moreover, due to the restrictions associated with legalization, as well as the exclusion of sex workers without citizenship or national status from the regulated sector, it is not uncommon for people to opt to work illegally in underground areas out of state view (Chapkis, 1997; Sullivan, 2010; see also Hydra e.V., 2015).

This regulatory approach is in contrast to decriminalization, which focuses on enabling sex workers to access their human rights and is supported internationally by those sex workers and allies who define sex work as a form of legitimate and socially valuable labour (NSWP, 2013). Contrary to legalization, where onerous polices and heavy state intervention attempt to manage and control the industry, decriminalized contexts remove prostitution-related offences from criminal law and instead rely on labour and health policies to regulate activities and to establish rights and protections for workers. Although sex workers are still protected by and subject to the criminal law in all work-related, private, and public activities, with decriminalization, sex workers enjoy improved workplace conditions and benefits as defined by employment standards and occupational health and safety provisions (Abel, 2014; Abel et al., 2010; Bindman, 1998).

Those who argue against decriminalization, such as prohibitionists who support the criminalization of clients, often claim that without criminal laws to protect them from exploitative "pimps," sex workers would be left vulnerable to violence. However, with decriminalization, workplace harms and grievances can be adjudicated under more appropriate federal, provincial, or municipal policies. For instance, in Canada there are existing Criminal Code provisions that protect against extortion, sexual assault, forcible confinement, and threat with a weapon, crimes that prohibitionists claim are inherent to sex work. In addition, provincial labour laws regulate aspects of employer-employee relationships and can protect against problematic managers or supervisors and unfair labour conditions. Businesses causing public disturbances, such as brothels, can face municipal fines and even forced closure if operating outside of designated zones. Indeed, in a decriminalized system, brothels and other commercial sex establishments would have to abide by the rules, regulations, and standards imposed on other businesses. Street solicitation, like many other public and outdoor activities, can be subject to nuisance, loitering, littering, and trespassing laws where appropriate. Regulation in the decriminalized context is established to support sex workers and communities. In a decriminalized system, sex workers could be eligible for worker's compensation, health and disability insurance, and statutory holidays under employment standards and occupational health and safety acts. They could also organize into unions, guilds, and associations to protect their labour rights with greater ease. Since decriminalizing its sex industry in 2003, New Zealand has seen an improvement in sex workers' access to labour protections (Abel, 2014; Abel et al., 2010) and enhanced relationships with law enforcement (Armstrong, 2017).

The Sex-Work-Is-Work Paradigm

Locating sex work as a form of labour not only challenges embedded stigmatic assumptions of deviance, immorality, and pathology but also opens a rich analytic point of entry to think through the issues explored in this collection, and indeed there are now many decades worth of literature advancing this paradigm (early examples include Bell, 1987; Chapkis, 1997; Stein, 1974). The writing of socialist feminist Thanh-Dam Truong (1990) has been influential in theorizing sexual work as a productive labour category and in empiricizing the value of sex workers' contributions to the economy. Others have similarly applied labour theory to the analysis of sex work (e.g., Bruckert and Parent, 2013; Law, 2016) or have used the concept of care work as a point of entry to think through the work of sex work (Rivers-Moore, 2016). Much of this scholarship builds on Hochschild's (1983) concept of emotional labour, drawing parallels to the deep and surface acting required in many service-sector jobs (e.g., Bernstein, 2007; Bruckert, 2002; Sanders, 2005; van der Meulen, 2010, 2012). In short, understanding sex work as a form of labour enables connections to be drawn between it and other forms of emotional, caring, and/or service work, as well as – importantly – between the working conditions and experiences of those employed in these respective industries. Such labour-based analyses support the argument that violence and other forms of criminal exploitation are not inherent features of sex work. Instead, they are produced by structural factors, including legal regimes that criminalize prostitution and illegalize migrants, the capitalist organization of the labour process, and gendered and racialized devaluations of work.

At the same time as alerting us to commonalities, thinking of sex work as work positions us to tease out nuances. Recognizing the occupational category, rather than job description, pushes us to think about labour processes and practices as well as the complex and varied ways that the work is organized; for example, the experience of independent sex workers who run their own businesses is very different from the work of service providers in massage parlours who are scheduled for shifts and receive a cut of the house fees that clients pay. The occupational category also alerts us to the role of third parties – those individuals who are neither the client nor the sex worker but who are integral to the sex industry, such as drivers, security, receptionists, and agency owners – whose policies, practices, and labour profoundly impact workers (see Bruckert and Law, 2013, 2018). And of course, thinking about sex work as service-sector employment highlights the similarities to consumers of other services; clients in the sex industry are purchasing a service – one that, as a number of authors in this collection demonstrate, may be sexual, erotic, and/or interpersonal (see also Atchison, 2010; Atchison, Vukmirovich, and Burnett, 2015).

Recognizing diversity also allows us to examine the operation of racism, classism, and citizenship within the specific hierarchies of a highly complex sex industry and the ways that sex workers' intersecting social locations affect their labour-related experiences. Histories of colonialism and racism have resulted in the eroticization of women who are considered to be different from the dominant group because of their ethnic, racial, and/or cultural backgrounds (Miller-Young, 2010, 2014; Nagle, 1997; Race and the sex industry, 2011; Raguparan, 2017; Ross, 2009). Kempadoo (1998) explains that this exoticization is as important as economic factors in positioning specific groups of women, particularly racialized women, in sex work.

This idea that sex work is nuanced and diverse is further reflected in the range of experiences of people in the industry. In recent decades, a growing body of literature written by sex workers, including scholarly books and articles as well as novels, blogs, and online magazines, has emerged that highlights the many layers of meaning that sex workers attach to their work (Aimee, Kaiser, and Ray, 2015; Bell, 1987; Dawn, 2010, 2013; Delacoste and Alexander, 1998; Leigh, 2004; Milne, 2005; Oakley, 2007; Sterry and Martin, 2009; see also http://www.eminism.org; https://kwetoday.com; and http://titsandsass.com). As is the case for workers in mainstream labour markets, for many sex workers their job is not *just* work. In addition to being an income-generating activity that allows them to purchase the necessities and sometimes the luxuries of life, sex work may also be an expression of sexuality, a space to explore intimacy, or an act of resistance to heteronormative gender tropes and rigid gendered expectations of respectability.

Social and Economic Justice for Sex Workers

Although the "sex-work-is-work" paradigm is fundamental to establishing and advancing sex worker rights and justice, it is important to include an analysis of situations where there are conditions of force or coercion, highly constrained options, or structural inequalities that limit income-generating options. For some sex workers, there may be a fine line between consent and coercion – or the "acceptable" limits of economic exploitation characteristic of so much precarious work. In the context of global neoliberal capitalism and severe economic and labour inequalities, justice necessitates enabling sex workers to live and work without discrimination based on occupation, race, gender, or sexuality; to access the material necessities of life and economic development; to live free from violence, detention, deportation, and arbitrary interference from the state; and to access healthcare and maintain bodily and sexual autonomy (for a comprehensive discussion of sex work and human rights, see Amnesty International, 2016a; NSWP, 2013). Removing barriers to social and economic justice not only necessitates changing laws and regulations, including those that criminalize sex work, but at a broader level also requires the redistribution of economic and other resources and the creation of conditions that foster social and economic equity.

Importantly, individuals in the sex industry who do not conceptualize their activities as work and those who are in situations of coercion, violence, or severe economic exploitation do not relinquish their entitlement to human rights and protection from harm. As we see in this collection, the penalization of sex work, including criminalization in any form, creates barriers to justice, including for those who may be most marginalized and vulnerable, such as youth or people experiencing trafficking or forced migration. There is abundant evidence to show that laws and policies, like those in Canada, directed toward eradicating prostitution and human trafficking produce widespread human rights violations (Amnesty International, 2016b; GAATW, 2007; Global Commission on HIV and the Law, 2012; Levy and Jakobsson, 2014). Similarly, we see that laws penalizing youth who sell sex are proactively creating harms rather that helping the people that they purport to assist (Bittle, 2013; NSWP, 2016a; Schaffner et al., 2016; WHO, 2015). Seen from this perspective, criminalizing aspects of sex work cannot be thought to improve sex workers' access to justice or quality of life, and indeed there is much to suggest the opposite.

Largely in response to human rights violations, and in an effort to improve their living and working conditions, sex workers around the world have been organizing for many decades; the international sex worker rights movement is now a global phenomenon (see Jeffrey, 2002; Kempadoo and Doezema, 1998; NSWP, 2016b). The movement's demands, such as sexual autonomy and self-determination, access to health information, broader social understandings of prostitution as work, and the eradication of violence against sex workers by state actors and others, are globally supported (see NSWP, 2013). That said, although many sex worker organizations in the Global South articulate their demands through a language of "rights" and "labour," their advocacy efforts speak to the local circumstances of the workers and are not simple reflections of North American or Euro-Western sex worker rights discourses (Kempadoo, 1998). Recognizing the organizing and resistance efforts of sex workers from the Global South challenges the portrayal of these women as homogeneous, ignorant, and easily duped (Mohanty, 1991), constructs that line up easily with discourses on sex slavery and trafficking (Agustín, 2007; Doezema, 2010).

Complicating the dichotomized narrative of the Global North and South are former state socialist countries in central and eastern Europe and in Russia. Fears over organized crime and trafficking in women from post-socialist territories have galvanized the contemporary international legal response to human trafficking (Suchland, 2015). Racialized constructions of legitimate victimhood are visible in the positioning of white women from such jurisdictions as passive and in need of protection (Andrijasevic, 2007) and of postsocialist territories as "lagging" behind the Western world (Koobak and Marling, 2014), highlighting the centrality of both race and imperialism to notions of agency, consent, and victimization.

International sex worker organizing has, importantly, sought to redefine these discourses of human trafficking and to position migrant sex workers as definitive sources of expertise on issues of forced and coerced labour in the global industry. As international attention to prostitution, migration for sex work, and sex tourism continues to increase, so too does sex worker activism against prohibitionist campaigns that largely define sex workers as victims (Pattanaik, 2002). Writers such as Agustín (2007), Andrijasevic (2010), Davies (2009), and Zheng (2010) capture the complexity of the situation of migrant workers in the sex industry, showing how workers' own experiences of labour and migration undermine dominant narratives of trafficking. These authors illustrate how women's migration projects are complex, develop from a variety of motivations and circumstances, and involve varying degrees of agency and coercion.

Introducing the Collection

In the context of recent regulatory shifts in Canada and the expanding Canadian and international sex worker rights movements that continue to challenge dominant discourses and narratives about sex workers' lives, we set out to develop an edited collection that brings together leading and emerging scholars, notable sex worker activists, and key movement allies. Building on an earlier collection by two of the editors, *Selling Sex: Experience, Advocacy, and Research on Sex Work in Canada* (van der Meulen, Durisin, and Love, 2013), this book represents a renewed intervention into, and engagement with, shifting legal and discursive frameworks in Canada. *Red Light Labour* features a small number of revised and updated chapters from *Selling Sex*, which demonstrates the connection between the two books, but we have substantially expanded the variety and diversity of topics presented. Most significantly, the social and legal context in Canada has changed considerably since *Selling Sex* was published five years ago. In what follows, many chapters engage directly with this new context, which includes both the Supreme Court's *Bedford* decision and PCEPA. As an editorial team, and as members of the global sex worker movement with over five decades of combined sex work research and advocacy experiences, we feel that dissemination of the most up-to-date research and discussion of lived experience are important.

Given the centrality of the state in sex workers' lives, we open the collection with a series of chapters that provide an in-depth analysis of the legislative and policy context in Canada, looking specifically at the ways that laws and those who uphold them have constructed, controlled, and criminalized sex workers and their loved ones, as well as their workspaces, colleagues, and clients. Part 1 begins with Emily van der Meulen and Elya M. Durisin's (Chapter 2) examination of the historical trajectory of Canadian prostitution policy from 1860 to the present, providing an overview of changes to federal and municipal regulation. They show how sex workers historically and today, whether conceptualized as victims or as criminals, have been subject to laws that rarely help and instead often result in harm.

Brenda Belak (Chapter 3) follows with an analysis of Canada's most notable legal ruling on sex work: *Canada (Attorney General) v. Bedford* (2013). Drawing on her legal expertise, Belak suggests that by looking at the decisions of the three levels of court, we can see how legal and political discourses on sex work shifted to include an acknowledgment of sex workers' health, safety, and human rights. Also advancing a legal analysis, Naomi Sayers (Chapter 4) explores municipal authority to regulate street-based sex work with a focus on the overrepresentation of Indigenous women in this sector of the industry. Sayers suggests that in the current context, including the National Inquiry into Missing and Murdered Indigenous Women and Girls, a critical examination of municipal bylaws is particularly crucial.

Ummni Khan (Chapter 5) shifts our focus to an analysis of law and policy directed at clients. Here, she contrasts the recent criminalization of the purchase of sexual services in Canada with various time periods when different social constructions of clients prevailed and criminal justice interventions were not perceived to be necessary. Kara Gillies and Chris Bruckert (Chapter 6) consider other key individuals involved in the commercial exchange of sexual services by examining the criminalization of sex workers' partners and third parties. Drawing on primary data from two research projects, their chapter shows that the conceptualization of partners and third parties as always already exploitative and predatory is overly simplistic and fails to account for the diversity of sex workers' experiences and relationships. With the recent changes and additions to Canada's anti–sex work laws, particularly the new provisions aimed at prohibiting advertising, Andrea Sterling's (Chapter 7) primary research with "high-end" escorts demonstrates other impacts of criminalization, such as effects on sex workers' social networks and their ability to communicate with clients. Sterling argues that the new advertising law has engendered a new risk-space for independent sex workers.

The next two chapters likewise draw on primary research to explicate regulatory contexts and impacts. Tamara O'Doherty, Hayli Millar, Alison Clancey, and Kimberly Mackenzie (Chapter 8) critique anti–human trafficking approaches and discourses in their study with criminal justice personnel, specifically Crown prosecutors and defence attorneys. By examining trafficking statistics, reporting practices, prosecutions, and convictions, they expose the exaggerated claims of human trafficking in Canada and show the implications of these misrepresentations for sex work organizations. Frances M. Shaver, John Bryans, and Isabelle Bhola (Chapter 9) similarly interviewed criminal justice personnel, relying specifically on the narratives of regulatory officials such as police and licensing officers as well as elected city and government officials. They examine such officials' views on the governance of sex work, finding variation in the perceptions of and responses to sex workers and the sex industry. Finally, Steven Bittle (Chapter 10) closes the first section of the collection with a look at youth engaged in sex work and various provincial policies aimed at "rescuing" them. From secure care to enhanced child welfare schemes, this chapter critically examines state responses in Alberta, British Columbia, and Manitoba to show how provincial governments individualize youth prostitution and ultimately fail to either protect or help young women.

Part 2 moves from analyses of law and policy to chapters that highlight the diverse and complex experiences of sex workers in Canada. Contributors in this section foreground a range of commercial sexual labour activities as well as the ways that discourses and narratives condition the experiences of selling sex, emphasizing the need to recognize the ever-present interaction between structure and agency in conceptualizations of sex work. The first three chapters present sex workers' personal narratives, illuminating the complex relationships between systems of privilege and oppression that give form to experiences of, and meanings associated with, sex work. Elizabeth James (Chapter 11) shares her perspectives as an Indigenous woman and second-generation sex worker for whom sex work is a way to meet class aspirations and desires for erotic exploration, reconciling her past and present from within the tension of living a life of duality. River Redwood (Chapter 12) complicates the relationship between masculinity and class by drawing on his long career as a male sex worker, sharing his story and dispelling common myths. Victoria Love (Chapter 13) likewise draws on her lengthy career in sex work and discusses subjective identities and investments in relation to her shifting class positionality. Collectively, these theorizations of sex work from the perspective of industry workers complicate the simplistic framing of sex workers as empowered workers, sexual rebels, or hapless victims by shedding light on their complex and contradictory feelings and experiences.

The next chapters foreground the relationship between sex workers and the social, economic, and political structures in which they work. Menaka Raguparan (Chapter 14) explores the experiences of racialized and Indigenous sex workers, unpacking the complex interactions between race, class, sexuality, and the capitalist market place. Marginalized within the normative labour market, racialized and Indigenous workers employ specifically raced and classed strategies to position themselves within the sex industry and paradoxically obtain economic rewards denied to them in their other economic roles. Nora Butler Burke (Chapter 15) bases her analysis in the everyday lived experiences of migrant trans women in Montreal, showing the intersection of criminal and immigration laws and how they function to regulate and control migrant sex workers. Andrea Krüsi, Brenda Belak, and Sex Workers United Against Violence (Chapter 16) present primary research on police enforcement strategies in Vancouver targeting the purchasers of sexual services and conclude that the criminalization and policing of clients creates negative outcomes for street-based sex workers' working conditions, health, and safety.

The last chapters of this section move to an examination of sex work in smaller centres and rural contexts, exploring the influence of geographic location. Stacey Hannem's (Chapter 17) research in a working-class region of Ontario describes the unique elements that condition sex work in this location and offers critical reflections about the role of drugs and third parties more broadly. Laura Winters and Gayle MacDonald (Chapter 18) provide an analysis of sex work in Newfoundland and Labrador, showing how social and geographic proximity, wilful blindness to the existence of sex work, and stigma based on cultural and religious understandings condition experiences of sex work in the province.

Whereas chapters in Part 2 challenge stereotypes and dominant discourses on sex work through powerful counternarratives, Part 3 moves on to consider some of the tactics employed, successes realized, and difficulties encountered by sex workers as they challenge legal repression and social/civic exclusion. While acknowledging the successes of the national sex workers rights movement in Canada, the chapters also serve to highlight the paradox that many ostensibly progressive social justice groups (e.g., organized labour and feminists) fail to align with, or actively work against, the efforts of sex workers to realize their human, labour, and social rights. The section starts with Mariana Valverde's (Chapter 19) critical examination of mainstream feminist engagement with sex work law reform. Reflecting on both the 1980s "sex wars" and more recent mobilization, she unpacks the failure of the women's movement to positively impact sex work policy. Like Valverde's cautionary tale, Becki Ross's (Chapter 20) contribution considers lost opportunities, examining why, in spite of their shared histories of persecution as "sexual outlaws," the potential allegiance between gay liberationists and "whorganizers" never materialized. The rise of whitened, neoliberal homonormativity and "gaybourhoods" that Ross examines is also at the heart of Morgan Page's observations (Chapter 21). Page brings her insights as a trans sex worker rights activist to the conversation, demonstrating how the decriminalization of homosexuality, anti–sex work laws, and gay gentrification coalesce in the struggle over trans sex workers' occupation of public space.

Exclusion is also a central theme for Robyn Maynard (Chapter 22), who critiques anti–sex work prohibitionists for appropriating the imagery and language of slavery to support policies that criminalize and further exacerbate the harms experienced by Black women in general and by those with perceived or real involvement in the sex industry in particular. The next chapter, by Elene Lam and Chanelle Gallant (Chapter 23), considers sex workers' exclusion from a different point of entry, arguing that because of isolation, racism, language differences, and anti-immigrant xenophobia, migrant sex workers' voices are absent from conversations about sex worker rights. Drawing on their experiences establishing North America's first grassroots organization of sex workers, migrants, and allies, they highlight the importance of, and strategies for, working with migrant sex workers.

The final three chapters of the collection examine the Canadian sex worker rights movement more specifically. Jenn Clamen and Kara Gillies (Chapter 24) consider organized labour's engagement in sex worker rights, asking where Canada's labour unions were during the *Bedford v. Canada* Charter challenge. Kerry Porth (Chapter 25) focuses on movement mobilization in the policy realm in response to PCEPA. She lays bare the stigma, discredit, and disrespect that sex workers encountered when they bravely spoke "truth to power" in the House of Commons and Senate hearings on the new legislation. The closing contribution by Sarah Beer (Chapter 26) documents the emergence of the national sex worker rights movement itself. It is fitting that the collection concludes by celebrating the resistance, resilience, and tenacity of generations of sex worker rights activists – the brave people who paved the way for the conversations we are having today.

Notes

This chapter includes updated and reprinted material from an earlier publication: van der Meulen, E., Durisin, E.M., and Love, V. (2013). Introduction. In E. van der Meulen, E.M., Durisin, & V. Love (Eds.), *Selling sex: Experience, advocacy, and research on sex work in Canada* (pp. 1–25). Vancouver, BC: UBC Press.

1 The strategic litigation initiated by Terri-Jean Bedford, Amy Lebovitch, and Valerie Scott in 2007 resulted in three different court cases, each of which is referenced differently. The first, presided over by Justice Susan Himel of the

Ontario Superior Court of Justice, is known as *Bedford v. Canada* (2010). The subsequent decision by the Court of Appeal for Ontario is referred to as *Canada (Attorney General) v. Bedford* (2012). Finally, the decision by the Supreme Court of Canada, which is the case most frequently referenced in this collection, is *Canada (Attorney General) v. Bedford* (2013). Many of the chapters refer to the legislative process as a whole as *Bedford v. Canada* or simply *Bedford*.

References

Abel, G. (2014). A decade of decriminalization: Sex work 'down under' but not underground. *Criminology and Criminal Justice, 14*(5), 580–92. https://doi.org/10.1177/1748895814523024

Abel, G., Fitzgerald, L., Healy, C., & Taylor, A. (2010). *Taking the crime out of sex work: New Zealand sex workers' fight for decriminalization.* Bristol, UK: Policy Press.

Agustín, L.M. (2007). *Sex at the margins: Migration, labour markets and the rescue industry.* New York, NY: Zed Books.

Aimee, R., Kaiser, E., & Ray, R. (2015). *$pread: The best of the magazine that illuminated the sex industry and started a media revolution.* New York, NY: Feminist Press.

Amnesty International (2016a). *Amnesty International policy on state obligations to respect, protect and fulfil the human rights of sex workers.* Retrieved from https://www.amnesty.org/en/documents/pol30/4062/2016/en/

Amnesty International. (2016b). *The human cost of 'crushing' the market: Criminalisation of sex work in Norway.* London, UK: Amnesty International.

Andrijasevic, R. (2007). Beautiful dead bodies: Gender, migration and representation in anti-trafficking campaigns. *Feminist Review, 86*(1), 24–44. https://doi.org/10.1057/palgrave.fr.9400355

Andrijasevic, R. (2010). *Migration, agency, and citizenship in sex trafficking.* New York, NY: Palgrave Macmillan. https://doi.org/10.1057/9780230299139

Armstrong, L. (2017). From law enforcement to protection? Interactions between sex workers and police in a decriminalized street-based sex industry. *British Journal of Criminology, 57*(3), 570–88. https://doi.org/10.1093/bjc/azw019

Atchison, C. (2010). *Report of preliminary findings for Johns' Voice: A study of adult Canadian sex buyers.* Retrieved from https://www.researchgate.net/publication/284371948_Report_of_the_Preliminary_Findings_for_Johns%27_Voice_A_Study_of_Adult_Canadian_Sex_Buyers

Atchison, C., Vukmirovich, D., & Burnett, P. (2015). *A report of the preliminary findings for Team Grant Project 4 – Sex, safety and security: A study of experiences of people who pay for sex in Canada.* Retrieved from https://www.researchgate.net/publication/281592683_A_Report_of_the_Preliminary_Findings_for_Team_Grant_Project_4_-_Sex_Safety_and_Security_A_Study_of_Experiences_of_People_Who_Pay_for_Sex_in_Canada

Baptie, T., Falle, N., Perrier, B., & Walker, M. (2014). *Brief submitted to the House of Commons Standing Committee on Justice and Human Rights regarding Bill C-36*

Protection of Communities and Exploited Persons Act. Retrieved from http://lawc.on.ca/briefsubmitted/

Barry, K. (1979). *Female sexual slavery.* Englewood Cliffs, NJ: Prentice-Hall.

Barry, K. (1995). *The prostitution of sexuality: The global exploitation of sexuality.* New York, NY: New York University Press.

Bell, L. (Ed.). (1987). *Good girls/bad girls: Feminists and sex trade workers face to face.* Toronto, ON: Seal.

Benoit, C., Atchison, C., Casey, L., Jansson, M., McCarthy, B., Phillips, R., ... Shaver, F.M. (2014). *A 'working paper' prepared as background to Building on the evidence: An international symposium on the sex industry in Canada.* Retrieved from http://www.nswp.org/resource/gender-violence-and-health-contexts-vulnerability-resiliencies-and-care-among-people-the

Benoit, C., Smith, M., Jansson, M., Magnus, S., Ouellet, N., Atchison, C., ... Shaver, F.M. (2016). Lack of confidence in police creates a 'blue' ceiling for sex workers' safety. *Canadian Public Policy, 42*(4), 456–68. https://doi.org/10.3138/cpp.2016-006

Bernstein, E. (2001). The meaning of the purchase. *Ethnography, 2*(3), 389–420. https://doi.org/10.1177/14661380122230975

Bernstein, E. (2007). *Temporarily yours: Intimacy, authenticity, and the commerce of sex.* Chicago, IL: University of Chicago Press. https://doi.org/10.7208/chicago/9780226044620.001.0001

Bindman, J. (1998). An international perspective on slavery in the sex industry. In K. Kempadoo & J. Doezema (Eds.), *Global sex workers: Rights, resistance, and redefinition* (pp. 65–68). New York, NY: Routledge.

Bittle, S. (2013). Still punishing to 'protect': Youth prostitution law and policy reform. In E. van der Meulen, E.M. Durisin, & V. Love (Eds.), *Selling sex: Experience, advocacy, and research on sex work in Canada* (pp. 279–96). Vancouver, BC: UBC Press.

Bowen, R., Bungay, V., & Zangger, C. (2015). *Making SPACES: Advancing recommendations for the off-street sex industry in Vancouver.* Vancouver, BC: Making SPACES Project.

Bruckert, C. (2002). *Taking it off, putting it on: Women in the strip trade.* Toronto, ON: Women's Press.

Bruckert, C., & Law, T. (2013). *Beyond pimps, procurers and parasites: Third parties in the incall/outcall sex industry.* Management in the sex industry project, Ottawa, ON. Retrieved from http://www.nswp.org/resource/beyond-pimps-procurers-and-parasites-mapping-third-parties-the-incalloutcall-sex-industry

Bruckert, C., & Law, T. (2018). The business of sex businesses: Management in the incall/outcall sector. In C. Bruckert & C. Parent (Eds.), *Getting past 'the pimp': Management in the sex industry* (pp. 56–71). Toronto, ON: University of Toronto Press.

Bruckert, C., & Parent, C. (2013). The work of sex work. In C. Parent, C. Bruckert, P. Corriveau, N. Mensah, & L. Toupin (Eds.), *Sex work: Rethinking the job, respecting the workers* (pp. 57–80). Vancouver, BC: UBC Press.

Bruckert, C., & Parent, C. (Eds.). (2018). *Getting past 'the pimp': Management in the sex industry.* Toronto, ON: University of Toronto Press.

Chapkis, W. (1997). *Live sex acts: Women performing erotic labor.* New York, NY: Routledge.

Davies, J. (2009). *My name is not Natasha: How Albanian women in France use trafficking to overcome social exclusion (1998–2001).* Amsterdam, Netherlands: Amsterdam University Press. https://doi.org/10.5117/9789053567074

Dawn, A. (2010). *Sub Rosa.* Vancouver, BC: Arsenal Pulp.

Dawn, A. (2013). *How poetry saved my life: A hustler's memoir.* Vancouver, BC: Arsenal Pulp.

Delacoste, F. & Alexander, P. (Eds.). (1998). *Sex work: Writings by women in the sex industry.* (2nd ed.). San Francisco, CA: Cleis.

Ditmore, M. (2005). Trafficking in lives: How ideology shapes policy. In K. Kempadoo, J. Sanghera, & B. Pattanaik (Eds.), *Trafficking and prostitution reconsidered: New perspectives on migration, sex work and human rights* (pp. 107–26). London, UK: Paradigm.

Doezema, J. (1998). Forced to choose: Beyond the voluntary v. forced prostitution dichotomy. In K. Kempadoo & J. Doezema (Eds.), *Global sex workers: Rights, resistance, and redefinition* (pp. 34–50). New York, NY: Routledge.

Doezema, J. (2010). *Sex slaves and discourse masters: The construction of trafficking.* New York, NY: Zed Books.

Dworkin, A. (2004). Pornography, prostitution, and a beautiful and tragic recent history. In C. Stark & R. Whisnant (Eds.), *Not for sale: Feminists resisting prostitution and pornography* (pp. 137–48). North Melbourne, Australia: Spinifex.

Ekberg, G. (2004). The Swedish law that prohibits the purchase of sexual services: Best practices for prevention of prostitution and trafficking in human beings. *Violence Against Women, 10*(10), 1187–218. https://doi.org/10.1177/1077801204268647

Ferris, S. (2015). *Street sex work and Canadian cities: Resisting the dangerous order.* Edmonton, AB: University of Alberta Press.

Farley, M. (2004). 'Bad for the body, bad for the heart': Prostitution harms women even if legalized or decriminalized. *Violence Against Women, 10*(10), 1087–125. https://doi.org/10.1177/1077801204268607

Farley, M., & Barkan, H. (1998). Prostitution, violence, and posttraumatic stress disorder. *Women and Health, 27*(3), 37–49. https://doi.org/10.1300/J013v27n03_03

GAATW (Global Alliance Against Traffic in Women). (2007). *Collateral damage: The impact of anti-trafficking measures on human rights around the world.* Retrieved from http://www.gaatw.org/Collateral%20Damage_Final/singlefile_CollateralDamagefinal.pdf

Global Commission on HIV and the Law. (2012). *Risks, rights and health.* New York, NY: United Nations Development Program.

Hannem, S., & Tigchelaar, A. (2016). Doing it in public: Dilemmas of images, voice, and constructing publics in public sociology on sex work. *Symbolic Interaction, 39*(4), 634–53. https://doi.org/10.1002/symb.260

Hochschild, A.R. (1983). *The managed heart: Commercialization of human feeling.* Berkeley, CA: University of California Press.

Hydra e.V. (2015). The German prostitution law: An example of the 'legalisation of sex work'. *Research for Sex Work,* (14), 13–15. Retrieved from http://www.nswp.org/resource/research-sex-work-14-sex-work-work

Jeffrey, L.A. (2002). *Sex and borders: Gender, national identity and prostitution policy in Thailand.* Vancouver, BC: UBC Press.

Kempadoo, K. (1998). Introduction: Globalizing sex workers' rights. In K. Kempadoo & J. Doezema (Eds.), *Global sex workers: Rights, resistance, and redefinition* (pp. 1–28). New York, NY: Routledge.

Kempadoo, K., & Doezema, J. (Eds.). (1998). *Global sex workers: Rights, resistance, and redefinition.* New York, NY: Routledge.

Koobak, R., & Marling, R. (2014). The decolonial challenge: Framing post-socialist central and eastern Europe within transnational feminist studies. *European Journal of Women's Studies, 21*(4), 330–43. https://doi.org/10.1177/1350506814542882

Krüsi, A., Pacey, K., Bird, L., Taylor, C., Chettier, J., Allan, S., ... Shannon, K. (2014). Criminalisation of clients: Reproducing vulnerabilities for violence and poor health among street-based sex workers in Canada – a qualitative study. *British Medical Journal Open, 4*(6), 1–10. http://dx.doi.org/10.1136/bmjopen-2014-005191

Law, T. (2016). *Managing the 'party': Third parties and the organization of labour in Ontario strip clubs.* (Unpublished doctoral dissertation). University of Ottawa, Ottawa, Ontario.

Leigh, C. (2004). *Unrepentant whore: Collected works of Scarlot Harlot.* San Francisco, CA: Last Gasp.

Levy, J., & Jakobsson, P. (2014). Sweden's abolitionist discourse and law: Effects on the dynamics of Swedish sex work and on the lives of Sweden's sex workers. *Criminology and Criminal Justice, 14*(5), 593–607. https://doi.org/10.1177/1748895814528926

Lyons, T., Krüsi, A., Pierre, L., Kerr, T., Small, W., & Shannon, K. (2017). Negotiating violence in the context of transphobia and criminalization: The experiences of trans sex workers in Vancouver, Canada. *Qualitative Health Research, 27*(2), 182–90. https://doi.org/10.1177/1049732315613311

Miller-Young, M. (2010). Putting hypersexuality to work: Black women and illicit eroticism in pornography. *Sexualities, 13*(2), 219–35. https://doi.org/10.1177/1363460709359229

Miller-Young, M. (2014). *A taste for brown sugar: Black women in pornography.* Durham, NC: Duke University Press. https://doi.org/10.1215/9780822375913

Milne, C. (Ed.). (2005). *Naked ambition: Women who are changing pornography.* New York, NY: Carroll and Graf.

Mohanty, C.T. (1991). Under Western eyes: Feminist scholarship and colonial discourses. In C.T. Mohanty, A. Russo, & L. Torres (Eds.), *Third World women and the politics of feminism* (pp. 51–80). Indianapolis, IN: Indiana University Press.

Nagle, J. (1997). Showing up fully: Women of colour discuss sex work. In J. Nagle (Ed.), *Whores and other feminists* (pp. 195–209). New York, NY: Routledge.

NSWP (Global Network of Sex Work Projects). (2013). *Consensus statement on sex work, human rights, and the law.* Retrieved from http://www.nswp.org/resource/nswp-consensus-statement-sex-work-human-rights-and-the-law

NSWP (Global Network of Sex Work Projects). (2016a). *Policy brief: Young sex workers.* Retrieved from http://www.nswp.org/resource/policy-brief-young-sex-workers

NSWP (Global Network of Sex Work Projects). (2016b). *Research for Sex Work*, (15). Retrieved from http://www.nswp.org/resource/research-sex-work-15-resistance -and-resilience

Oakley, A. (Ed.). (2007). *Working sex: Sex workers write about a changing industry.* Berkeley, CA: Seal.

Parent, C., Bruckert, C., Corriveau, P., Mensah, N., & Toupin, L. (Eds.). (2013). *Sex work: Rethinking the job, respecting the workers.* Vancouver, BC: UBC Press.

Pattanaik, B. (2002). Conclusion: Where do we go from here? In S. Thorbek & B. Pattanaik (Eds.), *Transnational prostitution: Changing global patterns* (pp. 217–30). New York, NY: Zed Books.

Race and the sex industry. (2011). [Special issue]. *$pread: Illuminating the Sex Industry, 5*(4).

Raguparan, M. (2017). 'If I'm going to hack capitalism': Racialized and Indigenous Canadian. sex workers' experiences within the neo-liberal market economy. *Women's Studies International Forum, 60,* 69–76. https://doi.org/10.1016/j.wsif.2016.12.003

Rivers-Moore, M. (2016). *Gringo gulch: Sex, tourism and social mobility in Costa Rica.* Chicago, IL: University of Chicago Press. https://doi.org/10.7208/chicago/9780226373553.001.0001

Ross, B.L. (2009). *Burlesque west: Showgirls, sex, and sin in postwar Vancouver.* Toronto, ON: University of Toronto Press.

Sanders, T. (2005). 'It's just acting': Sex workers' strategies for capitalizing on sexuality. *Gender, Work and Organization, 12*(4), 319–42. https://doi.org/10.1111/j.1468-0432.2005.00276.x

Scibelli, P. (1987). Empowering prostitution: A proposal for international legal reform. *Harvard Women's Law Journal, 10,* 117–57.

Schaffner, L., & Buhr, G., lewis, d., Roc, M., and Volpintesta, H. (2016). *Experiences of youth in the sex trade in Chicago.* New York, NY: Center for Court Innovation.

Shannon, K., Strathdee, S.A., Goldenberg, S.M., Duff, P., Mwangi, P., Rusakova, M., ... Boily, M. (2015). Global epidemiology of HIV among female sex workers: Influence of structural determinants. *Lancet, 385*(9962), 55–71. https://doi.org/10.1016/S0140-6736(14)60931-4

Shaver, F.M. (1985). Feminist defense of the decriminalization of prostitution. *Resources for Feminist Research, 14*(4), 38–39.

Stein, M. (1974). *Lovers, friends, slaves: The nine male sexual types, their psychosexual transactions with call girls.* Berkeley, CA: Berkley Publishing Corporation.

Sterry, D.H., & Martin, R. (2009). *Hos, hookers, call girls, and rent boys: Professionals writing on life, love, money, and sex.* Berkeley, CA: Soft Skull.

Suchland, J. (2015). *Economies of violence: Transnational feminism, postsocialism, and the politics of sex trafficking.* Durham, NC: Duke University Press. https://doi.org/10.1215/9780822375289

Sullivan, B. (2010). When (some) prostitution is legal: The impact of law reform on sex work in Australia. *Journal of Law and Society, 37*(1), 85–104. https://doi.org/10.1111/j.1467-6478.2010.00496.x

Truong, T.-D. (1990). *Sex, money, and morality: The political economy of prostitution and tourism in South East Asia.* London, UK: Zed Books.

van der Meulen, E. (2010). Reframing prostitution as sexual and emotional labour. In J.A. Jaworski (Ed.), *Advances in sociology research* (Vol. 6, pp. 305–13). New York, NY: Nova Science.

van der Meulen, E. (2012). When sex is work: Organizing for labour rights and protections. *Labour/Le Travail, 69,* 147–67.

van der Meulen, E., Durisin, E.M., & Love, V. (Eds.). (2013). *Selling sex: Experience, advocacy, and research on sex work in Canada.* Vancouver, BC: UBC Press.

Weitzer, R. (2005a). Flawed theory and method in studies of prostitution. *Violence Against Women, 11*(7), 934–49. https://doi.org/10.1177/1077801205276986

Weitzer, R. (2005b). New directions in research on prostitution. *Crime, Law, and Social Change, 43*(4–5), 211–35. https://doi.org/10.1007/s10611-005-1735-6

WHO (World Health Organization). (2015). *Technical brief: HIV and young people who sell sex.* Retrieved from http://www.who.int/hiv/pub/toolkits/hiv-young -sexworkers/en/

Wijers, M. (2001). Criminal, victim, social evil or working girl: Legal approaches to prostitution and their impact on sex workers. Paper presented at Seminario Internacional sobre Prostitución, Madrid, Spain, June 21–23. Retrieved from http://www.nswp.org/resource/criminal-victim-social-evil-or-working-girl -legal-approaches-prostitution-and-their-impact

Zheng, T. (Ed.). (2010). *Sex trafficking, human rights and social justice.* New York, NY: Routledge.

Cases

Bedford v. Canada, 2010 ONSC 4264.
Canada (Attorney General) v. Bedford, 2012 ONCA 186.
Canada (Attorney General) v. Bedford, 2013 SCC 72, [2013] 3 SCR 1101.

Legislation

Bill C-36, *Protection of Communities and Exploited Persons Act,* SC 2014, c. 25.
Criminal Code, RSC 1985, c. C-46.
Prostitution Reform Act, 2003, Act of Parliament USC Wellington, New Zealand.

PART 1

LAW AND POLICY CONTEXTS

The State and Beyond

2

Sex Work Policy
—————— Tracing Historical and
Contemporary Developments
EMILY VAN DER MEULEN AND ELYA M. DURISIN

Contemporary configurations of sex work policy in Canada have emerged out of a complex and contested history. Developing an understanding of this history is important in order to appreciate how sex workers have been constructed as subjects of political discourse. In this chapter, we trace federal policies on prostitution from just prior to Confederation in the 1860s to the contemporary context, ending with an often-neglected area of analysis: municipal regulation on licensing and zoning. This historical trajectory illustrates how sex work has been understood through competing frameworks, including struggles for political dominance in the context of shifting notions of acceptable feminine sexual behaviour; evolving feminist theorizing on sex work, colonization, and gentrification; and the ascendency of neoliberalism. Retrospectively, we see that the Canadian governmental response to prostitution policy at the federal level has intensified the criminalization of sex work and that municipalities have increasingly imposed various regulations.

Federal Prostitution Policy Development (1860–1915)

Before criminal law became the jurisdiction of the federal government in 1867, the criminalization of prostitution-related activities in Canada was primarily focused on provisions aimed at two areas: reducing residential brothels, street prostitution, and vagrancy; and "protecting" girls and women under twenty-one years of age from defilement through "false pretences" (McLaren, 1986). The laws were, in part, based on a social understanding of the monetary and proprietary value of a woman in relation to a male counterpart, namely her husband, brother, or father. Some cities explicitly encoded the sexual double standard by tolerating a certain level of prostitution in recognition "of the need to service the large surplus male population" (McLaren, 1986, p. 127). Other communities, however, saw prostitution as a nuisance, and police focused on reducing the trade. Prostitution was classified as a status offence, which meant that women could be subject to vagrancy charges and detention merely for *being* prostitutes.

Canadian criminal laws and social values at the time were greatly influenced by the moral and social purity movements in Britain, including those surrounding the Contagious Diseases Acts (CDAs) (Phoenix, 1999; Walkowitz, 1982), as well as the white slavery panic in the United States (Rosen, 1982). Canada implemented its own CDA from 1865 to 1870, which meant that women could be detained on the suspicion of having a venereal disease, as it was called at the time, and forcibly confined in a certified "lock hospital" for up to three months (McLaren, 1986; see also Khan, this collection). Because no certified hospitals existed, the Canadian CDA was never fully enacted, and it expired with very little impact in 1870.

In 1869, the year before Canada's CDA was to end, Canadian politicians passed a series of laws intended to regulate prostitution as a moral issue. An Act Respecting Vagrants, or the Vagrancy Act, maintained the existing status offence for prostitution and added new provisions that criminalized men who were a "keeper or inmate" of a bawdy-house, were "in the habit of frequenting such houses," or had "no peaceable profession ... [and] supports himself ... by the avails of prostitution" (*Criminal Code*, 1892, s. 207(j), (k), (l)). On paper, the Vagrancy Act targeted and criminalized the procurers, prostitutes, managers, and owners of bawdy-houses. In practice, however, sex-working women were disproportionately charged (Backhouse, 1991). Major social and political changes occurred at the federal level between the 1869 Vagrancy Act and the 1892 ratification of Canada's first Criminal Code. Legal historian Constance Backhouse (ibid.) has argued that these changes were a "response to a growing outcry from middle-class social reformers against the sexual exploitation of women" (p. 255). The campaign for social and moral reform, she continues, was really an attempt to eradicate sexual double standards and to encourage the same (white, female) standard of chastity and purity for both genders. Moral reformers saw the strengthening of family values as a way to save society from moral decay, and since women were viewed as the guardians of the family's welfare, they in particular needed to be shielded from male licentiousness; eradicating prostitution was seen as a good place to start. In response, Canadian laws pertaining to prostitution were developed into a highly complex series of provisions that sought to protect (white) women from the wiles of the procurer, pimp, and brothel keeper (McLaren, 1986).

The relationship between Indigenous women and early prostitution laws is likewise complex, as differing local laws existed before Confederation (see Backhouse, 1985; Boyer, 2009). As parts of a British colony, Canada's first provinces followed English common law and relied on statutes that targeted bawdy-houses and premises used for prostitution. These locations were considered one variety of "disorderly houses," believed to foster improper behaviours and to encourage forms of criminality (see *Disorderly Houses Act*, 1751; Russell, 1982).[1] In the post-Confederation context, an 1879 amendment to the 1876 Indian Act criminalized Indigenous women who were suspected of selling sex in bawdy-houses or other locations (see *An Act to Amend "The Indian Act, 1876,"* 1879). This amendment was intended to prevent racial mixing between Indigenous women and white settlers (Backhouse, 1985). The punishment for anyone found keeping these houses was a fine or imprisonment; enforcement of the law meant Indigenous women could be forced out of towns (Boyer, 2009). Indigenous women's sexuality was seen as threatening to the colonial project (Barman, 1997–98) and to the goal of settling Canada as a white nation. Indeed, many early settler communities located in the country's western provinces saw Indigenous women as causes of "vice" and threats to morality and restricted them from free access to such settlements (Carter, 1993). In 1892 the criminal laws in Canada were amalgamated in the first federal Criminal Code, which centralized the legal infrastructure of Canada's colonial regime. The Criminal Code adopted the earlier provisions from the Indian Act and with them much of the discriminatory thinking about Indigenous women, who were specifically targeted in early anti-prostitution laws (Begalka, 2016; Boyer, 2009; Carter, 1993; see also *Criminal Code*, 1892, s. 190).

With the first Criminal Code, Canadian federal laws included a wide-ranging series of provisions against prostitution and other "offences against morality," including: the seduction of "previously chaste girls" of fourteen to sixteen years of age as well as women under twenty-one "with promise of marriage"; the procuring of women who were under twenty-one and were not prostitutes or "of known immoral character"; the enticement of any woman or girl into a "house of ill-fame" for the purposes of prostitution; and the procurement of a girl or woman by her parent or guardian for "carnal connection" with a man (*Criminal Code*, 1892, ss. 181–82, 185(a), 185(b), 186). Bawdy-house offences, previously dealt with under the Vagrancy Act, were also made stricter and subsumed into the Criminal Code.

Despite the rhetoric of saving innocent girls and women from the evils of carnal knowledge and those who would force it upon them, the Criminal Code did not contain legislation directed at prostitutes' customers. It is here that the unique, and somewhat contradictory, social positioning of prostitution is most apparent. On the one hand, it was argued that prostitutes were victims in need of legal protection. On the other hand, it was thought that prostitution provided a necessary and inevitable outlet for male sexual needs, which should not be criminalized; therefore prostitution was both a necessary evil and a social evil or social ill (see also Khan, this collection). During the early twentieth century, as the moral reform movement grew and gained mainstream acceptance across North America, the positioning of prostitution as a necessary evil that could be regulated began to erode, and it became increasingly characterized as a social evil that needed to be prohibited through criminalization (Rosen, 1982), with women's sexual behaviour the key focus. This ideological and legislative shift also corresponded to the early twentieth century's white slavery panic (Ringdal, 2004), when Canadian and international policies were created to prohibit occurrences of white girls and women being trafficked into prostitution, primarily by racialized and immigrant men (Donovan, 2006).[2] Such policies must be understood within the larger social context of the time, which included colonial government and popular discourse positioning Indigenous people, especially women, as sexually licentious (Hunt, 2013), fear of immigration from countries with racialized populations, as well as the priority to settle Canada as a white nation (Doezema, 2010; Valverde, 2008). Thus the development of laws targeting prostitution, white slavery, and trafficking were part of a larger imperial and colonial project.

In the decades following the white slavery panic, the Canadian federal government did little to modify the Criminal Code in relation to prostitution. In effect, during the fifty-five years surrounding the enactment of the first Criminal Code, from 1860 to 1915, Canada's laws on prostitution developed from a set of segmented offences directed at protecting young women and girls and reducing street nuisances to complicated and far-reaching measures applied to a series of unlawful activities with increasingly stricter penalties (Shaver, 1996). For the next fifty-five years, from 1915 to 1970, the Criminal Code remained relatively unchanged in its criminalization of prostitution-related activities.

Recent Changes to Federal Legislation (1970–2000)

Since it had remained largely unmodified since 1892, part of the vagrancy section of the Criminal Code continued to read that any "common prostitute or night walker" found wandering the fields, streets, highways, or other public locations needed to "give a satisfactory account of herself" or risk arrest (Robertson, 2003; see also *Criminal Code*, 1892, s. 207(i)). Women could be charged for what they were presumed to be – sex workers – not for what they actually did. Police officers subjected women to overnight detentions and mandatory medical exams, which were legitimate according to the vagrancy provisions (Brock, 1998). It was not until 1972, when it was argued that the status offence was in violation of the 1960 Bill of Rights, that the sex work–related vagrancy legislation was revoked and replaced with a gender-neutral law that prohibited soliciting. Since the original bawdy-house and procuring sections of the Criminal Code were separate from the vagrancy section, they remained in effect along with the new soliciting offence. Thus *being* a prostitute was no longer illegal; instead, the law criminalized the activities that surrounded it.

In the years directly following the ratification of the solicitation law, both the police and the courts were unsure about how to interpret the legislation. Further, despite the gender neutrality in the wording of solicitation, police predominantly arrested and charged women. After six years of confusion and conflicting court decisions, in 1978 the Supreme Court ruled in *Hutt v. R.* (1978) that solicitation must be "pressing or persistent"; in other words, solicitation had to be an inconvenience, not a simple nod of the head to attract a client (Boritch, 2005; Jeffrey, 2004; Sturdy, 1997). Residents' groups, politicians, and the police publicly critiqued the Supreme Court decision: residents' groups claimed that street prostitution was increasing; municipalities attempted to control the trade through city bylaws, which were later deemed ultra vires, or invalid; and the police complained that they were left with little power to lay charges (Brock, 1998).

The late 1970s was also the time when sex workers – partially in response to increased public focus on their work – were beginning to form organizations around the world, including in North America (see also Beer, this collection). In 1977 Canada's first sex work organization, Better End All Vicious Erotic Repression (BEAVER), which soon changed its name to Committee

Against Street Harassment (CASH), was launched in Toronto. Not long after, in 1982, sex workers and allies in Vancouver created the Alliance for the Safety of Prostitutes (ASP), and in 1983 the Canadian Organization for the Rights of Prostitutes (CORP) was formed in Toronto. Also, at the same time, urban spaces were gentrifying as middle-class residents were increasingly moving from suburban areas into what were then becoming desirable downtown locations. Inner-city geographies, which had been home to sex workers and the urban poor, became contested spaces (see also Page, this collection; Ross, this collection). Further, the second wave of the women's movement was engaged in heated arguments over issues of gender and sexuality. These extra- and intra-movement debates, commonly called the sex wars, would see conceptualizations of prostitution and pornography as disputed terrain (Duggan and Hunter, 1995; Khan, 2014; Vance, 1984; see also Valverde, this collection).

With mounting pressure from the courts, police associations, residents' groups, and mayors of the country's large cities, the federal minister of justice, appointed by the then ruling Liberal Party of Canada, decreed that the national prostitution and pornography "problems" needed a national solution. In June 1983 the Special Committee on Pornography and Prostitution was created. Commonly called the Fraser Committee after its chairperson, Paul Fraser, it was mandated to research pornography and prostitution in Canada through a socio-legal frame (Special Committee on Pornography and Prostitution, 1985). During its nearly three years of public consultation and research, the committee heard from only a small number of sex workers.

Public reaction to the release of the committee's final report varied considerably, with the media focusing on the most controversial of its 105 recommendations – the loosening of bawdy-house laws. The Fraser Committee argued that it should be allowable for "small numbers of prostitutes to organize their activities out of a place of residence" and that the Criminal Code should not prevent "provinces from permitting and regulating small-scale, non-residential commercial prostitution establishments employing adult prostitutes" (Special Committee on Pornography and Prostitution, 1985, p. 684). Although sex workers and some women's organizations and civil liberties associations were in support of the findings, strong criticisms came from anti–sex work advocates in the women's movement, as well as from municipal politicians and representatives of religious groups (Brock, 1998).

There was a change in federal government from Liberal to Conservative leadership during the years of the Fraser Committee consultations, and it was newly appointed Minister of Justice John Crosbie who introduced Bill C-49 in the fall of 1985, immediately after the release of the Fraser Report. This new piece of legislation ignored much of the evidence and recommendations put forward by the Fraser Committee. Instead, it proposed to make "communication" for the purpose of engaging in prostitution a criminal offence for both sex workers and clients as well as to revoke the earlier standard that solicitation had to be pressing or persistent, ensuring that sex workers would be liable for arrest at the mere suggestion of sex. In addition, Bill C-49 proposed defining cars as public places, making it illegal to communicate about a commercial sexual exchange in a vehicle. These provisions would come to have devastating effects on sex workers in Canada.

Within six months and in direct contravention of the Fraser Committee's recommendations, Bill C-49 passed into law.[3] Shortly afterward, it became Section 195.1 of the Criminal Code (subsequently renumbered s. 213). Three years later, the mandatory review of the communication law found dramatic enforcement inequity, concluding that many sex workers "simply have longer criminal records" (DoJC, 1989, p. 118). The review also stated that the criminalization of communication had not succeeded in curbing prostitution, as originally intended, claiming that "the main effect was to move street prostitutes from one downtown area to another, thereby displacing the problem" (ibid., p. 119). In addition to being disproportionately charged and displaced, sex workers were also reporting an increase of violence on the streets and more punitive policing measures, including detentions, curfews, and strict bail conditions (Brock, 1998).

In the late 1980s, the constitutionality of the communication and bawdy-house laws was challenged on the basis that they violated the Charter of Rights and Freedoms, particularly freedom of expression (s. 2b) and the right to life, liberty, and security of the person (s. 7). In 1990 the Supreme Court upheld the constitutionality of both laws, concluding that the prohibition against keeping a common bawdy-house did not violate one's Charter right to freedom of expression and that although the communication section was an infringement on expression, this infringement was within reasonable limits (*Reference re ss. 193 and 195.1(1)(c) of the Criminal Code (Man.)*, 1990). Individually or together, neither law was deemed a violation of life, liberty, and security of the person.[4] The early 1990s saw three other Charter cases brought before the Supreme Court.[5] In each instance, the court ruled that when and if the prostitution laws infringed on one's rights, this infringement was a justifiable reasonable limit.

Outside of the courts, another governmental review of Canada's prostitution policy was initiated in 1992. Called the Federal-Provincial-Territorial Working Group on Prostitution, it focused primarily on youth and street-based sex work (Working Group, 1998). Among its recommendations, the Working Group suggested that youth prostitution laws be made easier to enforce and that sentences for procurers and customers should be increased and/or made mandatory (see also Bittle, this collection).

During this time period, violence against sex workers increased dramatically. Between 1991 and 1995, sixty-three known sex workers, sixty of whom were women, were murdered in Canada. It was thought that most were killed by men posing as clients (Lowman, 1998). In a study of violence toward sex workers in British Columbia before and after the implementation of the communicating law, Lowman and Fraser (1996) found that twelve sex workers were murdered in the six years preceding the legislative change (an average of two per year), compared to four murders in 1985 alone, the year that the new law was enacted. Murder rates in British Columbia continued to increase, with an average of five per year from 1986 through 1995. Lowman and Fraser (1996) argued that the communicating law created a symbolic marginalization of sex workers that contributed to their displacement and made them easier targets of violence.

Current Federal Sex Work Policy Contexts (2000–Present)

The most recent federal review of Canada's prostitution laws was initiated in response to continued violence against sex workers, an issue brought into sharp relief by the missing and murdered women from Vancouver's Downtown Eastside, many of whom were Indigenous. Called the Subcommittee on Solicitation Laws Review (SSLR), it included representation from each major political party and was mandated to review Canada's legal framework in order to make recommendations for reducing exploitation and violence (Davies, 2003). Over the course of 2005, the SSLR held consultations, both closed-session and public, with nearly 300 witnesses representing police services, community and residents' associations, women's groups, advocacy and rehabilitation organizations, researchers, and sex workers. Unlike the previous Fraser Committee, which saw only a limited number of sex workers, the SSLR heard, either directly or indirectly, from well over 100 (Clamen, 2005a, 2005b; Pivot Legal Society Sex Work Subcommittee, 2004). Despite their mobilizing and organizing efforts – supported by many researchers and advocates – sex workers' near unanimous endorsement of decriminalization did not convince the subcommittee. In their final report, SSLR members agreed on just six recommendations, including increased resources to combat youth sex work and trafficking, better education to prevent people from entering sex work, and resources for those who wished to leave. The Conservative Party representative's framing of sex work as exploitation and (most) sex workers as powerless to protect themselves may be one reason why the SSLR failed in its mandate.

At the time, and up until December 2014, prostitution and the sale of sexual services were not illegal in Canada, yet the laws that surrounded prostitution-related activities made it extremely difficult to work without breaking the law; sex workers were forced to choose between working safely and risking arrest. Four areas of federal law regulated how, where, and between whom transactions could take place, and each produced its own set of problems and dangers for workers. The first area of law criminalized keeping, being an inmate of, or being found in a common bawdy-house (*Criminal Code*, 1985, s. 210). Since Section 197.1 of the Criminal Code defined a common bawdy-house as any location that was "kept or occupied, or resorted to by one or more persons, for the purpose of prostitution or the practice of acts of indecency," it was unlawful for sex workers to work in any fixed location by themselves or with others. Further, Canadian case law dictated that neither sexual intercourse nor full nudity had to take place for the act to be considered prostitution; "the definition of prostitution merely requires proof that the woman offered her body for lewdness or for the purposes of the commission of an unlawful act in return for payment" (Bruckert, Parent, and Robitaille, 2003, p. 13). Therefore, the broad bawdy-house section of the Criminal Code encompassed many more workplaces than simply brothels; strip clubs, massage parlours, dungeons, and other locations were also (at least in principle) criminalized.

The second area of legislation added to the criminalization of a sex worker's work activities through the prohibition of directing or transporting, or offering to direct or transport, someone to a bawdy-house (*Criminal Code*, 1985, s. 211). This law applied to individuals who drove sex workers to their workplace as well as potentially to referrals among and between clients and sex workers when they were directing someone to an in-call. Thus Section 211 not only detracted from sex workers' business by prohibiting word-of-mouth recommendations but also added to their vulnerability by criminalizing drivers, who are often the first people to be contacted by workers in instances of an undesirable or difficult client and who are also responsible for safely transporting workers to various locations that could be considered bawdy-houses.

The third key area of law was related to procuring offences, including living on the avails of a sex worker's earnings and owning or operating an establishment where sexual services were provided (*Criminal Code*, 1985, s. 212). It further deemed guilty any individual who was "habitually in the company of a prostitute ... in the absence of evidence to the contrary." Canadian case law determined that the "habitually in the company of" relationship needed to be "parasitic" (*R. v. Bramwell*, 1993; *R. v. Celebrity Enterprises*, 1998; *R. v. Grilo*, 1991), yet the definition of "parasitic" remained vague (van der Meulen, 2010). In effect, this section exposed sex workers' partners and friends to charges of pimping, even if coercion could not be proven. It further disallowed employer-employee relationships and prevented sex workers from being able to organize unions in order to protect their labour rights. Section 212 additionally included specific provisions, with increased penalties, that prohibited paying for the sexual services of people under eighteen years of age.

Finally, the federal law used in the vast majority of prostitution-related charges criminalized public communication for the purposes of buying or selling sexual services and made it a crime to stop any motor vehicle or to "impede the free flow of pedestrian or vehicular traffic" in a manner that communicated for the purposes of prostitution (*Criminal Code*, 1985, s. 213). Communication was further prohibited in any public place, or place open to public view, including the inside of a car, hotel lobbies, restaurants, and bars. Because of this section, sex workers were often de facto forced to go with clients to private and potentially dangerous locations before the negotiation of sexual services could take place. This law was disproportionately used to criminalize sex workers in outdoor and public locations, yet Canadian research consistently demonstrated that outdoor sex work accounted for less than 20 percent of the overall sex trade (Lowman, 2005; Pivot Legal Society, 2006; Shaver, 1993).

Given the problematic aspects of these four laws and the resulting increased violence and discrimination, sex workers and allies engaged in social and legal efforts to remove them from the Criminal Code. In 2007 former sex worker Sheryl Kiselbach, together with a registered nonprofit society of current and former sex workers from Vancouver's Downtown Eastside, Sex Workers United Against Violence (SWUAV), filed a constitutional challenge in British Columbia against the prostitution-related legislation. The challenge was initially dismissed in 2008 because of a lack of standing, as Kiselbach was not a current sex worker, meaning that the laws did not impact her at the time of the court decision, and because as a group

SWUAV "cannot attract private interest standing by purporting to act in a representative capacity on behalf of its members" (*Downtown Eastside Sex Workers United Against Violence Society v. Canada (Attorney General)*, 2010, para. 15). In the fall of 2010, the BC Court of Appeal ruled that the constitutional challenge could indeed proceed and that SWUAV could be granted public interest standing. This was a significant decision in Canadian constitutional law. Since people who experience social and economic marginalization often encounter barriers to legal recourse, changes to the test of public interest standing enhanced access to justice for members of equality-seeking groups (Bailey and Chaisson, 2012).

Also beginning in 2007, there was another Charter challenge being developed by three current and former sex workers in Ontario: Terri-Jean Bedford, Amy Lebovitch, and Valerie Scott. Called *Bedford v. Canada* (2010), this challenge saw Justice Susan Himel of the Ontario Superior Court of Justice concur with the applicants and strike down three central provisions of Canada's prostitution laws, ruling that they violated Charter rights to freedom of expression and security of the person (see also Belak, this collection). The case proceeded to the Ontario Court of Appeal in 2012 and then to the Supreme Court of Canada in 2013, with the Supreme Court releasing its unanimous decision that the impugned sections of the Criminal Code were unconstitutional in December of that year (*Canada (Attorney General) v. Bedford*, 2013). The landmark *Bedford* decision affirmed the decades of work by sex workers, advocates, and researchers that showed the harms caused by the Criminal Code. Although the court upheld the unconstitutionality of the laws, it delayed invalidating them for one year to give the government time to draft new provisions that were constitutionally compliant.

Immediately following the *Bedford* decision, Minister of Justice Peter MacKay stated that the government would be looking into different options to ensure that criminal law responded to the harms caused by prostitution (*CBC News* 2013). Soon afterward, the Conservative-led government initiated an online public opinion poll advancing the criminalization of the purchase of sexual services as a viable policy option and went on to claim popular public support for criminalization despite the apparent methodological flaws of the poll's approach. In its bias toward policy options favoured by the government, the poll problematically positioned prostitution as inherently dangerous and sex workers as women needing to be rescued (Spalding, 2014).

Nevertheless, Bill C-36, the Protection of Communities and Exploited Persons Act (PCEPA), was introduced in June 2014, endorsing the criminalization of the purchase of sexual services for the first time in Canada. The proposed new legal framework on prostitution in fact contained provisions similar to those that had just been deemed unconstitutional, in addition to a number of new ones. As well as criminalizing the *purchase* of sex, PCEPA also proposed criminalizing communication for the purpose of *selling* sex if it occurred near daycares, playgrounds, or schools. It further included provisions aimed at receiving material benefit from sexual services and advertising sexual services (see also Sterling, this collection). Many commentators argued that these new laws were likewise unconstitutional, violated the spirit of the Supreme Court of Canada's *Bedford* decision, and would exacerbate violence against sex workers (Amon, 2014; Canadian Bar Association, 2014; Pivot Legal Society and Downtown Eastside Sex Workers United Against Violence, 2014). Despite wide critique and opposition, the new laws quickly passed the House of Commons and Senate policy processes (see also Porth, this collection) and came into force on December 6, 2014, the national day memorializing violence against women.

The change from a federal Conservative to federal Liberal government in October 2015 signalled the possibility of more legislative changes. In November of that year, Minister of Justice Jody Wilson-Raybould stated that she was "committed to reviewing the prostitution laws, and sitting down with [her] officials to assess the best options, and with those they affect directly" (Ball, 2015, n.p.). While there is reason for tempered optimism that the Liberal government will take steps to overturn PCEPA, history suggests that ideological divides over the framing of sex work will not be easily surmounted, particularly given the discursive linkages often made between sex work, morality, and exploitation; indeed, at the time of writing, there have been no clear indications that the federal prostitution laws will be revised.

From National to Municipal Regulations

Although the anti-prostitution criminal laws tend to be the focus of much sex work research and advocacy given the significance of those laws to sex workers' lives, municipalities also have a role to play. Cities are not empowered to regulate prostitution directly, as the criminalization of sexual services can happen only at the federal level through the Criminal Code. However, many municipalities have attempted to control and limit aspects of the sex industry through various zoning bylaws and licensing schemes and thus approach the matter indirectly through the powers they have available (see also Sayers, this collection). Despite various restrictions – unlike criminal law, municipal bylaws cannot prohibit certain acts absolutely, and unlike civil law, they cannot regulate personal relationships – cities do have significant powers regarding property, both private and public, and how it is used. For example, they can regulate spaces and activities by imposing noise bylaws, garbage bylaws, and rules about the use of parks and sidewalks. Especially in a decriminalized context, if that is to be achieved in Canada in the future, municipal policies will become exceedingly important, as they will be the prime regulatory framework governing sex workers' lives.

Although the extent of municipal powers can differ slightly from location to location, cities in Canada generally have the power to administer and revoke business and individual licences as well as inspect business premises for bylaw adherence. They also have jurisdiction over where businesses can be located within the city boundaries, the sorts of signage they are allowed to display, and the type and price of licences they require. The full extent of these regulations varies by province and according to local pressures and desires. Indeed, a municipality is able to restrict the number of certain kinds of establishments or licences, such as for taxi drivers and street-food vendors, and can implement exorbitantly high licensing fees for business owners and workers, effectively deterring individuals from working in particular sectors (Pivot Legal Society, 2006). These tactics are much more common for sex industry businesses than for others. Although the direct purchase of sexual services has now been deemed illegal in Canada, there are numerous aspects and areas of the sex industry that skirt around the Criminal Code, such as erotic massage and dancing/stripping. In these instances, municipal bylaws play a substantial regulatory role.

Regulating Buildings and Their Uses through Zoning

In North America zoning is one of the biggest legal "sticks" that municipalities can wield against individuals or businesses. If you buy a home or business premise in good faith and later find out that the previous owners had built an illegal addition, you can be compelled to tear it down at your own expense for no reason other than that it contravenes the local zoning bylaw. Although this rarely occurs, the likelihood of it happening dramatically increases if a neighbour makes a complaint to the city. Since municipal zoning regulations are so complex – the City of Toronto's zoning bylaw is longer than the federal Income Tax Act – it is very difficult for the average person to know what is and is not legal. And since zoning variances or exceptions are easily obtained, looking at the neighbour's house to judge the legality of your own will not be helpful since they may have received a variance that you might well be denied.

Generally, municipalities are divided into different zoning or land-use areas that regulate the types of development that can occur there, including residential zones, industrial zones, and commercial zones, among others. However, the zoning rules do not amount to a coherent overall system. There are different rules in different neighbourhoods, even on different blocks, and it is not uncommon for areas within one city to have their own separate bylaws. To determine where sex industry establishments can exist, some municipalities have instituted bylaws that prohibit massage parlours or escort agencies from setting up businesses in residential neighbourhoods; instead, sexual service establishments are relegated to industrial zones far from the downtown core and thus far from readily accessible public transit.

The assumed purpose of these bylaws is to prevent residential zones from having sex businesses in their vicinity, but their consequence is that it can be much more difficult and dangerous for sex workers to get to and from work (van der Meulen and Durisin, 2008). Conversely, in other municipalities such as Vancouver, licensed body rub parlours are permitted to provide services only in the "Downtown District" (Pivot Legal Society, 2006). Indeed, each municipality can institute its own zoning regulations that specify which sex industry establishments are permitted and in which zones. Businesses that violate the zoning bylaws can face stiff penalties; for example, the penalty in Vancouver is up to $10,000 (City of Vancouver, Bylaw No. 3575, s. 8.2).

The complexity and lack of uniformity of zoning rules can encourage political interference with planning decisions. Someone who wants a zoning variance for a property or business might be more likely to call a city councillor than to spend the money on a planning lawyer. In return, the councillor may be more willing to support the constituent's request, as it can build political capital if the request is unlikely to upset other members of the community. This politicization of zoning has serious implications for those involved in businesses that might be unpopular and can lead to "not in my back yard" sentiments.

Regulating Small Entrepreneurs through Licensing

In addition to zoning bylaws, licensing is a common measure through which municipalities restrict and control local sex-related businesses. Ironically, whereas large corporations such as banks, factories, offices, and warehouses can establish themselves in any industrially or commercially zoned building without needing municipal permission, the self-employed entrepreneurs who operate variety stores, drive taxis, or sell hot dogs on the street are often subject to expensive, time-consuming, and onerous regulations. In Canadian cities, there are two primary types of licences for regulating and, in many cases, deterring the sex trade: business licences for owners, managers, and operators of sex industry establishments; and licences for the individual workers themselves.

Mandating that business owners and operators must have a licence to manage their establishment provides an effective way for municipalities to "control the number and nature of businesses within their boundaries, ensure compliance with health and safety guidelines, and collect licensing fees for city revenue" (Pivot Legal Society, 2006, p. 36). To get a business licence, the business owner will be required to fill out the necessary paperwork at the local city hall – including his or her personal contact information – and submit to a criminal record check. Municipalities can refuse to grant a business licence if the applicant has a criminal record. As a condition of granting the licence, it is not uncommon for operators of body rub parlours and dating services, for example, to have to agree that they will supply the city and/or the local police with the names and addresses of their employees, and cities can set licence fees without much, if any, scrutiny. Thus business owners' licence fees can be quite expensive and considerably higher than for almost all other licences. Not surprisingly, establishments that commonly provide sexual services to clients are also subject to considerably more bylaws, both in number and in severity, than most other businesses (Pivot Legal Society, 2006).

In addition to owner/operator licenses, municipalities can set rules regrding licensing for individual sex workers. Since licensing systems are not subject to much legal scrutiny, municipalities have a great deal of leeway in deciding what activities they will regulate. Municipalities will, therefore, differ in what licences they require and for what areas of work. For example, in Ontario, the City of Windsor requires licences for escorts, whereas neither Toronto nor Ottawa do. Although escort licensing is not common among most other cities, many do require licences for exotic dancers and massage or body rub attendants. It is somewhat peculiar for municipalities to mandate licences for exotic dancers or massage attendants while exempting restaurant workers, bartenders, and non-erotic masseuses from the same requirement. In places where police crackdowns on body rub parlours are common and where municipalities restrict the number of body rub licences that they grant to individual workers, some workers circumvent the regulation by working under licences for holistic-health or health-enhancement practitioners or by working without a licence in unregulated parlours.

Like the fees for business owners and operators, the annual cost of a sex worker's licence can be very high – a distinct barrier for many who might want to work in regulated indoor locations. Further, if a sex worker receives a licence in one municipality, it is not transferable to another; sex workers must apply for and purchase licences in each city where they work. For some, such as exotic dancers who travel as part of their job, this can be very expensive.

In instances where a licensed massage attendant provides sexual services in a licensed massage parlour, her client could nonetheless be charged for purchasing sexual services under the federal Criminal Code provisions, she could have her municipal licence revoked or suspended, and she could perhaps be fined for violating the terms of the bylaw (Pivot Legal Society, 2006). Illustrative of the complex interaction and layering of municipal and federal regulations, municipalities themselves are not permitted to regulate prostitution, and purchasing sexual services remains criminalized even if a worker has a city-issued licence to provide body rub services. Bylaw fines can vary widely within and between jurisdictions. In Vancouver, for example, fines range from $250 to $10,000. If the licensed sex worker is convicted of the offence, a permanent notice could be placed in her city record, which could then prevent her from gaining a licence in future. Further, if her fines go unpaid, she could be charged with contempt of court and face imprisonment.

Licensing schemes present a particularly important feature for sex businesses insofar as the business or the person is subject to immediate unannounced inspections that would likely be deemed unconstitutional in other circumstances. Police enforcing the criminal law are not supposed to enter a private business without cause. For instance, without probable cause, a police officer cannot go into a department store and start questioning staff or request to see the day's cash intake. However, at any time and for no reason, police can enter a business that is municipally licensed, such as a strip club or massage parlour, and demand to see the workers' licences.[6]

Zoning and licensing bylaws are not only complicated and confusing but can also be onerous for sex workers who might not know how to navigate the complex bureaucracy of many city halls or how to access the specific bylaw details (Bruckert, Parent, and Robitaille, 2003; Lewis and Maticka-Tyndale, 2000). Sex workers in Canada have reported that licensing does not improve their workplace conditions, their safety, or their ability to organize for better rights (Pivot Legal Society, 2006; van der Meulen and Durisin, 2008). It is rare for people working in licensed sex industry establishments to speak out against abuses, as any attempt to rectify exploitative working conditions could lead to federal criminal charges, bylaw fines, licence cancellation, or even the closure of the business itself (Pivot Legal Society, 2006; van der Meulen and Durisin, 2008; van der Meulen, 2010).

Conclusion

Far from being straightforward or self-evident, the evolution of federal prostitution laws to their current configuration, along with the rules and regulations set out by municipalities, shows a variety of competing interests acting on terrain that is practically and discursively complex and particularly uneven for sex workers. The sex workers' movement in Canada has made impressive strides in articulating sex workers' perspectives at the federal and municipal levels, yet sex workers today remain bound in webs of criminalization and regulation whereby access to legal protections is legitimated only when they are conceptualized as victims. When seen as criminals in violation of one of the many federal laws or municipal bylaws that continue to govern their work and lives, sex workers in both indoor and outdoor environments can be targeted by diverse officials, including police and municipal licensing and standards officers (see also Shaver, Bryans, and Bhola, this collection). As the following chapters show, the new legal regime that is beginning to emerge in the post-PCEPA context is one where sex workers' safety strategies have been disrupted, antagonistic relationships with police and other regulatory officials continue to persist, and stigma and discrimination remain.

Notes

This chapter is a shortened, revised, and updated amalgamation of two previous publications: van der Meulen, E., Durisin, E.M. and Love, V. (2013). Introduction. In E. van der Meulen, E.M. Durisin, and V. Love (Eds.), *Selling sex: Experience, advocacy, and research on sex work in Canada* (pp. 1–25). Vancouver, BC: UBC Press; and van der Meulen, E., and Valverde, M. (2013). Beyond the Criminal Code: Municipal licensing and zoning bylaws. In E. van der Meulen, E.M. Durisin, and V. Love (Eds.), *Selling sex: Experience, advocacy, and research on sex work in Canada* (pp. 314–22). Vancouver, BC: UBC Press.

1 Thank you to Melanie Begalka and Brenda Belak for the legal feedback and research.

2 Contemporary research has produced conflicting reports as to the actual instances of white girls and women being lured into prostitution, with many suggesting
that the panic was unfounded and that it did not accurately describe women's
entry into prostitution (Backhouse, 1985; McLaren, 1986).

3 The vote was 111 for to 35 against.

4 Over the ten-year period following the enactment of the communication law,
from 1986 to 1995, between 6,000 and 10,000 prostitution-related charges were
generally laid per year (Duchesne, 1997). Although the communication section
of the law was deemed a reasonable infringement of freedom of expression and
freedom of speech, 92 percent of the 7,165 charges laid in 1995 alone came under
that section.

5 *R. v. Stagnitta* (1990); *R. v. Skinner* (1990); *R. v. Downey* (1992).

6 This situation also applies to any establishment holding a liquor licence, where
police may enter without cause.

References

Amon, J. (2014, June 18). Canada's prostitution bill a step in the wrong direction.
Ottawa Citizen. Retrieved from http://ottawacitizen.com/news/politics/joseph-
amon-canadas-prostitution-bill-a-step-in-the-wrong-direction

Backhouse, C. (1985). Nineteenth-century Canadian prostitution law: Reflection of
a discriminatory society. *Social History/Histoire sociale, 18*(36), 387–423.

Backhouse, C. (1991). *Petticoats and prejudice: Women and law in nineteenth-
century Canada.* Toronto, ON: Osgoode Society.

Bailey, J., & Chaisson, A. (2012). On being 'part of the solution': Public interest standing after SWUAV SCC. *Canadian Journal of Poverty Law, 1*(1), 121–44.

Ball, D.P. (2015, November 27). New justice minister says she'll listen to sex
workers on prostitution reforms. *The Tyee.* Retrieved from http://thetyee.ca/
News/2015/11/27/Justice-Minister-on-Sex-Work/

Barman, J. (1997–98). Taming Aboriginal sexuality: Gender, power, and race in British Columbia, 1850–1900. *BC Studies,* (115–16), 237–66.

Begalka, M. (2016). *The Indian Act and origins of bawdy house laws in Canada.*
(Unpublished memorandum). Vancouver, BC: Pivot Legal Society.

Boritch, H. (2005). The criminal class revisited: Recidivism and punishment in
Ontario, 1871–1920. *Social Science History, 29*(1), 137–70.

Boyer, Y. (2009). First Nation's women's contributions to culture and community
through Canadian Law. In G. Guthrie Valaskakis, M. Dion Stout, & E. Guimond
(Eds.), *Restoring the balance: First Nations women, community, and culture*
(pp. 69–96). Winnipeg, MB: University of Manitoba Press.

Brock, D. (1998). *Making work, making trouble: Prostitution as a social problem.*
Toronto, ON: University of Toronto Press. https://doi.org/10.3138/9781442676930

Bruckert, C., Parent, C., & Robitaille, P. (2003). *Erotic service/erotic dance establishments: Two types of marginalized labour.* Ottawa, ON: Law Commission of Canada.

Canadian Bar Association. (2014). *Bill C-36, Protection of Communities and
Exploited Persons Act.* Retrieved from https://www.cba.org/CMSPages/GetFile.
aspx?guid=506f61b6-ecdb-441d-9879-f4a1f3bd3f04

Carter, S. (1993). Categories and terrains of exclusion: Contructing the 'Indian woman' in the early settlement era in western Canada. *Great Plains Quarterly, 13*(3), 147–61.

CBC News. (2013, December 20). Supreme Court strikes down Canada's prostitution laws. Retrieved from http://www.cbc.ca/news/politics/supreme-court-strikes -down-canada-s-prostitution-laws-1.2471572

Clamen, J. (2005a). *Recommendations for law reform: A sex worker rights perspective.* (Unpublished manuscript).

Clamen, J. (2005b). *Submission to the Subcommittee on Solicitation Laws of the Standing Committee on Justice, Human Rights, Public Safety and Emergency Preparedness.* (Unpublished manuscript).

Davies, L. (2003, February 9). *Libby succeeds: Parliamentary committee to review sex trade laws.* (News release). Retrieved from http://www.libbydavies.ca/

Doezema, J. (2010). *Sex slaves and discourse masters: The construction of trafficking.* New York, NY: Zed Books.

DoJC (Department of Justice Canada). (1989). *Street prostitution: Assessing the impact of the law.* Ottawa, ON: Communications and Public Affairs.

Donovan, B. (2006). *White slave crusades: Race, gender, and anti-vice activism, 1887–1917.* Chicago, IL: University of Illinois Press.

Duchesne, D. (1997). *Street prostitution in Canada.* Ottawa, ON: Canadian Center of Justice Statistics.

Duggan, L., & Hunter, N.D. (1995). *Sex wars: Sexual dissent and political culture.* New York, NY: Routledge.

Hunt, S. (2013). Decolonizing sex work: Developing an intersectional Indigenous approach. In E. van der Meulen, E.M. Durisin, & V. Love (Eds.), *Selling sex: Experience, advocacy, and research on sex work in Canada* (pp. 82–100). Vancouver, BC: UBC Press.

Jeffrey, L.A. (2004). Prostitution as public nuisance: Prostitution policy in Canada. In J. Outshoorn (Ed.), *The politics of prostitution: Women's movements, democratic states and the globalization of sex commerce* (pp. 83–102). London, UK: Cambridge University Press.

Khan, U. (2014). *Vicarious kinks: Sadomasochism in the socio-legal imaginary.* Toronto, ON: University of Toronto Press.

Lewis, J., & Maticka-Tyndale, E. (2000). Licensing sex work: Public policy and women's lives. *Canadian Public Policy, 26*(4), 437–49. https://doi.org/10.2307/3552610

Lowman, J. (1998). Prostitution law reform in Canada. In the Institute of Comparative Law in Japan (Ed.), *Toward comparative law in the 21st century* (pp. 919–46). Tokyo, Japan: Chuo University Press.

Lowman, J. (2005). *Submission to the Subcommittee on Solicitation Laws of the Standing Committee on Justice, Human Rights, Public Safety and Emergency Preparedness.* (Unpublished manuscript).

Lowman, J., & Fraser, L. (1996). *Violence against persons who prostitute: The experience in British Columbia.* (Technical Report No. TR1996–14e). Ottawa, ON: Department of Justice Canada.

McLaren, J.S. (1986). Chasing the social evil: Moral fervour and the evolution of Canada's prostitution laws, 1867–1917. *Canadian Journal of Law and Society, 1,* 125–65. https://doi.org/10.1017/S0829320100001034

Phoenix, J. (1999). *Making sense of prostitution.* New York, NY: Palgrave. https://doi.org/10.1057/9780333985472

Pivot Legal Society. (2006). *Beyond decriminalization: Sex work, human rights and a new framework for law reform.* Retrieved from http://www.nswp.org/resource/beyond-decriminalization-sex-work-human-rights-and-new-framework-law-reform

Pivot Legal Society and Downtown Eastside Sex Workers United Against Violence. (2014). *Brief to the Senate Committee on Legal and Constitutional Affairs.* Retrieved from http://www.parl.gc.ca/Content/SEN/Committee/412/lcjc/Briefs/C-36/C-36_brief_PIVOT_Legal%20Society(Pacey-Porth)_E.pdf

Pivot Legal Society Sex Work Subcommittee. (2004). *Voices for dignity: A call to end the harms caused by Canada's sex trade laws.* Retrieved from http://old.nswp.org/resource/voices-dignity-call-end-the-harms-caused-canadas-sex-trade-laws

Ringdal, N.J. (2004). *Love for sale: A world history of prostitution.* New York, NY: Grove.

Robertson, J.R. (2003). *Prostitution.* Ottawa, ON: Library of Parliament.

Rosen, R. (1982). *The lost sisterhood: Prostitution in America, 1900–1918.* London, UK: Johns Hopkins University Press.

Russell, J.S. (1982). The offence of keeping a bawdy-house in Canadian criminal law. *Ottawa Law Review, 14*(1), 270–313.

Shaver, F. (1993). Prostitution: A female crime? In E. Adelberg & C. Currie (Eds.), *In conflict with the law: Women and the Canadian criminal justice system* (pp. 153–73). Vancouver, BC: Press Gang.

Shaver, F.M. (1996). The regulation of prostitution: Setting the morality trap. In B. Schissel & L. Mahood (Eds.), *Social control in Canada* (pp. 204–26). London, UK: Oxford University Press.

Spalding, D. (2014, February 18). Government prostitution survey full of "loaded" questions. *Ottawa Citizen.* Retrieved from http://ottawacitizen.com/news/national/government-prostitution-survey-full-of-loaded-questions

Special Committee on Pornography and Prostitution. (1985). *Pornography and prostitution in Canada: Report of the Special Committee on Pornography and Prostitution.* (Vol. 1). Ottawa, ON: Canadian Government Publishing Centre.

Sturdy, S. (1997). *Prostitution in Canada.* Retrieved from http://records.viu.ca/www/crimweb/Student/Sturdy.htm

Valverde, M. (2008). *The age of light, soap, and water: Moral reform in English Canada, 1885–1925.* Toronto, ON: University of Toronto Press.

van der Meulen, E. (2010). Illegal lives, loves, and work: How the criminalization of procuring affects sex workers in Canada. *Wagadu: A Journal of Transnational Women's and Gender Studies, 8,* 217–40.

van der Meulen, E., & Durisin, E.M. (2008). Why decriminalize? How Canada's municipal and federal regulations increase sex workers' vulnerability. *Canadian Journal of Women and the Law, 20*(2), 289–312.

Vance, C. (Ed.). (1984). *Pleasure and danger: Exploring female sexuality.* Boston, MA: Routledge.

Walkowitz, J.R. (1982). *Prostitution and Victorian society: Women, class, and the state.* New York, NY: Cambridge University Press.

Working Group (Federal-Provincial-Territorial Working Group on Prostitution). (1998). *Report and recommendations in respect of legislation, policy and practices concerning prostitution-related activities.* Ottawa, ON: Department of Justice Canada.

Cases

Bedford v. Canada, 2010 ONSC 4264.

Canada (Attorney General) v. Bedford, 2012 ONCA 186.

Canada (Attorney General) v. Bedford, 2013 SCC 72, [2013] 3 SCR 1101.

Downtown Eastside Sex Workers United Against Violence Society v. Canada (Attorney General), 2010 BCCA 439.

Hutt v. R. (1978), 82 DLR (3d) 95.

R. v. Bramwell (1993), 86 CCC (3d) 418 (BC CA).

R. v. Celebrity Enterprises (1998), 41 CCC (2d) 540 (BC CA).

R. v. Downey, [1992] 2 SCR 10.

R. v. Grilo (1991), 64 CCC (3d) 53 (ON CA).

R. v. Skinner, [1990] 1 SCR 1235.

R. v. Stagnitta, [1990] 1 SCR 1226.

Reference re ss. 193 and 195.1(1)(c) of the Criminal Code (Man.), [1990] 1 SCR 1123.

Legislation

An Act to Amend "The Indian Act, 1876," SC 1879, c. 34.

Bill C-36, *Protection of Communities and Exploited Persons Act,* SC 2014, c. 25.

City of Toronto Municipal Code, *Licensing,* Article 31, No. 545–394, Chapter 545 Licensing.

City of Vancouver, Bylaw No. 3575, *Zoning and Development Bylaw.*

City of Vancouver, Bylaw No. 4450, *License Bylaw* (23 September 1969).

Criminal Code, 1892, 55–56 Vict., c. 29.

Criminal Code, RSC 1985, c. C-46.

Disorderly Houses Act, 1751, 25 Geo 2, c. 36 (UK) (repealed).

3

Bedford v. Canada
A Breakthrough in the Legal Discourse

BRENDA BELAK

When the Supreme Court of Canada struck down three Criminal Code provisions concerning prostitution in 2013, it marked a watershed moment for sex workers and for Canadian legal history. The court recognized for the first time something that sex workers themselves had said for years: efforts to keep prostitution out of sight put sex workers' lives and rights at risk. The *Bedford* decision shifted the legal and political discourse around sex work from a focus on nuisance and public order to a focus on health, safety, and human rights. The case, which was years in the making, produced a voluminous evidentiary record, most of it research conducted with sex workers about their own experiences. *Bedford* set Canada's sex work laws on a new course. It also changed the public face of sex work, as sex workers stepped forward to demand recognition as experts in their own lives and joined with allies to create a national movement devoted to law reform.

The case began in 2007 when three current and former sex workers in Ontario applied to the Ontario Superior Court of Justice for a declaration that three of the Criminal Code offences regarding prostitution were unconstitutional.[1] Prostitution had been defined by previous case law as "lewd acts for payment for the sexual gratification of the purchaser" (*R. v. Bedford*, 2000). It was not illegal, but many of the activities surrounding it were. The three women applicants – Terri-Jean Bedford, Amy Lebovitch, and Valerie Scott – had decades of experience between them providing sexual services for money in a variety of circumstances, both on the street and indoors. The applicants risked considerable reputational jeopardy identifying as having engaged in sex work in a case of this magnitude and public interest; however, they considered the hardships that sex workers continued to suffer under the laws significant enough to justify the high level of exposure.

The applicants challenged the laws that prohibited keeping a bawdy-house (s. 210), defined in Section 197 of the Criminal Code as a fixed location at which prostitution was offered; living on the avails of another's prostitution (s. 212(1)(j)); and communicating in public for the purposes of prostitution (s. 213(1)(c)). They alleged that enforcement of these provisions put their lives and the lives of other sex workers at risk, infringing their rights to liberty and security of the person under Section 7 of the Charter of Rights and Freedoms. They also asserted that the restrictions on communicating infringed the constitutional guarantee of freedom of expression under Section 2(b) of the Charter. The provision against public communication was historically the most widely enforced of the prostitution laws, used to scapegoat street-based sex workers for public annoyances often unrelated to sex work, including noise, littering, and drug use, and to keep sex work out of public view.

Bedford at the Ontario Superior Court of Justice: The Initial Application

The application, heard by the Ontario Superior Court of Justice in October 2009, was opposed by the attorney general of Canada, with the attorney general of Ontario and three conservative religious organizations as the only interveners at this level of court.[2] During the seven days of hearings, Justice Susan Himel heard two strongly opposing views. The applicants argued that the challenged laws materially contributed to the violence faced by sex workers, whereas the respondents argued that the risks and harms flowing from sex work were inherent to the activity itself, not caused by the laws. Justice Himel considered the evidence of current and former sex workers, advocates, politicians, police officers, and numerous social science researchers put forward by the applicants and respondents, as well as the interveners' arguments. She reviewed more than 25,000 pages of evidence, amassed over the previous two and a half years and submitted in an eighty-eight-volume joint application record, which included expert reports, parliamentary studies, newspaper articles, legislation, and excerpts from *Hansard* (the transcripts of parliamentary debates) (*Bedford v. Canada*, 2010, para. 84).

Justice Himel released her decision on September 28, 2010, striking down the three impugned laws because they infringed Section 7 of the Charter. She found that sex workers were unable to employ measures to reduce threats to their physical safety without breaking the law, which was not in keeping with the requirement according to the principles of fundamental justice that laws infringing security of the person cannot be arbitrary, overbroad, or grossly disproportionate. The infringement was not saved under Section 1 of the Charter as a reasonable limit demonstrably justified in a free and democratic society; thus she determined that the laws could not be upheld. Justice Himel made very specific findings about the way that sex work occurs in Canada and about what that means for sex workers' safety:

> With respect to section 210, the evidence suggests that working in-call is the safest way to sell sex; yet, prostitutes who attempt to increase their level of safety by working in-call face criminal sanction. With respect to section 212(1)(j), prostitution, including legal out-call work, may be made less dangerous if a prostitute is allowed to hire an assistant or a bodyguard; yet, such business relationships are illegal due to the living on the avails of prostitution provision. Finally, section 213(1)(c) prohibits street prostitutes, who are largely the most vulnerable prostitutes and face an alarming amount of violence, from screening clients at an early, and crucial stage of a potential transaction, thereby putting them at an increased risk of violence.
>
> In conclusion, these three provisions prevent prostitutes from taking precautions, some extremely rudimentary, that can decrease the risk of violence towards them. Prostitutes are faced with deciding between their liberty and their security of the person. Thus, while it is ultimately the client who inflicts violence upon a prostitute, in my view the law plays a sufficient contributory role in preventing a prostitute from taking steps that could reduce the risk of such violence. (*Bedford v. Canada*, 2010, paras. 361–62)

With specific regard to the principles of fundamental justice, Justice Himel found that the bawdy-house provision (s. 210) was overbroad because it went far beyond the objective of preventing public nuisance, making it an offence to do sex work from any fixed location. She found that the prohibition against living on the avails of prostitution (s. 212(1)(j)) was arbitrary and grossly disproportionate because it actually made sex workers more vulnerable to violence and exploitation by increasing their dependence on abusive third parties. She also found that it was overbroad because it captured all sex workers' relationships with others, including those that were safety-enhancing (see *Canada (Attorney General) v. Bedford*, 2013, para. 21). Finally, Justice Himel found that the public-communicating provision

(s. 213(1)(c)) was grossly disproportionate because it prevented sex workers from adequately screening their clients, while providing only a small social benefit. She also found that it infringed the freedom of expression guarantee under Section 2(b) of the Charter. Justice Himel found that it would be inappropriate to suspend the declaration of the laws' invalidity (*Bedford v. Canada*, 2010, para. 538) because of the danger that their continuing enforcement posed to sex workers' lives. The decision was heralded as a victory, not just for the three applicants but also for sex worker rights movements across Canada and throughout the world.

Bedford at the Ontario Court of Appeal

Unsurprisingly given the arguments they put forth, the attorneys general of Canada and Ontario appealed Justice Himel's decision. In addition to the original parties, the Court of Appeal heard submissions from a large number of interveners, including organizations focused on sex work, HIV/AIDS, and civil liberties, which supported the health, safety, and human rights arguments of the applicants, as well as anti–sex work women's organizations, which supported the governments' arguments for upholding the laws (see also Beer, this collection).[3] On March 26, 2012, the Ontario Court of Appeal rendered its judgment, affirming Justice Himel's ruling that the bawdy-house law was unconstitutional. It also found that the "living on the avails" provision infringed Section 7 of the Charter but could be saved by reading in words so that the prohibition applied only to those who lived on the avails of prostitution in circumstances of exploitation (*Bedford v. Canada*, 2012, para. 6). It overturned Justice Himel's decision on the communicating law, with Justices James MacPherson and Eleanore Cronk dissenting. The Court of Appeal found that the restrictions on communicating met the goal of protecting residential neighbourhoods from nuisances in a way that was not overbroad or grossly disproportionate in its impacts on sex workers' safety. Neither the applicants nor the defendants were happy with this decision. In particular, sex workers were deeply concerned that upholding the communicating law meant that the most vulnerable sex workers would continue to face arrests, harassment by police, prosecution, and violence.

Bedford at the Supreme Court of Canada

At the end of October 2012, the Supreme Court of Canada granted leave to hear Canada's and Ontario's appeals on the bawdy-house and "living on the avails" provisions and the applicants' cross-appeal on the communicating provision. Canada's highest court heard the case at a one-day hearing on June 13, 2013, with interventions by many of the same parties that had appeared previously, as well as new ones.[4] Those supporting the applicants addressed experiences of Indigenous women in sex work, sex work and women's autonomy, and technical aspects of legal fact finding and decision making. Those supporting the government addressed experiences of Asian women in sex work, issues of morality, and the value of human life in Canadian culture. One intervener, the United Nations HIV/AIDS Secretariat, did not take a position on the outcome of the litigation but rather intervened to ensure that the court was apprised of international human rights and public health standards regarding sex work in the context of the global HIV pandemic. Hearings at the Supreme Court of Canada are highly condensed, with parties granted one hour each for oral argument and interveners granted just ten minutes each. Thus all the arguments presented were very focused.

Six months after the hearing, on December 20, 2013, in a unanimous decision written by Chief Justice Beverley McLachlin, the Supreme Court affirmed Justice Himel's findings and struck down all three laws. Most importantly for sex workers, the Supreme Court of Canada affirmed key factual findings by Justice Himel and drew legal conclusions that the laws, individually and in combination, made sex work more dangerous. The court ruled that the evidence "amply supported" (*Canada (Attorney General) v. Bedford*, 2013, para. 300) the finding that the safest form of sex work was independent work from a fixed location and that out-call work was not as safe as in-call. This difference was particularly evident when sex workers were precluded by virtue of the "living on the avails" provision from hiring those who were not exploitative and could instead make sex work safer, such as drivers, receptionists, or security guards. It also found that prohibiting sex work from fixed locations inhibited sex workers from establishing a regular trusted clientele and from employing safeguards to reduce risks (paras. 64 and 67, affirming *Canada (Attorney General) v. Bedford*, 2012, para. 421). The prohibition on bawdy-houses likewise prevented provision of preventative health measures and resort to safe houses where sex workers could see their clients (para. 64). Finally, the court found that screening clients for intoxication or propensity toward violence was a key security practice; street-based sex workers were often precluded from employing such measures under the communicating law because of their overriding concerns for negotiating with clients as quickly as possible to avoid police attention and arrest (paras. 69–71, citing *Canada (Attorney General) v. Bedford*,

2012, paras. 301, 421, 432). Enforcement of communicating laws also displaced sex workers to unfamiliar areas where they were less able to avail themselves of help if needed (para. 70, citing *Canada (Attorney General) v. Bedford*, 2012, paras. 331, 502). All three provisions were therefore found to infringe Section 7 guarantees of liberty and security of the person, with the Supreme Court writing,

> The prohibitions at issue do not merely impose conditions on how prostitutes operate. They go a critical step further, by imposing *dangerous* conditions on prostitution; they prevent people engaged in a risky – but legal – activity from taking steps to protect themselves from the risks. (Para. 60, emphasis in original)

On the issue of causation and whether the laws produced the harm that sex workers experienced, the attorneys general of Ontario and Canada had argued that sex workers chose to engage in an inherently risky activity, coming into harm's way through their own actions rather than through the operation of the laws (*Canada (Attorney General) v. Bedford*, 2013, para. 79). They argued that the real source of harm was violent third parties (para. 84). The Supreme Court rejected these arguments and found that there was a "sufficient causal connection" between the effect of the laws and the harms they caused to sex workers:

> It is certainly conceivable ... that some street prostitutes would not refuse a client even if communication revealed potential danger. It is also conceivable that the danger may not be perfectly predicted in advance. However, that does not negate the application judge's finding that communication is an essential tool that can decrease risk. The assessment is qualitative, not quantitative. If screening could have prevented one woman from jumping into Robert Pickton's car, the severity of the harmful effects is established. (Para. 158)

The Supreme Court also found that because of the way that the laws worked together, they could not be considered in isolation but were "intertwined" and had an "impact on each other." Any new legal regime would need to consider the interconnected nature of various legal provisions:

> Greater latitude in one measure – for example, permitting prostitutes to obtain the assistance of security personnel – might impact on the

constitutionality of another measure – for example, forbidding the nuisances associated with keeping a bawdy-house. The regulation of prostitution is a complex and delicate matter. It will be for Parliament, should it
choose to do so, to devise a new approach, reflecting different elements of
the existing regime. (Para. 165)

Perhaps mindful of the deadlock experienced by the Parliamentary Subcommittee on Solicitation Laws Review, which failed to reach a consensus
on law reform in 2006 after two years of hearings and consultations, the
Supreme Court concluded that "moving abruptly from a situation where
prostitution is regulated to a situation where it is entirely unregulated would
be a matter of great concern to many Canadians" (*Canada (Attorney General) v. Bedford*, 2013, para. 168).

Thus, instead of making an immediate declaration of invalidity, as Justice
Himel had done, the Supreme Court delayed the invalidation of the three
laws, giving the government a year to choose whether it would legislate further in the area or allow prostitution to be unregulated under the criminal
law, as was the case with abortion (see *R. v. Morgentaler,* 1988).

Lessons from *Bedford*

The findings of fact in *Bedford* changed the legal and political landscape for
sex work in Canada for those who make the law as well as those who interpret it. *Bedford* established that there is great variety in how and where sex
work takes place and that rather than being a public nuisance, most sex
work happens indoors and is invisible to the general public. The *Bedford*
decision demolished the notion that relationships between sex workers and
others are necessarily parasitic, replacing it with factual evidence that working and living with others enhances sex workers' safety and reduces the isolation that many sex workers experience. The decision further affirmed sex
workers' assertions that they engage in very specific practices to assess the
potential risks of any given interaction with a client in order to provide
themselves with greater control and a means of escape if necessary. Despite
arguments by the attorneys general of Canada and Ontario and anti–sex
work interveners painting sex workers as hapless victims, the picture that
emerges from the court decisions is one of diverse, practical individuals
navigating a host of situations, with the laws acting as constant impedi-
ments. In addition, the *Bedford* case brought home the idea that sex work
laws function together and must be considered as an interconnected system

in terms of the impacts they have, and it importantly established that the harms of our criminal laws must be assessed on the basis of their impact on the constitutional rights of those most affected.

Conclusion

Bedford was a critical turning point in the legal dialogue around sex work in Canada. It allowed courts to see sex workers as human beings – rational actors attempting to keep themselves safe under a criminal law regime that stigmatizes them, their relationships with others, and the people they work with. After a century of justifying and upholding the prostitution laws, our courts paused to seriously deliberate on the damage those laws were doing to the human rights of sex workers. The disappointing postscript to *Bedford* is that the laws drafted and implemented by the Conservative federal government in response to the decision did not protect and promote sex worker rights. On December 6, 2014, after a cursory consultation process that sidelined sex workers and their allies, the government enacted Bill C-36, the Protection of Communities and Exploited Persons Act, which criminalizes purchasing sexual services for the first time in Canada. The new provisions not only replicate the harms of the laws struck down in *Bedford* but also go further by constraining client communications and other safety-enhancing measures among all sex workers, including indoor workers, who previously had less interaction with law enforcement (see also Krüsi, Belak, and Sex Workers United Against Violence, this collection; Sterling, this collection). As we see in many of the chapters in this collection, the impacts of this new legislation are being felt by sex workers across the country.

Notes

The views expressed in this chapter are those of the author and have not been endorsed by the BC Supreme Court.

1 At the same time as *Bedford* was proceeding through the courts, sex workers in Vancouver, led by Sex Workers United Against Violence (SWUAV) and Sheryl Kiselbach and represented by Pivot Legal Society, were pursuing their own challenge, which was thwarted by procedural objections from the attorney general of Canada. SWUAV intervened in the *Bedford* case at the Supreme Court of Canada, along with PACE Society and Pivot Legal Society.
2 These organizations were the Christian Legal Fellowship, Real Women of Canada, and the Catholic Civil Rights League.

3 At the Court of Appeal, a large number of organizations intervened to support the applicants' argument that the provisions should be struck down: the Canadian Civil Liberties Association; a coalition made up of Providing Alternatives Counselling and Education Society, Downtown Eastside Sex Workers United Against Violence Society, and Pivot Legal Society; the Canadian HIV/AIDS Legal Network; the British Columbia Centre for Excellence in HIV/AIDS; the British Columbia Civil Liberties Association; and both POWER and Maggie's: Toronto Sex Workers Action Project, two peer-run sex worker organizations in Ottawa and Toronto respectively. The Women's Coalition for the Abolition of Prostitution – made up of the Canadian Association of Sexual Assault Centres, the Native Women's Association of Canada, the Canadian Association of Elizabeth Fry Societies, Action ontarienne contre la violence faite aux femmes, La concertation des luttes contre l'exploitation sexuelle, Le regroupement québécois des centres d'aide et de lutte contre les agressions à caractère sexuel, and the Vancouver Rape Relief Society – intervened on the side of the government to argue that the provisions should be upheld.

4 The sex worker organizations Maggie's and POWER were denied intervener status at the Supreme Court, where new interveners included Aboriginal Legal Services of Toronto Inc., the attorney general of Quebec, Asian Women Coalition Ending Prostitution, the David Asper Centre for Constitutional Rights, the Evangelical Fellowship of Canada, the HIV and AIDS Legal Clinic of Ontario, the Secretariat of the Joint United Nations Program on HIV/AIDS, and the Simone de Beauvoir Institute of Concordia University.

Cases

Bedford v. Canada, 2010 ONSC 4264.
Canada (Attorney General) v. Bedford, 2012 ONCA 186.
Canada (Attorney General) v. Bedford, 2013 SCC 72, [2013] 3 SCR 1101.
Canada (Attorney General) v. Downtown Eastside Sex Workers United Against Violence Society, 2012 SCC 45, [2012] 2 SCR 524.
R. v. Bedford (2000), 184 DLR (4th) 727 (CA).
R. v. Morgentaler, [1988], 1 SCR 30.

Legislation

Bill C-36, Protection of Communities and Exploited Persons Act, SC 2014, c. 25.
Canadian Charter of Rights and Freedoms, part 1 of the Constitution Act, 1982, being Schedule B to the Canada Act 1982 (UK), 1982, c. 11.
Criminal Code, RSC 1985, c. C-46.

4

Municipal Regulation of Street-Based Prostitution and the Impacts on Indigenous Women
——— A Necessary Discussion

NAOMI SAYERS

In 2006 the Ontario Ministry of Municipal Affairs and Housing introduced Bill 130, the Municipal Statute Law Amendment Act. The intent of the bill was to give municipalities "more tools and greater flexibility to creatively serve their residents" (Gerretsen, 2006, n.p.), thus providing Ontario municipalities broad bylaw-making powers. For instance, municipalities may pass bylaws related to public nuisance, "including matters that, in the opinion of council, are or could become or cause public nuisances" (ibid., s. 128). Sometimes, these powers extend over into a federal power, like the regulation of certain criminal activities. Courts, however, have reluctantly refused to narrowly interpret a municipality's bylaw-making powers for not being within its jurisdiction to pass such laws. When it comes to Parliament's ability to regulate prostitution, there is very little discussion about municipalities also regulating prostitution in relation to their bylaw-making powers, like those listed above. This situation is important to highlight given that the majority of street-based prostitutes, such as Indigenous women and drug-dependent women, come from marginalized backgrounds. Unfortunately, governments rarely consider this reality.

This chapter explores municipalities' broad bylaw-making powers by examining the regulation of street-based prostitution, the effects of the discussions about such regulation, although limited, on Indigenous women's realities, and the right of Indigenous women, especially those who engage in selling and trading sex, to engage in policy and law reform initiatives as active agents, especially in light of the launch of the National Inquiry into Missing and Murdered Indigenous Women and Girls (Government of Canada, 2016). Organizations and individuals involved with women working on the street argue that "Indigenous women make up 70% of visible (street-based) sex workers" (Ontario Native Women's Association, 2016, p. 6). Yet it is street-based prostitution that forces governments to consider concerns about safety, properties, and ultimately the community. When regulation by any level of government targets the most marginalized individuals, there is often little benefit extended to them.

In British Columbia the lieutenant governor established the Missing Women Commission of Inquiry and named the Honourable Wally T. Oppal as its commissioner in 2010, with a mandate to examine the police investigations into women reported missing in Vancouver's Downtown Eastside (Missing Women Commission of Inquiry, 2013a). This provincial inquiry was fundamentally different from the recently established National Inquiry into Missing and Murdered Indigenous Women and Girls, whose mandate is quite broad in comparison (Government of Canada, 2016). However, the latter's mandate intends to build off of British Columbia's inquiry. Oppal's (2012b) limited mandate prevented him from commenting on the validity of Canada's prostitution laws. When discussing marginalization in the context of missing and murdered women in the Downtown Eastside, Oppal (2012a) writes,

> Marginalization is closely related to the condition of endangerment and vulnerability to predation, creating the climate in which the missing and murdered women were forsaken. Three overarching social and economic trends contribute to the women's marginalization: retrenchment of social assistance programs, the ongoing effects of colonialism, and the criminal regulation of prostitution and related law enforcement strategies. (p. 10)

Despite valid reasons related to the well-being of the public for regulating street-based prostitution, such public interest reasons should not overshadow other options for providing greater safety and support for the most marginalized in the sex trade: Indigenous women.

Current Case Law Governing Street-Based Prostitution

Courts have been reluctant to decide against a municipality's power to regulate certain activities, like prostitution, that also fall under Parliament's regulatory powers. This is particularly true if the municipality crafts laws that regulate activities under its broad bylaw-making powers (see also van der Meulen and Durisin, this collection). A 1983 decision by the Supreme Court, for example, declared a City of Calgary bylaw prohibiting certain uses of the city's streets, including for prostitution and related purposes, to be constitutionally invalid (*Westendorp v. The Queen*, 1983, para. 7). The court recognized that the bylaw extended beyond control of the streets and targeted certain activities (i.e., prostitution) related to "what is said by a person, referable to the offer of sexual services" (para. 16). The court also noted that the bylaw targeted only prostitution-related activities and that it did not provide benefit to other individuals, like the "control and enjoyment of property" (para. 16). It is thus reasonable to presume that a municipality may regulate against street-based prostitution if the bylaw provides benefits to other individuals. Leading up to the Supreme Court decision, the Alberta Court of Appeal, however, held that a municipality may enact a bylaw when it acts as a "preventative measure" (para. 20). The Supreme Court disagreed and clarified the Court of Appeal's reasoning by holding that the City of Calgary had confused its bylaw-making powers with Parliament's power to regulate criminal activities (para. 21). This is what is called a jurisdictional issue, when one level of government's legislative powers encroaches upon another's (i.e., the division of powers in Canada's Constitution Act of 1867).

Thirty years later, following the ruling in *Canada (Attorney General) v. Bedford* (2013), wherein Canada's top court declared three prostitution provisions, including one targeting street-based prostitution, to be invalid for violating the Charter (see also Belak, this collection), similar jurisdictional issues related to street-based prostitution have arisen. In 2014 the federal government introduced Bill C-36, the Protection of Communities and Exploited Persons Act (PCEPA), and in doing so reintroduced provisions similar to those struck down by the court the year previous, including provisions prohibiting street-based prostitution (Protection of Communities and Exploited Persons Act, SC 2014, c-25, s 213). The newly enacted street-based sex work law targets the regulation of traffic, namely "stopping or impeding traffic" (ibid., marginal notes).[1] PCEPA did what the Supreme Court said the City of Calgary could not do, namely regulate street-based prostitution for the purposes of prohibiting certain uses of the street.

When it comes to interpreting the scope and validity of a municipality's bylaw, courts presume all bylaws to be validly enacted unless there is a clear contradiction with federal legislation or a clear constitutional violation

(*114957 Canada Ltée (Spraytech, Société d'arrosage) v. Hudson (Town)*, 2001, para. 41). Courts will also not rely on Charter principles unless there is genuine ambiguity in the wording of the bylaw (*Bell ExpressVu Limited Partnership v. Rex*, 2002, para. 62). This practice leaves the door wide open for municipalities to regulate street-based prostitution according to their bylaw-making powers.

With Bill C-36 passed into law, the Ottawa Police Service's website indicates that it intends to enforce this new legislation (Ottawa Police Service 2017a). To date, there have been as many as nine arrests in so-called john sweeps, which are policing initiatives to target clients of street-based prostitutes as opposed to targeting people offering and selling sexual services (*CBC News*, 2016). The Ottawa Police Service (2017a) has also requested "supports to assist those in the sex trade" as well as necessary "legislative tools to address community concerns related to sex trade activities in our communities." A bylaw targeting street-based prostitution as a whole, as opposed to just the clients, may provide the Ottawa Police Service with a legislative tool for addressing community concerns. However, many street-based prostitutes come from marginalized communities. Relying on legislative tools to marginalize an already overmarginalized group would not and should not be justified when placed within a Charter-based analysis. Despite some people and institutions favouring these bylaws regulating street-based prostitution, necessary discussions must take place that centre Indigenous women as active agents and community members.

The National Inquiry and Concerns for Women in the Sex Trade

Concerns regarding street-based prostitution rarely acknowledge women in the sex trade as community members. The focus on regulating street-based work is intended to do away with prostitution as a whole. The perception is that to get rid of prostitution, one must get rid of the prostitute. These two separate but related premises – that people in prostitution are not members of the community and that community concerns are always focused on displacing these same people from the community – are important to highlight because discussions on the regulation of street-based prostitution rarely examine the effects of these premises in reality, namely the marginalization of street-based prostitutes. Laws and other forms of regulation (e.g., bylaws) have real consequences, especially in the lives of Indigenous women. This statement is evidenced by the high rates of missing and murdered Indigenous women, whose realities may include engaging in prostitution.

At the time that the Honourable Wally T. Oppal was named commissioner of British Columbia's Missing Women Commission of Inquiry, he was a former judge, politician, and lawyer who had been recognized for his work on criminal justice issues (Missing Women Commission of Inquiry, 2013b). Within the commission's report, Oppal (2012b) defined marginalization as a "social process by which individuals and groups are relegated to the fringe of society," and he connected marginalization to "social exclusion" and "social disadvantage" (p. 78). Together, these concepts "systematically [block people] from rights, opportunities and resources that are normally available in a society" (ibid., p. 78). The majority of discussions on the regulation of street-based prostitution create environments that marginalize and exclude street-based prostitutes from communities, which dehumanizes this same class of individuals.

Even as discussions dehumanize people in prostitution by not seeing them as community members who can benefit from the same rights as others, these discussions also prevent input from those directly involved in the sex trade, such as prostitutes themselves. Prostitutes would have to "out" their status, which could lead to increased police surveillance and police harassment (*Canada (Attorney General) v. Downtown Eastside Sex Workers United Against Violence Society*, 2012, para. 71). These same concerns extend to outing oneself in other public processes, like community consultations concerning prostitution. In the context of the National Inquiry into Missing and Murdered Indigenous Women and Girls, this type of outing is troubling since Indigenous women who engage in prostitution would have to disclose being a prostitute in order to be seen as having access to the same rights as other Indigenous women.

After I published an op-ed in the *Ottawa Citizen* calling on the national inquiry to ensure that Indigenous sex trade workers are heard (Sayers, 2016), I received an invitation from the minister of Indigenous and northern affairs, Carolyn Bennett (2016), to present at the pre-inquiry consultations. Yet I know all too well the risks in choosing to participate in discussions about the regulation of the industry or about prostitution in general. Immediately following my testimony to the House of Common's Standing Committee on Justice and Human Rights in 2014, for example, I received harassing tweets, emails, and letters from people who identify as anti-violence advocates or as "abolitionists" seeking to abolish the sex trade and from people employed by such groups (see also Porth, this collection). For the pre-inquiry consultations in 2016, I went alone and arrived on the second day. I found prohibitionists and their supporters occupying an entire row of chairs. The consultation facilitator – an Indigenous woman who is a prominent community leader and who aligns with prohibitionist views on sex work – explained at the outset that this was not a day "for politicking" and asked attendees to leave politics at the door. Still, the president of a prominent Native women's organization occupied Minister Bennett's time as soon as the minister stepped into the room.

Then, later that day, an employee of this same group stood up to speak and called for an end to prostitution. At that moment, I decided not to speak because I did not want to be seen as "politicking," as I had assumed that the facilitator meant zero discussion of policies on prostitution and no calls for the inclusion of the experiences of Indigenous women who sell or trade sexual services. As potentially the only person in the room who identified as someone with such experience and who supported the human rights of people in the sex trade, including the right to live free from violence, I feared an increase in harassment similar to what I had experienced during and after testifying before the House of Commons committee. I sat alone and in silence. Hence the national inquiry engaged in a process that effectively silenced Indigenous women who have sex trade experience and who do not support the criminal regulation of prostitution.

Even as discussions tend to fixate on the high numbers of Indigenous women in street-based prostitution, the focus is mostly on getting Indigenous women *out* of prostitution while ignoring why they go into it in the first place. Oppal (2012b) outlined some of these reasons in his final report, such as the social conditions in which Indigenous women live every day, including forced displacement and racism or racist policies as a result of colonialism (see also James, this collection). It is also these same women who are likely to be reported missing or murdered, as demonstrated by British Columbia's Missing Women Commission of Inquiry. Although the limited mandate of the provincial commission prevented Oppal from commenting on the validity of the prostitution provisions, he was not precluded from discussing prostitution and related laws in general and their effects on prostitutes. Thus he noted that criminal regulation, especially of street-based prostitution, has been applied unevenly, most notably within different cities across Canada (Oppal 2012b, p. 99), that the emphasis is on "curbing the visibility of prostitution" (p. 100), and that the focus is mostly on street-based prostitution despite the fact that it makes up only 5 to 20 percent of the entire industry (p. 100). When the attention is on street-based prostitution, the effects include displacing people to more unsafe areas or forcing them to hastily enter a client's vehicle (*Canada (Attorney General) v. Bedford*, 2013, para. 158).[2]

The effects of street-based regulation are especially noticeable given that street-based prostitutes experience the highest rates of violence. Oppal (2012b) comments on this violence: "The murder rate of adult women engaged in street prostitution is estimated to be between 60 and 120 times the rate of other adult women" (p. 104). The Ottawa Police Service (2017b) released a notice to people in the sex trade "in light of a potential pattern of homicides involving sex trade workers in the City of Ottawa," although it paradoxically also advised this same group to take "more time than usual before getting into a vehicle," which would increase the risk of police surveillance, police harassment, and ultimately arrest.

With the National Inquiry into Missing and Murdered Indigenous Women and Girls, it is imperative for discussions not to ignore that the realities of street-based prostitutes are worsened by the continued criminal and related regulation of street-based prostitution. The effects of criminal regulation were made clear in Oppal's report (2012b) on missing women in Vancouver's Downtown Eastside. The government continues to ignore these realities when these laws are still on the books, especially the solicitation provisions. Oppal may have had a limited mandate in conducting British Columbia's Missing Women Commission of Inquiry, but there is ample opportunity for the national inquiry to examine the validity of prostitution and related laws. When individuals and organizations call for decriminalization, it is essential to highlight that these calls do not mean repealing provisions targeting human trafficking; it is Canada's obligation as a signatory of the United Nations (2000) protocol to end human trafficking. Still, the discussions concentrate on the alleged increase in human trafficking when a state decriminalizes prostitution (Harvard Law School, 2014). Although human trafficking does happen, the suggestion that it increases when a state decriminalizes prostitution is a distraction from the lived realities of women, especially Indigenous women, in prostitution. These realities reveal that they are more likely to be reported missing, if ever missed at all, or to be found murdered. Even policing strategies that are aimed at targeting only clients tend to backfire; the police leave street-based prostitutes with little to no option but to hurriedly enter cars out of fear that the client can face arrest (see also Krüsi, Belack, and Sex Workers United Against Violence, this collection). People in prostitution must risk their own lives because of these kinds of policing strategies. The police then ironically provide tips on how to avoid situations of violence, such as taking more time than usual before getting into a vehicle.

Conclusion

If policing agencies and communities are concerned about street-based prostitution, there should be a focus on working to support these women before they enter the profession. And if the Canadian government is truly concerned about addressing the issue of missing and murdered Indigenous women and girls, there have to be substantive discussions about what pushes Indigenous women into the sex trade in the first place. There should be practical responses like working to end the continued marginalization of Indigenous women, especially marginalization through the criminal regulation of prostitution and related strategies.

Notes

1 It should be highlighted that the constitutional challenge in *Canada (Attorney General) v. Bedford* (2013) did not affect any other provisions regulating communication for the purposes of prostitution, as only Section 213(1)(c) was challenged and repealed. However, it is alleged that PCEPA did not substantively amend this provision, although the new legislation did amend the intent of this provision by explicitly referring to "stopping or impeding traffic." If and when this provision is challenged, the courts will look to the intent in order to determine whether the amendment is within Parliament's power to pass such a provision while striking a balance of any rights infringement with the intent of the provision. This balancing is important to highlight because the courts have repeatedly upheld provisions that fall under a provincial power and a federal power to make laws if the purpose of either the provincial or federal law is of "roughly equal importance" (*R. v. Keshane*, 2012, para. 18). It will be necessary for sex worker rights groups to consider this equivalence in the event that such a challenge is brought forward since many opposing groups that agree with the regulation of prostitution often argue that the increase of traffic affects their businesses or enjoyment of property. I am not suggesting, however, that a prostitute's right to work freely and safely should not be prioritized; rather, I am merely commenting on current case law that discusses these constitutional doctrines.

2 Although some people suggest that the laws de facto force prostitutes into more unsafe areas – an assessment with which I agree – I do not qualify "force" since it is the term used in the decision of *Canada (Attorney General) v. Bedford* (2013).

References

Bennett, C. (2016, February 6). Wd love you to join us on the 15th for the Ottawa consultation @kwetoday @OttawaCitizen #MMIW #cdnpoli. [Tweet]. Retrieved from https://twitter.com/Carolyn_Bennett/status/696132029570744320

CBC News. (2016, February 26). Men arrested in daytime john sweep in Vanier, police say. Retrieved from http://www.cbc.ca/news/canada/ottawa/vanier-john -sweep-prostitution-afternoon-1.3465811

Gerretsen, J. (2006, June 15). *Introduction of bills: Municipal Statute Law Amendment Act, 2006*. Retrieved from http://www.ontla.on.ca/house-proceedings/ transcripts/files_html/2006-06-15_L091.htm#PARA314

Government of Canada. (2016, October 11). *About the independent inquiry*. Retrieved from https://www.aadnc-aandc.gc.ca/eng/1470140972428/1470141043933

Harvard Law School. (2014, June 12). *Does legalized prostitution increase human trafficking?* [Web log post]. Retrieved from https://orgs.law.harvard.edu/ lids/2014/06/12/does-legalized-prostitution-increase-human-trafficking/

Missing Women Commission of Inquiry. (2013a). *About this commission*. Retrieved from http://www.missingwomeninquiry.ca

Missing Women Commission of Inquiry. (2013b). *Honourable Wally Oppal, Q.C., Commissioner of Inquiry*. Retrieved from http://www.missingwomeninquiry.ca/ wally-oppal/

Ontario Native Women's Association. (2016, February). *Sex trafficking of Indigenous women in Ontario*. Retrieved from http://www.onwa.ca/upload/documents/ report-sex-trafficking-of-indigenous-wom.pdf

Oppal, W.T. (2012a). *Forsaken: The report of the Missing Women Commission of Inquiry: Executive summary*. Retrieved from http://www.missingwomeninquiry. ca/wp-content/uploads/2010/10/Forsaken-ES-web-RGB.pdf

Oppal, W.T. (2012b). *Forsaken: The report of the Missing Women Commission of Inquiry: Volume 1*. Retrieved from http://www.missingwomeninquiry.ca/wp -content/uploads/2010/10/Forsaken-Vol-1-web-RGB.pdf

Ottawa Police Service. (2017a). *Community concerns on prostitution*. Retrieved from https://www.ottawapolice.ca/en/safety-and-crime-prevention/Community -Concerns-on-Prostitution.asp

Ottawa Police Service. (2017b). *Sex trade workers*. Retrieved from https://www. ottawapolice.ca/en/safety-and-crime-prevention/Sex-Trade-Workers.asp

Sayers, N. (2016, February 4). MMIW inquiry needs to look at sex work. *Ottawa Citizen*. Retrieved from http://ottawacitizen.com/opinion/columnists/naomi -sayers-mmiw-inquiry-needs-to-look-at-sex-work

United Nations. (2000). *Protocol to prevent, suppress and punish trafficking in persons, especially women and children, supplementing the United Nations Convention against Transnational Crime*. Retrieved from http://www.osce.org/ odihr/19223?download=true

Cases

114957 Canada Ltée (Spraytech, Société d'arrosage) v. Hudson (Town), 2001 SCC 40, [2001] 2 SCR 241.

Bedford v. Canada, 2010 ONSC 4264.

Bell ExpressVu Limited Partnership v. Rex, 2002 SCC 42, [2002] 2 SCR 559.

Canada (Attorney General) v. Bedford, 2013 SCC 72, [2013] 3 SCR 1101.

Canada (Attorney General) v. Downtown Eastside Sex Workers United Against Vio-lence Society, 2012 SCC 45, [2012] 2 SCR 524.

R. v. Keshane, 2012 ABCA 330.

Westendorp v. The Queen, [1983] 1 SCR 43, 1983 CanLII 1 (SCC).

Legislation

Bill 130, *Municipal Statute Law Amendment Act,* 2006, SO 2006, c. 32.

Bill C-36, *Protection of Communities and Exploited Persons Act,* SC 2014, c. 25.

Canadian Charter of Rights and Freedoms, Part 1 of the *Constitution Act, 1982,* being Schedule B to the *Canada Act 1982* (UK), 1982, c. 11.

Criminal Code, RSC 1985, c. C-46.

5

From Average Joe to Deviant John
The Changing Construction of Sex Trade Clients in Canada

UMMNI KHAN

The socio-legal significance of sex trade clients in Canada has been unstable and contested over the past century and a half, but different discourses have dominated at different times. In the early Victorian era, for example, clients were generally tolerated, understood as ordinary men who were simply satiating their naturally robust libido (Backhouse, 1985). In the late nineteenth century, clients' vulnerability to acquiring sexually transmitted infections became a social concern (McLaren, 1986). Later, in the second half of the 1900s, the male client started to become more visible as an object of inquiry and social control, with this problematization intensifying over the past few decades. The recent criminalization of purchasing sexual services in Canada in 2014, along with the proliferating anti-prostitution discourse found in ideologically driven studies, the media, and pop culture, has constructed the man who buys sex as a veritable sexual deviant – a danger to women and to society in general.

Two things should be noted before beginning an analysis of the ways that clients have been constructed in the past 150 years. Female clients exist but have been entirely overlooked by anti-prostitution advocates. The experiences of transgender, gender-non-binary, and gender-variant clients have also been ignored. My focus on male clients should thus be interpreted not as support for the notion that sex buying is an inherently cis male activity but as a reflection of, and engagement with, the dominant narratives of clients. The other preliminary issue to address is the interconnection between the treatment and characterization of different participants in the sex trade. Although I focus on client characterizations, this necessarily involves exploring the socio-legal understanding of sex workers, as there is an inter-connection between sex worker and client constructions.

Evolving Attitudes toward Clients

The Necessary Evil – Tolerance of Sex Work

The recent criminalization of clients in Canada stands in stark contrast to historical understandings of sex work (see also van der Meulen and Durisin, this collection). There is, in fact, a long history in theology, philosophy, political discourse, and sexology that accepts men buying sexual services as the natural, if not necessarily the ideal, order of things.[1] In the Victorian era, Irish political theorist William Lecky (1838–1903) used the most stigmatizing, yet paradoxically glorifying, language to describe the social good that sex workers accomplished: "Herself the supreme type of vice, she is ultimately the most efficient guardian of virtue ... On that one degraded and ignoble form are concentrated the passions that might have filled the world with shame ... the eternal priestess of humanity, blasted for the sins of the people" (Lecky, 1890, quoted in L'Espérance, 1979, p. 317). Backhouse (1985) further points out that some Victorian moralists also saw prostitution as preferable to masturbation or to the seduction of "pure" women. For married men, prostitution would satisfy husbands who had surplus passion, and it effectively acted as a form of marital birth control. Such attitudes understood sex work as a safety valve to accommodate the natural overflow of male lust, which could not always be contained by the institution of marriage.

At the end of the 1800s, sexology provided scientific support for the hydraulic theory of male sexuality, suggesting some men needed an outlet for surplus desire, lest they turned to perversity.[2] Within this ideological script, the naturally lustful man was inversely mirrored by the inherently chaste woman. The sex worker was thus rendered a deviant form of woman, a fallen woman. Regardless of their actual identity, these fallen women were constructed as "throwbacks to a primoridial phase of racial development" (McClintock, 1992, p. 81) and, from the perspective of the middle-class gaze, were usually read as working-class women inclined to indecency. This narrative of sex workers as socially useful deviants and of sex work as serving a public good can be characterized as the "necessary evil" perspective.

The Inevitable Evil – Minimizing the Supposed Harm of Sex Work
Slightly different from conceptualizing prostitution as a necessary evil is the "inevitable evil" perspective. Like necessary evil, this perspective still sees purchasing sex as an "irregular indulgence of a natural impulse" (Walkowitz, 1982, p. 71). Unlike the "necessary evil" perspective, however, it does not credit sex work as producing any substantial social good but rather reluctantly accepts that it is impossible to fully eradicate this misconduct. The most that society can achieve is to control and regulate sex work, thereby minimizing its harmful effects, notably the nuisance that supposedly accompanies some forms of sex work and the presumed spread of disease. Historically, in response to both issues, sex workers bore the brunt of criminal regulation and punishment. The laws that implicated clients during the Victorian and post-Confederation era were minimal. For example, in 1839 clients could be charged for being a "habitual frequenter" of a brothel, and in 1915 this offence was updated to simply being "found in" a brothel (McLaren, 1992, para. 52; McLaren and Lowman, 1990, p. 37). However, the evidence suggests that there was very little enforcement of the laws (Backhouse, 1985; McLaren, 1986; Strange and Loo, 1997). In contrast, sex workers were targeted by a number of bawdy-house and vagrancy laws that were, indeed, enforced against them (McLaren, 1986). Furthermore, in 1865 Canada's Contagious Diseases Act, which remained in force for only five years and was based on the more robust Contagious Diseases Acts in the United Kingdom from 1864 to 1886, allowed the forced hospitalization of any sex worker perceived to be suffering from a venereal disease for up to three months; there was no comparable regulation for clients similarly suspected (Backhouse, 1985). The "inevitable evil" perspective thus replaced the image of the sex worker as "ignoble" but nonetheless the "priestess of humanity" (Lecky, 1890, quoted in L'Espérance, 1979, p. 317) with the image of the sex worker as a social nuisance and contagion. In this ideological framework, clients were given a pass for their contribution to perceived nuisance and were figured as potential victims of disease-carrying sex workers. As discussed below, it was not until the 1970s that clients would be more directly targeted by the law.

The Social Evil – Eradication of Sex Work
In tension with the construction of sex workers as fallen women who serve the greater good, as a social nuisance to the community, or as disease carriers who infect innocent men is the stereotype of the victim sex worker.

This approach may not be any more empowering than the nuisance or disease discourse; indeed, the two frameworks often intersect (Strega, Janzen, Morgan, and Brown, 2014). Nonetheless, when sex workers are positioned as inherent victims – whether of life circumstances, biological disposition, evil men, or their own purportedly bad choices – new ideological narratives are produced. Such narratives have existed throughout the past 150 years (and longer), but their interrelationship with client construction has evolved significantly in recent decades.

Around the time of Confederation, reformers in the social purity movement, who vehemently opposed the tolerance or mere regulation of prostitution, were gaining ground (Backhouse, 1985; McLaren, 1986). For such campaigners, prostitution was not a necessary or inevitable evil but a social evil. Then, as now, those who claimed to oppose sex work from a victim-centric perspective often conflated prostitution with sex trafficking, called white slavery in the late nineteenth century. The inflammatory concept of white slavery invokes a very specific storyline of an innocent, white female being kidnapped and forced into sexual servitude by an unscrupulous, racialized man. However, as McLaren (1992) and Valverde (2008) have pointed out, white slavery was a malleable concept fed by contradictory narratives that could be used to condemn any perceived form of sexual exploitation, whether the participants in the activity recognized it as such or not. So-called white slaves were often apportioned some blame for their plight. Nonetheless, blame was also spread to other figures, most prominently the perceived trafficker. This narrative featured evil men, and sometimes evil women, who lured or abducted females and prostituted them, both locally and internationally.

Significantly, the client also enters the stage as a wrongdoer in the "social evil" literature. Although in most cases he plays a minor role, some women's rights organizations at the time pointed out the sexist ways that sex workers were singled out for stigma, whereas clients were effectively ignored. The National Council of Women of Canada, for example, stated in its 1913 annual report, "One of our greatest weaknesses has been that we have construed this social evil as a female proposition ... Some of us think the social evil is a masculine proposition; certainly we shall never accomplish much until we lay upon the man the heavier end of this burden of guilt" (quoted in Valverde, 2008, pp. 93–94). For these middle-class feminists, the sex workers were partly excused because it was assumed that poverty, a substandard upbringing, and desperation drove them to the trade, whereas the man was understood simply to be satisfying lascivious desires.

Aside from feminist advocates critical of sexual double standards, most anti-prostitution reformers did not tend to focus their disapproving gaze on clients. However, two specific types of othered clients did surface in both the feminist and the conservative social purity literature: aristocratic clients and racialized clients. Whereas the selling of sexual services was understood to be caused by a working-class vice, vulnerability, or disposition, the buying of sexual services was sometimes blamed on the decadence of wealthy aristocratic men (Valverde, 2008). Fear of contamination and corruption thus implicated both the upper and the lower classes. An increase in immigration also incited fears of racialized masculinity. In particular, Chinese, Japanese, African, and East Indian migrants were caricatured as savage and thus as having sexual appetites that posed a threat to Canadian values, female virtue, and white purity (McLaren, 1992; Valverde, 2008).

Clients as Objects of Inquiry

Although aristocratic and racialized men were the subject of some commentary regarding the sex trade around the turn of the century, it was not until mid-century that the peculiarization of the client as a definable category began to take shape, particularly in psychology, psychiatry, psychoanalysis, and related fields. A key text in this regard was sexologist Alfred Kinsey and colleagues' study *Sexual Behavior in the Human Male* (Kinsey, Martin, and Pomeroy, 1948), which found that 69 percent of males had had at least one experience with a sex worker. Although the statistic established the prevalence of the behaviour, the question itself contributed to the classification of buying sexual services as a discrete activity worthy of examination. Similarly, famed American psychologist Albert Ellis (1959) published the article "Why Married Men Visit Prostitutes." He offered a variety of answers, some of which blamed the wife for being sexually stingy, or blamed circumstance such as illness or work-related reasons, or blamed the man for being neurotic, craving partner variety, or enjoying the illicitness. A British article by Gibbens and Silberman (1960) researched the same question but cast both married and unmarried clients as primarily neurotic subjects. It is notable that their analysis pathologized buying sex, partly by associating it with other "perversions," including masochism, sadism, and voyeurism.

The literature on the client as an object of inquiry continued to increase after this time, with a more intense proliferation in the past twenty-five years. Current-day scholarship and policy on clients can be divided into three categories: epidemiological, sociological, and prohibitionist. Disease-management scholarship still focuses on sex workers, although clients have recently joined the ranks of contagions (Atchison and Burnett, 2016; Faugier and Cranfield, 1995; Leonard, 1990; Shannon, Strathdee, Shoveller, Rusch, Kerr, and Tyndall, 2009; Smith and Seal, 2008). Although this perspective can reproduce some of the "inevitable evil" ideology, there is some recent destigmatizing literature on client engagement with safer sex practices as well (Atchison and Burnett, 2016). The sociological realm more broadly addresses client characteristics, motivations, and risks. Much of this empirical work de-exceptionalizes clients, finding that they are not fundamentally different from men who do not purchase sexual services (Benoit et al., 2014; Sanders, 2008). One subset of clients garnering scholarly and activist attention are those with disabilities, who may experience barriers to erotic expression and fulfilment due to ableist logics or to health challenges that require specialized knowledge on the part of a sexual partner (Fritsch, Heynen, Ross, and van der Meulen, 2016; Liddiard, 2014; Wotten and Isbister, 2010). Access to sexual services can thus have a profound effect on the rights and well-being of clients with disabilities. The sociological literature has also demonstrated that the criminalization of clients is associated with increased risk of violence for sex workers (Amnesty International, 2016; Krüsi et al., 2014; see also Krüsi, Belak, and Sex Workers United Against Violence, this collection).

In contrast, the prohibitionist stance deems all clients deviants and criminals (see also Durisin, van der Meulen, and Bruckert, this collection). Although we have seen that this perspective was historically embraced by feminist-inspired social purity reformers at the turn of the nineteenth century, it gained influence in the 1990s, partly due to Sweden's new approach to prostitution, which officially deemed the activity to be a form of violence against women (Swedish Institute, 2010). The so-called Swedish model criminalizes purchasers of sexual services, along with managers and other third parties, but technically not sex workers. Although the latest enactment of this legislation in Sweden is gender-neutral, its ideology is premised on the construction of a deviant male client and a victimized female worker. Kulick's (2005) analysis of the discursive process that reifies clients into "perverts" demonstrates a reiteration of older psychological ideologies, which pathologize desire for sex outside of a loving committed relationship. But the fact that medical language is being harnessed to explain buying sexual services does not mean that clients escape punishment; on the contrary, they are criminalized for their perceived psychological deficiencies, which purportedly violate women's rights. By substituting the rhetoric of morality with the rhetoric of pathology and gender equality, the Swedish approach to criminalizing clients has had a powerful impact on a global scale as countries reform their own prostitution laws (Skilbrei and Holmström, 2016).

This outcome has been seen in Canada. Canadian prohibitionist literature tends to consist of sensationalist, unsubstantiated morality tales that use isolated incidents of violent men posing as clients as emblematic of the essential character of the "john." Benjamin Perrin's (2010) *Invisible Chains: Canada's Underground World of Human Trafficking* and Victor Malarek's (2009) *The Johns: Sex for Sale and the Men Who Buy It* exemplify this strategy. Both of these general-reading books conflate sex work with sex trafficking, imply that there is something inherently violent in desiring sex without commitment, provide no citations of their major "truth" claims, rely heavily on law enforcement officers' anecdotal horror stories, and specifically promote the Swedish approach. It should be noted that the prohibitionist literature often claims to be based on sociology or psychology; however, as Lowman (2013) and others (Khan, 2015; Weitzer, 2005) have shown and as the recent Supreme Court decision in *Canada (Attorney General) v. Bedford* (2013) has determined, such studies are irrevocably flawed on an empirical level. Unfortunately, this evidence-informed insight has not swayed governmental bodies. For example, former Conservative member of Parliament Joy Smith's report on "tackling the demand" positions sex work as inherently harmful to women and girls – while typically ignoring male and gender-non-binary sex workers – and champions the Swedish model as Canada's best option (Smith, 2014b). Moreover, in justifying Canada's basic adoption of this approach in Bill C-36, the Protection of Communities and Exploited Persons Act (PCEPA), the former Conservative government relied heavily on reports sponsored by Sweden that claim its own policies on prostitution have been a success (Government of Canada, 2014), despite ample evidence to the contrary. Whether from a feminist or a family-values perspective, prohibitionism reproduces the moral panic of social evil and white slavery – although it is now called the "violence against women" framework or the human-trafficking perspective (Benedet, 2007; Farley, 2004; Government of Canada, 2014; Smith, 2014a).

The "Social Evil" Redux: The Client as Sex Deviant and Criminal
With the implementation of PCEPA in 2014, the prohibitionist perspective has now been legally entrenched in Canada, and clients are subject to a variety of formal and informal punishments. Section 286.1 of the Criminal Code, entitled "Commodification of Sexual Activity," designates the purchase of sex as a hybrid offence, subject to either an indictable or summary

conviction. The punishment ranges from a minimum fine of $500 to a maximum jail term of five years. But before guilt is established or a verdict released, the informal punishment can begin, significantly without any due process. Police officers can send shaming letters to *suspected* clients driving in areas associated with sex work, which could be received or intercepted by family members or employers (Khan, 2015). Using public-shaming tactics, police in Canada (as well as the United States and elsewhere) often release the names of arrested suspected clients to the media. Although some accused men have alleged that such tactics infringe their right to life, liberty, and security of the person as protected by Section 7 of the Charter of Rights and Freedoms, formal legal challenges have not been successful to date (*R. v. Mercer*, 2016).

Another pretrial tool that can be used to exert social control over suspected clients is the so-called john school. These are court diversion programs that allow persons arrested for purchasing sexual services to opt for an educational program, instead of facing a trial and possible conviction. John schools came into Canada in the mid-1990s and were seen as an innovative, cost-effective, and victim-centred response to the "problem" of prostitution (Wortley, Fischer, and Webster, 2002). They have been a relatively consistent feature of client stigmatization and sex work criminalization ever since, although some police services reported a decline in their use while the laws were being constitutionally challenged, most notably in relation to *Bedford* (Rotenberg, 2016). As PCEPA has now firmly established client criminalization in Canadian law, john schools seem to have become re-entrenched as a standard practice (ibid.).

John schools operate by charging alleged clients a fee in the range of $500 to $1,000, which funds a workshop that they must attend. During my primary research on john schools, conducted in 2011, I observed attendees, who were figured as would-be criminals and, thanks to the grace of the criminal justice system, had been given a "second chance" through john school.[3] The day often began with a Crown lawyer outlining the sex work–related laws in Canada and the conditions for successfully completing the diversion program. This person was followed by various other guest speakers, who engaged with a range of ideologies that constructed clients in diverse, but always pejorative, ways.

Typically, a woman identifying as an "ex-prostituted woman" shared a heart-wrenching story of the abuse, poverty, and addiction that had led her to the sex trade. She then generalized this story to all sex work, chastised the men for driving the demand, and construed them as perpetrators of violence against women, even if unwittingly so. Another shaming speaker was the representative of the neighbourhood association, who lectured the men on the ways that sex work harmed the community by reducing property values and making non-sex-working women feel unsafe. In one such session, the community resident analogized participants in the sex trade to "cockroaches that come out at night," thus equally stigmatizing both sex workers and clients. Needless to say, such vermin analogies have an extraordinarily dehumanizing effect, justifying punitive laws and creating the conditions for violence against sex workers (Lowman, 2000).

From a harm reduction perspective, a nurse also presented on the health risks of buying sexual services, sometimes showing menacing close-ups of genitals with sexually transmitted infections and always providing safer-sex information. Bringing the same message closer to home, some john schools featured a wife or girlfriend, who revived the discourse on the sex worker as disease vector. Like the "ex-prostituted woman," she gave a moving personal account of contracting a sexually transmitted infection from her husband, who had – unbeknownst to her – been visiting sex workers.

A final frequent speaker worthy of mention was the former sex buyer, who identified as a recovering sex addict. This speaker offered a medical diagnosis to explain the social problem of purchasing sexual services, building on some of the mid-century pathologization literature steeped in psychological discourses. Offering the most sympathy, he encouraged the attendees to consider their behaviour within an addiction model and to seek out counselling, along with peer assistance.

John school presents a fascinating amalgam of narratives that produce clients as deviants who are harmful to society, communities, sex workers, non-sex-working women, their own families, and themselves. It is built on hyperbole, moralistic understandings of good and bad sex, distorted and uncited statistics, and anecdotal evidence. It also has a disproportionate effect on racialized and working-class clients (Fischer, Wortley, Webster, and Kirst, 2002), echoing the earlier racist impact of the "social evil" discourse. Although stigmatizing, dehumanizing, and shaming, it offers redemption by the end of the program if the suspected clients recommit to coupled, noncommercial, normative sexuality.

Conclusion

An analysis of the evolving construction of sex work reveals the contradictions and role reversals of its participants through different eras and in different discourses. In some sectors, sex workers were at once reviled and revered for the "dirty work" they did in containing male sexual excess, which protected families and virtuous women. But this characterization was in tension with those who saw them as disease carriers contaminating decent people. Both of these constructions have given way to the sex worker as quintessential victim, although she still retains the taint of deviancy. She must be "rescued" from her deviant lifestyle, compelled to recognize her own degradation, and coerced to leave the trade if necessary. In contrast, clients were once an overlooked character in mainstream prostitution debates. But they have also been, at times, endowed with victim status because of their supposedly heightened vulnerability to sexually transmitted infections. But now, second only to the caricature of the pimp and the trafficker, clients have been cast as inherent deviants.

At the forefront of the fight against this negative construction of clients are sex workers themselves. Sex workers have attested to the humanity of their clients (Ross, 2007; Sycamore, 2000) and to the ways that client stigmatization and criminalization intensify sex workers' vulnerability to violence, while undermining their ability to earn a living (Kohn, 2016; Nikiforuk, 2014). Moreover, sex workers are talking back to the ideologies that have demeaned them and their clients. For example, in a widely circulated article published in the magazine *Vice*, "A Letter from a Sex Worker to a Wife about Her Cheating Husband," April Adams (2015) asserts, "I am the secret ingredient in a lot of healthy marriages." In this epistolary communique, she refutes the disease-vector stereotype, pointing out the safety precautions that characterize what I assume to be escort work. She further explains that her married clients want more sex than their wives do and that thanks to professionals like her, everyone gets the level of sexual contact that they desire. This perspective, of course, echoes the "necessary evil" framework, but it removes the evil. Because Adams takes pride in her services, her description rejects the deviancy label and positions sex work as care work for the wife as well as the husband. She also implicitly challenges Ellis's (1959) piece on why married men seek out paid sex by rejecting the blame game. Neither the wife nor the husband is at fault; their libidos are simply incompatible. Yet despite, or more likely *because* of, their criminalization and deviantization, clients themselves have not en masse created a movement to promote the sex-work-is-work framework or to defend their own rights to due process, liberty, expression, and dignity. Nonetheless, a small amount of emerging work that is centred on the voices of clients (Atchison, n.d.) or that is written by a client (Brown, 2013; Kron, 1998; Loebner, 1998;

Schafer, 2015) shows a wide range of desires, motivations, and personality types within the group. Such interventions, along with those of sex workers themselves, are crucial for the sex worker rights movement, as they demonstrate that, intrinsically, buying or selling sexual services is no more or less prone to producing violence, harm, or exploitation than any other type of care work, sexual practice, or commercial exchange.

Notes

The Social Sciences and Humanities Research Council of Canada supported the research for this chapter.

1 For example, during the development of the early Christian church, Saint Augustine of Hippo (354–430) reluctantly tolerated the existence of prostitution for the greater good: "If you do away with harlots, the world will be convulsed with lust" (quoted in Ditmore, 2006, p. 51). In the medieval era, theologian and philosopher Thomas Aquinas cited Augustine in his support for legal tolerance of prostitution, even as he vehemently objected to the activity on moral grounds (Dever, 1996).

2 For example, prominent sexologist Richard von Krafft-Ebing not only seemed to accept that many men would inevitably buy sex but even suggested that male homosexuality could be treated through the services of female sex workers (cited in Oosterhuis, 2000, p. 56).

3 My knowledge of the john school agenda is based on interviews conducted with the organizers of these programs in Edmonton, Hamilton, Ottawa, Toronto, Saskatoon, Sudbury, Vancouver, Windsor, Winnipeg, and the Peel Region of southern Ontario. I also observed two john school sessions in person and one on video.

References

Adams, A. (2015, January 18). A letter from a sex worker to a wife about her cheating husband. *Vice*. Retrieved from http://www.vice.com/en_uk/article/nnqgab/a-letter-from-a-sex-worker-to-a-wife-about-her-cheating-husband

Amnesty International. (2016). *Amnesty International policy on state obligations to respect, protect and fulfil the human rights of sex workers*. Retrieved from https://www.amnesty.org/en/documents/pol30/4062/2016/en/

Atchison, C. (n.d.). *Johns' Voice: Providing a safe space for sex buyers to be heard*. Retrieved from http://www.johnsvoice.ca/

Atchison, C., & Burnett, P.J. (2016). The social dynamics of safe sex practices among Canadian sex industry clients. *Sociology of Health and Illness, 38*(6), 939–56. https://doi.org/10.1111/1467-9566.12416

Backhouse, C. (1985). Nineteenth-century Canadian prostitution law: Reflection of a discriminatory society. *Social History/Histoire sociale, 18*(36), 387–423.

Benedet, J. (2007). Pornography and prostitution in Canada: The dangers ahead. In J. DiCaro (Ed.), *Pornography: Driving the demand in international sex trafficking* (pp. 306–20). Los Angeles, CA: Captive Daughters Media.

Benoit, C., Atchison, C., Casey, L., Jansson, M., McCarthy, B., Phillips, R., ... Shaver, F.M. (2014). *A 'working paper' prepared as background to Building on the Evidence: An International Symposium on the Sex Industry in Canada.* Retrieved from http://www.nswp.org/resource/gender-violence-and-health-contexts -vulnerability-resiliencies-and-care-among-people-the

Brown, C. (2013). *Paying for it.* Montreal, QC: Drawn and Quarterly.

Dever, V.M. (1996). Aquinas on the practice of prostitution. *Essays in Medieval Studies, 13,* 39–50. Retrieved from http://www.illinoismedieval.org/ems/VOL13/ dever.html

Ditmore, M.H. (2006). *Encyclopedia of prostitution and sex work.* Westport, CT: Greenwood.

Ellis, A. (1959). Why married men visit prostitutes. *Sexology, 25,* 344–47.

Farley, M. (2004). Bad for the body, bad for the heart: Prostitution harms women even if legalized or decriminalized. *Violence Against Women, 10*(10), 1087–25. https://doi.org/10.1177/1077801204268607

Faugier, J., & Cranfield, S. (1995). Reaching male clients of female prostitutes: The challenge for HIV prevention. *AIDS Care, 7*(1), 21–32. https://doi. org/10.1080/09540129550126795

Fischer, B., Wortley, S., Webster, C., & Kirst, M. (2002). The socio-legal dynamics and implications of 'diversion': The case study of the Toronto 'John School' diversion program for prostitution offenders. *Criminology and Criminal Justice, 2*(4), 385–410. https://doi.org/10.1177/17488958020020040201

Fritsch, K., Heynen, R., Ross, A.N., & van der Meulen, E. (2016). Disability and sex work: Developing affinities through decriminalization. *Disability and Society, 31*(1), 84–99. https://doi.org/10.1080/09687599.2016.1139488

Gibbens, T., & Silberman, M. (1960). The clients of prostitutes. *British Journal of Venereal Diseases, 36*(1), 113–17.

Government of Canada. (2014, June 4). *Statement by the minister of justice regarding legislation in response to the Supreme Court of Canada ruling in Attorney General of Canada v. Bedford et al.* (News release). Retrieved from https://www.canada. ca/en/news/archive/2014/06/statement-minister-justice-regarding-legislation -response-supreme-court-canada-ruling-attorney-general-canada-v-bedford-al -.html?wbdisable=true

Khan, U. (2015). 'Johns' in the spotlight: Anti-prostitution efforts and the surveillance of clients. *Canadian Journal of Law and Society, 30*(1), 9–29. https://doi. org/10.1017/cls.2014.27

Kinsey, A.C., Martin, C.E., & Pomeroy, W.B. (1948). *Sexual behavior in the human male.* Philadelphia, PA: W.B. Saunders Co.

Kohn, S. (2016, November 9). *The problem with criminalizing sex workers' clients.* Retrieved from https://www.opensocietyfoundations.org/voices/problem -criminalizing-sex-workers-clients

Kron, J. (1998). My sexual encounters with sex workers: The effects on a consumer. In J. Elias (Ed.), *Prostitution: On whores, hustlers and johns* (pp. 204–7). New York, NY: Prometheus.

Krüsi, A., Pacey, K., Bird, L., Taylor, C., Chettiar, J., Allan, S. ... Shannon, K. (2014). Criminalisation of clients: Reproducing vulnerabilities for violence and poor health among street-based sex workers in Canada – a qualitative study. *British Medical Journal Open, 4*(6), 1–10. https://doi.org/10.1136/bmjopen-2014-005191

Kulick, D. (2005). Four hundred thousand Swedish perverts. *GLQ: A Journal of Lesbian and Gay Studies, 11*(2), 205–35. https://doi.org/10.1215/10642684-11-2-205

Lecky, W.E.H. (1890). *History of European morals: From Augustus to Charlemagne.* (Vol. 2). New York, NY: D. Appleton.

Leonard, T.L. (1990). Male clients of female street prostitutes: Unseen partners in sexual disease transmission. *Medical Anthropology Quarterly, 4*(1), 41–55. https://doi.org/10.1525/maq.1990.4.1.02a00040

L'Espérance, J.L. (1979). Woman's mission to woman: Explorations in the operation of the double standard and female solidarity in nineteenth century England. *Social History/Histoire sociale, 12*(24), 316–38.

Liddiard, K. (2014). 'I never felt like she was just doing it for the money': Disabled men's intimate (gendered) realities of purchasing sexual pleasure and intimacy. *Sexualities, 17*(7), 837–55. https://doi.org/10.1177/1363460714531272

Loebner, H.G. (1998). Being a john. In J. Elias (Ed.), *Prostitution: On whores, hustlers and johns* (pp. 221–25). New York, NY: Prometheus.

Lowman, J. (2000). Violence and the outlaw status of (street) prostitution in Canada. *Violence Against Women, 6*(9), 987–1011. https://doi.org/10.1177/10778010022182245

Lowman, J. (2013). Crown expert-witness testimony in *Bedford v. Canada:* Evidence-based argument or victim-paradigm hyperbole? In E. van der Meulen, E.M. Durisin, & V. Love (Eds.), *Selling sex: Experience, advocacy, and research on sex work in Canada* (pp. 230–50). Vancouver, BC: UBC Press.

Malarek, V. (2009). *The johns: Sex for sale and the men who buy it.* New York, NY: Arcade.

McClintock, A. (1992). Screwing the system: Sex work, race, and the law. *Boundary 2, 19*(2), 70–95. https://doi.org/10.2307/303534

McLaren, J.P. (1986). Chasing the social evil: Moral fervour and the evolution of Canada's prostitution laws, 1867–1917. *Canadian Journal of Law and Society, 1*, 125–65. https://doi.org/10.1017/S0829320100001034

McLaren, J.P. (1992). *Recalculating the wages of sin: The social and legal construction of prostitution in Canada, 1850–1920.* Winnipeg, MB: University of Manitoba Press.

McLaren, J.P., & Lowman, J. (1990). Enforcing Canada's prostitution laws, 1892–1920: Rhetoric and practice. In M.L. Friedland (Ed.), *Securing compliance: Seven case studies* (pp. 21–87). Toronto, ON: University of Toronto Press. https://doi.org/10.3138/9781442679696-004

Nikiforuk, C. (2014, June 17). Listen to sex workers, kill Bill C-36. *Ricochet.* Retrieved from https://ricochet.media/en/9/listen-to-sex-workers-kill-bill-c-36

Oosterhuis, H. (2000). *Stepchildren of nature: Krafft-Ebing, psychiatry, and the making of sexual identity.* Chicago, IL: University of Chicago Press.

Perrin, B. (2010). *Invisible chains: Canada's underground world of human trafficking.* Toronto, ON: Penguin Canada.

Ross, M.S. (2007). Dear john. In A. Oakley (Ed.), *Working sex: Sex workers write about a changing industry* (pp. 211–18). Berkeley, CA: Seal.

Rotenberg, C. (2016). Prostitution offences in Canada: Statistical trends. *Juristat, 36*(1), 4–24. Retrieved from http://www.statcan.gc.ca/pub/85-002-x/2016001/article/14670-eng.pdf

Sanders, T. (2008). *Paying for pleasure: Men who buy sex.* Cullompton, UK: Willan.

Schafer, P. (2015, August 4). Diary of a sex tourist. *Vantage.* Retrieved from https://medium.com/vantage/diary-of-a-sex-tourist-2d73817d23df

Shannon, K., Strathdee, S.A., Shoveller, J., Rusch, M., Kerr, T., & Tyndall, M.W. (2009). Structural and environmental barriers to condom use negotiation with clients among female sex workers: Implications for HIV-prevention strategies and policy. *American Journal of Public Health, 99*(4), 659–65. https://doi.org/10.2105/AJPH.2007.129858

Skilbrei, M., & Holmström, C. (2016). *Prostitution policy in the Nordic region: Ambiguous sympathies.* New York, NY: Routledge.

Smith, J. (2014a, April 15). Prostitution isn't a nuisance, it's violence against women. *Huffington Post.* Retrieved from http://www.huffingtonpost.ca/joy-smith-mp/canada-prostitution-law_b_4782305.html

Smith, J. (2014b). *The tipping point: Tackling the demand for prostituted/trafficked women and youth.* (First report). Retrieved from http://freethem.ca/wp-content/uploads/2014/02/The-Tipping-Point-MP-Joy-Smith-Full-Report-FEB-12-2014.pdf

Smith, M.D., & Seal, D.W. (2008). Motivational influences on the safer sex behavior of agency-based male sex workers. *Archives of Sexual Behavior, 37*(5), 845–53. https://doi.org/10.1007/s10508-008-9341-1

Strange, C., & Loo, T.M. (1997). *Making good: Law and moral regulation in Canada, 1867–1939.* Toronto, ON: University of Toronto Press.

Strega, S., Janzen, C., Morgan, J., & Brown, L. (2014). Never innocent victims: Street sex workers in Canadian print media. *Scandinavian Journal of Immunology, 79*(3), 6–25.

Swedish Institute. (2010). *The ban against the purchase of sexual services: An evaluation 1999–2008.* (Selected extracts of the Swedish government report SOU 2010:49). Retrieved from https://ec.europa.eu/anti-trafficking/publications/ban-against-purchase-sexual-services-evaluation-1999-2008_en

Sycamore, M.B. (2000). *Tricks and treats: Sex workers write about their clients.* New York, NY: Harrington Park.

Valverde, M. (2008). *The age of light, soap, and water: Moral reform in English Canada, 1885–1925.* Toronto, ON: University of Toronto Press.

Walkowitz, J.R. (1982). *Prostitution and Victorian society: Women, class, and the state.* Cambridge, MA: Cambridge University Press.

Weitzer, R. (2005). Flawed theory and method in studies of prostitution. *Violence Against Women, 11*(7), 934–49. https://doi.org/10.1177/1077801205276986

Wortley, S., Fischer, B., & Webster, C. (2002). Vice lessons: A survey of prostitution offenders enrolled in the Toronto John School Diversion Program. *Canadian Journal of Criminology, 44*(4), 369–402.

Wotten, R., & Isbister, S. (2010). A sex worker perspective on working with clients with a disability and the development of Touching Base Inc. In R. Shuttleworth & T. Sanders (Eds.), *Sex and disability: Politics, identity and access* (pp. 155–78). Leeds, UK: Disability.

Cases

Bedford v. Canada, 2010 ONSC 4264.
Canada (Attorney General) v. Bedford, 2013 SCC 72, [2013] 3 SCR 1101.
R. v. Mercer (2016), NSPC 48.

Legislation

Bill C-36, *Protection of Communities and Exploited Persons Act,* SC 2014, c. 25.

Pimps, Partners, and Procurers
Criminalizing Street-Based Sex Workers' Relationships with Partners and Third Parties

KARA GILLIES AND CHRIS BRUCKERT

There is a small body of literature that examines third parties in the Canadian indoor sex industry (e.g., Benoit et al., 2014; Bowen, Bungay, and Zangger, 2015; Bruckert and Law, 2013, 2018; Gillies, 2013). This literature challenges presumptions of deviance by documenting the reasons indoor sex workers elect to work for or with third parties, including improved access to occupational health and safety measures (e.g., screening, safe calls, and the presence of others), training and mentorship, protocols for client negotiations, and business services (e.g., administration, advertising, and booking). Some sex workers lack the interest, resources, time, or skills to run a business, and others prefer "to leave the work of client management and public relations to a third party because of the emotional labour and infringement on personal space" (Gillies, 2013, p. 271). This scholarship also unpacks the impact of third-party criminalization by highlighting, for example, the exclusion of workers from protective labour legislation, the inhibition of clear communication between clients and sex workers, the constrained training of new sex workers, the limited access to criminal justice, and the encouragement of wilful ignorance on the part of third parties (in particular, see Bruckert and Law, 2013, pp. 86–89). Criminalization notwithstanding, there is, generally speaking, a measure of recognition that indoor sexual commerce may operate in a similar manner to other service-sector businesses, and there is an openness to the possibility that drivers, security persons, and owners of escort agencies provide valuable services to indoor sex workers.

Such normative framing largely disappears when the street-based sex industry is under consideration.[1] Here, a narrative of violence, disorder, and pathology is superimposed – a tendency that in itself reflects classist stereotypes that presume community, solidarity, and social cohesion to be middle-class norms absent in underclass spaces. Such a framing deviantizes street economies and cultures at the same time as it invisibilizes not only structural and social inequality but also the strategies and tactics that people employ to navigate and survive on the margins of mainstream society. The broad brush strokes of legal, political, and media discourse that construct individuals (i.e., third parties or partners) who assist street-based sex workers as exploitative and predatory individuals are a case in point. It is therefore appropriate to ask street-based sex workers about the people who assist them, the roles and responsibilities of these individuals, and the nature of their relationships. When we do so, we immediately recognize complexity – in place of the stereotypical pimp, we see street managers, intimate partners, manager-partners, drug dealers, contractors, and peer facilitators; it is these roles and their attendant relationships that we unpack in the first section of this chapter.

The chapter draws on two qualitative research projects in order to examine the complexity of relationships in the context of street-based economies and cultures. The first, "Bound by Law: How Canadian Protectionist Policies in the Areas of Both Rape and Prostitution Limit Women's Choices, Agency and Activities,"[2] was undertaken by Kara Gillies and Nora Currie (Currie and Gillies, 2006); the second, "Rethinking Management in the Sex Industry,"[3] was directed by Chris Bruckert. Our combined data for this chapter include interviews with forty-eight women with street-based sex work experience in Edmonton, Toronto, Ottawa, Montreal, or Halifax,[4] forty-four of whom identified as cisgender and four as transgender, as well as interviews with twelve street-based third parties in Toronto, Ottawa, and Halifax, five of whom were men and seven of whom were women, including one trans woman. After examining the findings that emerged from our analysis of the data regarding various third-party roles,[5] we consider the current regulatory context created by the Protection of Communities and Exploited Persons Act (PCEPA), reflecting on what the criminalization of many third-party activities means for sex workers.

Personal and Professional Relationships: Street-Based Sex Workers

As the street-based sex industry has transformed over the past decades, the prevalence of the "players" described by Milner and Milner (1972) has diminished and changed. The sex workers and street managers with whom we spoke described a professional business relationship with clearly articulated expectations. Robert, a street manager in Halifax, explained, "Times have changed. It's not like it used to be back in the day where, 'Hey, you get out there,' whack, whack, whack ... That's not like that nowadays because they won't stay with you. They don't need that. So it's almost like there's a contract. You negotiate a kind of 'this is what I'll do.'" The reciprocal arrangement accords the manager a measure of control over when, where, and how sex workers labour in exchange for the manager's services, which may include deterring and/or preventing violence (e.g., being in the vicinity and/or reachable and/or recording client information) or intervening in cases of crisis. Managers may also provide industry advice on safety, income-generating strategies, and tactics to evade law enforcement, as well as manage and safeguard money, post bail, and secure work and personal supplies.

Although the (frequently) gendered roles and some features of the relationship bear markers of the archetypical pimp, there are also elements that stand in stark contrast to the trope. For example, many participants noted that sex workers are neither "turned out" nor recruited but rather select the individuals for whom they work. If they are giving all or most of their income to their manager and living with that individual, there is the expectation that an acceptable standard of living will be maintained (e.g., housing, food, clothes, and funds). According to our research participants, ties with managers are severed when the latter fail to fulfil their responsibilities. Chelsea, a street-based sex worker in Toronto, explained that "after they tell me everything that they're going to do for me, well, if they don't follow through ... Well, you know what? You don't want to take care of me like you promised, bye-bye, honey. Next." Moreover, whereas some workers spoke of violent discipline, others experienced strategies that echoed those of managers in mainstream labour sectors, including generating competition among workers: "He would always throw the other girls in my face. 'You know how much money she makes?' ... It made me feel like shit, but it also made me work ... It was like those workplace-fucking-challenges" (Candy, street-based sex worker, Toronto).

Just like other social actors, sex workers may share their lives with one or more intimate partners. In some of these relationships, the male partner also generates income, whereas in others, the conventional gender-labour script is inverted, with the male partner providing support or assistance in the couple's home life (e.g., childcare), in her work (e.g., security), and/or in their leisure activities (e.g., procurement of drugs). As Lisa, a Toronto sex worker, pointed out, when an intimate partner does not contribute to this sort of an arrangement, it is criminalized and deviantized only in the context of sex work: "If I was a nurse and I lived with a boyfriend who had no job, and he was just kind of sponging off me, there's no law for that. He's considered an asshole. But he's not considered criminal."

As is the case in other intimate relationships, some partners are abusive. Indeed, a number of participants described not only physical, sexual, emotional, and financial abuse but also the dynamics and escalation that sometimes characterize intimate-partner violence (Walker, 2001): "Mine fell into a relationship, and I guess I got hooked on him, and I'd do anything for him, and I couldn't leave. Even though he was beating me" (Kammy, street-based sex worker, Halifax). In short, when we take off moral blinders, we see that these women, along with an estimated 4 percent of all women in Canada (Government of Canada, 2016), are in abusive relationships: "It's about control, no matter what. I think that's the bottom line. You know, no matter if you're a sex trade worker or if you're just the average Joe, you know, it's about control for men" (Clarisse, street-based sex worker, Halifax).

Some workers have a manager and some a partner, or both, or neither; however, in some cases, the two roles coexist in a manager-partner hybrid: "Man-slash-pimp. I say 'pimp' because he pimped me out and 'man' because I loved him" (Candy, street-based sex worker, Toronto). On the one hand, as we saw above, partners of sex workers may provide some assistance to the worker (e.g., driving, security, or obtaining illicit substances) but not exercise control over the worker's labour process or practices. On the other hand, complex power relations can emerge when the two roles coexist and managerial authority is layered over the gender privilege enjoyed by male partners. When the male partner is also the manager of other workers (e.g., "wives-in-law," who may or may not live with the couple), the female partner, in addition to engaging in sex work, sometimes assumes managerial and disciplinary responsibility for "their business."

Drawing on powerful negative tropes of evil drug dealers and exploitative pimps, the drug dealer who provides third-party services to sex workers has emerged as indisputably malevolent in the public imagination. When we unpack the nature of the relationship, however, the easy vilification and homogeneity of the construct appears misplaced. Of course, individuals, including sex workers, sometimes exchange sexual favours for drugs; for sex workers, such an arrangement eliminates the need to solicit clients and expedites access to drugs. According to our research participants, there are also times when the business interests of sex workers and their dealers coincide in a mutually advantageous manner. Sex workers may enact an introduction or purchase substances for a client who, for example, wants to "party," or they may meet individuals who wish to purchase sexual services at a dealer's home.

Some dealers, in addition to selling substances, also provide street-based sex workers with particular services, such as procuring clients and service-provision space. These arrangements are not, in and of themselves, either positive or negative. When dealers secure clients for sex workers – who either pay the dealer a fee or, if the client pays the dealer directly, may be compensated by the dealer in drugs – sex workers do not have to solicit clients on the street and then purchase substances. In other words, having a third party make the arrangements can be more convenient, less time-consuming, and reduce the risk of theft and arrest. At the same time, however, a worker's ability to negotiate the terms of her services may be restricted in these instances: "So there's like no room to negotiate condom use" (Amy, street-based sex worker, Montreal). Similarly, having a location to provide services for clients with whom one is "partying" can increase security because of the presence of other people and because of the reduced risk of being apprehended, or it can increase risk if those present are themselves threatening. Street-based sex workers' drug dealers, who, as our research participants reminded us, may also be their friends, can also be a resource when they are in need of protection or redress. Amy explained that when a gang demanded protection money, the sex workers "called in their dealers and said if you want our business, get these guys the fuck out of here – and they did" (see also Pitts, 2016). In this context, it would appear that stereotypes may work to sex workers' advantage; after all, the ability to evoke the scary dealer-pimp trope could have a deterrent effect on potential aggressors.[6]

As is the case in the in-call and out-call sectors (see Bruckert and Law, 2018), some third parties are contractors – individuals who provide, on a fee-per-service basis, specific services to sex workers (e.g., protection by being in the vicinity and deterrence by taking licence plate numbers). One such arrangement was described by Lily, a street-based sex worker in Toronto: "There used to be a parking lot where we'd go, and there would be a guy there who'd be protection, right? ... He said, 'Roll down the window if there's anything. You know, you yell.'"

Finally, some of these contractors are peer facilitators – current or former sex workers who draw on their experiential knowledge and, in exchange for money or drugs, provide valuable services, including obtaining clients, security, advice, and space to see clients. These fluid, informal relationships and roles destabilize dominant pimp tropes around gender, exploitation, and the role of drugs. They also draw into question the ascription of master status (Hughes, 1945); in practice, providing services to sex workers becomes one way for economically and socially marginalized street-involved individuals to "get by." Star, who organized appointments and allowed workers to use her room in a supportive-housing facility, framed this as "just my day-to-day survival and getting along, getting what I need and what I want and helping somebody out at the same time."

The typology sketched above provides a point of entry to think about the range of relationships that street-based sex workers have with third parties. Of course, the categories are not definitive, as other relationships may well exist that did not emerge in our research, nor are they necessarily mutually exclusive. For example, our participants advised us that some drug dealers have parallel and occasionally intersecting businesses as sex industry managers, that a sex worker's boyfriend may also sell drugs, and that a manager may be uninvolved in their partner's sex work but manage other workers. We see echoes of the stereotypes in some of these roles and relationships, and violence, drugs, and abuse are sometimes, but certainly not always, a factor. That said, even when this is the case, these elements do not necessarily manifest in stereotypical ways, nor does the relationship conform to the "pimp" archetype. This disjuncture notwithstanding, all these individuals are vulnerable to criminalization – an issue to which we now turn.

Criminalization of Sex Workers' Relationships

The complexities of these relationships, their varied benefits for workers, and the contexts in which they occur are largely absent from Canada's prior and current laws governing sex workers' partners and the third parties for, or with whom, they work. Indeed, the very existence of criminal laws specific to sex workers' professional and personal relationships exposes an othering of sex work and underlying assumptions about the (problematic) character, motives, and agency of the actors involved. In particular, the construct of the "pimp" surfaces and is reinforced in Canadian jurisprudence, such as the declaration in *R. v. Downey* (1992) that "the pimp personifies abusive and exploitative malevolence" (p. 36) and the case's reference to "the cruel, pernicious and exploitative evil of the pimp" (p. 32). This trope continued during the 2014 parliamentary hearings leading up to PCEPA, with Minister of Justice Peter MacKay asserting that this "bill would crack down on those predators, pimps, and johns who fuel the demand for this inherently dangerous activity" (Government of Canada, 2014a).

The panic about the malevolent "pimp," combined with the government's stated objective of discouraging the exploitation, commercialization, and institutionalization of sex work, underpins Criminal Code sanctions against procuring (s. 286.3) and receiving a material benefit from another person's sex work (s. 286.2). The procuring provision makes it illegal to "cause, induce or have persuasive effect" (*Deutsch v. The Queen*, 1986, para. 32) on someone to offer or provide sex work services as well as to facilitate the purchase of sexual services, even without compensation or material benefit. This situation criminalizes the beneficial role that both personal and business parties play in connecting workers with clients, including security measures such as screening and holding money. It is also to exercise direction, control, or influence over a sex worker's movements if it is for the purpose of facilitating her sex work. Not only does this restriction criminalize managers, but given that directing workers' movements is a common and legitimate supervisory duty, it also criminalizes the sorts of supportive services provided by boyfriends, contractors, and peer facilitators.

The "material benefits" provision of the Criminal Code, which purports to prevent exploitation by criminalizing financial or other material benefits to third parties, negates sex workers' agency and exposes the paternalistic assumption that women in the sex trade lack the judgment and capacity to determine who should receive their earnings and why. Further, as with the prior "living on the avails" offence, absent evidence to the contrary, that a person lives with or is in the habitual company of a sex worker is proof of material benefit. This presumption speaks to the stigma and normative understanding that sex workers cannot be legitimate objects of affection and that anyone who seeks intimacy with such an (immoral) woman has an ulterior and malevolent motive. The courts have upheld this "reverse onus" on the grounds that sex workers are fearful of testifying against "pimps" (*R. v. Downey*, 1992, p. 12) – a "fact" not supported by empirical evidence but embraced by judicial "common sense" (Valverde, 2003).

This approach creates conditions favourable to having abuse from intimate partners dismissed in favour of prosecuting a sex work–related charge. As Clarisse in Halifax said about her abusive partner, "I wanted him charged with assault. But never [with] living off the avails because he never made me do anything that I didn't choose to do." Moreover, framing domestic violence as pimping not only invisibilizes these women's experiences but also serves as a powerful disincentive to seek police assistance and legal redress. Sex workers are mindful that if their partner is labelled a pimp, they are outed as a sex worker, and the ascription of *that* identity can have significant consequences for, among other things, travel, custody of children, and future interactions with police and courts.

PCEPA codifies exceptions to the "material benefits" provision that were previously established in "living on the avails" jurisprudence, such as a material benefit occurring in the context of a "legitimate living relationship" (*Criminal Code*, 1985, s. 286.2 (4)(a)), as the result of a "legal or moral obligation" (s. 286.2(4)(b)), and/or in consideration for a service or good offered to the general public (s. 286.2(4)(c)). In deference to *Bedford*, PCEPA adds the new exception of offering a good or service exclusively to a sex worker provided that the benefit is proportionate to the value and that the person did not "counsel or encourage" the other party to engage in sex work (s. 286.2(4)(d)). These exceptions flow from prior attempts to legally distinguish between beneficial or neutral relationships and those that are exploitative or otherwise harmful; this endeavour is evidenced in jurisprudence (e.g., see *R. v. Barrow*, 2001; *R. v. Downey*, 1992; and *R. v. Grilo*, 1991) and articulated in *Bedford* in regard to the former "living on the avails" provision:

> The law punishes everyone who lives on the avails of prostitution without distinguishing between those who exploit prostitutes (for example, controlling and abusive pimps) and those who could increase the safety and security of prostitutes (for example, legitimate drivers, managers, or bodyguards) ... In these ways, the law includes some conduct that bears no relation to its purpose of preventing the exploitation of prostitutes. (*Canada (Attorney General) v. Bedford*, 2013, para. 142)

Subjective and normative concepts such as legitimacy and morality, combined with stereotypes and assumptions about sex work, street culture, and drug use, raise concerns regarding their application to street-based sex workers, especially those who are drug-using or in nonstandard personal or work relationships. Would several sex workers living together with their shared "man" and turning their money over to him be considered to be in a "legitimate living arrangement"? Or would working on the street to provide for a partner with a substance dependency – which in most other contexts would be considered supporting a person with a disability – be accepted as a "moral obligation"?

Nor are these legal exceptions absolute. In a further display of paternalism predicated on myths about sex workers as victims and their affiliates as inherently exploitative, the government revokes these exceptions in specific circumstances partly to capture "persons who initially pose as a benevolent helper and thereby appear to be entitled to one of the exceptions" (Government of Canada, 2014b, p. 7). The first such exception to the exceptions occurs when the person uses, threatens to use, or attempts to use violence, intimidation, or coercion in relation to the sex worker from whom the material benefit is derived (*Criminal Code*, 1985, s. 286.2(5)(a)). However, the abuse need not be committed for the purpose of materially benefiting from the sex worker or coercing someone to engage in sex work activities. Violence, intimidation, or coercion of any sort, for any purpose, and in any context nullifies otherwise applicable exceptions and thus locates the material benefit as a de facto form of criminal exploitation. Once again, we see the complexity of the contexts and experiences of violence against women sex workers reduced to a simplistic and problematic "pimp" narrative.

Sex-working women's narratives also trouble the "material benefits" exceptions in relation to drugs. As it stands, someone who provides a drug, alcohol, or other intoxicating substance to a sex worker for the purpose of "aiding or abetting" that person to offer or provide sex work services from which the third party materially benefits is considered to be engaged in exploitation and excluded from the legal exceptions (*Criminal Code*, 1985, s. 286.2(5)(c)). Notably, the law captures the act of *assisting* someone to engage in sex work through the provision of substances and does not require that drugs be provided for a nefarious purpose such as vitiating consent or coercing or manipulating someone to provide sexual services or turn over her earnings. Indeed, multiple troubling assumptions underlie this provision. It implies that drugs inevitably have a debilitating impact, that sex workers who use drugs are necessarily incapacitated, that women develop an automatic and harmful dependency on anyone who supplies them with substances, and that people who supply substances to sex workers are poised or planning to exploit them (see also Hannem, this collection). The first assumption is countered by some women's narratives that reveal that drug or alcohol use in some contexts works to facilitate cognitive and behaviour functioning. Terry, a street-based sex worker in Halifax, said, "If I don't have [my drugs] on a daily basis, then I can't function properly, and that's not good. That's really not good." In that context, a partner, manager, or dealer providing a substance could be considered to be assisting in a harm reduction strategy. For example, it isolates the woman from the risks and challenges of procuring drugs. In fact, generally speaking, it is not uncommon for male partners to source and supply drugs for women users (Miller and Neaigus, 2002). The no-substances provision of the Criminal Code (1985, s. 286.2(5)(c)) also reinforces the stereotype of the addled, risk-taking, drug-using street-based sex worker and overlooks the resourcefulness, skill, and perseverance that are exercised on a daily basis by people who are drug-using – including the drug-dependent – and who are street-involved.

Perhaps the most far-reaching exception to the "material benefits" exceptions is the prohibition on "commercial enterprises" (*Criminal Code*, 1985, s. 286.2(5)(e)). The construction of a material benefit occurring in the context of a commercial enterprise as necessarily exploitative undermines the many benefits that sex workers state can flow from working for a third party. That the term "commercial enterprise" is understood to be broad enough to provide "flexibility to the courts to find different types of enterprises, including informal ones, to be 'commercial'" (Government of Canada, 2014b, p. 7) suggests that, given the right elements, a street-based manager and his supportive services could be criminalized under this section.

Conclusion

In this chapter, we have demonstrated that the laws criminalizing the partners and third parties of street-based sex workers are a flimsy house of cards balancing on moral conventions, class-based prejudice, and the stigmatic assumption that sex workers are incompetent subjects incapable of operating in their own best interests and in need of rescue. The laws further construct the men with whom sex workers share their work and personal lives as always already predatory and abusive and the state as the mechanism for salvation. In practice, the legal regime works to the detriment of some of the most marginalized sex workers (see Sayers, this collection). There is a profound and highly disturbing irony here. It is these women, who are isolated, made vulnerable, and consistently denied access to police protection and redress (Shaver and Lewis, 2005), who are most in need of the sorts of support and the interventions provided by third parties.

Notes

1 For exceptions, see Pitts's (2016) analysis of street-based sex workers' engagement with drug dealers and Bruckert and Parent (2018).

2 The sex work component of the "Bound by Law" study interviewed twenty-five street-based and indoor sex workers about their experiences of working for third parties and about the impact of the procuring laws. This study was approved by the Status of Women Ethics Board.

3 The "Rethinking Management" study, which examined the street-based, in-call, out-call, and strip sectors, interviewed seventy-five third parties and fifty-two sex workers who either hired or worked with or for third parties (see Bruckert and Parent, 2018). The study was funded by the Social Sciences and Humanities Research Council of Canada and was approved by the University of Ottawa Research Ethics Board.

4 The sex-working women were between the ages of twenty-three and fifty-three, and most had considerable experience in the sex industry, the range being from three to thirty-eight years and the average being sixteen years. Twenty-one participants identified as white, nine as Indigenous, and six as Black.

5 To ensure rigour and consistency, all interviews were reviewed and coded. In particular, we attended to the roles of third parties and to the relationships between sex workers and the individuals they worked for, worked with, or hired, which in some cases included intimate partners. The typology presented in this chapter is grounded in findings that emerged from these data. To ensure that the model was comprehensive (i.e., that there were no outliers), a reverse reading was undertaken.

6 See Hannem and Bruckert (2016) for a discussion on the use of the pimp stereotypes to advantage in indoor spaces.

References

Benoit, C., Atchison, C., Casey, L., Jansson, M., McCarthy, B., Phillips, R., ... Shaver, F.M. (2014). *A 'working paper' prepared as background to Building on the Evidence: An International Symposium on the Sex Industry in Canada*. Retrieved from http://www.nswp.org/resource/gender-violence-and-health-contexts-vulnerability-resiliencies-and-care-among-people-the

Bowen, R., Bungay, V., & Zangger, C. (2015). *Making SPACES: Advancing recommendations for the off-street sex industry in Vancouver*. Vancouver, BC: Making SPACES Project.

Bruckert, C., & Law, T. (2013). *Beyond pimps, procurers and parasites: Third parties in the incall/outcall sex industry*. Retrieved from http://www.nswp.org/resource/beyond-pimps-procurers-and-parasites-mapping-third-parties-the-incalloutcall-sex-industry

Bruckert, C., & Law, T. (2018). The business of sex businesses: Management in the incall/outcall sector. In C. Bruckert & C. Parent (Eds.), *Getting past 'the pimp': Management in the Canadian sex industry* (pp. 73–100). Toronto, ON: University of Toronto Press.

Bruckert, C., & Parent, C. (2018). *Getting past 'the pimp': Management in the Canadian sex industry*. Toronto, ON: University of Toronto Press.

Currie, N., & Gillies, K. (2006). *Bound by law: How Canada's protectionist public policies in the areas of both rape and prostitution limit women's choices, agency and activities*. Ottawa, ON: Status of Women Canada.

Gillies, K. (2013). A wolf in sheep's clothing: Canadian anti-pimping law and how it hurts sex workers. In E. van der Meulen, E.M. Durisin, & V. Love (Eds.), *Selling sex: Experience, advocacy and research on sex work in Canada* (pp. 269–78). Vancouver, BC: UBC Press.

Government of Canada. (2014a, June 12). *House of Commons Deabates*. (Vol. 147, No. 102, 2nd Session, 41st Parliament). Retrieved from http://www.ourcommons.ca/DocumentViewer/en/41-2/house/sitting-102/hansard

Government of Canada. (2014b). *Technical paper: Bill C-36, Protection of Communities and Exploited Persons Act*. Retrieved from http://www.justice.gc.ca/eng/rp-pr/other-autre/protect/p1.html

Government of Canada. (2016). *Family violence in Canada: A statistical profile, 2014*. Ottawa, ON: Canadian Centre for Justice Statistics.

Hannem, S., & Bruckert, C. (2016). 'I'm not a pimp, but I play one on TV': The moral career and identity negotiations of third parties in the sex industry. *Deviant Behavior, 38*(7), 824–36. https://doi.org/10.1080/01639625.2016.1197700

Hughes, E.C. (1945). Dilemmas and contradictions of status. *American Journal of Sociology, 50*(5), 353–59. https://doi.org/10.1086/219652

Miller, M., & Neaigus, A. (2002). An economy of risk: Resource acquisition strategies of inner city women who use drugs. *International Journal on Drug Policy, 13*(5), 409–18. https://doi.org/10.1016/S0955-3959(02)00119-6

Milner, C., & Milner, R. (1972). *Black players: The secret world of black pimps*. New York, NY: Little Brown and Co.

Pitts, A.J. (2016). Remembering Bedford: Impacts of criminalisation of street-based sex work. *Research for Sex Work*, (15), 29–30. Retrieved from http://www.nswp.org/resource/research-sex-work-15-resistance-and-resilience

Shaver, F.M., & Lewis, J. (2005). *Safety, security and the well-being of sex workers: A report submitted to the House of Commons Subcommittee on Solicitation Laws*. Montreal, QC: Sex Trade Advocacy Research (STAR).

Valverde, M. (2003). *Law's dream of a common knowledge*. Princeton, NJ: Princeton University Press.

Walker, L. (2001). *The battered women's syndrome*. (2nd ed.). New York, NY: Springer.

Cases

Canada (Attorney General) v. Bedford, 2013 SCC 72, [2013] 3 SCR 1101.
Deutsch v. The Queen, [1986] 2 SCR 2, 1986 CanLII 21 (SCC).
R. v. Barrow, 2001 CanLII 8550 (ON CA).
R. v. Downey, [1992] 2 SCR 10.
R. v. Grilo (C.A.), 1991 CanLII 7241 (ON CA).

Legislation

Bill C-36, *Protection of Communities and Exploited Persons Act*, SC 2014, c. 25.
Criminal Code, RSC 1985, c. C-46.

7

New Risk-Spaces, New Spaces for Harm
——— The Effects of the Advertising Offence on Independent Escorts

ANDREA STERLING

Prior to the ascension of Canada's new prostitution legislation, independent escorts were primarily criminalized in instances where they hosted a client at a location that they themselves had arranged, often referred to as an "in-call" and prohibited under the former bawdy-house provisions. Many escorts, especially those who had a higher socio-economic position relative to other sex-working populations, who did not work for third parties, and who provided only "out-call" services, meeting clients in their hotels or private residences, tended to feel insulated from the criminal laws surrounding sex work. This situation changed in 2014, however, when the federal Conservative government adopted Bill C-36, the Protection of Communities and Exploited Persons Act (PCEPA), in response to the Supreme Court of Canada's decision in *Canada (Attorney General) v. Bedford* (2013) (see Belak, this collection). With *Bedford,* the laws prohibiting sex workers from seeing clients in a bawdy-house were deemed unconstitutional, so independent escorts technically became less criminalized than in the past. However, as PCEPA introduced a new offence to the Criminal Code aimed at curtailing the advertisement of sexual services, many escorts felt directly affected by the legislative changes.

The new advertising provision criminalizes "everyone who knowingly advertises an offer to provide sexual services for consideration" (Bill C-36, 2014, s. 286.4). To find clients, independent escorts place paid advertisements on websites dedicated to hosting sex-related services. Given this new advertising provision, however, both the administrator of such a website and an escort who mentions another worker in her advertisement could be vulnerable to prosecution for advertising an offer to provide a sexual service for remuneration. Despite the provision that grants immunity from prosecution for anyone who advertises their *own* sexual services (*Criminal Code*, 1985, s. 286.5(1)), the research highlighted in this chapter suggests that many independent escorts now feel as though their relationship to the law has been altered. In examining independent escorts' changing relationship to the law, this chapter presents findings from in-depth interviews about the new advertising restrictions, looking specifically at the implications for their social networks and ability to communicate with clients. These narratives show that the advertising restrictions have affected sex workers' risk-management strategies, leaving them vulnerable to new potential harms.

Primary Research with Independent Escorts

The study upon which this chapter is based includes semi-structured interviews with eighteen cisgender female sex workers in Montreal and Toronto. The women all worked as "high-end" independent escorts, which is defined here as sex workers who manage all aspects of their own business, including branding, advertising, scheduling, and communicating with clients; charge hourly rates ranging from $300 to $600, with an average of $400; and offer extended engagements, most typically dinner dates, with a four-hour dinner date ranging from $1,200 to $1,900 and a twelve-hour overnight engagement starting at $3,500.[1] Most participants reported seeing two or three clients per week and spoke of travelling with clients often, the frequency of their travel being an indicator of their status as "elite courtesans." The women with whom I spoke were thus among the upper strata of Canadian independent escorts (see also Love, this collection; Raguparan, this collection).

The participant group included three Black women, one of whom identified as mixed-race, two Asian women, and fifteen white women, with ages ranging from the mid-twenties to early forties. All of their advertising took place online, as did most of their communication with clients. Every woman in this study had a personal website that contained a detailed biography, photo galleries, and information about her rates and services. All reported putting considerable amounts of time and money into their websites – including hiring web designers and photographers – referring to this task as "branding." Advertising and promotion of this kind, although imperative for meeting their clientele, were also financially costly. Two research participants had more than one work persona, with a separate website for each pseudonym. To promote their personal websites, these independent escorts placed profiles on various paid-advertising websites, or ad sites, which operate like online classified listings. The cost of placing an ad on such sites can range from $70 to $600 monthly. Interview transcripts were analyzed using an inductive and iterative approach. Data collection and analysis occurred simultaneously, with themes emerging from the data. Data were coded with NVivo software using an open-coding method. The findings presented in this chapter typify the most prominent themes in the data.

Effects of the Advertising Offence on Social Networks

As the world of independent escorts is necessarily clandestine, it can be very isolating for many women (Bernstein, 2007; Bungay, Halpin, Atchison, and Johnston, 2011). Despite the hermitic nature of their work, the women with whom I spoke had managed to forge valuable friendships and social networks by meeting other escorts during "duos," where one client pays two escorts to join him at the same time. Whether the initial meeting led to a close friendship or the women remained only work colleagues, the resultant social networks were valued for numerous reasons. As Amber explained,

> It helped me a lot when I was getting established to have other workers that would post photos of me with them and promote duo bookings. I learned how to be good at my job and how to market myself properly from other escorts. We love to work together because it's fun, you have company, it feels safer, and it's a good way to meet other people and expand your network of both clients and workers.

Davies and Evans (2007) claim that intuition is a key risk-management strategy used by sex workers which comes from experience and that, without it, workers new to the business, or newbies, may not possess the skills required to assess the risk level of certain situations. Newbies will often look to more experienced sex workers who can provide mentorship to make up for their lack of intuition (Bruckert and Law, 2013; Lewis, Maticka-Tyndale, Shaver, and Schramm, 2005; Whittaker and Hart, 1996).

Independent escorts also share material resources within their social networks; for example, twelve participants shared an in-call space with other workers. These spaces comprise communally rented condos that enable each escort to host her clients, as opposed to frequently booking hotel rooms. Most attributed a significant portion of their income to their ability to host clients in these shared locations. They described the spaces as upscale and well maintained, attributes that were consistent with their branding and that catered to their clients' expectations. Despite escorts' high hourly rates, the cost of running such a space would be unaffordable for any one escort on her own or would seriously compromise her earning capacity; by sharing with each other, they increase their financial stability while feeling safe and comfortable.

Although many of the women with whom I spoke were, in a way, competing for the same clientele, they often promoted each other through booking duos or recommended each other to clients. Posting a list of their duo partners on their websites was a frequently mentioned advertising technique that increased their website traffic and, in turn, led to more bookings. Similarly, banner exchanges – an Internet advertising technique wherein affiliated websites display links to each other's sites – is another way that escorts help each other gain exposure. Some women told me that they received more website traffic from other escorts' websites than from any of their paid advertisements.

In the months prior to and following the implementation of PCEPA, various sex worker and allied organizations produced and disseminated information sheets about the changing legislation in an attempt to help sex workers understand and navigate the new laws, including the new restrictions on advertising (e.g., see Canadian Alliance for Sex Work Law Reform, 2015; Canadian HIV/AIDS Legal Network, Pivot Legal Society, and Stella, 2014; Stella, 2015). Many of these information sheets suggested that mentioning another sex worker, such as a duo partner, in an advertisement may render a sex worker vulnerable to prosecution under the advertising offence. In this study, thirteen of the participants appear to have adhered to this advice by removing all references to other escorts from their websites after PCEPA came into force, including removing both duo sections and banner exchanges. Although three participants cited the information sheets as the impetus for the adjustments, most simply emulated the changes that they noticed on other escorts' websites.

These website changes were described by the research participants as extremely negative insofar as they threatened the viability of their social networks. As Amber explained, "I feel that [advertising duos] have always been nothing but beneficial, and we don't do that anymore because we're all intimidated by the new laws and unsure of how they're going to apply to us, so everyone is cautious. And we can't give each other the support because no one really knows what's going to happen." Contrary to the expressed purpose of PCEPA, which is to "denounce and prohibit the purchase of sexual services" because of the supposed "exploitation that is inherent in prostitution and the risks of violence posed to those who engage in it" (Bill C-36, 2014, preamble), the new advertising offence has actually made independent escorts feel more vulnerable to criminalization. To avoid criminalization, the women in this study reported making changes that threatened the important social networks they had developed to receive information and support and to increase their economic viability.

Effects of the Advertising Offence on Communication with Clients

Communicating with clients is an essential risk-management strategy used by sex workers. Independent escorts include information about their rates and services in their online advertisements so that clients know what to expect before contacting them. When sex workers are unable to clearly negotiate with their clients, the potential for miscommunication increases, as does the risk of encountering a frustrated or aggressive client (Bruckert and Law, 2013). Two major Canadian paid-ad sites have changed their policies in response to PCEPA and thus no longer publish sex worker advertisements that contain references to specific sexual acts and will not link to an escort's website that contains such terms. The restrictions that these ad sites have implemented are meant to protect the owners and managers of the sites from the new anti-advertising sanctions in the Criminal Code. Indeed, by banning references to sexual acts in sex workers' ads, the ad sites may be able to claim that they did not *knowingly* advertise the sexual services of another person and thus be exempt from prosecution. Yet escorts are not subject to the same legal scrutiny as third-party ad sites; they are immunized from prosecution for advertising their own services, and it is only the advertisement of another's services that is criminalized. Twelve of the research participants incorrectly assured me that advertising their own sexual services had become a crime, with ten citing the ad sites themselves as their main source of legal information in this regard.

The restrictions imposed by ad sites had created problems for at least three of the women in this study. Hannah, for example, had two work personas, one as an independent escort and another as an erotic masseuse. Her massage website used to explicitly list the acts that she would, and would not, perform. However, she removed the list when the advertising offence was implemented and was concerned that not being able to clearly explain her boundaries could expose her to violence or aggression from clients. Hannah described her fears:

> My massage website is very explicit. It says, "You cannot touch my vagina." If I can't put that on my site, then someone might show up expecting more because usually a massage is known to have extras ... So if someone was to come to me and expect it to be like in a massage parlour, then they're going to be disappointed. That's where dangerous things can happen. I don't want an angry dude in my condo when I'm by myself.

Hannah believed that the advertising-related strategies she had developed prior to PCEPA in order to stay safe were no longer viable. Although she was aware that she was technically allowed to list sexual services on her personal massage website because of her immunity from prosecution for advertising her own services, she had removed these references to avoid being banned from the third-party ad sites that now disallow that kind of information from being posted. Hannah told me that if she were to stop using these ad sites, it would be nearly impossible for her to meet new clients. Thus, despite knowing that it could render her vulnerable to an aggressive client, she had acquiesced to the restrictions imposed by the ad sites in order to sustain her business.

Cynthia, who identified as mixed-race, often encountered clients who assumed she provided anal sex – a service she did not offer. She attributed this assumption to the fetishization of Black women's buttocks, consistent with postcolonial scholarship on stereotypes about Black women's sexualities (e.g., see Bernardi, 2006; Nash, 2014; Rahier, 2014). As a response to these assumptions, Cynthia had used the euphemism "I don't speak Greek" in her advertisements to indicate that she did not provide anal sex, a phrase that is commonly used in the sex industry. Due to the new advertising restrictions, however, she had removed this reference from her advertisements and website. By the time of her interview, Cynthia had already met one new client who had assumed that she "speaks Greek" when he booked an appointment. Alhough this particular incident did not result in conflict with the client, like Hannah, Cynthia worried that other clients would try to push her boundaries or become aggressive.

Betty had also removed references to sexual acts from her advertisements. Although this change had not directly exposed her to potential conflict, it had affected her business in a different way. The majority of Betty's income came from seeing couples, and she had a website that focused exclusively on this market. Betty told me that she had found it difficult to market herself to couples without using words such as "ménage à trois" or "threesome." Instead, she had added various images of three items to her website, such as a trio of hearts or three sets of bare feet sticking out of a rumpled bed, trying to indicate that she specialized in work with couples. She believed that the implied meaning of these photos had been lost on potential clients. Having experienced a marked loss of income since the introduction of the advertising offence, Betty felt as though adherence to the new ad-site guidelines had negatively affected her brand and her business.

The negative effect on income generation was felt by all of the research participants, who reported a significant decline in business due to PCEPA, an outcome that itself had the potential to lead to other negative consequences. As Betty explained, "There's research that shows when the general volume of clients is reduced, you lose good clients and get more dangerous clients." Similarly, Amy told me that her business had significantly slowed down, and she felt that she could no longer be as selective about whom she decided to see:

> I already have way less business. There's some clients I didn't like because they were too aggressive or creepy or whatever, and I used to refuse to see them again. But my first thought when I heard about the advertising stuff was that I should probably email them now. And I also regretted always being so strict with references ... A lot of the time if you are really strict, some clients will just stop writing you 'cause they don't want to give their real name, which they really don't want to do now ... So this law says I'm a victim or whatever, which I never was, but now in order to not go to jail, I have to do things that are actually really scary. How does that even make sense?

Conclusion

Sex work advocates, academics, and legal professionals have criticized PCEPA because they believe that the legislation "will recreate and exacerbate all of the harms faced by sex workers" (Hollett, 2014, para. 3) and that it "undermines the spirit of the *Bedford* decision" (Canadian Bar Association, 2014, p. 41). The Supreme Court of Canada ruled in *Bedford* that the previous laws criminalized sex workers' risk-management strategies and were thus unconstitutional (see also Belak, this collection). The court advised legislators to ensure that any new laws would protect sex workers' Charter rights (*Canada (Attorney General) v. Bedford*, 2013). Instead of prioritizing sex workers' safety and dignity, the Conservative government's legislative response framed sex work as inherently exploitative and focused on eliminating it through criminalizing purchasers and third parties (Government of Canada, 2014). Research suggests that this approach will be harmful for street-based sex workers (see also Krüsi, Belak, and Sex Workers United Against Violence, this collection; Sayers, this collection).

Given that the majority of sex work in Canada takes place indoors (Weitzer, 2005), it is also necessary to consider the impact of this legislation on indoor sex workers, such as the independent escorts in this study. Sex workers represent an extremely varied and heterogeneous group (Agustín, 2005; Bernstein, 2007; McCarthy, Benoit, and Jansson, 2014; Sanders, 2004), and in many ways the Internet functions for independent escorts as strolls do for outdoor workers since sex workers use these spaces to meet clients, form social networks, and negotiate the terms and conditions of their work (Sanders, Scoular, Campbell, Pitcher, and Cunningham, 2018).

The criminalization of Internet advertising has the potential to lead to negative implications for indoor workers in a similar way that the criminalization of public communication has led to very serious negative consequences for street-based workers, partly by limiting their ability to effectively negotiate and communicate with their clients, which has left them unable to adequately assess risk levels in a public space. This is not to say that either the types or frequency of harm experienced by outdoor sex workers and independent escorts are homogenous and unaffected by structural factors. Rather, I argue that not only has PCEPA exacerbated the existing harms faced by already marginalized sex workers, but it has also created a new risk-space where the harms identified in *Bedford* have been translated and written into the lives of independent escorts. As Amy so clearly articulated, "We're not able to communicate the way we want to work. It kind of feels like the Internet version of the communications law, like we can't negotiate the terms and it's more dangerous."

As the narratives presented here illustrate, the independent escorts in this study felt that they were new potential targets of law enforcement efforts and thus that they had to take precautions to mitigate the risk of prosecution under the advertising offence. These precautions, or what Candice described as having to be "a lot more careful," have limited some participants' abilities both to effectively communicate with clients and to maintain strong social networks with other escorts. The advertising offence has created a new risk-space for independent escorts where the potential for the harms associated with isolation and miscommunication has seeped into a category of sex workers who previously felt insulated from criminalization, which further demonstrates the need for immediate legislative reform.

Note

1 The research was approved by the University of Toronto's Research Ethics Board, and data were collected in 2015–16.

References

Agustín, L.M. (2005). New research directions: The cultural study of selling sex. *Sexualities, 8*(5), 618–31. https://doi.org/10.1177/1363460705058400

Bernardi, D. (2006). Interracial joysticks: Pornography's web of racist attractions. In P. Lehman (Ed.), *Pornography: Film and culture* (pp. 220–43). New Brunswick, NJ: Rutgers University Press.

Bernstein, E. (2007). Sex work for the middle classes. *Sexualities, 10*(4), 473–88. https://doi.org/10.1177/1363460707080984

Bruckert, C., & Law, T. (2013). *Beyond pimps, procurers and parasites: Mapping third parties in the incall/outcall sex industry.* Retrieved from http://www.nswp. org/resource/beyond-pimps-procurers-and-parasites-mapping-third-parties -the-incalloutcall-sex-industry

Bungay, V., Halpin, M., Atchison, C., & Johnston, C. (2011). Structure and agency: Reflections from an exploratory study of Vancouver indoor sex workers. *Culture, Health and Sexuality, 13*(1), 15–29. https://doi.org/10.1080/13691058.20 10.517324

Canadian Alliance for Sex Work Law Reform. (2015). *Criminalizing advertising of sexual services: Impacts and consequences.* Retrieved from http://www. safersexwork.ca/wp-content/uploads/2014/07/Infosheet-on-Criminalizing -Advertising.pdf

Canadian Bar Association. (2014). *Bill C-36, Protection of Communities and Exploited Persons Act.* Retrieved from https://www.cba.org/CMSPages/GetFile. aspx?guid=506f61b6-ecdb-441d-9879-f4a1f3bd3f04

Canadian HIV/AIDS Legal Network, Pivot Legal Society, & Stella. (2014, June 25). *Reckless endangerment – Q&A on Bill C-36: Protection of Communities and Exploited Persons Act.* Retrieved from http://www.aidslaw.ca/site/reckless -endangerment-qa-on-bill-c-36-protection-of-communities-and-exploited -persons-act/?lang=en

Davies, K., & Evans, L. (2007). A virtual view of managing violence among British escorts. *Deviant Behavior, 28*(6), 525–51. https://doi.org/10.1080/016396 20701316830

Government of Canada. (2014). *Technical paper: Bill C-36, Protection of Communities and Exploited Persons Act.* Retrieved from http://www.justice.gc.ca/eng/rp-pr/other-autre/protect/p1.html

Hollett, K. (2014, November 6). Bill C-36: A backgrounder. *Pivot Blog.* Retrieved from http://www.pivotlegal.org/bill_c_36_a_backgrounder

Lewis, J., Maticka-Tyndale, E., Shaver, F.M., & Schramm, H. (2005). Managing risk and safety on the job: The experiences of Canadian sex workers. *Journal of Psychology and Human Sexuality, 17*(1–2), 147–67. https://doi.org/10.1300/J056v17n01_09

McCarthy, B., Benoit, C., & Jansson, M. (2014). Sex work: A comparative study. *Archives of Sexual Behavior, 43*(7), 1379–90. https://doi.org/10.1007/s10508-014-0281-7

Nash, J.C. (2014). Black anality. *GLQ: A Journal of Lesbian and Gay Studies, 20*(4), 439–60. https://doi.org/10.1215/10642684-2721366

Rahier, J.M. (2014). Stereotypes of hypersexuality and the embodiment of blackness: Some narratives of female sexuality in Quito, Ecuador. In J.M. Rahier (Ed.), *Blackness in the Andes: Ethnographic vignettes of cultural politics in the time of multiculturalism* (pp. 147–74). New York, NY: Palgrave Macmillan. https://doi.org/10.1057/9781137272720_8

Sanders, T. (2004). A continuum of risk? The management of health, physical and emotional risks by female sex workers. *Sociology of Health and Illness, 26*(5), 557–74. https://doi.org/10.1111/j.0141-9889.2004.00405.x

Sanders, T., Scoular, J., Campbell, R., Pitcher, J., & Cunningham, S. (2018). *Internet sex work: Beyond the gaze.* London, UK: Palgrave Macmillan.

Stella. (2015). *Advertising and the law.* Retrieved from http://www.nswp.org/sites/nswp.org/files/Advertising%20and%20the%20Law,%20Stella%20-%20March%202015.pdf

Weitzer, R. (2005). New directions in research on prostitution. *Crime, Law, and Social Change, 43*(4–5), 211–35. https://doi.org/10.1007/s10611-005-1735-6

Whittaker, D., & Hart, G. (1996). Research note: Managing risks: The social organization of indoor sex work. *Sociology of Health and Illness, 18*(3), 399–414. https://doi.org/10.1111/1467-9566.ep10934742

Cases

Bedford v. Canada, 2010 ONSC 4264.
Canada (Attorney General) v. Bedford, 2013 SCC 72, [2013] 3 SCR 1101.

Legislation

Bill C-36, *Protection of Communities and Exploited Persons Act,* SC 2014, c. 25.
Criminal Code, RSC 1985, c. C-46.

8

Misrepresentations, Inadequate Evidence, and Impediments to Justice

——————— Human Rights Impacts of Canada's Anti-Trafficking Efforts

TAMARA O'DOHERTY, HAYLI MILLAR, ALISON CLANCEY, AND KIMBERLY MACKENZIE

In Canada the academy, governments, nongovernmental organizations, and the media have portrayed human trafficking as a growing and pervasive problem that is difficult to prosecute (Perrin, 2010; Public Safety Canada, 2012). These mainstream sources offer simplistic explanations as to why this may be the case, arguing either that trafficked persons are unwilling to come forward or that law enforcement authorities need to do more to identify trafficked persons (Ferguson, 2012). Largely absent from these claims are critical analyses of the formulation of the anti-trafficking laws and their effects on the very communities that such laws are supposed to "protect," as well as discussions about the complex and intersecting socio-cultural, economic, legal, safety, and other reasons why "trafficked persons" may not come forward to report victimization. Mainstream claims often fail to address the many institutional factors that affect a decision to prosecute, such as a failure to meet charge-approval standards due to concern about the reliability of evidence or about victim/witness testimony leading to a determination that a case will not be successfully prosecuted.[1] Moreover, there are many factors related to historical oppression that explain why certain communities, particularly criminalized or otherwise marginalized communities, do not rely on the police or the criminal justice system to address their victimization and other forms of exploitation (Barrett, 2013; Hunt, 2015).

Anti–human trafficking law enforcement and awareness campaigns focus almost exclusively on situations of commercial sex trafficking. This narrow focus neglects the many other forms of labour exploitation that exist in every country, including Canada (Dandurand and Chin, 2014; Kaye and Hastie, 2015), and ignores the fact that sexual violence occurs within the context of labour exploitation generally and in precarious work sectors specifically. An absence of empirical knowledge uptake by the academy, governments, nongovernmental organizations, and the media is confounding given that a growing number of international and Canadian publications on this topic identify the harms of misrepresentation and the "collateral damage" of anti-trafficking laws on immigrant and migrant sex workers (Amnesty International, 2016; CASWLR and Pivot Legal Society, 2016; GAATW, 2007).

The resulting unidimensional and frequently racialized media-generated images commonly shown in the news and other sources lead one to believe that the sex trafficking of women and girls is a prolific and growing problem that exists solely in relation to commercial sex work, that traffickers are racialized or immigrant men who are getting away without being adequately punished, and that our criminal and immigration laws are ineffective (De Shalit, Heynen, and van der Meulen, 2014; Ferguson, 2012; Toupin, 2013). Such images, alongside an exaggerated and singular sex-trafficking narrative, have facilitated the expansion of some aspects of our anti-trafficking laws and have increased the severity of applicable penalties (Weitzer, 2012, 2015). In spite of few convictions since being introduced in 2005, the anti-trafficking provisions in the Criminal Code of Canada were amended in 2010, 2012, 2014, and 2015. These amendments included an increase in the number of offences from three to six, an increase in the corresponding maximum penalties, and the introduction of mandatory minimum sentences.

In addition to lacking a sound evidentiary basis, this expansion of criminal justice policy demonstrates a clear pattern of "crimmigration" (Stumpf, 2006) – the convergence of the criminal and immigration laws that are ostensibly used to "protect" migrant women as workers, students, and visitors (see also Butler Burke, this collection). For example, in July 2012 the Immigration and Refugee Protection Act (IRPA) and its associated regulatory provisions were amended to include a provision on "protecting foreign nationals from exploitation." The amendments enabled immigration officers to deny work permits for foreign nationals seeking to work in a sector "where there are reasonable grounds to suspect a risk of sexual exploitation" (Government of Canada, 2012, para. 7). These amendments prohibit all foreign nationals, whether visitors, students, or labourers, from working in sex-related businesses, including exotic dance establishments, massage parlours, and escort services (see also Lam and Gallant, this collection). Employers found to be in violation of Subsection 185(b) of the IRPA potentially face fines of up to $50,000 or up to two years in prison. At the same time, at the federal level there has been little discussion or assessment either of the effectiveness of national anti-trafficking laws and protectionist immigration policies or of the actual impacts of anti-trafficking campaigns and law enforcement measures on trafficked persons or on those thought to be most at risk of being trafficked.

After receiving requests to participate as "expert" panel discussants regarding the situation of human trafficking in Canada and in view of their own recognized knowledge deficits in this area, two of this chapter's authors, Millar and O'Doherty, sought to create a collaborative study with the Supporting Women's Alternative Network (SWAN) Vancouver Society. SWAN is an outreach organization that supports immigrant, migrant, and racialized indoor sex workers in Greater Vancouver. Together, they successfully applied for a BC Law Foundation grant to conduct a small independent study critically assessing the formulation and effects of anti-trafficking laws in Canada (for the full report, see Millar and O'Doherty, 2015). The academic-community partnership was intended not only to investigate the scope of Canadian anti-trafficking legal efforts but also to develop SWAN's capacity to conduct empirical research that the organization could then use for advocacy and education on the effects of anti-trafficking measures experienced by immigrant and migrant sex workers. This partnership featured a knowledge uptake model where SWAN's experiential knowledge – about the real and/or perceived effects of immigration and criminal anti-trafficking laws on their frontline work and the communities they serve – could be directly transmitted to academic and legal audiences. The study was also intended to contribute to the scant available evidence derived from socio-legal research on human trafficking in Canada.

Over the course of twenty months, the study collected data to assess the implementation of Canada's national anti–human trafficking laws following the ratification of the 2002 United Nations Protocol to Prevent, Suppress and Punish Trafficking in Persons, Especially Women and Children (hereafter, the Trafficking Protocol), including Canada's compliance with its definitional, prosecution, prevention, and protection provisions. The study comprised three components: an analysis of the relevant legislative framework and jurisprudence, interviews with SWAN members to learn about their perspectives on the formulation and enforcement of anti-trafficking legal measures, and interviews with eight practitioners and legal experts within the criminal justice system (e.g., law enforcement officials, Crown prosecutors, defence attorneys, and policy analysts) to ascertain their views on Canada's national anti-trafficking laws.[2] The study was intended to provide greater clarity on the state of legal anti-trafficking efforts, while exploring some of the consequences of such measures for immigrant, migrant, and racialized sex workers.

This chapter presents some key findings of the study, which examined human-trafficking cases prosecuted in Canada between 2002 and 2014. The study's findings expose some of the main consequences of a single narrative and exaggerated representations of human trafficking, not only for SWAN and the immigrant and migrant sex workers it supports but also in relation to the ability of the criminal justice system to successfully prosecute human-trafficking cases and to adequately respond to all trafficked persons. These results demonstrate the pressing need for more nuanced representations that better reflect the complex needs of those with lived migration and sex work experiences as the only way to create truly responsive services in order to meet those needs. Misrepresentations and exaggerations perpetuate marginalization and ultimately contribute to a systemic inability to address exploitation in effective ways.

The Canadian Legal Framework and Jurisprudence

Like most countries, and due in part to the challenges identified above, we know relatively little about the actual nature and extent of human trafficking in Canada (Toupin, 2013). To further obscure matters, government agency reports exaggerate human-trafficking statistics by including not only investigations and prosecutions of violations of immigration and criminal prohibitions against trafficking in persons, contrary to Section 118 of the IRPA and Section 279.01 and its subsidiary provisions of the Criminal Code, but also investigations of a vague category labelled "related offences" (Royal Canadian Mounted Police, 2014). The trafficking-related category includes a range of offences – such as assault, sexual assault, drug-related offences, prostitution-related offences, and weapons-related criminal offences, in addition to immigration offences like document fraud – that are subjectively and variously defined by the reporting government agency and that cannot be independently verified.[3] Indeed, the study's three attemps via the Access to Information Act to ascertain the basis of the federal government's published statistics on this category were denied.

Official government publications typically include statistics on both investigations and charges, in addition to data on prosecutions and convictions

(Karam, 2016). This expansive decription of trafficking statistics allows for the inclusion of cases where human-trafficking charges were ultimately dismissed, whether in instances when there was an acquittal or plea negotiation, when charges were withdrawn or stayed for a variety of reasons often related to evidence and witness credibility, or when there was a divergence in prosecution rates between provinces where police laid charges and provinces where prosecutors laid charges. The net effect of these official reporting practices, especially when combined with media reports about law enforcement investigations of human trafficking, is to amplify the appearance of human trafficking across the country. Indeed, research participants from within the criminal justice system suggested that they had witnessed a steady expansion of the activities falling under the general scope of human trafficking as a way of justifying the resources spent to counter it. The interviewees remarked that there had yet to be any empirically verifiable data demonstrating the scope and nature of human trafficking in Canada, with many quick to point out that this paucity of data did not mean that human trafficking was not occurring; rather, it was a statement reflecting the need for a more robust evidentiary basis to support corresponding legal efforts. In brief, the available government statistics appear to provide limited clarity about the actual scope and nature of human trafficking in Canada because there are significant problems with the way that cases are reported and represented by criminal justice and other government agencies (Ogrodnik, 2010).

One of the goals of the study was to determine the exact number of human-trafficking prosecutions in Canada through both immigration and criminal prohibitions. The findings show that there had been relatively few – under twenty – international and/or domestic trafficking prosecutions resulting in a conviction, which is surprising given the level of public, media, and governmental attention to the issue. The findings, affirmed by the Canadian Centre for Justice Statistics (Karam, 2016), indicate that there were a total of thirty-three immigration and criminal prosecutions between June 2002 and December 2014 that, contrary to both the IRPA (s. 118) and the Criminal Code (s. 279), resulted in either a conviction or another legal outcome, such as charges being withdrawn, a stay of proceedings, a full acquittal on all charges, or a partial acquittal for a trafficking offence. Of the thirty-three prosecutions, only seventeen concluded with trafficking-specific convictions, including two mixed-verdict convictions, thus falling considerably short of the data for the study period presented by sources such as the annual US Trafficking in Persons Reports (United States Department of State, 2001–15), which combined the broader trafficking-related category with the trafficking-specific category and asserted that there had been 104 human-trafficking convictions in Canada.

In reality, four of the thirty-three prosecutions (*R. v. Domotor,* 2011, 2012; *R. v. Ladha,* 2013; *R. v. Ng,* 2007, 2008; *R. v. Orr,* 2013, 2015) involved alleged international cross-border trafficking; the remaining twenty-nine involved domestic trafficking. Three of the thirty-three cases were IRPA prosecutions, including one alleged cross-border sex-trafficking case and two cases related to non–sexual labour trafficking. Two of the three IRPA prosecutions resulted in acquittals on the trafficking-specific charges at trial, and one resulted in an acquittal on appeal. The majority of the thirty-three cases involved allegations of domestic sex trafficking and, as evidenced by the cross-criminal charges, clearly related to commercial sex. Consistent with Roots's (2013) findings, our study's criminal justice research participants suggested that rather than targeting new exploitative activities, the Criminal Code's human-trafficking sections appeared to be used to prosecute cases that would historically have been considered "pimping," now criminalized under the provisions respecting material benefits (s. 286.2) and procuring (s. 286.3) in the Criminal Code (previously under s. 212).[4]

Rather remarkably, the study was unable to find any trafficking-specific prosecutions among the thirty-three cases that resulted in convictions for alleged migrant sex trafficking.[5] Nevertheless, the absence of charges and prosecutions is not indicative of an absence of incidents. Instead, these findings may simply point to the inability of the formal justice system to adequately respond to the victimization of groups whose members are marginalized and/or criminalized (Hunt, 2015). At the same time, the cases found by the study do not support the many official claims about transnational trafficking in Canada, especially the extent of such trafficking, the countries of origin, and the ethnicities of trafficked persons, along with purported links to organized crime (Ferguson, 2012). Indeed, the study found only one case (*R. v. Domotor,* 2011, 2012) involving multiple accused with cross-charges pertaining to an organized criminal group and involving labour exploitation – not commercial sex.

In addition to the focus on transnational human trafficking, the singular narrative in Canada claims that the domestic trafficking of Indigenous women and girls is a major concern. The prosecuted cases found by the study, however, do not support these official claims. In this regard, Indigenous persons justifiably lack faith in the Canadian justice system to effectively respond to their victimization and/or exploitation in view of a lengthy history of colonization and ongoing oppression (van der Meulen,

Yee, and Durisin, 2010). As well, some observers contend that trafficking cases involving Indigenous complainants are underinvestigated or are not prosecuted as trafficking offences (Hunt, 2015). Low reporting rates occur in combination with other systemic and institutional challenges regarding testimony in court and witness cooperation, among other legal issues, that may affect the investigation and/or prosecution of cases (Kaye and Hastie, 2015).

Notably, Canada is not alone in its relatively few prosecutions and a low number of convictions for human-trafficking offences. Internationally, based on data from the United Nations Office on Drugs and Crime, Kangaspunta (2015) indicates that for every one hundred people suspected of trafficking in persons, forty-five are prosecuted and that of those prosecuted, twenty-four are convicted at the court of first instance. Kangaspunta cites various possible reasons for low prosecution and conviction rates globally, including the potential infrequency of trafficking offences, the hidden nature of human traf-ficking, limited national criminal justice capacity to effectively investigate and prosecute or to adequately sanction such offences, and corruption. Other experts, such as Gallagher (2016) and Farrell, DeLateur, Owens, and Fahy (2016), also point out that criminal prosecutions are still in their early stages.

Consequences of a Single Narrative and Exaggerated Representations

Our research details various negative impacts of misrepresenting human trafficking as a singular and hyper-idealized narrative. First, it is evident that immigrant and migrant sex workers are subject to heightened state surveillance in various policy domains, which adversely affects their access to health services and safety and their overall well-being.[6] Second, the vic-tims of noncommercial sex labour exploitation or sexual exploitation in other precarious labour contexts are relatively invisible as a result of a uni-dimensional presentation of human trafficking as sexual exploitation. Third, the inaccurate representations appear to negatively affect prosecu-tions and to make securing convictions difficult. The conflation of sex work and trafficking has become so entrenched in Canada that it is now virtually impossible to discuss commercial sex without including human trafficking. For example, in 2014, when introducing the new criminal laws targeting commercial sex under Bill C-36, the Protection of Communities and Exploited Persons Act (PCEPA), Minister of Justice Peter MacKay refer-enced human trafficking twelve times in his seventeen-minute speech, in spite of the fact that PCEPA was created after *Canada (Attorney General) v. Bedford* (2013) to replace prostitution-related laws, not anti-trafficking laws (see Belak, this collection). Notably, PCEPA simultaneously introduced significant amendments to Canada's criminal anti-trafficking laws, suggesting that, from a national policy perspective, commercial sex and trafficking in persons are intertwined. This conflation is equally evident in Canadian law enforcement units that are tasked with investigating human-trafficking allegations, which are frequently part of vice units, and in official government publications that almost always present human trafficking in association with commercial sex.

This conflation of commercial sex work and human trafficking is one of the most troubling and frustrating issues facing SWAN members and, indeed, other sex work organizations across the country. The realities for immigrant and migrant sex workers in Canada can vary considerably; however, based on their outreach work and provision of supportive services, SWAN staff and board members felt that human trafficking has little to do with their clientele. Since 2008, SWAN has only supported one woman who considered herself trafficked. Instead, the staff and board members suggested that portraying immigrant and migrant sex workers as victims grossly misrepresents the diversity, resilience, and independence of their clientele. These sex workers resist the label of trafficking victim and its associated stigma. The participants in the study indicated that oversimplifying issues of consent in the context of adult commercial sex ignores the differing degrees of agency exercised by diverse individuals in varying circumstances and the systemic causes that result in immigrant and migrant women choosing sex work. SWAN participants pointed to the barriers that immigrants and migrants face in the Canadian labour market – such as being unable to obtain work in their field because of language barriers, their lack of Canadian work experience, and/or policies against acceptance of their foreign credentials – as being key to understanding why immigrant and migrant women sell sex. They further suggested that society's moralistic views of sex influence conceptions of agency. Racism was also identified as a significant issue affecting the perceived agency of Asian immigrant and migrant sex workers, which accords with official narratives, especially those in the annual US Trafficking in Persons Reports (United States Department of State, 2001–15), about whom transnational trafficked persons in Canada are presumed to be.

SWAN members not only affirmed the negative consequences of the stigma affecting sex workers generally but also pointed to a number of specific concerns about the effects of criminalization and expanding state regulation when commercial sex is conflated with human trafficking. They explained that misrepresentations lead to increased state surveillance both within and outside of the criminal justice system, which in turn affects service provision and service access.[7] In relation to other legal policies and law enforcement practices, SWAN identified several situations that have become increasingly common since the introduction of PCEPA (O'Doherty, 2015), which is based on an end-demand, asymmetrical criminalization ideology. Sex workers, their clients, and third parties who manage, own, or otherwise facilitate adult commercial sex are concerned about the impact of the new criminal laws. SWAN members reported managers refusing to keep condoms on their premises or even forbidding the organization to continue providing outreach because of their concern that either activity would be perceived as indicating that commercial sex was occurring and result in law enforcement actions against the establishment.

Research participants also reported that raids designed to "rescue" women from situations of human trafficking have major negative results. The immigrant, migrant, and racialized women with whom SWAN works are overwhelmingly permanent residents or Canadian citizens employed in legal sex establishments with business licenses and without immigration-related problems. Raids frequently result in the closure of workplaces and often force sex workers to move from licensed establishments to unlicensed, harder to reach, and less safe working environments; they do not "free enslaved women." Instead, raids and other similar law enforcement actions result in a reduction in sex workers' access to health, safety, and well-being. Further, these actions lead immigrant, migrant, and racialized sex workers to become increasingly reluctant to contact police in the event of an experience of violence or exploitation.

The study data also suggest that the negative impacts of representing a singular narrative of human-trafficking victims in the context of commercial sex work alongside an overly simplistic portrayal of victims of extreme violence creates problems for those who attempt to enforce the laws in this politicized context. Criminal justice policy in general has become increasingly politicized in Canada (Ismaili, Sprott, and Varma, 2012), and discussions of human trafficking feature widely diverging views on fundamental issues such as agency, consent, and the definition of exploitation (Wijers, 2015). The criminal justice personnel who participated in the study expressed frustration about the "infusion of politics" into their law enforcement work in this area. Moreover, they were aware of the lack of reliable government data and the problems with the transparency of government representations related to human trafficking. One participant suggested that government-funded research reporting findings that contrasted with mainstream representations or that did not otherwise support the ideological mandate of the federal Conservatives' majority government remained unpublished or simply vanished altogether. A lack of independent (i.e., non–government sponsored) research, serious barriers against access to information, a lack of transparency related to governmental data, and official publications that appear to deliberately amplify the scope of investigations, prosecutions, and convictions concerning trafficking in persons combine to cast doubt on the empirical validity of much of the Canadian government's research on human trafficking and many of its related policy documents. The media further compound the situation, for there is heavy media coverage when a charge is laid or an investigation uncovers alleged human-trafficking activities or victims, but there is no corresponding follow-up coverage when the charges are subsequently dropped or result in acquittal. Equally troubling, some journalists now appear to be describing their investigations as research.[8]

The study data support existing literature and evidence (Chuang, 2015; Ferguson, 2012; Kaye and Hastie, 2015; Ogrodnik, 2010; Wijers, 2015) about the challenges that criminal justice personnel face in attempting to apply laws in a highly politicized context. Due to a lack of agreement about the specific point at which exploitation occurs, meeting evidentiary thresholds in court is difficult, notwithstanding that Canadian immigration and criminal offences arguably should be easier to prosecute in view of departures from the more rigorous offence elements anticipated by the Trafficking Protocol.[9] Some of the research participants (i.e., the Crown prosecutors) argued for more expansionist definitions, whereas others (i.e., the defence attorneys) argued that such expansionism was not necessarily in the interests of groups whose members are perceived to be at risk of being trafficked. The study data suggest that the reductive narrative of human trafficking as predominantly an issue of extreme sexual exploitation is a major impediment to prosecuting cases successfully. Four criminal justice interviewees discussed the challenges they faced in preparing their cases for trial, explaining that there were difficulties in establishing witness credibility, in proving a total absence of consent, and in persuading judges about the level of subjective fear for safety required in the criminal offence of human trafficking in relation to proving psychological coercion as opposed to overt physical violence. One problem that interviewees pointed out was that the Criminal

Code's specific anti-trafficking offence was still relatively new and that because there were so few cases, very few people across Canada had experience with human-trafficking prosecutions. In addition, the same issues that lead to sexual assault acquittals (i.e., witness credibility and reasonable doubt concerning consent) are exacerbated in the context of human trafficking because popular (and media-idealized) notions of what human trafficking entails do not correspond well with the reality of trafficked persons or with the required legal evidentiary burdens.

The study's criminal justice research participants suggested that the cases that have emerged thus far are complex and that gradations of exploitation and control feature prominently. Public awareness campaigns that are focused on sensational depictions of human trafficking – including the use of extreme violence, the international kidnapping dimension, and sexual assault – are not representative of the cases in which our interviewees were involved as prosecutors, defence attorneys, or expert witnesses. Indeed, the thirty-three Canadian cases examined were multifaceted, often involving varying levels of consent to exploitative working conditions, and they rarely included the extreme version of physical exploitation depicted both in Hollywood movies such as *Taken, The Whistleblower,* and *Human Trafficking (The Conversation,* 2016) and in most campaigns for anti-trafficking awareness (De Shalit, Heynen, and van der Meulen, 2014). Some of the interviewees expressed frustration in their attempts to convince judges and juries of the complex realities of those victimized by exploitative relationships. This obstacle was most evident at trial since the legal burden of proof in criminal cases (i.e., beyond a reasonable doubt) is difficult to meet. If defence counsel can successfully establish doubt about a complainant's consent or doubt as to whether an alleged victim truly feared for her or his safety, the accused is entitled to an acquittal. In this way, overly simplistic and hyper-idealized depictions of human trafficking appear to contribute to an inability to secure convictions at trial. This conclusion is evidenced by the study's prosecution case data: relatively few convictions have been secured (i.e., 17 cases between 2002 and 2014), as compared with the number of police-reported charges recorded by Statistics Canada (i.e., 299 offences of trafficking in persons cleared, respresenting charges against 374 persons, including 353 adults and 21 youths, between 2006 and 2014).

Cumulatively, these findings suggest that a singular and exaggerated narrative grossly misrepresents the complexity of trafficking and may result in unintentional harms to the very individuals anti-trafficking laws purport to protect. Exploitation exists on a spectrum and affects all forms of labour;

our current political and public attention to exploitation as solely existing in marginalized and precarious forms of labour such as commercial sex work renders invisible the exploitation that occurs elsewhere. Here, our analysis of immigration and criminal cases has exposed an almost singular focus on prosecuting human trafficking in the context of commercial sex work, especially for cases involving pimping and minor victims, to the exclusion of other forms of labour exploitation. Four of the criminal justice interviewees suggested that the unilateral focus on commercial sex has made it difficult to enforce laws against other forms of labour exploitation. These interviewees further asserted that this narrow focus is unwarranted; other forms of labour exploitation are likely more common than sexual exploitation, yet the other forms of labour exploitation warrant little media or criminal justice attention in Canada.

Conclusion

The data emerging from this research demonstrate some of the many challenges of enforcing laws related to trafficking in persons for the purpose of labour exploitation within a system of criminalization, as well as a singular narrative overwhelmingly focused on sexual exploitation in the commercial-sex sector. Several interviewees noted that positive action, such as extending labour rights to workers with precarious status and proactively using other systems of law, such as municipal-bylaw enforcement, could function more effectively to prevent labour exploitation from occurring in the first place, unlike a system of criminalization after the fact. A change in legal approach would necessarily involve expanding understandings of human trafficking to include other forms of labour beyond commercial sex and more subtle forms of labour exploitation beyond physical coercion. Indeed, awareness campaigns that rely on extremism or that depict exploitation in unidimensional ways not only lead to law enforcement approaches that negatively affect the labour and human rights of immigrant and migrant sex workers but also make it difficult to persuade juries, and even judges, about less extreme but still harmful forms of exploitation occurring in other contexts. There are far more cases of partial consent to exploitative labour or consent to precarious and informal labour due to a lack of economic or migration opportunities (West Coast Domestic Workers Association, 2013).

The study data further raise the concern that labour-exploitation cases become more difficult to investigate and prosecute in a context of sensationalism and the intersection of criminal and immigration law. If our goal is to improve labour conditions and to reduce the exploitation of vulnerable labourers, such as immigrant and migrant sex workers, we need to reconsider our reliance on inflated statistics and unidimensional depictions. In this regard, we note that Canadian criminal prosecutions of trafficking in persons are in their infancy and that relatively few convictions have been secured. There is an absence of appellate jurisprudence to draw on, and there are few criminal justice professionals with expertise in investigating, prosecuting, and trying such cases. At the same time, the study data point to the vital importance of ensuring that the voices of those most directly affected by anti-trafficking legal efforts – especially experiential and historically marginalized communities – are fully considered by those who develop and amend Canadian laws to ensure that law reform efforts are inclusive and truly evidence-informed and rights-based.

Notes

1 There are varying approaches – including whether the police or Crown approves charges – and standards for federal and provincial prosecutions to proceed across Canada. For example, British Columbia is one of only two provinces where the provincial Crown must approve charges. In British Columbia the decision to prosecute is based on whether there is a *substantial likelihood* of conviction and on whether the prosecution is deemed to be in the public interest. The Public Prosecution Service of Canada, representing the federal Crown, bases the decision to prosecute on similar citeria, but the threshold is arguably lower, namely whether there is a *reasonable* prospect of conviction given the available evidence at trial and whether the prosecution serves the public interest. However, other provinces and territories have standards that differ from these (e.g., *reasonable likelihood*), and as our interviews suggest, the decision to prosecute is to some extent personality-driven.

2 The study's qualitative research approach was based on principles of grounded theory and was conducted using NVivo software. Although the data reflect the interview schedule created in collaboration with the research team, the interview participants were given the opportunity to raise issues independently of the schedule. The study endeavoured to include commonalities between interviewees as well as any contrasting perspectives or unique viewpoints.

3 This government statistical practice of referring to "related" trafficking offences that are outside the ambit of the actual immigration or criminal offence provisions seems unusual when compared with how other criminal offences are represented. For example, by way of contrast, official reports on "prostitution-related" offences refer to prostitution-specific provisions of the Criminal Code, such as procuring and living on the avails. Likewise, "terrorism-related" offences refer to terrorism-specific provisions of the Criminal Code, such as financing or facilitating

terrorism, and generally do not refer to other types of tangentially related criminal offences.

4 Here, the study looked at police-reported crime statistics on charging patterns that suggested an inverse relationship between charges for prostitution-related offences and trafficking-specific offences during the interval between prostitution-related offences being constitutionally challenged and struck down and the introduction of Bill C-36, the Protection of Communities and Exploited Persons Act (PCEPA), in 2014. Police-reported crime statistics on the number of persons charged with the offence of trafficking in persons indicate that there was an increase from 36 charges in 2011 to 50 charges in 2012, 72 charges in 2013, and 173 charges in 2014. In the same period, the number of persons charged with prostitution-related offences declined from 1,583 in 2011 to 1,254 in 2012, 1,202 in 2013, and 314 in 2014, when the new laws came into effect (data obtained from Statistics Canada, 2017).

5 There was a partial acquittal in *R. v. Ng* (2007, 2008), where the defendant was acquitted of trafficking-specific charges but convicted of other offences.

6 See CASWLR and Pivot Legal Society (2016), which documents this increased surveillance nationally, including raids on sex work establishments that combine the enforcement of border laws, criminal laws, and bylaws.

7 This situation is particularly apparent in the medical field. Sex workers need to be able to access safe and nonjudgmental healthcare; however, SWAN has observed that with increasing interventions suggested for medical staff, especially in the form of online training modules and webinars, sex workers have reported intrusive and inappropriate questioning, resulting in their reluctance to fully disclose sexual and physical health concerns and even their reluctance to access health services at all (Clancey, Khushrushahi, and Ham, 2014).

8 See, for example, a *Globe and Mail* article by Grant (2016) that is part of a reporting series described as an "investigation" of trafficking in persons.

9 Both the IRPA's and Criminal Code's definitions of "trafficking in persons" fall short of the more rigorous offence elements contemplated by the Trafficking Protocol, which defines it as consisting of three offence elements: an action (e.g., recruiting, transferring, and harbouring), the means by which control over a person is achieved (e.g., force, fraud, and deception), and the purpose of exploiting a person's labour or service. The IRPA's offence of trafficking in persons largely omits the exploitation element, whereas the Criminal Code's offences largely omit the means. The omission of these offence elements in Canadian legal definitions should make it easier to successfully prosecute an offence of trafficking in persons.

References

Amnesty International. (2016). *Amnesty International policy on state obligations to respect, protect and fulfil the human rights of sex workers.* Retrieved from https://www.amnesty.org/en/documents/pol30/4062/2016/en/

Barrett, N. (2013). *An assessment of sex trafficking.* Toronto, ON: Canadian Women's Foundation, Task Force on Trafficking of Women and Girls in Canada.

CASWLR (Canadian Alliance for Sex Work Law Reform) & Pivot Legal Society. (2016). *Joint submission for Canada's review before the UN Committee on the Elimination of All Forms of Discrimination against Women, 65th session.* Retrieved from http://tbinternet.ohchr.org/Treaties/CEDAW/Shared%20Documents/CAN/INT_CEDAW_NGO_CAN_25385_E.pdf

Chuang, J.A. (2015). The challenges and perils of reframing trafficking as 'modern-day slavery'. *Anti-Trafficking Review,* (5), 146–49. https://doi.org/10.14197/atr.20121559

Clancey, A., Khushrushahi, N., & Ham, J. (2014). Do evidence-based approaches alienate Canadian anti-trafficking funders? *Anti-Trafficking Review,* (3), 87–108. https://doi.org/10.14197/atr.20121435

The Conversation. (2016, January 20). Movies and myths about human trafficking. Retrieved from http://theconversation.com/movies-and-myths-about-human-trafficking-51300

Dandurand, Y., & Chin, V. (2014). *Uncovering labour trafficking in Canada: Regulators, investigators, and prosecutors.* Vancouver, BC: International Centre for Criminal Law Reform.

De Shalit, A., Heynen, R., & van der Meulen, E. (2014). Human trafficking and media myths: Federal funding, communication strategies, and Canadian anti-trafficking programs. *Canadian Journal of Communication, 39*(3), 385–412. https://doi.org/10.22230/cjc.2014v39n3a2784

Farrell, A., DeLateur, M., Owens, C., & Fahy, S. (2016). The prosecution of state-level human trafficking cases in the United States. *Anti-Trafficking Review,* (6), 48–70. https://doi.org/10.14197/atr.20121664

Ferguson, J. (2012). *International human trafficking in Canada: Why so few prosecutions?* (Unpublished doctoral dissertation). University of British Columbia, Vancouver, British Columbia.

GAATW (Global Alliance Against Traffic in Women). (2007). *Collateral damage: The impact of anti-trafficking measures on human rights around the world.* Retrieved from http://www.gaatw.org/Collateral%20Damage_Final/singlefile_CollateralDamagefinal.pdf

Gallagher, A. (2016). Editorial: The problems and prospects of trafficking prosecutions: Ending impunity and securing justice. *Anti-Trafficking Review,* (6), 1–11. https://doi.org/10.14197/atr.20121661

Government of Canada. (2012). *Operational bulletin 449.* Retrieved from http://www.cic.gc.ca/ENGLISH//resources/manuals/bulletins/2012/ob449.asp

Grant, Tavia. (2016, February 15). Indigenous Affairs minister says new approach needed to tackle trafficking. *Globe and Mail.* Retrieved from https://www.theglobeandmail.com/news/national/indigenous-affairs-minister-says-new-approach-needed-to-tackle-trafficking/article28762556/

Hunt, S. (2015). Representing colonial violence: Trafficking, sex work, and the violence of law. *Atlantis: Critical Studies in Gender, Culture, and Social Justice, 37*(2), 25–39.

Ismaili, K., Sprott, J., & Varma, K. (2012). *Canadian criminal justice policy: Contemporary perspectives.* Toronto, ON: Oxford University Press.

Kangaspunta, K. (2015). Was trafficking in persons really criminalised? *Anti-Trafficking Review*, (4), 80–97. https://doi.org/10.14197/atr.20121545

Karam, M. (2016). *Trafficking in persons in Canada, 2014. Juristat*, 36(1), 3–10. Retrieved from http://www.statcan.gc.ca/pub/85-002-x/2016001/article/14641 -eng.pdf

Kaye, J., & Hastie, B. (2015). The Canadian Criminal Code offence of trafficking in persons: Challenges from the field and within the law. *Social Inclusion*, 3(1), 88–102. https://doi.org/10.17645/si.v3i1.178

Millar, H., & O'Doherty, T. (2015). *The Palermo protocol and Canada: The evolution and human rights impacts of anti-trafficking laws in Canada (2002–2015)*. Retrieved from https://icclr.law.ubc.ca/publication/the-palermo-protocol -canada-the-evolution-and-human-rights-impacts-of-anti-trafficking-laws-in -canada-2002-2015/

O'Doherty, T. (2015). *Victimization in off-street commercial sex*. (Unpublished doctoral dissertation). Simon Fraser University, Burnaby, British Columbia.

Ogrodnik, L. (2010). *Towards the development of a national data collection framework to measure trafficking in persons*. Ottawa, ON: Canadian Centre for Justice Statistics. Retrieved from http://www.statcan.gc.ca/pub/85-561-m/85 -561-m2010021-eng.pdf

Perrin, B. (2010). *Invisible chains: Canada's underground network of human trafficking*. Toronto, ON: Viking Canada.

Public Safety Canada. (2012). *National action plan to combat human trafficking*. Ottawa, ON: Public Safety Canada.

Roots, K. (2013). Trafficking or pimping? An analysis of Canada's human trafficking legislation and its implications. *Canadian Journal of Law and Society*, 28(1), 21–41. https://doi.org/10.1017/cls.2012.4

Royal Canadian Mounted Police. (2014). *Project safekeeping 2013*. Ottawa, ON: Royal Canadian Mounted Police.

Statistics Canada. (2017). Table 252–0051, incident-based crime statistics by detailed violations. (CANSIM database). Retrieved from http://www5.statcan. gc.ca/cansim/a26?lang=eng&id=2520051

Stumpf, J. (2006). The crimmigration crisis: Immigrants, crime, and sovereign power. *American University Law Review*, 56(2), 367–419.

Toupin, L. (2013). Clandestine migrations by women and the risk of trafficking. In C. Parent, C. Bruckert, P. Corriveau, M.N. Mensah, & L. Toupin (Eds.), *Sex work: Rethinking the job, respecting the workers* (pp. 111–36). Vancouver, BC: UBC Press.

United States Department of State. (2001–15). *Trafficking in persons reports (2001–2015), Country narratives: Canada*. Washington, DC: United States Department of State.

van der Meulen, E., Yee, J., & Durisin, E.M. (2010). Violence against Indigenous sex workers: Combating the effects of criminalisation and colonialism in Canada. *Research for Sex Work*, (12), 35–37. Retrieved from http://www.nswp.org/ resource/research-sex-work-12-sex-work-and-violence

Weitzer, R. (2012). Sex trafficking and the sex industry: The need for evidence-based theory and legislation. *Journal of Criminal Law and Criminology*, 101(4), 1337–69.

Weitzer, R. (2015). Researching prostitution and sex trafficking comparatively. *Sexuality Research and Social Policy, 12*(2), 81–91. https://doi.org/10.1007/s13178 -014-0168-3

West Coast Domestic Workers Association. (2013). *Access to justice for migrant workers in British Columbia.* Retrieved from http://www.wcdwa.ca/wp-content/ uploads/2014/03/Access-to-Justice-for-Migrant-Workers_WCDWA_FINAL_ 30_07_20131.pdf

Wijers, M. (2015). Purity, victimhood and agency: Fifteen years of the UN Trafficking Protocol. *Anti-Trafficking Review,* (4), 56–79. https://doi.org/10.14197/ atr.20121544

Cases

Canada (Attorney General) v. Bedford, 2013 SCC 72, [2013] 3 SCR 1101.
R. v. Domotor, [2011] OJ No. 6357.
R. v. Domotor, [2012] OJ No. 3630.
R. v. Ladha, 2013 BCSC 2437.
R. v. Ng, [2007] BCJ No. 1338, 2007 BCSC 880.
R. v. Ng, 2008 BCCA 535.
R. v. Orr, 2013 BCSC 1883.
R. v. Orr, 2015 BCCA 88.

Legislation

Bill C-36, *Protection of Communities and Exploited Persons Act,* SC 2014, c. 25.
Criminal Code, RSC 1985, c. C-46.
Immigration and Refugee Protection Act, SC 2001, c. 27.

9

Perceptions of Sex Work
Exploring the Narratives of Police and Regulatory Officials

FRANCES M. SHAVER, JOHN BRYANS, AND ISABELLE BHOLA

Current scholarly work on the sex industry relies heavily on responsibiliza-tion and victimization discourses that reinforce the marginalization of sex workers and undermine their human and civil rights. Two spheres of analy-sis related to these discourses predominate. One focuses on sex workers and their perceptions of and experiences with the police (Benoit et al., 2016; Krüsi, Kerr, Taylor, Rhodes, and Shannon, 2016; Scoular and O'Neill, 2007; Sherman et al., 2015; Williamson, Baker, Jenkins, and Cluse-Tolar, 2007), and the other analyzes the stigmatic assumptions inherent in the laws that reinforce the vulnerability of sex workers by undermining their human and civil rights (Bruckert and Hannem, 2013; Canadian HIV/AIDS Legal Net-work, 2007; Sampson, 2014). This chapter introduces a third sphere of analysis by focusing on the narratives of regulatory officials – including the police – and on their perceptions of sex workers. By doing so, it identifies two frameworks in addition to the victimization and responsibilization per-spectives: autonomy and vulnerability.

Canadian prostitution laws are built into the Criminal Code and apply across all provinces and territories. Yet official data show selective variation in the enforcement of the law among different municipalities (Shaver et al., 2015; Wagenaar and Altink, 2012). Thus we begin with the assumption that place matters and with the hypothesis that policing culture is an important factor in both the enforcement patterns adopted and the perceptions held about the people involved in the sex industry. The term "policing culture" refs to the shared and legitimated ways that laws and regulations are used by those regulating sex work to fulfil their objectives. Policing culture includes formal institutional legacies and contexts, as well as the more informal and often unconscious social norms that are established and maintained by training, daily practices, and social control mechanisms (Armstrong, 2017; Dewey and St. Germain, 2014; Paoline, 2003).

In this chapter, we examine policing culture by exploring perceptions of, and responses to, sex workers and the sex industry that are found in the narratives of regulatory officials. We are also interested in the action options available to regulatory officials that are implied by each narrative, such as supporting those exiting the sex trade while abandoning those who remain, as well as supporting harm reduction, reducing risk, and including sex workers in policy decisions. To this end, we interviewed municipal, justice, and policing representatives in Canadian municipalities about their interactions with people involved in the sex industry and about their views regarding the governance of sex work. Within this chapter, we address two objectives that informed our project: first, to analyze variation, if any, in policing cultures surrounding sex work and sex workers; second, to better understand the main characteristics of that variation.

Research on Perceptions of Sex Work(ers)

The data for this chapter are drawn from a multiproject, community-based study that occurred in 2013 and 2014 in six Canadian municipalities: Victoria, British Columbia; Calgary and Fort McMurray, Alberta; Kitchener-Waterloo, Ontario; Montreal, Quebec; and St. John's, Newfoundland and Labrador.[1] These sites were selected from a sample of ninety-three census metropolitan areas on the basis of census measures reflecting various social and institutional factors such as population size, mobility, education, income, and provincial jurisdiction. The aim was to obtain a broad cross-section in order to represent the diversity of social, political, and cultural contexts that are likely to affect the organization and practices related to the sex industry in Canada. Research team members surveyed and conducted interviews with 218 sex workers, 258 clients, 35 spouses or intimate partners of sex workers, 55 sex industry managers (i.e., 38 in escort services and 17 in massage businesses), 58 people who provide social services related to the sex industry, and 64 regulatory officials who are responsible for creating or enforcing laws and regulations (i.e., 27 police officers, 17 justice and licensing officials, and 20 elected city and government officials).[2] The present analysis is based on the 64 regulatory officials. Their transcripts were coded using NVivo 10 software in a two-step process. The first involved assignments of codes corresponding to the specific questions in the interview guide. The second incorporated a review of these codes, multiple readings of selected sections, and the identification of emerging themes. Once there was agreement on the revised set of dimensions by the first author and the research assistants, the transcripts were coded accordingly.

The regulatory officials with whom we spoke had an average of 14.6 years on the job, with years worked ranging from one to thirty-seven. Fifty-six percent identified as female and 44 percent as male. Their ages ranged from 30 to 69, with the average being just over 47. In terms of ethnicity, 1.6 percent identified as a visible minority, and none identified as Indigenous. Contrary to our expectations, their experience with people involved in the sex industry was limited. Regular interactions with off-street sex workers were rare: only 7.8 percent reported such interactions, and regular interactions with owners/managers or clients was even rarer, at 3 percent each. However, just over half, or 51.6 percent, reported regular contact with street-based workers. The exposure to street-based sex workers increased to 73.4 percent when both regular and occasional contacts were taken into account, but there was no substantial increase regarding exposure to others.

All four sex work frameworks or conceptualizations discussed below are found in the respondent interviews, but victimization is by far the most pervasive, and vulnerability is the least pronounced. This pattern is repeated in five of the six study locations.[3] These results are not surprising given the limited exposure our respondents have to off-street workers and others involved in the industry. The overwhelming tendency to see street-based sex workers as "risky" and "at risk" sets the conditions for the victimization narrative to predominate. We also examined the prevalence of the narratives across the three types of regulatory official. Victimization is the most common regardless of the type of official, although police and city officials are more likely to adopt this perspective than justice officials. What is surprising in this case is the extent to which all three types, including the police and the justice officials, support the autonomy narrative.

Theoretical Frameworks and Sex Work Conceptualizations

Since the late 1990s and with the increasing awareness of the missing and murdered women in Vancouver's Downtown Eastside, there has been a discursive shift away from seeing sex workers as deviant or criminal and toward seeing them as victims (see also Khan, this collection). Public and media narratives now reflect a greater concern for the health and safety of those involved in the sex industry (Krüsi et al., 2016; Matthews, 2005; Sanders and Soothill, 2011). Policing culture has changed as well, especially in response to the publication of *Forsaken,* a report on the failure of police to investigate the missing and murdered women (Oppal, 2012; see also Sayers, this collection).[4] Rather than reflecting a greater concern for health and safety, however, policing narratives rely heavily on responsibilization and victimization discourses. As Krüsi et al. (2016) and others have shown, responsibilization and victimization coexist with stigmatizing assumptions about sex workers as victimized or vulnerable. They argue that responsibilization is presented as protecting victims from risk but that it reinforces a distinction between responsible sex workers who exit or stop doing sex work and those "risky" subjects who continue to sell sex. Indeed, those who exit are supported, whereas those who remain are held responsible for their own downfall and may be subject to sanctions and restrictions (Scoular and O'Neill, 2007).

Although the scholarship on responsibilization and victimization is insightful, there are some shortfalls in the argument. First, even where sex workers are referred to as victims, the regulatory options available tend to transform sex workers into agents by making them responsible for their actions. It is assumed that they have a choice to stay or to leave. Job retraining and counselling therapies tend to be the programs of choice, and when sex workers fail or refuse to leave the sex trade, they are most often left to fend for themselves. Second, in speaking with regulatory officials, we found more variation than implied by the responsibilization narrative. This variation provides some insights regarding other perspectives and options for regulators. The initial analysis of our regulatory respondents revealed two important variations: one where the choice to enter and stay in sex work is considered legitimate; and one where victims are identified as those who cannot become, or who are not, full agents.

Our initial analysis of the interviews thus encouraged us to look beyond responsibilization and victimization. To this end, we identified two additional perspectives – autonomy and vulnerability – and organized our research to more systematically explore how and to what extent these narratives are used and what characteristics of the respondents or their contexts appear related to the use of these narratives. The following qualitative analysis provides an in-depth look at each of the four frameworks and their associated regulatory options.

Responsibilization

This framework includes an *implied* acknowledgment that sex workers, even if seen as victims, are able to make choices. Responsibilization is about getting sex workers to the point where they have enough agency to make a choice, preferably the choice to exit sex work, but refusing to exit is also a choice. Rejecting an exiting program or continuing to use drugs and work in "risky" situations, however, is clearly not the "preferred" response to help. Thus any consequences that sex workers then suffer are their own fault. Although difficult to distinguish from victimization, the key to the responsibilization framework is that it includes a judgment of the worker and/or the worker's decision. Regulatory options and responses include convincing sex workers to exit and supporting them in this endeavour, abandoning them to their own devices (i.e., "you made your bed so lie in it"), and minimal harm reduction initiatives. Interview excerpts from regulatory officials in Victoria and St. John's provide clear examples of how sex workers are being held accountable for their actions and decisions:

> Sex workers have chosen this. Therefore, they need to deal with the consequences. So if they get sexually assaulted or they get beat up or robbed, well they've chosen that lifestyle, so deal with it. (Police Officer, Victoria VIPO-902)

> We have a saying here that you're responsible for your own safety. So I guess the onus falls somewhat on the person involved to protect themselves in whatever way they can. I mean policies and guidelines around how it's regulated still probably won't protect you in every situation. (City Official, St. John's SJCO-553)

The preferred choice for sex workers in the responsibilization narrative is to exit the industry. Regardless of the circumstances, exiting is *always* offered:

> When we encounter sex trade workers, under any circumstance, one of the things that is always offered is the opportunity to exit the lifestyle. And more often than not, the offer is rejected. Because each woman – I liken it to a drug addict that has to reach rock bottom before they're willing to accept help. (Police Officer, Calgary CAPO-651)

Autonomy

Unlike the implied acknowledgment of agency in the responsibilization framework, the narrative here includes an *explicit* acknowledgment that sex workers are agents who are able to make choices. They are seen as individuals who have chosen to engage in sex work and who may choose, at some later date, to exit the industry or to keep working. Autonomy options and responses include harm reduction programs, risk reduction initiatives, and the inclusion of sex workers in policy decisions. Interview excerpts from a justice official in St. John's and a city official in Montreal provide clear examples of sex workers fitting this framework:

> I don't look at them as bad people. They're not bad people. I don't judge them and say, "You're a slut," or "You're this or that." People do what they need to do. There's always a reason for behaviour, and I always say that. Like in all the programs we do, there is a reason for a behaviour. (Justice Official, St. John's SJJO-557)

And a city official in Montreal insisted that all interventions must be based on respect:

> Any intervention must be based on respect for the autonomy of the victims. We work with them at their level. A comprehensive and concerted approach. That is what we absolutely want to promote. Also, an approach aimed at prevention, protection, and some prosecution. At first, I wasn't too comfortable with the prosecution aspect, but now that I've been around for a while, I understand the logic. (City Official, Montreal MOCO-206)

Agency is part of all of the autonomy narratives but is particularly noticeable in several interviews from Victoria. A city official described the director of a community-development project as one who recognized that people who are sex workers have a lot of qualities that are "entrepreneurial in spirit" and thought that they could help to revitalize the commercial area. She continued,

> We're looking at creating a more vibrant downtown or village here. So we kind of put two and two together and said, "Well, wouldn't it be great if there was an opportunity for sex workers to be entrepreneurs?" Still run their own business and be their own boss. (City Official, Victoria VICO-957)

Assumptions of agency also include seeing sex work as legitimate work. The next example is from a city official in Kitchener-Waterloo who described the opinions of her eighty-two-year-old mother:

It should be decriminalized, absolutely. She says, "What is the difference between a girl going out for dinner with a guy and then having sex with him because he bought her dinner, or a woman who sells herself for sex? What's the difference?" And she said this actually about a week ago, and I thought, "Yeah." (City Official, Kitchener-Waterloo KWCO-306)

Finally, recognizing sex workers as agents includes listening to and getting input from them when making decisions about the sex industry. A Victoria police officer explained what it means to understand that they are vulnerable:

Just like getting out of your car and saying, "How's it going?" How would I know what they have to deal with if I don't get out and say that? I wouldn't. So does decriminalization sound like a good idea? Probably. Yeah. But let's ask them. (Police Officer, Victoria VIPO-005)

A similar sentiment was echoed by a justice official in St. John's:

Let's find out the reasons why these people are doing this. Let's find out if they want to take themselves out of it. If they don't, that's their decision. We can't make decisions for people, and I think that's where the stigma with the police comes from because they feel the police are telling me what to do; the police are making decisions for me. (Justice Official, St. John's SJJO-557)

Victimization

The victimization framework depicts sex workers as victims or suggests that they had no choice but to become sex workers because of their upbringing. It also includes any reference indicating that sex workers (as victims) have little or no capacity to become agents because of their history of abuse, drug use, mental health issues, or similar conditions. Individual workers are seen as being victimized by others or by life circumstances. Regulatory options and responses include teaching individual safety strategies, prosecuting the victimizers (i.e., clients and sex-business owners and managers), and other paternalistic or protectionist approaches (e.g., incarcerating them for their own good).

The capacity for agency is limited or nonexistent in the victimization perspective, mostly because of the strong links presumed to exist between sex work, drugs, and violence. In addition, the violence and abuse are most often linked to other individuals or to personal life circumstances rather than to structural constraints. This perspective was reflected in the interviews with regulators in Montreal and St. John's:

> But me, my girls walk the streets, these are women who are dealing with severe drug addictions. There is also often mental health issues. They don't take their medication and they, they are on crack. That is my, that's my reality. (Police Officer, Montreal MOPO-212)

> But the drug habit has a lot to do with why they're into prostitution. (Police Officer, St. John's SJPO-550)

As with the responsibilization narrative, victimization options for action often include attempts to teach safety strategies and risk reduction. However, such regulatory options also include the prosecution of victimizers and more protectionist responses since victims are often treated as unable to act as agents, a key requirement for responsibilization approaches. The regulatory options associated with victimizers may even include incarcerating them for their own good:

> We said we're gonna bring them all before the courts, we're gonna detain them, bring them before the courts, johns and ... And then they get some court orders put in place for the girls for their benefit. (Police Officer, St. John's SJPO-550)

Vulnerability
From the perspective of vulnerability, there is an acknowledgment that the work environment is "risky" and potentially violent. However, the risks and most of the violence are seen as being linked to social-structural and more systemic constraints (e.g., the laws that are in place). Thus sex workers are seen as having limited opportunities to become agents. This is considered to be a form of systemic victimization rather than one linked to individual choice or life circumstances. Regulatory options and responses include the elimination of structural constraints and the minimization of risk.

The distinction between *being a victim* and *being vulnerable* is an important one, especially if the long-term goal is to build respect for sex workers, improve their working conditions, and address health and safety issues. The latter approach grounds vulnerability in a broad framework that recognizes individuals as having several different qualities or statuses that define them socially: their gender (i.e., female, male, transgender, etc.), their age (i.e., young or old), and their job (e.g., firefighter, coal miner, nurse, or night-shift worker). Thus they may find themselves at risk due to any one of these social qualities. In addition, the potential for risk may also be linked to the environment in which they find themselves (Becker, 1966) or to the structural constraints under which they operate. In any event, the responsibility for keeping safe and avoiding danger cannot be placed entirely on the individual sex worker. Structural and organizational changes become necessary, as does the development of policies that promote the employment, human rights, and citizenship of sex workers (Sanders and Campbell, 2007). Conversely, the victim-centred approach seriously limits the possibilities for making changes. It tends to rely on one social quality to define individual sex workers (i.e., their master status as a sex worker) without regard for any of the other aspects of their lives or persons. As a consequence, there is a tendency to rely on changing individual perceptions or the individual alone, with "the responsibility for keeping safe and avoiding danger ... placed entirely with the individual sex worker" (ibid., p. 12).

Several of the regulatory officials we interviewed recognized the importance of this distinction. A police officer from Victoria – one who thinks of sex workers as agents rather than victims – was careful to point out the difference between *being a victim* and *being vulnerable* in a potentially risky or dangerous situation:

> If you're working at a Subway at 1:00 a.m. in an area with no other staff, you're by yourself, there's no video cameras, you're not a victim but you're vulnerable. So there's a big difference, you know? ... Yeah. So it's by virtue of sometimes your gender or sometimes your profession and sometimes where you are at what time of the day. When you have something that somebody else wants and they're of the mindset to take it, then whether you're engaging willingly in the act or not [there is risk]. (Police Officer, Victoria VIPO-003)

A similar perspective is reflected in the response of a city official in St. John's:

> I think it's something that should be looked at from the point of view of, you know, if you have two consenting adults, for lack of a better word, that are willing to engage in that for a trade of money or whatever it might be, then I think sometimes the criminalization of that obviously adds to the stigma, but on top of that, it might kind of lead others to be able to take advantage

of [people] – whether it's male or female – who are maybe more vulnerable than them. (City Official, St. John's SJCO-553)

A key feature of the vulnerability narrative is that risk and the potential for violence are linked to systemic constraints rather than to individual characteristics or failure. A Victoria police officer, speaking about the court ruling in the *Bedford v. Canada* (2010) Charter challenge, explained how archaic laws put people at risk:

> Definitely agree with the opinions of the Superior Court of Ontario with regards to some of the archaic ways of the written legislation in regards to communication for the purpose, mostly that, [but] even living off the avails, where it penalizes people who are supporting sex trade workers. So I think the, the judge who made those decisions is making them from a really thoughtful considerate perspective. Now, now we need to decide what we're going to do with that. I do think that the current, the way that the laws are written, puts our sex trade workers at risk. (Police Officer, Victoria VIPO-602)

In summary, our findings show that the four narrative types contain key implications regarding the agency of sex workers and the legitimacy of sex work. The responsibilization perspective assumes that workers are agents but rejects the legitimacy of the work, whereas the autonomy approach accepts both the agency of the workers and their work. The victimization approach questions their agency while focusing on their individual capacities to overcome individual limitations, with the vulnerability approach also questioning their agency but focusing on social-structural problems. Each approach makes the case for specific regulatory programs and options as well. Responsibilization supports those who exit and abandons those who remain, autonomy programs include harm reduction and a willingness to include sex workers in policy decisions, victimization approaches include protectionist programs, and vulnerability responses seek to reduce structural constraints.

Conclusion

In this chapter, we have analyzed variations in the perspectives of regulatory officials regarding sex work and sex workers – that is, police officers, justice and licensing officials, and elected city and government officials. The data support the existence of reasonably coherent and distinct frameworks or conceptualizations used by regulatory officials when describing, understanding, and responding to sex work and sex workers. In many respects, the data reinforce the validity of sex workers' perceptions of the police and other officials as both responsibilizing and victimizing (Benoit et al., 2016; Krüsi et al., 2016; Scoular and O'Neill, 2007; Sherman et al., 2015; Williamson et al., 2007), as well as the stigmatic assumptions found to be inherent in the laws that undermine the human and civil rights of sex workers (Bruckert and Hannem, 2013; Canadian HIV/AIDS Legal Network, 2007; Sampson, 2014).

To better understand the main characteristics of each, we identified a number of variations on the two typical narrative frameworks currently found in the literature: responsibilization and victimization. We also showed that this literature tends not to treat them as distinct but considers victimization to be an initial stage in the process of responsibilization – a stage that must be ultimately denied since sex workers are redefined as agents with responsibility for the challenges that they face if they do not seek to exit the job. We found additional evidence for regulatory officials who accept and support sex workers as agents but without the insistence that they exit the job (e.g., the autonomy framework). We also found evidence for regulators who argue that victimization can often be a consequence of systemic conditions and constraint – in addition to the more individual-based dynamics of workers, clients, or victimizers.

This research provides a baseline for future study analyzing the relative outcome of those environments on the health and safety of sex workers. By recognizing and refining the greater number of frameworks and perceptions, it acknowledges the existence of new options and opportunities for action on the part of regulatory officials. We are encouraged by the hints that the use of particular narratives are a feature of the type of regulator role, the location, or the direct encounters between sex workers and regulatory officials. We have also noticed how these conceptualizations have changed since the late 1990s, when the police investigations into women missing from Vancouver's Downtown Eastside began and the report of the Honourable Wally T. Oppal (2012) was published. All of these findings reinforce our hypothesis that an improved understanding of policing culture and the perspectives of regulatory officials will help us to design more coherent and effective policies for improving the health and safety of sex workers.

Notes

This research was funded by the Institute of Gender and Health, part of the Canadian Institutes of Health Research. Bill Reimer assisted with the SPSS analysis, for which we are grateful. We also thank those who participated in the interviews; without their input, this chapter would not have been possible.

1 Data were collected during the window in which Canada's prostitution laws were being constitutionally challenged by current and former sex workers (*Canada (Attorney General) v. Bedford*, 2013) but prior to December 2014, when the new laws were enacted (Bill C-36, 2014). Under the pre-2014 legal regime, the Criminal Code criminalized keeping or being in a common bawdy-house, living on the avails of prostitution, and communicating in public for the purpose of prostitution.
2 For more information on the project, see http://www.understandingsexwork.ca/.
3 Fort McMurray was excluded from the analysis by location because there were too few participants for a reliable comparison.
4 The Missing Women Commission of Inquiry was established in September 2010 by the lieutenant governor of British Columbia. Mandated to inquire into and make findings of fact as well as to recommend necessary changes, the Honourable Wally T. Oppal produced a four-volume report focusing on police failures to investigate the disappearance of the women. The report also tells the story of the missing and murdered women in Vancouver's Downtown Eastside, who "were forsaken by society at large and then again by the police" (Oppal, 2012, p. 11).

References

Armstrong, L. (2017). From law enforcement to protection? Interactions between sex workers and police in a decriminalized street-based sex industry. *British Journal of Criminology, 57*(3), 570–88. https://doi.org/10.1093/bjc/azw019

Becker, H.S. (1966). *Outsiders: Studies in the sociology of deviance.* New York, NY: Free Press.

Benoit, C., Smith, M., Jansson, M., Magnus, S., Oullet, N., Atchison, C., ... Shaver, F.M. (2016). Lack of confidence in police creates a 'blue ceiling' for sex workers' safety. *Canadian Public Policy, 42*(4), 456–68. https://doi.org/10.3138/cpp.2016-006

Bruckert, C., & Hannem, S. (2013). Rethinking the prostitution debates: Transcending structural stigma in systemic responses to sex work. *Canadian Journal of Law and Society, 28*(1), 43–63. https://doi.org/10.1017/cls.2012.2

Canadian HIV/AIDS Legal Network. (2007). *Not up to the challenge of change: An analysis of the report of the Subcommittee on Solicitation Laws.* (Briefing paper). Retrieved from http://www.aidslaw.ca/site/not-up-to-the-challenge-of-change-an-analysis-of-the-report-of-the-subcommittee-on-solicitation-laws/?lang=en

Dewey, S., & St. Germain, T. (2014). 'It depends on the cop': Street-based sex workers' perspectives on police patrol officers. *Sexuality Research and Social Policy, 11*(3), 256–70. https://doi.org/10.1007/s13178-014-0163-8

Krüsi, A., Kerr, T., Taylor, C., Rhodes, T., & Shannon, K. (2016). 'They won't change it back in their heads that we're trash': The intersection of sex work-related stigma and evolving policing strategies. *Sociology of Health and Illness, 38*(7), 1137–50. https://doi.org/10.1111/1467-9566.12436

Matthews, R. (2005). Policing prostitution: Ten years on. *British Journal of Criminology, 45*(6), 877–95. https://doi.org/10.1093/bjc/azi046

Oppal, W.T. (2012). *Forsaken: The report of the Missing Women Commission of Inquiry*. Retrieved from http://www.missingwomeninquiry.ca/obtain-report/

Paoline, E.A., III. (2003). Taking stock: Toward a richer understanding of police culture. *Journal of Criminal Justice, 31*(3), 199–214. https://doi.org/10.1016/S0047-2352(03)00002-3

Sampson, L. (2014). 'The obscenities of this country': Canada v. Bedford and the reform of Canadian prostitution laws. *Duke Journal of Gender Law and Policy, 22*, 137–72.

Sanders, T., & Campbell, R. (2007). Designing out vulnerability, building in respect: Violence, safety and sex work policy. *British Journal of Sociology, 58*(1), 1–19. https://doi.org/10.1111/j.1468-4446.2007.00136.x

Sanders, T., & Soothill, K. (2011). The policing of pleasure: 'What kind of police service do we want?' *Police Journal, 84*(2), 110–24. https://doi.org/10.1350/pojo.2011.84.2.557

Scoular, J., & O'Neill, M. (2007). Regulating prostitution: Social inclusion, responsibilisation and the politics of prostitution reform. *British Journal of Criminology, 47*(5), 764–78. https://doi.org/10.1093/bjc/azm014

Shaver, F.M., Reimer, B., Jansson, M., Casey, L., Benoit, C., & Reist, D. (2015). Variation in Canadian social and legal environments related to the implementation of prostitution laws: Exploring how place matters. Paper presented at the 2nd International Conference on Public Policy in the session Prostitution Policy and Sex Work Governance – Design, Implementation, and Evaluation, Milan, Italy, July 3.

Sherman, S.G., Footer, K., Illangasekare, S., Clark, E., Pearson, E., & Decker, M.R. (2015). 'What makes you think you have special privileges because you are a police officer?' A qualitative exploration of police's role in the risk environment of female sex workers. *AIDS Care, 27*(4), 473–80. https://doi.org/10.1080/09540121.2014.970504

Wagenaar, H., & Altink, S. (2012). Prostitution as morality politics or why it is exceedingly difficult to design and sustain effective prostitution policy. *Sexuality Research and Social Policy, 9*(3), 279–92. https://doi.org/10.1007/s13178-012-0095-0

Williamson, C., Baker, L., Jenkins, M., & Cluse-Tolar, T. (2007). Police-prostitute interactions. *Journal of Progressive Human Services, 18*(2), 15–37. https://doi.org/10.1300/J059v18n02_03

Cases

Bedford v. Canada, 2010 ONSC 4264.

Canada (Attorney General) v. Bedford, 2013 SCC 72, [2013] 3 SCR 1101.

Legislation

Bill C-36, *Protection of Communities and Exploited Persons Act,* SC 2014, c. 25.

10

Protecting Victims Sexually Exploited through Prostitution?

————— Critically Examining Youth Legal and
Policy Regimes

STEVEN BITTLE

Contemporary debates regarding Canadian prostitution laws bristle with disquiet over the sexual exploitation and abuse of women involved in sex work. An example is the aftermath of the Supreme Court's historic decision in *Canada (Attorney General) v. Bedford* (2013), a case that precipitated legal reforms and confirmed what many sex workers, along with numerous activists and academics, had long argued: the country's anti-prostitution laws placed sex workers in violent situations by forcing them to meet their clients in secluded locales so as to avoid running afoul of the law (van der Meulen, Durisin, and Love, 2013). Critics, including many prohibitionist and anti-prostitution women's groups, immediately decried the court's decision, arguing that it effectively condoned the sexual exploitation of women by legitimizing the commodification of women's sexual services. The then Conservative federal government quickly followed suit, signalling its preference for new legislation that purports to protect women seen to be victimized through prostitution while criminalizing the so-called perverts and sexual miscreants who purchase their sexual services. Girded by this discourse of prostitution as abuse and victimization, in 2014 the federal government introduced Bill C-36, the Protection of Communities and Exploited Persons Act (PCEPA), which, among other things, criminalizes the purchase of sexual services (see also Porth, this collection).

Although the victim discourse marks a new and still contested (and contestable) development in the state's response to adult sex work, it constitutes the predominant means of understanding and responding to youth involvement in prostitution in this country.[1] Terms and phrases such as "exploitation," "sexual abuse," "the commercial sexual exploitation of children," "victims of trafficking," and "sexual slavery" are commonplace in academic and policy circles related to the prevention and control of youth in sex work (Barnett, 2011). In keeping with this dominant narrative, several jurisdictions across Canada have at their disposal various measures meant to "rescue" young women from sexual exploitation through prostitution. These strategies include secure care legislation and enhanced child welfare schemes that permit authorities to detain young prostitutes for their own "protection," programs that encourage youth to end the abuse they suffer through prostitution, and (largely unfulfilled) promises to criminalize male "sexual predators," notably customers and men thought to be pimps (Barnett, 2011; Busby, 2003; Martin, 2002). Similar victim-orientated laws exist in other jurisdictions, including "safe harbor" laws in several American states aimed at redefining and addressing youth in prostitution as human-trafficking victims (Mehlman-Orozco, 2015).

Critics argue that state laws, policies, and programs rooted in the sexual abuse and exploitation discourse ultimately fail to protect or help youth engaged in sex work. Secure care, for instance, is an unduly harsh measure that pushes prostitution underground and drives youth away from the possible protective services of police and from accessing (increasingly disappearing) social supports that they may want or need (Busby, 2003). The Canadian federal government's 2014 decision to criminalize the purchase of sexual services does little to assuage these concerns since sex workers, including youth, will continue to meet clients in secluded locales in order to avoid authorities. Critics further point to the dearth of evidence on the effectiveness of secure care (Kidd and Liborio, 2011) and to concerns that it reinforces colonial responses by detaining young Indigenous people in the sex trade via an industry of support systems that fail to address the historic and systemic exploitation of Indigenous women and girls (Hele, Sayers, and Wood, 2015; see also Sayers, this collection). In this respect, the "rhetoric of victimhood" (Phoenix, 2002a, p. 361) does little to challenge the material and social conditions that make sex work a viable option for some young people (Busby, 2003; Martin, 2002; Phoenix, 2007). Regardless, the sexual exploitation discourse continues apace, constituting the hegemonic common sense that animates the state's legal and policy response to sex work.

This chapter critically examines official state responses to youth prostitution in Canada that are rooted in the language of sexual abuse and exploitation. The chapter argues that treating young women engaged in sex work as "always and already victims" (Phoenix, 2002a, p. 354) individualizes the youth prostitution phenomenon, that a familial ideology underpins efforts to confront youth prostitution as sexual exploitation, and that, despite official rhetoric to the contrary, the extant legal and policy nexus reaffirms the state's coercive control of young women under eighteen years of age engaged in sex work. These conditions are particularly damaging for Indigenous youth, whose experiences with the state's efforts to "help" and "protect" them are wrapped up in a history of colonialism (Hele, Sayers, and Wood, 2015; JJ, 2013). Whereas youth who accept their victim identity are provided with counselling and support, even if this "help" is not of their choosing, those who resist their victim status are labelled as problematic and detained "for their own protection" and/or risk criminalization through their marginalized status as street-involved youth (Busby, 2003; Phoenix, 2002a, 2002b). In essence, the state treats youth working in prostitution as victims "*except* when they are offenders" (Phoenix, 2002b, p. 69, emphasis in original), (re)confirming the historically rooted distinction "between good women and bad women" (Brock, 2000, p. 80).

To develop these arguments, the chapter interrogates youth prostitution's legal and policy regimes in the Canadian provinces of Alberta, British Columbia, and Manitoba. The youth prostitution–related measures in these jurisdictions are empirical exemplars of the political and cultural appetite of recent decades to tackle the sexual abuse and exploitation of young women through prostitution. The chapter addresses the state's response to women under the age of eighteen engaged in sex work, as they constitute the primary target of these initiatives (Busby, 2003). Young men and queer youth under eighteen involved in prostitution, whose experiences are marginalized by the sexual abuse discourse and who are subject to different forms of regulation and control, are therefore beyond the scope of this discussion (see also McIntyre, 2008; Visano, 1987). What is more, the following does not deny that many young women experience harms through their involvement in sex work; instead, in order to situate youth sex work within its broader socio-legal context, the goal is to transcend debates about harm and victimization, as well as those that fixate on whether a particular policy or program properly balances an individual youth's rights with the state's duty to protect. Although many young women involved in sex work do experience "some form of victimization and exploitation," this does not mean that they are "all victims waiting to be saved" (Phoenix, 2007, p. 91), nor should it negate the reality that, as sex workers themselves explain, "the need for money is perhaps the most significant factor informing the lives of young people who sell sex" (NSWP, 2016, p. 8).

For critical socio-legal feminist scholars, the state's laws and policies, including the measures examined in this chapter, are mutually constitutive of the gendered, racialized, and class conditions of the broader social formation; that is, law is both repressive and productive in that it controls and punishes certain individuals and groups while also reinforcing and (re)producing the very ideological and material conditions that give rise to young women's subordination (Chunn and Lacombe, 2000; Comack, 2006; Smart, 1995; Snider, 2006; van der Meulen and Durisin, 2008). From this perspective, as Chunn and Lacombe (2000) submit, law is a gendering practice that plays a significant role in constructing categories of woman and girls. Law is thus part of a hegemonic process in which various discourses coalesce within state institutions and practices and under historically contingent conditions to (re)create dominant social formations (Chunn and Lacombe, 2000; Comack, 2006). Never predetermined or absolute, these processes reflect ongoing ideological struggles about the nature of gender, race, and class relations in society. As Chunn and Lacombe (2000) suggest, "Far from being fixed and immutable, state, law and patriarchy are historically and culturally specific constructs embedded in particular social relations, and they assume new forms with different content over time" (p. 9). Law, including secure care and related child welfare schemes, is a site where meanings are contested and certain beliefs take root to animate law as legislation and as practice (Comack, 2006; Comack and Balfour, 2004).

What follows draws insight from this socio-legal feminist scholarship to demonstrate how current responses to youth sex work in Canada reinforce and reproduce gender, race, and class relations. It documents the dominant knowledge claims that animate official responses to youth prostitution, unearthing the "meanings and assumptions embedded in different forms of language use, ways of making sense of the world, and their corresponding practices" (Comack, 2006, p. 61). As we shall see, (re)conceptualizing youth in prostitution as always already victims of sexual abuse and exploitation inspires a range of repressive and ineffectual legal and policy innovations that reinforce a "constructed normality about gender stereotypes and gender power relations" (Bonnycastle, 2000, p. 61). Although young women are punished and controlled under the guise of protection, the conditions that give rise to youth prostitution continue unabated.

Historical Contradictions of Youth Prostitution Law and Policy

Official responses to youth prostitution in Canada historically oscillate between treating young prostitutes as fallen women who require punishment and treating them as victims in need of sympathy and protection (Brock, 2000). In many instances, however, we find a blurring between these seemingly contradictory positions, resulting in what Busby (2003) describes as a perpetual "slippage between criminal justice and social welfare responses" (p. 104). We also see that, in practice, it is young women in prostitution who face censure and control due to their actions, whereas the men who procure their sexual services are relatively unfettered to pursue, in prevailing heterosexual terms, their (supposedly biologically determined) sexual proclivities. Even under the limited circumstances where the actions of male customers are subject to moral approbation, such as with recent trends in defining the male customers of all sex workers as sexual predators, both the nature and the extent of the state's response pale in comparison to the regulation and control of women and girls (Busby, 2003; Martin, 2002). Whether they are conceived of as deviants or victims, women sex workers are "quintessentially gendered criminals," as Martin (2002) argues, "cast as immoral, sexually loose, irresponsible breeders of poverty and disorder and punished accordingly" (p. 363).

The contemporary rhetoric of the sex worker as victim has its roots in the knowledge claims of twentieth-century moral reformers, who significantly shaped early prostitution laws in arguing that prostitution was an affront to women's purity (Backhouse, 1985, 1991; Minaker, 2006). During this time, many young women, particularly those from immigrant and working-class backgrounds, found themselves serving lengthy sentences in women's reformatories under the pretense that it was necessary to save them from immorality, to eliminate vice, and to attain social purity (Brock, 2000). As we shall see, and as Minaker (2006) argues, these strategies to help "erring females" (p. 81) were harbingers of the protectionist discourses that animate state responses to youth prostitution today.[2]

Contemporary youth prostitution law and policy were developed in the 1980s within the context of growing concerns about sexual offences against children and youth. At the forefront of this transformation was the work of the Committee on Sexual Offences against Children and Youth (Badgley Committee, 1980–84), mandated by the federal government to conduct nationwide research and consultations concerning childhood sexual abuse.

The report of the Badgley Committee (1984) argued that addressing the harms that young prostitutes "bring upon themselves" required using the criminal law against them "so that social intervention can take place" (p. 1046). Sharply criticized for individualizing the causes of youth prostitution and misconstruing punishment as help (Busby, 2003; see also Brock, 1998; Lowman, 1987), the report's recommendation nevertheless set the tone for creating sexual offences that hinged on differentiating between adults and youth (Brock, 1998). As Lowman (2001) notes, the report represented a "decisive point in the Canadian literature because it helped introduce the idea that although the Canadian age of consent is 14 [which has since been raised to 16], prostitution involving 14 to 17 year-olds is a form of sexual abuse" (p. 2).

The sexual abuse and exploitation discourse gained further momentum in the years following the Badgley Committee's (1984) report, creating new "ways of objectifying and speaking the truth" (Burchell, 1996, p. 31) and fuelling various legal and policy reforms. In 1986, for instance, Ottawa enacted legislation criminalizing the purchase or attempted purchase of the sexual services of a young person under the age of eighteen (*Criminal Code*, 1985, s. 212(4)). It quickly became evident, however, that this law would fall into a state of virtual disuse (Hornick and Bolitho, 1992; Lowman and Fraser, 1996). According to Busby (2003), the perception among law enforcement was, and is, that "gathering evidence for these cases is very difficult and therefore charges against those who exploit minors are almost never laid" (p. 104). The alternative was to charge young sex workers under the communicating law (even if less frequently than in the past) or with offences such as drug crimes that are often associated with life on the streets. However, despite failing to produce a "crackdown" on male customers, the enactment of sexual procurement legislation signalled the growing belief that young women who engaged in sex work were victims of sexual abuse and exploitation. The recent criminalization of the purchase of sexual services only further cements this sentiment given that all sex workers are deemed to be victims and their customers to be sexual predators (see also Khan, this collection).

During the 1990s several municipal task forces and federal and provincial initiatives concluded that youth prostitution constituted child sexual abuse and should be dealt with accordingly (British Columbia Ministry of Attorney General, 1996; Forsyth Report, 1997; Manitoba Child and Youth Secretariat, 1996). Key among these developments was the Alberta Task Force on Children Involved in Prostitution (1996–97), charged with exploring programs for addressing youth prostitution. Its resulting Forsyth Report (1997) made its philosophical orientation clear in arguing that children involved in prostitution, "if not abused while at home, are certainly victims of sexual abuse when they are used by either a pimp or john" (p. 3). The report recommended a system of "collaborative case management," more procuring charges, a media campaign to raise public awareness about the issue, and most prominently, secure care legislation to provide "legislative support for a continuum of services for children involved in prostitution" (ibid., p. 3).

On February 1, 1999, in response to the Forsyth Report, the Province of Alberta became the first and still only Canadian jurisdiction to enact secure care legislation in order to address the sexual exploitation of children and youth in prostitution. The Protection of Children Involved in Prostitution Act, amended in 2007 as the Protection of Sexually Exploited Children Act to "reflect the true circumstances of these children's lives" (Government of Alberta, 2007, n.p.), empowers police and child welfare workers to detain children involved in, or at risk of becoming involved in, prostitution. A judge must approve the power to apprehend, although the police can do so without a court order if they believe the youth is in serious and imminent danger (Government of Alberta, 2010). Unless there is a "suitable" guardian, authorities will place the young person (most commonly a young woman) in a "protective safe house," where she is held for up to five days, "to ensure the safety of the child and to assess the child" (ibid., p. 6); more specifically, the state conducts "tests for drug and alcohol use, sexually transmitted diseases, HIV and pregnancy" (Busby, 2003, p. 105). The Act also permits the Children and Youth Services director to apply for two additional periods of detainment of up to twenty-one days each so that the youth can receive further treatment and counselling to break the "cycle of abuse" (Government of Alberta, 2010, p. 7).

Alberta's secure care legislation is the most visible and controversial response to the redefinition of youth prostitution as sexual abuse and exploitation. Other jurisdictions contemplated similar measures, including British Columbia, where the Secure Care Working Group advocated a "safe care" strategy, as well as Saskatchewan, Nova Scotia, and Ontario, but they have yet to enact secure care laws. Nevertheless, many jurisdictions still drew from the sexual abuse and exploitation discourse to form their own youth prostitution–related policies and programs. In British Columbia, for instance, the government has established community-action teams, comprising service providers, police, government officials, and community members, to help eliminate "the exploitation of children and youth through prostitution" (BC – MPSSG, 2011a, n.p.). It has also published a handbook for parents and teachers to identify risk factors for youth involvement in prostitution and has proclaimed a "stop the sexual exploitation of children and youth awareness week" (BC – MPSSG, 2011b, n.p.). Meanwhile, as part of its sexual exploitation strategy, the Manitoba government has amended the Child and Family Services Act to increase penalties to a maximum of a $50,000 fine and two years in prison for "causing a child to be in need of protection" (Government of Manitoba n.d.).[3] Special sexual exploitation investigators work with Street Reach programs set up throughout the province, which operate similarly to British Columbia's community-action teams, to strengthen the "safety net for youth who have been sexually exploited or are at high risk of being victimized" (Government of Manitoba, 2009, n.p.). The Manitoba government also participates in an annual "stop child sexual exploitation" awareness week.

Recent provincially based developments further demonstrate a deepening and extending of the sexual abuse discourse within the context of youth prostitution law and policy. Some jurisdictions now have laws to "rescue" and "protect" young women who are defined as victims of trafficking and sexual slavery (Barnett, 2011). In 2012, for instance, the Government of Manitoba enacted the Child Sexual Exploitation and Human Trafficking Act, which introduces restraining or protection orders against those who traffic and/or sexually exploit youth (i.e., pimps) and enables victims to sue their traffickers for damages (Manitoba Justice, n.d.). A private member's bill tabled in Ontario's legislature in 2016, dubbed the Saving the Girl Next Door Act, contains similar provisions (see also *CBC News*, 2016). Although the issue of trafficking remains highly controversial – some observations, for instance, point to the absence of reliable data on the nature and extent of trafficking (Bergman, 2012; Gosnell-Myers, 2012) – and beyond the scope of this chapter, it points to an ongoing transformation in official strategies to regulate and control youth in sex work. The current legal and policy landscape is unambiguous in its premise that youth engaged in sex work, regardless of circumstance, are victims of sexual abuse and exploitation who require protection (Busby, 2003; Martin, 2002). However, this approach fails to address the material and social conditions that give rise to youth prostitution, effectively reinforcing and reproducing status quo gender, race, and class inequities (Martin, 2002; Snider, 2006).

As noted earlier, the aftermath of the *Bedford* decision in 2013 marks the most recent shift in Canada's prostitution laws, albeit at the federal level, to a legal regime that obscures the punishment of sex workers under the guise of protecting them from sexual exploitation. As other chapters in this collection demonstrate, instead of respecting the Supreme Court's decision to remedy the troubling fact that Canada's prostitution laws forced many sex workers to meet clients in secluded and dangerous areas so as to avoid legal censure – a policy decision with deadly consequences for many women – the government instead prohibited public communicating for the purposes of prostitution when youth are nearby, in addition to implementing other anti-prostitution provisions. Regrettably, this decision means that sex workers, including youth, will continue to be at risk of violence from abusive men as they seek ways to conduct their business beyond criminal justice scrutiny. In addition, adult sex workers may now be reluctant to provide young women in sex work with advice, companionship, or support since the new law criminalizes the sale of sexual services within the vicinity of anyone under the age of eighteen. This decision places young women in sex work in dangerous situations, as they are left to work on their own. It would thus appear that, regardless of whether the state views sex workers as deviants or victims, the dominant belief prevails that prostitution is a female crime that requires some form of punishment and control.

Individualizing the Youth Prostitution "Problem"

As the predominant discourse that animates the state's legal and policy framework, the definition of youth prostitution as sexual abuse and exploitation abstracts the individual sex worker from her social circumstances, obscuring the broader social conditions that shape a young woman's decision to work in prostitution (Martin, 2002; Phoenix, 2002a, 2002b). Further, as this discourse was taken up by, and interpreted through, an increasingly neoliberal lens, the individual became responsible both for her decision to prostitute and for making the "prudent" choice (see Hannah-Moffat, 2001) to end her abuse. These expectations are acutely gendered in that (predominantly) male third parties are not held to the same account (Busby, 2003; Martin, 2002) and that the advent of neoliberalism compounds the feminization of poverty, drastically reducing social programs and employment opportunities for young street-involved women (Martin, 2002; see also Chunn and Gavigan, 2004; Mosher and Hermer, 2010).

In Western societies, law derives its legitimacy through claims of "fairness, stability and justice" (Woodiwiss, 2006, p. 525; see also Comack, 2006; Fudge and Cossman, 2002; Smart, 1989). Naffine (1990) argues that law asserts this status by abstracting individuals from their complex and varied social contexts to "examine the merits of their individual cases" (p. 52). Despite the reality that we are not all "equally located structurally" (Morrison, 1995, p. 213) and critical examinations of law that debunk its claims to neutrality (Chunn and Lacombe, 2000), this legal sleight of hand ensures that everyone is treated as "free, capable and competitive" (Comack, 2006, p. 22) subjects whose social circumstances are irrelevant to rendering legal judgments. Law therefore obscures and individualizes complex social matters, as Snider (2006) reminds us, rendering legal institutions and practices incapable of delivering "empowerment or amelioration" (p. 323) to the very populations that they claim to defend.

The current youth prostitution legal and policy environment in Canada abstracts the female sex worker from her social context by formalizing her status as a victim of sexual abuse and exploitation. Underpinning Alberta's secure care legislation, for example, is the principle that "sexually exploited children are victims of sexual abuse" who require "protection services and support" (Government of Alberta, 2010, p. 5). Similarly, the Manitoba government has amended its Child and Family Services Act to "deter predators and protect children in danger of being harboured and sexually exploited" (Government of Manitoba, n.d.), and the British Columbia government notes that the "sexual exploitation of children and youth is never considered prostitution or consensual" (BC – MPSSG, 2011a, n.p.; see also Manitoba Family Services and Consumer Affairs, 2011). These official positions underscore the notion that young women are sexually exploited and abused through their involvement in prostitution, regardless of their individual circumstances and varied histories.

Viewing youth in prostitution as "always and already victims" (Phoenix, 2002a, p. 367) obscures the conditions that make sex work a viable option for some young women. There is an extensive literature documenting how many young women in prostitution ran away from or were thrown out of emotionally, physically, and sexually abusive home environments – the abuse being committed primarily by male family members and acquaintances (Gosnell-Myers, 2012; Kidd and Liborio, 2011; O'Neill, 2001). This literature further demonstrates that following the decision to run away, the desire for autonomy and money pulled some young women to the streets and that the situational poverty of street-involved youth, along with a steady male demand for sexual services, made sex work a feasible survival option. These factors are particularly germane for understanding the overrepresentation of young Indigenous women in prostitution, whose experiences are also shaped significantly by a history of colonialism and exploitation by the state (Brock, 1998; Gosnell-Myers, 2012; Hele, Sayers, and Wood, 2015; JJ, 2013). Unfortunately, however, these complex factors are ignored, or pushed to the background, in favour of directing the legal and policy lens almost exclusively at the abuse that can occur in the context of exchanging sexual services for money (Phoenix, 2002a). As a result, there is a silencing of some young women's desire to exercise their autonomy and develop a life outside of an abusive home environment; dominant voices equate prostitution with sexual coercion and exploitation, not with a decision that young people make within a particular gendered, racialized, and class context (see also James, this collection; Love, this collection).

Phoenix (2002a) argues that framing youth prostitution as sexual abuse and exploitation conflates important sociological differences between the sexual abuse that young women experience in "intimate and/or familial relationships" (p. 367) and the commercial exchange of sexual services. In particular, Phoenix suggests that "the relationships and activities constituting the institution of prostitution have little meaning outside of the exchange of sex for money" (ibid.). Although she does not deny that young women may experience harm and abuse through their involvement in sex work, her point is that reducing prostitution to "another form of child abuse" glosses over the "economic, political and ideological" (ibid.) context – the very elements that make prostitution possible. Absent this recognition, abuse and exploitation in prostitution become something to confront and control, not an indication of larger structural problems that require transformation.

The abstraction of youth in prostitution from their social circumstances also emerges through the convergence of legal and sexual abuse discourses with neoliberal ideals that celebrate the accomplishments of the white, male captain of industry and that downplay the need for, and effectiveness of, state-sponsored social welfare programs (Fudge and Cossman, 2002). Growing concerns with declining corporate profit levels and economic recessions throughout the 1980s and early 1990s helped to propel the now well-documented "tectonic shift" in public policy toward privatization (ibid., p. 3). This transformation allowed influential neoliberal voices to caution against "government overreach and overload" and to question the state's responsibility for addressing social and economic ills (Rose and Miller, 1992, p. 198; see also Fudge and Cossman, 2002). The state responded by reshaping its regulatory responsibilities in pro-business and market-friendly ways, freeing up corporate capitalists to pursue avenues of unprecedented wealth – and, ironically, corporations to commit serious and devastating crimes (Snider, 2009). The state also disassembled its welfare regime, introducing crippling cutbacks to unemployment insurance and to provincial transfers for "welfare, social services, and post-secondary institutions" (Fudge and Cossman, 2002, pp. 15–16). And with the state largely out of the social welfare business, matters of poverty, homelessness, and unemployment became individual problems – problems that advanced the already-problematic state of the feminization of poverty (Comack and Balfour, 2004). The dominant neoliberal message was, and is, that overcoming poor social circumstances is a choice, one that individuals, along with their families and communities, must work to achieve (ibid.).

Neoliberal ideals are evident throughout various measures that attempt to address youth sex work as sexual abuse and exploitation. For instance, the British Columbia government's Secure Care Working Group (1998) argues that some *"out of control"* (p. 5, emphasis added) children and youth resist help and therefore place *"themselves* at a great risk of harm" (p. 16, emphasis added). Likewise, the Alberta government's Forsyth Report (1997) acknowledges the victim status of young prostitutes but also demands that they "take *responsibility* for their actions" (p. 11, emphasis added) and understand that there are consequences for their decisions, including whether to leave the streets. That Alberta's secure care legislation permits authorities to detain youth in prostitution so that they can receive treatment to "break the cycle of abuse" (Deis et al., 2000, n.p.; see also Government of Alberta, 2010) underscores the belief that the decision to engage in sex work – or to be sexually exploited – is an individual choice. Echoing Carlen's (2002) critique of neoliberal reforms of women's imprisonment is the view that "the problem is in their heads, not their social circumstances" (p. 235).

The development of various community-based initiatives, including sexual exploitation awareness weeks, community-action teams, and tool kits for parents and communities to identify youth at risk of sexual exploitation, also reflects dominant neoliberal ideals. More than benevolent attempts by the state to coordinate efforts against youth prostitution, these measures reflect the state backing away from its claim to be the sole provider of safety and security, recasting the issue as a normative problem to be addressed through community and state (correctional) partnerships (Garland, 2000). In situations where the state enlists Indigenous communities to address the sexual exploitation of young Indigenous women (BC – MPSSG, 2011a; Government of Manitoba, 2009), this reconfiguration of responsibilities obscures the complex socio-economic factors that give rise to Indigenous youth involvement in sex work, conditions that fade to the background in favour of strategies that focus on the exploitation that occurs within the context of prostitution (Hele, Sayers, and Wood, 2015). In this respect, as Garland (2000) notes, the neoliberal state acts "through civil society and not upon it" (p. 348).

Reinforcing Familial Ideology

Current youth prostitution law and policy also reinforce a dominant familial ideology, espousing the benefits of the "idealized white, Christian, heterosexual, bourgeois, patriarchically organized family" (Martin, 2002, p. 361). Regardless that many young women who are engaged in sex work describe their home environments as intolerable, a perception shaped by their experiences of sexual, physical, and emotional abuse in the family unit (Lowman, 1987), the patriarchal family remains a primary solution to the youth prostitution "problem"; young women must be returned to it or with proper intervention encouraged to stay. Underlying this commitment is a hegemonic belief that the nuclear family is the most obvious and normal place for women and men to fulfil their socially ascribed gender roles and responsibilities (Chunn and Lacombe, 2000). It also conforms to neoliberal knowledge claims that the family is a more appropriate vehicle for delivering the care and support that was once considered within the state's charge (Fudge and Cossman, 2002). Within this context, the youth's best interests are synonymous with maintaining the family unit (Boyd, 2000), whether it is the traditional family or a state substitute, such as foster care.

Examples of this familial ideology emerge through the development and implementation of different youth prostitution–related policies and programs. For instance, both the Forsyth Report and the Secure Care Working Group argued for empowering the family to protect young prostitutes and to remove them from the sex trade. As the Forsyth Report (1997) suggested, "Parents wishing to help and support their children to leave prostitution often feel powerless and at the mercy of social service agencies and police ... This is not helpful or supportive of families" (p. 29). Alberta's secure care framework therefore provides for the family's active involvement in a young person's care while she is in protective confinement (Government of Alberta, 2010). Families also play a central role in educational programs and in strategies to prevent the sexual exploitation of children and youth. "Education is a parent's best weapon against sexual exploitation; you can never know too much when protecting your children," notes Alberta Children and Youth Services (2011, n.p.). Similarly, the BC government funds educational programs and support services for parents of sexually exploited youth, which include helping parents to determine whether their children are on the verge of being coerced into a life of prostitution and removing them from sexually exploitative circumstances (BC – MPSSG, 2011a).

This situation should not deny that families are caring and supportive environments for many young people or that the state does not recognize through these initiatives that some children and youth experience abuse in the family. However, the ultimate goal of keeping young women in, or returning them to, the family unit overshadows the role of harmful familial relationships in shaping some young women's decision to engage in sex work. The centrality and supremacy of the nuclear family, along with the gender-based power imbalances that contribute to the harm of young women, are reinforced and reproduced, not challenged or transformed (Martin, 2002). It is the decision to leave the family that becomes problematic, not the organization of the patriarchal family itself.

Youth Still Criminalized and Controlled

The redefinition of youth prostitution as sexual abuse and exploitation also helps to reinforce a "disturbing hypocrisy" (Martin, 2002, p. 364) in that the state affords some young women sympathy and protection as victims of sexual abuse and exploitation, whereas it criminalizes and punishes those who reject their victim identity, refuse care, or continue their involvement in prostitution (Busby, 2003; Phoenix, 2002a, 2002b). As Phoenix (2002b) argues, equating youth prostitution with child sexual abuse "reconstructs the 'problem' of youth prostitution in a binary fashion: as child (sexual) abuse, except where voluntarism can be established in which case it is a crime problem" (p. 78). We therefore find a continued blurring of "criminal justice and social welfare responses" (Busby, 2003, p. 104), a historically rooted contradiction that ultimately holds the erring female to account for her engagement in sex work (Minaker, 2006).

Secure care punishes and controls young women in prostitution through their forced detainment and treatment, despite the questionable adequacy of this strategy for dealing with this phenomenon. After all, those who face detention in "protective confinement" to help them end their abuse are the young women in sex work, not the "predators" who procure their sexual services. There is no such thing as secure care treatment for male customers! In addition, many young prostitutes report negative experiences with child welfare services, citing their distrust and suspicion of "any helping agency" (Nixon et al., 2002, p. 1039). Ellis (2016), for instance, reports that many youth whom the state deems "troubled" or "troublesome," and therefore in need of some form of social welfare intervention, often perceive the state's helping efforts as punishment, not assistance. Focus group discussions confirm that young female prostitutes in Alberta identify secure care as an "ineffective and even counter-productive" (Busby et al., 2000, p. 13) form of punishment in which many detainees "simply sleep out their time before being released back to the street" (Busby, 2003, p. 120). Forcing young women into secure care therefore risks discouraging them from voluntarily seeking help from service agencies, and it drives youth sex work underground, where people are even more vulnerable to violence and exploitation.

Non-secure-care strategies also increase the governance and control of young female prostitutes. For instance, in British Columbia and Manitoba, community-action teams share information and work with communities to identify youth at risk of sexual exploitation and to safeguard those perceived as trapped in the sex trade. Although these coordinating efforts appear laudable, we cannot overlook that the comprising agencies (i.e., police, social welfare officials, and service providers) typically structure their work around "traditional child protection methods" (Phoenix, 2007, p. 85). This means that there will be instances when the police will doff their "helping hat" to detain young women who persistently prostitute or who commit a street crime (for a discussion of this in the US context, see Mehlman-Orozco, 2015). In addition, these coordinating strategies are limited to providing help in the form of counselling and educating youth about the dangers of sexual exploitation and are not equipped to address the material and social conditions that shape some young women's decision to work in prostitution.

Finally, we need to situate the control of many youth sex workers within their street-involved realities. In recent decades, as the state was busy befriending business, it was simultaneously sharpening its teeth when it came to dealing with traditional street crimes (Garland, 2001; Wacquant, 2009). Despite official rhetoric citing the demise of the overly burdensome and bureaucratic state, those who do not measure up to dominant neoliberal ideals have come under greater surveillance and control (Comack and Balfour, 2004). These individuals include young women working in prostitution who risk being charged with prostitution-related offences (particularly if they resist their victim identity through persistent involvement in sex work), as well as with crimes associated with life on the street, such as theft and drug use (Busby, 2003; Mehlman-Orozco, 2015). It would thus appear that, as a result of dominant neoliberal thinking, there is improved (economic) freedom for the privileged few but greater state control of marginalized and disadvantaged young women.

Conclusion

This chapter demonstrates the problems associated with (re)conceptualizing young women in prostitution as victims of sexual abuse and exploitation. As the dominant knowledge claim that animates the state's legal and policy response, it abstracts young females in sex work from their complex social histories, particularly young Indigenous women, individualizing the decision to prostitute and overshadowing the gender, race, and class inequalities that make prostitution both plausible and possible (Phoenix, 2002a). It also reinforces and reproduces a familial ideology wherein the ultimate goal is to return young women to, or keep them in, the patriarchal family unit, despite its inherent gender power imbalances (Martin, 2002). There is no room for agency here and no acknowledgment that the decision to engage in sex work is made in conditions that are not of a young person's choosing (Phoenix, 2007). The young female sex worker is either a victim of sexual abuse and exploitation who requires help and protection, essentially a euphemism for incarceration, or an erring female who needs to be punished and controlled (Phoenix, 2002a, 2002b). Recent developments in prostitution-related law and policy, including different anti-trafficking measures and the federal government's criminalization of the purchase of sexual services, only cement the victim discourse and the concomitant contradictions that effectively punish sex workers under the cloak of protection. It would thus appear that the duality of the good girl versus the bad girl is firmly entrenched (Minaker, 2006), ensuring that young people in sex work continue to face the burden for the regulation and control of youth prostitution.

These observations are not meant suggest that the state, and through it law and policy, automatically or necessarily contributes to the ongoing marginalization of young sex workers. The factors underlying the desire to help are too complex for such a simple formula. What is more, there are signs of resistance to the sexual abuse and exploitation discourse (JJ, 2013), underscoring that this language is constitutive of larger ideological struggles that are never complete and always subject to change (Chunn and Lacombe, 2000). In addition to the fact that Alberta remains the only Canadian jurisdiction to have enacted secure care legislation, there have been attempts, albeit unsuccessful, to challenge its constitutionality (see *Alberta (Director of Child Welfare) v. K.B.*, 2000), and service providers question the wisdom of locking up young women in the name of protection (Busby, 2003). However, despite these dissenting voices, the victim-oriented approach to youth in sex work continues to shape the legal and policy landscape, effectively reinforcing and reproducing the "material and ideological conditions" (Smart, 1995, p. 144) within which youth prostitution flourishes. The challenge therefore becomes finding ways to transcend the hegemonic status quo in order to situate youth prostitution within its broader social, economic, gendered, and historical context.

In the end, characterizing young women in prostitution as victims of sexual abuse and exploitation might make for good politics, providing a convenient and easy target so that governments can *seem* to be doing something about youth prostitution, but it fails to deal with root causes. Quite simply, young women are incarcerated for their own "protection," whereas the conditions that give rise to youth involvement in prostitution remain untouched. Instead of casting the regulatory lens down the social hierarchy at young, marginalized women, the state should redirect its efforts toward the "underlying structural constraints (race, class and gender inequalities)" (Minaker, 2006, p. 93). Developing intervention strategies around these matters stands a far better chance of ameliorating the lives of young women working in prostitution than efforts that purport to do so under the guise of protection.

Acknowledgment

Thank you to Samantha McAleese for her research assistance and Jennifer Kilty for her helpful comments on an earlier version of this chapter. The usual disclaimers apply.

Notes

This chapter is a revised and updated version of my previous work in this area (see Bittle, 2013).

1 Throughout the chapter, I use terms such as "youth engaged in sex work" and "youth involved in prostitution," unless referring specifically to programs and initiatives that employ the language of "sexually exploited" or "sexually abused" youth.

2 See van der Meulen and Durisin, this collection, for a discussion of how the history of prostitution law in Canada, including the Protection of Communities and Exploited Persons Act (PCEPA) of 2014, reveals that sex workers of all ages were (and are) subject to discriminatory legislation and unequal law enforcement.

3 The Manitoba government launched its sexual exploitation strategy, dubbed Tracia's Trust, in response to the suicide death of Tracia Owen, a fourteen-year-old Indigenous youth with an extensive history of abuse and neglect, contact with child welfare officials, drug use, and involvement in prostitution. A coroner's inquest recommended changes to the province's child welfare provisions and services in order to combat drug use and sexual exploitation of young people on the streets (Guy, 2008).

References

Alberta Children and Youth Services. (2011). *Child sexual exploitation*. Edmonton, AB: Government of Alberta. Retrieved from http://humanservices.alberta.ca/

Backhouse, C. (1985). Nineteenth-century Canadian prostitution law: Reflection of a discriminatory society. *Social History/Histoire sociale, 18*(36), 387–423.

Backhouse, C. (1991). *Petticoats and prejudice: Women and law in nineteenth century Canada*. Toronto, ON: Osgoode Society.

Badgley Committee (Committee on Sexual Offences against Children and Youth). (1984). *Sexual offences against children*. Ottawa, ON: Department of Supply and Services.

Barnett, L. (2011). *Prostitution in Canada: International obligations, federal law, and provincial and municipal jurisdiction*. Ottawa, ON: Legal and Social Affairs Division, Parliamentary Information and Research Service. Retrieved from https://lop.parl.ca/Content/LOP/ResearchPublications/2011-119-e.htm

BC – MPSSG (British Columbia Ministry of Public Safety and Solicitor General) (2011a). *Preventing sexual exploitation of children and youth*. Retrieved from https://www2.gov.bc.ca/assets/gov/public-safety-and-emergency-services/crime-prevention/community-crime-prevention/publications/crime-prev-series2-sexual-exploitation-children-youth.pdf

BC – MPSSG (British Columbia Ministry of Public Safety and Solicitor General) (2011b). *Stopping the sexual exploitation of children and youth*. Retrieved from http://pssg.gov.bc.ca/404redirect.html

Bergman, A.L. (2012). For their own good? Exploring legislative responses to the commercial sexual exploitation of children and the Illinois Safe Children Act. *Vanderbilt Law Review, 65*(5), 1361–400.

Bittle, S. (2013). Still punishing to 'protect': Youth prostitution law and policy reform. In E. van der Meulen, E.M. Durisin, & V. Love (Eds.), *Selling sex: Experience, advocacy, and research on sex work in Canada* (pp. 279–96). Vancouver, BC: UBC Press.

Bonnycastle, K. (2000). Rape uncodified: Reconsidering Bill C-49 amendments to Canadian sexual assault laws. In D.E. Chunn & D. Lacombe (Eds.), *Law as a gendering practice* (pp. 60–78). Toronto, ON: Oxford University Press.

Boyd, S. (2000). Custody, access, and relocation in a mobile society: (En)gendering the best interests principle. In D.E. Chunn & D. Lacombe (Eds.), *Law as a gendering practice* (pp. 158–80). Toronto, ON: Oxford University Press.

British Columbia Ministry of Attorney General. (1996). *Community consultation on prostitution in British Columbia: Overview of results.* Victoria, BC: Ministry of Attorney General.

Brock, D.R. (1998). *Making work, making trouble: Prostitution as a social problem.* Toronto, ON: University of Toronto Press. https://doi.org/10.3138/97814426 76930

Brock, D.R. (2000). Victim, nuisance, fallen women, outlaw, worker? Making the identity 'prostitute' in Canadian criminal law. In D.E. Chunn & D. Lacombe (Eds.), *Law as a gendering practice* (pp. 79–99). Toronto, ON: Oxford University Press.

Burchell, G. (1996). Liberal government and techniques of the self. In A. Barry, T. Osborne, & N. Rose (Eds.), *Foucault and political reason: Liberalism, neoliberalism and rationalities of government* (pp. 19–36). Chicago, IL: University of Chicago Press.

Busby, K. (2003). The protective confinement of girls involved in prostitution. In K. Gorkoff & J. Runner (Eds.), *Being heard: The experience of young women in prostitution* (pp. 103–25). Halifax, NS: Fernwood.

Busby, K., Downe, P., Gorkoff, K., Nixon, K., Tutty, L., & Ursel, E.J. (2000). *Examination of innovative programming for children and youth involved in prostitution.* Retrieved from http://www.sfu.ca/campuses/vancouver.html

Carlen, P. (2002). New discourses of justification and reform for women's imprisonment in England. In P. Carlen (Ed.), *Women and punishment: The struggle for justice* (pp. 220–36). Portland, OR: Willan.

CBC News. (2016, June 20). Saving the girl next door: Proposed law aims to stop human trafficking hubs. Retrieved from http://www.cbc.ca/news/canada/sudbury/sudbury-hub-trafficking-1.3643556

Chunn, D.E., & Gavigan, S. (2004). Welfare law, welfare fraud, and the moral regulation of the 'never deserving poor.' *Social and Legal Studies, 13*(2), 219–43. https://doi.org/10.1177/0964663904042552

Chunn, D.E., & Lacombe, D. (2000). Introduction. In D.E. Chunn & D. Lacombe (Eds.), *Law as a gendering practice* (pp. 2–18). Toronto, ON: Oxford University Press.

Comack, E. (Ed.). (2006). *Locating law: Race/class/gender connections.* (2nd ed.). Halifax, NS: Fernwood.

Comack, E., & Balfour, G. (2004). *The power to criminalize: Violence, inequality and the law.* Halifax, NS: Fernwood.

Deis, M., Rokosh, K., Sagert, S., Robertson, B., & Kerr-Fitzsimmons, I. (2000). *A historical act – Bill 1: Protection of children involved in prostitution.* Edmonton, AB: Government of Alberta.

Ellis, K.H. (2016). 'He's got some nasty impression of me he has': Listening to children in the secure estate. *British Journal of Social Work, 46*(6), 1553–67. https://doi.org/10.1093/bjsw/bcv114

Forsyth Report (Alberta Task Force on Children Involved in Prostitution). (1997). *Children involved in prostitution.* Edmonton, AB: Ministry of Family and Social Services.

Fudge, J., & Cossman, B. (2002). Introduction. In B. Cossman & J. Fudge (Eds.), *Privatization, law and the challenge to feminism* (pp. 3–37). Toronto, ON: University of Toronto Press.

Garland, D. (2000). The culture of high crime societies: Some preconditions of recent 'law and order' policies. *British Journal of Criminology, 40*(3), 347–75. https://doi.org/10.1093/bjc/40.3.347

Garland, D. (2001). *The culture of control: Crime and social order in contemporary society.* Chicago, IL: University of Chicago Press.

Gosnell-Myers, G. (2012). *Far from home: Experiences of sexually exploited Aboriginal youth in Vancouver, B.C.* Prepared for the Office of the Federal Interlocutor for Métis and Non-Status Indians. Retrieved from http://www.firstpeoplesgroup.com/mnsiurban/PDF/women_children_youth_families/Gosnell-Myers_G-Far_From_Home_SEY_(2012).pdf

Government of Alberta. (2007). *New law better protects sexually exploited children.* (News release). Alberta Children's Services.

Government of Alberta. (2010). *Protection of sexually exploited children and youth.* Retrieved from https://open.alberta.ca/publications/6045967

Government of Manitoba. (n.d.). *Responding to sexual exploitation: Tracia's Trust legislation and law enforcement.* Retrived from https://www.gov.mb.ca/fs/traciastrust/legislation.html

Government of Manitoba. (2009, May 11). First 'Stop Child Sexual Exploitation Awareness Week' proclaimed in Manitoba. (News release). Retrieved from http://www.gov.mb.ca/

Guy, J. (2008, January 11). *The Fatality Inquiries Act in the matter of Tracia Owens.* (Report on Inquest of the Honourable Judge John Guy, Provincial Court of Manitoba). Retrieved from http://www.manitobacourts.mb.ca/

Hannah-Moffat, K. (2001). *Punishment in disguise: Penal governance and federal imprisonment of women in Canada.* Toronto, ON: University of Toronto Press. https://doi.org/10.3138/9781442678903

Hele, C., Sayers, N., & Wood, J. (2015, September 14). What's missing from the conversation on missing and murdered Indigenous women and girls. *The Toast.* Retrieved from http://the-toast.net/2015/09/14/whats-missing-from-the-conversation-on-missing-and-murdered-indigenous-women/

Hornick, J.P., & Bolitho, F. (1992). *A review of the implementation of the child sexual abuse legislation in selected sites: Studies on the sexual abuse of children in Canada.* Ottawa, ON: Ministry of Supply and Services.

JJ. (2013). We speak for ourselves: Anti-colonial and self-determined responses to young people involved in the sex trade. In E. van der Meulen, E.M. Durisin, & V. Love (Eds.), *Selling sex: Experience, advocacy, and research on sex work in Canada* (pp. 74–81). Vancouver, BC: UBC Press.

Kidd, S.A., & Liborio, R.M.C. (2011). Sex trade involvement in São Paulo, Brazil and Toronto, Canada: Narratives of social exclusion and fragmented identities.

Youth and Society, 43(3), 982–1009. https://doi.org/10.1177/0044118X103 79127

Lowman, J. (1987). Taking young prostitutes seriously. *Canadian Review of Sociology and Anthropology, 24*(1), 99–116. https://doi.org/10.1111/j.1755-618X.1987. tb01073.x

Lowman, J. (2001). *Identifying research gaps in the prostitution literature.* Ottawa, ON: Research and Statistics Division, Department of Justice Canada.

Lowman, J., & Fraser, L. (1996). *Violence against persons who prostitute: The experience in British Columbia.* Ottawa, ON: Department of Justice Canada.

Manitoba Child and Youth Secretariat. (1996). *Report of the Working Group on Juvenile Prostitution.* Winnipeg, MB: Manitoba Child and Youth Secretariat.

Manitoba Family Services and Consumer Affairs. (2011). *Responding to sexual exploitation: Tracia's Trust.* Retrieved from http://www.gov.mb.ca/

Manitoba Justice. (n.d.). *The Child Sexual Exploitation and Human Trafficking Act.* Retrieved from https://www.gov.mb.ca/justice/csehtact.html

Martin, D. (2002). Both pitied and scorned: Child prostitution in an era of privatization. In B. Cossman & J. Fudge (Eds.), *Privatization, law and the challenge to feminism* (pp. 355–402). Toronto, ON: University of Toronto Press. https://doi. org/10.3138/9781442678774-011

McIntyre, S. (2008). *Under the radar: The sexual exploitation of young men – Western Canadian edition.* Calgary, AB: Hindsight Group. Retrieved from http:// www.hindsightgroup.com/Resources/Documents/UnderTheRadar%20Low%20 Res.pdf

Mehlman-Orozco, K. (2015). Safe harbor policies for juvenile victims of sex trafficking: A myopic view of improvements in practice. *Social Inclusion, 3*(1), 52–62. https://doi.org/10.17645/si.v3i1.56

Minaker, J. (2006). Sluts and slags: The censuring of the erring female. In G. Balfour & E. Comack (Eds.), *Criminalizing women: Gender and (in)justice in neo-liberal times* (1st ed., pp. 79–94). Halifax, NS: Fernwood.

Morrison, W. (1995). *Theoretical criminology: From modernity to post-modernity.* London, UK: Cavendish.

Mosher, J., & Hermer, J. (2010). Welfare fraud: The constitution of social assistance as crime. In J. Mosher & J. Brockman (Eds.), *Constructing crime: Contemporary processes of criminalization* (pp. 17–52). Vancouver, BC: UBC Press.

Naffine, N. (1990). *The law and the sexes: Exploration in feminist jurisprudence.* Sydney, Australia: Allen and Unwin.

Nixon, K., Tutty, L., Downe, P., Gorkoff, K., & Ursel, J. (2002). The everyday occurrence: Violence in the lives of girls exploited through prostitution. *Violence Against Women, 8*(9), 1016–43. https://doi.org/10.1177/107780120200800902

NSWP (Global Network of Sex Work Projects). (2016). *Policy brief: Young sex workers.* Retrieved from http://www.nswp.org/resource/policy-brief-young-sex -workers

O'Neill, M. (2001). *Prostitution and feminism: Towards a politics of feeling.* Cambridge, UK: Polity.

Phoenix, J. (2002a). In the name of protection: Youth prostitution policy reform in England and Wales. *Critical Social Policy, 22*(2), 353–75. https://doi.org/10.1177/02610183020220020901

Phoenix, J. (2002b). Youth prostitution policy reform: New discourse, same old story. In P. Carlen (Ed.), *Women and punishment: The struggle for justice* (pp. 67–93). Portland, OR: Willan.

Phoenix, J. (2007). Governing prostitution: New formations, old agendas. *Canadian Journal of Law and Society, 22*(2), 73–94. https://doi.org/10.1017/S0829320100009364

Rose, N., & Miller, P. (1992). Political power beyond the state: Problematics of government. *British Journal of Sociology, 43*(2), 173–205. https://doi.org/10.2307/591464

Secure Care Working Group. (1998). *Report of the Secure Care Working Group.* Commissioned by the Minister of Children and Families. Victoria, BC: Province of British Columbia.

Smart, C. (1989). *Feminism and the power of the law: Essays in feminism.* London, UK: Routledge. https://doi.org/10.4324/9780203206164

Smart, C. (1995). *Law, crime and sexuality.* London, UK: Sage.

Snider, L. (2006). Making change in neo-liberal times. In G. Balfour & E. Comack (Eds.), *Criminalizing women: Gender and (in)justice in neo-liberal times* (1st ed., pp. 323–42). Halifax, NS: Fernwood.

Snider, L. (2009). Accommodating power: The common sense of regulators. *Social and Legal Studies, 18*(2), 179–97. https://doi.org/10.1177/0964663909103634

van der Meulen, E., & Durisin, E.M. (2008). Why decriminalize? How Canada's municipal and federal regulations increase sex workers' vulnerability. *Canadian Journal of Women and the Law, 20*(2), 289–311.

van der Meulen, E., Durisin, E.M., & Love, V. (Eds.). (2013). *Selling sex: Experience, advocacy, and research on sex work in Canada.* Vancouver, BC: UBC Press.

Visano, L. (1987). *This idle trade: The occupational patterns of male prostitution.* Concord, ON: VistaSana Books.

Wacquant, L. (2009). *Punishing the poor: The neoliberal government of social insecurity.* Durham, NC: Duke University Press. https://doi.org/10.1215/9780822392255

Woodiwiss, A. (2006). International law. *Theory, Culture and Society, 23*(2–3), 524–25. https://doi.org/10.1177/026327640602300296

Cases

Alberta (Director of Child Welfare) v. K.B. (2000), 279 AR 328, [2000] AJ No. 1570 (QB) (QL) [KB (QB)].

Bedford v. Canada (Attorney General), [2010] OJ No. 4057 (Ont. Sup. Ct.).

Canada (Attorney General) v. Bedford, 2013 SCC 72, [2013] 3 SCR 1101.

Legislation

Bill 158, *Saving the Girl Next Door Act*, 2016. Legislative Assembly of Ontario.
Bill C-36, *Protection of Communities and Exploited Persons Act*, SC 2014, c. 25.
Child and Family Services Act, CCSM, c. C80.
Criminal Code, RSC 1985, c. C-46.
Protection of Children Involved in Prostitution Act, SA 1999, c. P-19.3.
Protection of Sexually Exploited Children Act, RAA 2000, c. P-30.3.

PART 2

DIVERSE EXPERIENCES

Examining Places, Spaces, and Types of Work

11

Indigenous, Indoors, and Incognito
Thoughts and Experiences of an Irish and Ojibwe Female Sex Worker

ELIZABETH JAMES

I am a status, card-carrying "Indian" with an Anishinaabe-Ojibwe mother and a white, Irish father. I share many elements in common with the life stories of Indigenous women in Canada, including poverty, generational trauma, and the living legacy of the residential school system. I also grew up off-reserve in a mid-sized city in eastern Ontario and am able to "pass" as a white woman. My experience in the sex industry has always been indoors and has included selling sex as a youth and an adult, webcam stripping, self-employed erotic massage, and girlfriend-style escort companionship. Given my family history and sex industry experiences, I exist at the crossroads of a stigmatized and marginalized yet privileged reality. In this chapter, I attempt to challenge dominant perspectives about people who sell sex, particularly Indigenous women. The salience of intersecting identities comes into sharp relief in the ways that poverty, abuse, colonization, and privilege resonate in my experiences and those of my sex-working family. I hope to show that although my life choices may differ from yours, at the end of the day, just like any other worker trying to make a living, I have experiences and multiple, layered identities that decry society's "othering" and one-dimensional stereotypes.

Childhood and Experiences of Generational Trauma

Although I grew up in a medium-sized city close to a major urban centre and am able to pass as white, I was not spared many of the negative experiences that are all too common to Indigenous childhoods: poverty, abuse, addiction, and a general lack of stability (see Campbell, 1973). When I think of my early years, I remember much pain and confusion. My family was, and still is, very dysfunctional. Around the age of seven, my parents separated, and my siblings and I lived under my mother's roof. Things were difficult for her; she missed my father and was very lonely. I can understand now why she wanted to escape the challenges and monotony of being a single mother; she did not come home until very late most nights and awoke after we left for school. My brother and I, the youngest of the five children, were mostly on our own.

There is a history of severe alcohol and drug addiction on both the Irish and Ojibwe sides of my family, a result of the cyclical generational pain of colonial domination, other exclusions, and brokenness. Episodes of my mother's instability occurred throughout my childhood. That instability I now understand, too. She was born on a western Ontario reserve into a family where there was conflict, addiction, and violence. Her experiences of residential school abuse, racism, familial separation, and sexual violence meant that she never completed high school and was not given the tools necessary to be successful in this society. Her inadequate preparation for life and experiences of trauma severely impacted her and, later, her children. At the age of ten, I watched helplessly as she forced me to be her audience as she systematically tried to drink herself to death in retaliation to my father leaving her. She somersaulted down our back porch; fearing for her life, neighbours called for help. I remember feeling ashamed about being barefoot at the hospital after she and I were rushed there in the ambulance.

I understand my mother more clearly now, having learned about colonization and her experiences of systemic racism. It is difficult not to repeat cycles of abuse, even if you know how wrong they are and how awful they feel. My brother, who raised me in my mother's absence, was excessively violent. Being at school and away from the dysfunction of home felt like being on a vacation, but being improperly dressed, unkempt, and constantly hungry simultaneously provoked shame. I escaped this abuse and neglect by voraciously reading any book I could get my hands on – library books, Harlequin romances, or other erotic novels discarded by my mother. I learned more from reading than many children learn from attentive and educated families. All the erotica may not have been the best choice for a prepubescent girl, but I was at the top of my class – at least until high school, when puberty hit.

Early Encounters with Sex Work

My older sister was a street-based sex worker during most of my childhood. Perhaps she was influenced in some way by my mother, who expected the men she picked up at the bars for one-night stands to leave her with money.[1] I remember being quite young when I heard my sister and her friend talk about working the streets, calling where they worked "the track." They referred to themselves as "streetwalkers," sometimes they had what they called "pimps" as boyfriends, and they showered us with presents bought with money they had earned. Their generosity, economic success, and open-mindedness influenced me and contributed to my acceptance of sex work as a conceivable, albeit unusual and stigmatized, profession. Their work in prostitution fascinated me at the time. I knew that they were not being "good" girls, but I was also impressed by their lifestyles. It made sense to me, a sentiment that was reinforced by the positive links made between sexuality, sex appeal, and consumerism in books, in movies, and on television.

I was the youngest of my immediate family, with a relentless curiosity about the world, and forbidden images of sex captured my imagination. Immersed in a sexually repressed yet sexually obsessed society, influenced by the sexual norms of my family and friends, and with the only affordable options for entertainment being reading, television, and socializing, I developed a keen interest in sex at a relatively early age. Poverty, neglect, and abuse may have influenced my choice to lose my virginity at the age of twelve, but when I consider that choice and my adolescent sexual explorations, the driving factor was a natural curiosity. Sex can be fascinating, fun, and rewarding in so many ways.

Although I would have had sex when I was twelve regardless, it just so happened that my "first" also ended up being my first client – my initiation into sex was also my initiation into selling sex. I often babysat for my sister or one of her sex-working friends at night when they "hit the track." On several occasions, my sister disappeared for days or weeks at a time, going to Montreal or Toronto to party and work. It became such a regular occurrence that we stopped worrying. Once, when I was staying at her place for a couple of weeks, a guy called and left several messages for my sister. Eventually, he suggested that I spend time with him. I was feeling really isolated and bored, and I was intrigued by his invitation. My uncle was living at the house and helping me with the kids, so after everyone was asleep, I went to meet the guy at his place. He was a seventeen-year-old university student. He was respectful, attractive, and never pushy. Overall, it was a good experience. Of course, it would have been better if I had had sex before – that first time was a bit painful. I saw him several times, knowing what I was getting myself into. My pathway to sex work was complex, but I made many decisions in the process. I was certainly young by most standards, but even looking back, I recognize that I possessed a wisdom and maturity beyond my years.

Class Aspirations, Erotic Explorations, and Revisiting Sex Work

Shortly afterward, when I was thirteen, I moved with my mother and brother to a town close to the reservation where my mother was born so that we could spend time with my grandmother, who was dying. My darker-skinned brother fell in with a "gangster-styled" clique of Natives, smoking weed, drinking, and engaging in crime – things he had been involved with in our hometown as well. In contrast, I aspired to middle-class goals and values. I wanted to fit in with the preppy, mostly white students, who had rich parents and nice clothes and spent time at the lake, went camping, attended proms, and had house parties. I struggled to fit in, but I was also an attractive, white-passing female. I found my first real job at fifteen and used my earnings to fund my goals of fitting in. Eventually, however, a small town with a gang-involved brother was not where I felt I belonged.

At sixteen, I moved back to the city where I grew up. Staying with my sister and her boyfriend for five months, I struggled financially. I was propositioned yet again by one of my sister's clients while at the store where he worked. We met at a low-end motel, and I remember feeling deeply ashamed that I went ahead with it. I felt even more ashamed about my living situation. My sister lived in an apartment complex known locally as the "ghetto," and I wanted to escape. Having found work at a coffee shop, I moved into a house with roommates in a nice neighbourhood, returned to high school, and was soon dating a popular, middle-class senior. I never shared with him or anyone else that I had sold sex. For three years, I felt that I was able to fit into my boyfriend's middle-class lifestyle. I worked several jobs, and I struggled, spending all my money on clothes, socializing, and "keeping up with the Joneses."

My life seemed to be going great until my relationship ended and I realized how alone I was. His friends, who were also my friends when we were a couple, remained his friends after we broke up. I felt like I was starting over with nothing. I began to focus on the educational goals that had previously been my priority; I took out a loan for basic computer courses, with plans to begin university as soon as I could. With my new skills, I got a job working in sales for a company that did high-end kitchen renovations, and I started school the following year. Working around thirty hours a week and with no familial support, I struggled in university, especially when my changing career aspirations led me to pursue a bachelor of science. I was unable to invest enough time in studying and was constantly exhausted.

During this time, I left my high-paying sales job for a career-oriented but low-paying and entry-level job in healthcare. My living expenses increased when my ex-boyfriend moved out, yet my employment income had dropped. Stressed, I decided to embrace my inner wild-child. While exploring Craigslist's "Casual Encounters" online personal ads, I was intrigued by a posting from a gentleman who was looking to attend a swingers club on a night for couples and single ladies. My interest piqued, I courageously went alone. I began attending the club regularly. There, I met a woman named Jay who did erotic massage (i.e., a sensual, nude massage with a "happy ending" manual release). I thought of her immediately after a moment of frustration at the grocery store near my work. Still dressed in my healthcare scrubs, I felt defeated when I saw the "Insufficient Funds" message on the debit terminal's screen. An unexpected tuition payment had been drawn from my account. I left the store that busy Saturday afternoon embarrassed – and with no groceries.

Considering my finances, my struggles to balance work and school, and my clear desire for sexual adventure, I decided to try erotic massage. After a handful of clients, I quit my straight job; I loved massage. For me, the sharing of affection, intimacy, and attention was invigorating. Earning twenty times my hourly wage afforded me more time to spend on my studies, although I was initially distracted from school by the newfound wealth and sense of empowerment. It was the best job I have ever had. I remember feeling excited about the opportunities that I could now enjoy, like living without roommates, travelling, shopping, eating at restaurants, and going out for entertainment, and I remember the secure feeling of not living paycheque to paycheque.

I began by sharing Jay's "studio," a room in a two-bedroom apartment set up with a massage table, towels, a large wall mirror, and candles everywhere. I paid one-third of what I made from each client as a fee for my use of the space (see also Gillies and Bruckert, this collection). I created a simple website with my photos, rates, and services, and I began advertising on escort review boards, Craigslist, and several other sex industry sites (see also Sterling, this collection). I remember excitedly answering emails from potential clients at school, enjoying the financial freedom and sexual intrigue I had discovered. After some emailing back and forth, we would set up a session, usually for an hour. Jay wisely advised me to always provide a professional and fair service, never end the session early, and draw out the sexual "happy ending" part(s) as long as possible. After lathering up together in the shower, I would give a full-body therapeutic (yet sensual) massage, hopping up on the table midway through to perform a body-slide, rubbing my chest all over clients' backs and buttocks. I would encourage them to watch the sensual show in the mirror. After I had turned them over to a face-up position, with more body-sliding and sexual touching, the session culminated in a slowly rising sexual experience achieved through a good sense of balance, oiled up breasts, and slippery hands exploring their erogenous zones.

I worked independently and could determine my own boundaries and services. I decided for the most part to follow Jay's lead and offer manual stimulation only, although I broke these self-imposed rules when I felt like it. I had oral and vaginal sex with certain clients, but because I did not ask for extra money, I did not consider myself a prostitute. I joked that I was simply taking my "pick of the litter." After a few months, I began to work from my own home. I turned my former roommate's room into a studio, and once school was finished for the year, I offered massage on a full-time basis.

Shifting Conceptions of Stigma and Living Life Incognito

A couple of years after beginning my massage career, I started offering select clients "full service," or the "girlfriend experience" (i.e., kissing, cuddling, oral sex, and vaginal sex). I was worried about being out publicly, but as time passed, I began offering these services openly in my advertisements. I am learning to get past my internalized whore stigma and to just do what I want, but reconciling my shame about sex, my job, and society's judgments is something I continue to struggle with. However, I enjoy my work, the clients I see, and the benefits that this kind of work offers, including having the time (and money) for reading, studies, and travel.

Many people may not appreciate that I see most of my clients as professional friendships. Some I have been seeing since I started massage nearly ten years ago, and we have come to know one another over the years (see also Love, this collection). We check in with each other about how life is going and know personal details about each other, yet we maintain a professional distance that informs the boundaries of our relationship in a respectful and caring manner. Having been employed in the healthcare industry, I see striking similarities between the emotional labour (Hochschild, 2003) required there and in the sex industry. My work with my clients involves a physical/sexual aspect as well as an affectionate, playful, and intellectual intimacy. Being naked with one another and expressing our sexuality leaves us in a vulnerable position, yet the level of care I offer to clients ensures that our time together becomes a safe space where we are able to relax, share our thoughts, and really connect with one another, something that I feel is missing from too many people's lives.

Being an indoor sex worker privileges me relative to street-based sex workers in a lot of ways. I am less worried about law enforcement, and I am able to interact with my clients in a relaxed, safe, and comfortable environment. I do not have to worry about being considered a public "nuisance." Although I work in a secure environment, I fear many things and necessarily live a life of duality. I currently work out of a condo that I share with another sex worker. Neither of us lives there, and if our landlord were to drop in unexpectedly, we would have some explaining to do. The bedroom is set up like a massage parlour, outfitted with a massage table, a bed, and large wall mirrors, and there are only linens, lingerie, and toiletries in the closets. This type of setup is one of many I have had over the years, and in many ways it is ideal – a safe space with a colleague and security. I am certainly relatively privileged, but I also worry that I will be reported, like I was years ago when someone anonymously called the landlord of an apartment where I lived and worked. I had to move only months after settling in. Feeling insecure about one's living situation is awful. I do not work from my current apartment, yet I worry that my neighbours know what I do and are watching me to see whether I bring clients home. If my neighbours notice male friends visiting, will they think I am seeing clients? Can they tell I do not belong in this upscale high-rise building? Although I realize that these feelings are due to the trauma of losing my place years ago, they still impact me. It feels like I am always just one step away from catastrophe. To mitigate the risk, I self-consciously project a professional, middle-class, conservative, and quiet image. Even though I do not work from home, it is hard knowing that, more than likely, my neighbours would not want me in the building if they knew about my job. Feeling unwanted is a form of societal punishment as well.

The stigma that results in the "othering" of sex workers relies on symbolic violence (see Bourdieu, 1989), something I have known all my life but am only now starting to understand. According to many, including anti-prostitution advocates and those who endorse Canada's new prostitution laws, sex workers are victims (see Durisin, van der Meulen, and Bruckert, this collection). Yet it is exactly because of criminalization and marginalization that we cannot educate our society about who we are and what our needs are. For sex workers, speaking openly could mean losing family, friends, future employment opportunities, our homes, and so much more (see also Porth, this collection). Many sex work–specific regulations are unnecessary and even harmful but somehow remain entrenched in law.

Speaking as an Indigenous woman and generational sex worker, I am not interested in focusing on the relationship between being a sex worker and being abused. Correlation is not causation! Lives are messy. Exploring the histories of abused Indigenous people reveals struggles with poverty, intergenerational trauma, colonization, addiction, disconnected families, racism, and societal exclusion. All of these factors can come together, creating a perfect storm that constrains options and pushes Indigenous people toward doing sex work. For most, it is neither a dream job nor a lifelong endeavour, but neither is working in the fast-food industry, as a janitor, or as a soldier. The choice to do sex work is not for everyone, but I believe, in this moment, it is the right choice for me.

Note

1 Indigenous women are three times more likely than non-Indigenous women to experience "generational sex work," having a family member currently or previously engaged in selling sex (Bingham, Leo, Zhang, Montaner, and Shannon, 2014).

References

Bingham, B., Leo, D., Zhang, R., Montaner, J., & Shannon, K. (2014). Generational sex work and HIV risk among Indigenous women in a street-based urban Canadian setting. *Culture, Health and Sexuality, 16*(4), 440–52. https://doi.org/10.10 80/13691058.2014.888480

Bourdieu, P. (1989). Social space and symbolic power. *Sociological Theory, 7*(1), 14–25. https://doi.org/10.2307/202060

Campbell, M. (1973). *Halfbreed*. Toronto, ON: McClelland and Stewart.

Hochschild, A.R. (2003). *The managed heart: The commercialization of human feeling*. Berkeley, CA: University of California Press.

12

Myths and Realities of Male Sex Work

————— A Personal Perspective

RIVER REDWOOD

My life as a sex worker started one night when I was riding the streetcar home from a concert with my high school boyfriend. We were both sixteen years old. An older guy sat down behind us, told us it was his birthday, and offered us money if we'd get off the streetcar and beat his ass with his belt. For every lash we gave him, we got two dollars. I'd charge much more by today's standards, but being the curious boys we were, we found it hard to say no. The guy ended up having a great birthday, it was fun for us both, and we got a good workout beating the guy's butt bright red. My friend and I still joke about it today – and both of us continue to do sex work: he's a hardcore leather-master top, a graduate of the London School of Economics who holds a senior position in government; I'm a forty-seven-year-old gay male porn performer, producer, and director. I'm also a male escort and have turned tricks in alleyways, stairwells, parks, and cars; I've operated out of apartments, condos, dungeons, and hotels. I've had a long list of sugar daddies and can't even begin to tell you how many men I've slept with – it's definitely well into the several thousands. My life might seem really different or outrageous compared to most people's lives, but in reality I'm just a normal guy. Over my working years, I've found that my biggest challenges have not come from sex work but from people's misperceptions, stereotypes, and prejudices. This chapter attempts to challenge some myths and presents some realities about sex work and sex workers by drawing on my personal experiences working in the sex industry.

Sex Workers Are Regular People

My partner and I have been together for twenty years, I pay a mortgage and bills, and I have held down several well-paid "straight" jobs. I don't currently, and never have, had a problem with substance use. I'm attractive and work out regularly, but I'm not a body builder or a supermodel. Like most types of work that directly involve the body, such as ballet or acting, there is pressure in male sex work to have a certain type of physique. I'm happy with how I look and often get praised for my body by my clients, but I personally think I'm a regular Joe. In other words, not only am I a male sex worker with a lengthy history in the sex industry, but at the end of the day, I'm also a lot like everybody else.

Male sex workers are everywhere. There really is no shortage of guys out there having sex for money, yet in discussions of sex work, male workers and their experiences are often ignored. It's rare for male sex workers to speak for ourselves in our own words. Few people seem to want to talk publicly about the nitty-gritty of hooking up and having gay sex, let alone spend time thinking about the realities of men paying other guys to have sex. Yet it's the everyday reality for myself and an entire world of people I know and love dearly.

There are many reasons why men start doing sex work; people enter it at different points in their lives, for different reasons, and in many different ways. Some men choose sex work because they enjoy the work and lifestyle. Others do it for a short period of time as an experiment or fantasy or simply to see what it's like. Some do it part-time for fun and to make extra money. Others do it because they simply have no other options. Like all occupations, it's best when you are in control of what you are doing and have choices about the job. I have done sex work out of necessity to meet my basic survival needs, but I'm much happier when I have other options. I've also worked in some terrible "straight" jobs because I've simply had to do them. Lots of people are stuck in jobs they don't like, and sometimes a job is the only means to an end. I'm happy to say that this is not my reality. I'm my own boss; I get to set my own hours and to pick who, where, when, and how I work. I may not have a pension plan or health benefits but, when you look at it, being a male sex worker really isn't very different from any other kind of freelance job.

I can't imagine how different and limited my world would have been if I had not had the opportunity to engage in sex work. It has allowed me to make good money, meet people, travel, and develop insights about society and myself. Most importantly, it has helped me to grow into a much fuller, better, and more rounded human being.

Sex Work Can Be a Good Job

I left what can only be described as an extremely dysfunctional home at age seventeen. I quickly realized that I had limited options, and the idea of working at a minimum wage job for the rest of my life was totally unappealing. At the time, I had a job in a shoe store that paid $6.25 an hour; I also had a sugar daddy with a luxury condo. One perfect summer day, I was dreading having to leave his place for another long, boring shift of drudgery for little pay. My trick wasn't happy to see me go either. He asked me how much money I would make that day at the shoe store; I was sad to say that it was about $50. He offered me $300 to call in sick and spend the day with him hanging out and drinking by the pool. It doesn't take a rocket scientist to figure out which was the better choice.

The crucial components of male sex work, like many other types of work, include listening to the client, communication, and acting out a role (Sanders, 2005). The mechanics don't have to be that difficult, but they do involve a distinct set of skills. Indeed, sex work takes skill and ability like anything else in life. Although sex work is stigmatized in ways that other jobs are not, at the end of the day, it is a job like any other.

However, because of this stigma and the stereotypes about sex work, it can be very difficult for me to get a non–sex industry job (Law, 2013). Although I have a range of skills and experiences, I'm often forced to leave things off my resume or just plain lie in job interviews. For example, I can edit and direct commercial movies; I've produced a number of films that are sold in stores across the country, some of which have been nominated for international awards. I've spent a good chunk of my time learning about and working with video equipment and editing software. My interpersonal skills are the best in town. Sounds like the perfect dude to hire for your next commercial project, right?

The problem is that my work experience has been sex-related. If I apply for work at a "straight" company that produces non-porn films or deals with non-sex-related material, this is a major issue. I have a few pieces of work that are passable for a mainstream audience (e.g., the thirty-second commercial I did for men's jock straps), but my best work is my porn films. For instance, I once met with an employment counsellor to create a resume. When I included my full videography, porn, sex work, gay activist work, awards, and community-group involvement, my resume filled five pages. But when I cut out everything that was gay- or sex-related, I ended up with a skimpy page and a half. It was hardly an accurate description of my abilities. I'm skilled enough to work for CBC, but it's not likely I'll ever be given the chance.

When a mainstream employer wants to see my portfolio, I can't just walk into an interview, pull out my best collection of porn pieces, and say, "look at the special effects in this video," or "don't you just love the angle of the camera for the cum-shot?" or "doesn't the lighting design create the perfect environment for the anal-sex dungeon scene?" Many sex workers have great professional skills, but they can't put them on their resumes for fear of stigma or due to the simple fact that their work isn't recognized as legitimate work. If they have worked in a strip club, escort agency, bathhouse, or massage parlour, they are forced to come up with a different name or alternative for how they've been employed. In other words, they are made to lie.

Stigma, Stereotypes, and Homophobia Are Harmful

Through my experience doing sex work, I've become acutely aware of the striking similarities between issues related to male and female sex work. I've found that the stereotypes surrounding female sex workers can also be applied to men who work in the sex industry. For example, by mainstream societal standards, sex workers are often portrayed as people with worthless or disposable bodies who are doing a horrific job against their will (Hoigard and Finstad, 1992; Jeffreys, 2004; MacKinnon, 2005). Sex workers are also commonly positioned as victims of abuse who are exploited by some older, nasty male figure (Barry, 1979; Dworkin, 1981). We are viewed as unethical, diseased, and suffering from post-traumatic stress disorder (Farley and Barkan, 1998). The list of myths goes on and on.

Male sex workers, especially those of us who are gay, face many of the stigmatic assumptions and much of the discrimination that women do, but we have the additional burden of dealing with even greater invisibility and increased marginalization. There is a lack of services and social supports, and there are the pressures of masculine stereotypes and intense homophobia both from straight people and within the gay community itself.

There are stereotypes attached to many jobs, such as the idea that bankers are conservative and uptight, but none of these stereotypes can be equated to the harshness and discrimination that comes with being labelled a sex worker. It seems that no matter what people do for a living, even if their jobs have negative outcomes for others or the environment, they still get more respect than a person turning tricks on a street corner; people simply do not get labelled as sick or diseased for doing their job like sex workers do.

Sex-negative and homophobic attitudes can be extremely damaging to our health and well-being. Too often, I've seen male sex workers who have internalized negative homophobic beliefs engage in self-destructive behaviour. These men are often ashamed of the work they do and are sometimes even ashamed of their clients. They are harmed by repressive and sex-shaming systems and institutions, whether religious, legal, cultural, social, governmental, or medical. In these circumstances, is it any wonder why some people might find sex work unappealing?

I've found that the best way to deal with these pressures is to surround myself with people who have a similar belief system, such as a community of gay and straight sex workers who have a variety of genders, are sex positive, and possess nonjudgmental attitudes. I often find myself gravitating toward these people so that I can be open about what I do and who I am. I am much more closeted in mainstream environments, and it takes time before I'll fully disclose my past to someone. After a time of testing the waters has passed and trust has been built, I'll disclose my work, but otherwise I find that it is often just not worth the effort.

Sex work stigma and homophobia are particularly evident in the context of healthcare. For example, when I disclose to a doctor that I'm a gay man or a sex worker, I'm often met with a host of questions, usually not at all related to the reason why I'm there. Suddenly, my queerness and my sex work become the sole focus of who I am as a patient. Doctors want to do a battery of STI and HIV tests regardless of how clear I make it that I practise only safe sex and already get tested regularly. It's as though everything I say needs to be second-guessed and I can't be trusted. I often find myself forced into the role of sex educator when I really just want to be treated for something like an in-grown toenail!

Sex Work and Pornography Are Not Always Exploitative

Everyone I know, including my seventy-year-old mother, has at some point viewed a piece of pornography. Yet few people attempt to understand or comprehend what's involved in the making of pornography. It's much easier to label certain things as "bad," to go along with stereotypes, and to ignore the many shades of grey in people's experiences of making porn.

We shouldn't be so quick to say that the porn industry is bad just because people are getting paid to perform sex. Pornography is hardly the only industry we should be focusing on when we talk about labour abuses and unfair work practices; as has been widely documented, harm and exploitation are abundant in non–sex industry workplaces (Vosko, 2006; Worker's Action Center, 2007). Although there is intense racism, classism, and ageism present in the sex industry, my feeling is that these "isms" and biases in male sex work reflect the power dynamics that exist in the larger society and within the capitalist economy itself.

One time, I was working on an amateur porn film with a group of guys; the film involved shooting an orgy scene. One of the guys had never done anything like that before, and he was extremely nervous about what was going to happen. We talked about it for a long time, and he was given many choices and chances to opt out of activities. Needless to say, after the day was done and he'd had sex with his fill of beautiful men, he couldn't stop talking about how great the shoot was. In fact, for months afterward, he begged to be cast in another movie.

Since working in gay and straight porn, I have found stories like this to be common. Most of the people on the set, both in front of the camera and behind it, are glad to be there, and the work tends to be fun and respectful. I have never seen people forced to do something that they didn't want to do; if I did, I would head straight out the door. Unless you're pumping someone full of Viagra, it's difficult for a man to perform in porn if he doesn't want to be doing it. Further, pornography is a highly controlled and regulated industry; there are a ton of rules and regulations that govern what we can and can't do on and off screen. Why don't such stories get told more often? Why do we tend to focus on the negative stories and stereotypes about working in porn?

Due to the stigma surrounding pornography, many sex workers feel that they cannot be open with family, friends, and service providers about their line of work (see also Winters and MacDonald, this collection). Can you imagine Hollywood actors not being allowed to talk about the movies they're making? This double standard allows for the further exploitation of sex workers since it prevents them from accessing services that protect people working in other industries, like employment standards and worker's compensation. No one is ever going to stop pornography or prostitution from taking place, nor should they try. It will always be around, and the sooner that society embraces this reality, the better things will be for everyone. In my view, people working in the sex industry need to be empowered to have control over their bodies and workspaces and to have the freedom to celebrate what they do.

Pornography Is about Acting and Performing

For nearly every porn film I have been involved with, the end result doesn't look anything like the process of making the film. A single scene can take many hours to set up and shoot, involving many different angles, stops, and starts. All of the materials from the day of the shoot are then chopped down and compressed into a few minutes. This means that all of the humour and joking on set are cut and that the viewer never sees the lights or other crew in the room. Even the personality of the performers gets dropped onto the cutting room floor. The final product is a reflection of what the producers and director think the consumer wants to buy. The names, situations, and narratives in porn are usually, if not always, fake.

In my mind, porn is best described as idealized sexual fiction. It's not the best place for people to learn about sexual communication; it is merely there to be enjoyed for what it is. If you saw Superman jump out a window in a movie, you wouldn't try to emulate the feat in reality because you know that it's fake and that you would get hurt if you tried. It's the same with porn. Yet many people fall into the trap of believing that porn sex is real sex, which can cause no end of problems for them. It's critically important for people to understand that what they are seeing in front of a camera is a performance by actors who are acting out a prescribed role that often does not reflect who they are or what they do in real life. If people believe that what they are viewing is genuine, they are setting themselves up for a big disappointment.

Clients Can Be Nice, Sweet, and Normal Guys

My ideal client is someone who is clean, treats himself and me with respect, understands the rules I set, doesn't pressure me to change things, and agrees to pay me for the service I provide. The vast majority of my clients fall into this category. A lot of the guys I meet are nervous, shy, or just looking to have some "no strings attached" fun. Quite often, they have fantasies that they want to experience, as well as needs that they want fulfilled. As a sex worker, I often take on the job of reproducing fantasies for other people. This task can be a lot of fun to do – something I take pride in and enjoy.

Client relationships are often about projecting secret fantasies onto me. Some like to take the role of a mentor or enjoy having me there for companionship. They can fall in love with the person they think I am or even with the real me if I decide to share that part of myself. I can't lie and say that every trick I've turned has been great or that I've never had a bad experience, but can anyone say that about any job they have worked in? I've definitely had my share of both crappy and fun experiences! For me, doing sex work is 99 percent good and 1 percent not so cool. I think that these are really good odds and probably much better than other workers' job satisfaction.

When I do have a bad client, it's usually someone who is really messed up by societal factors, their family life, or their own prejudices or stereotypes. It's not some happy-go-lucky guy looking for some dick to suck but someone who is deeply hurt and struggling with his own core issues; he needs help more than anything else. If sex education were better, it would go a long way to improving the lives of these men and their families. Ultimately, we're all suffering in the current system of silence and sexual ignorance.

Before Canada's new prostitution regulations came into effect in 2014, sex workers faced barriers to organizing and teaching each other techniques or running workshops about how to screen clients. Currently, under Bill C-36, the Protection of Communities and Exploited Persons Act, we experience even more stigmatization and limitations on our choices. We also can't form unions and demand basic labour rights and protections (see also Clamen and Gillies, this collection). This situation is frustrating to me and shows disregard for sex workers' realities and our safety. Those of us with first-hand experience could and should be allowed to share our experiences with other people working in the profession.

Men Can Be Victims of Sexual Assault

When a man is sexually assaulted, it is rare for him to be seen as a victim. More often, he will believe, or will be made to feel, that the assault was his own fault because he wasn't masculine enough. This situation is compounded if you're a male sex worker and get assaulted by another man. I would never call the police to help me if there was an issue related to the work that I do. I shudder at the thought of how they would react and deal with the situation. If anything, I view the police as being more dangerous then the most horrendous trick. For similar reasons, I would never choose to engage with the legal system. My hesitation to engage with the law is not unique but is a common feeling among many male sex workers, and it leaves us extremely vulnerable and unprotected against violence and assault.

Moreover, if a male sex worker is assaulted, there are very few services and supports he can access. Rape crisis and sexual assault centres aren't places that my male sex worker friends, or for that matter my female sex worker friends, would consider calling in an emergency. It's a sad reality that it's often better to deal with an assault on your own or with close friends than to risk the ignorance and abuse of a professional. A clear message is being sent that my life experiences, safety, and needs are unimportant. Fortunately, I do have a group of people in my life that I can count on for support, and through hard work I have been able to identify doctors and other professionals who treat me with respect and don't regard my sex work as an issue.

Sex Workers Are Stigmatized as Drug Users with STIs

Too often, sex work and drugs are automatically linked in people's minds. If I say that I'm a sex worker, people often draw the conclusion that I'm also a drug user. Some sex workers use drugs – just like some accountants and lawyers – but not all of us do. And for those of us who do, it's not necessarily a problem in our work or personal lives. I started to see a client who was a doctor when I'd moved to a different part of the city. I saw him over several months, and he started to deteriorate after a while; he was a nice guy but looked like he hadn't been sleeping. Then he wouldn't show up for our appointments, and one day I went to his office and found the door closed. Eventually, I learned that he had lost his medical licence because of a crystal meth addiction. I saw him homeless and on the street a year later. A lot of people can become addicted to substances for a lot of different reasons, but nobody would ever say this man started using crystal meth because he was a doctor.

I don't think that sex work has to be about drugs. There are lots of people who do drugs in a range of different fields. Rich people are simply better able to hide their drug-use problems than those with less money. People will do what they have to do in order to get what they need; some may end up stealing or doing sex work to pay for substances. Penalizing, blaming, and judging people for their addictions are not going to help them. I personally have never used chemical drugs and do not have any desire to start doing so. Other than the occasional use of marijuana, drugs aren't a part of my life. I can't say this for a lot of the lawyers I know! There are definitely sex workers who party when they are working, but there are lots who don't.

Just like with drugs, people love to assume that because I have sex for work, I must be walking around with a ton of sexually transmitted infections.

This too is an unfair assumption that reflects the extent to which sex workers are stigmatized. We never think about a nurse or doctor being surrounded by sick people and touching their bodies all day. It's assumed that because they are professionals, they care about protecting themselves, but for sex workers, well, it's a different story.

I personally don't know anyone who wants to get sick or get an infection. Sex workers are not out looking to give people HIV and certainly aren't in a hurry to get it. Since I am a gay man who has had no shortage of sex and is open about it, people assume I must have HIV. There's no dodging the issue, and it's another layer of stigma and fear that gets piled on to male sex workers. Sometimes, it feels like people want me to be punished by getting HIV, that I somehow deserve it for being sexually active.

I have had sex with lots of people who are HIV positive, and it doesn't scare me because I understand how the virus is transmitted and how to protect myself. Medical treatment has changed HIV infection to a chronic condition that can be manageable for people who are able to access HIV care. Sex workers, however, still face systemic barriers to HIV treatment and prevention. Given what is known today about HIV and its transmission (Joint United Nations Program on HIV/AIDS, 2012), why have we not done away with bad laws that criminalize sex work and further increase the risk of HIV? Why do we continue to criminalize people who are HIV positive and fail to disclose their HIV status (Global Commission on HIV and the Law, 2012), and why do we force people who are HIV positive to hide in a tightly sealed closet of stigma and silence?

Pre-exposure prophylaxis (PrEP) is an anti-retroviral medication that can both treat and prevent HIV infection. It has reduced the fears of many gay men about catching HIV (see Rodger et al., 2014) and could potentially improve sex workers' abilities to protect ourselves from becoming infected. Some sex workers have fears that PrEP will increase pressure from clients and third parties to offer services without condoms. Male sex workers also experience this pressure, but for those who choose to engage in condomless sex, PrEP provides a layer of protection that didn't exist before. From my perspective, PrEP has freed up a range of choices, and although it is not a cure, it can hugely reduce the anxieties surrounding sex and HIV transmission. PrEP is a great alternative tool for male sex workers who want another choice or an additional option for preventing HIV transmission, as well as for clients who choose to take PrEP for similar reasons.

Even with the potential benefits of PrEP, it's often assumed that sex workers don't know what we are doing when looking after our health. In fact, the majority of sex workers I know are super comfortable with condoms and know how to use them properly. Safer-sex supplies are integral to our work, and we use them regularly. Can you imagine a construction worker not knowing how to wear a hard hat or safety boots? In my experience, sex workers communicate about sex and sexual health directly with their clients, and just like the construction worker, they know the tools of their trade.

Not All Male Sex Workers Are Gay and Have Male Clients

Although the majority of a male sex worker's clients are other men, this doesn't mean that women never hire us; they definitely do and can sometimes be quite aggressive about it. I had a friend who worked as a stripper for women in Montreal. He was often paid to go into the back area to do private lap dances, and some of the women would open their shirts and ask him to ejaculate on their breasts. For some men, this would be a dream job! My friend, however, would never do it because of the potential implications. He was concerned that the women might return to the bar with his cum on their breasts and threaten to charge him with assault. It wasn't worth the risk no matter how much money he was offered.

Many people believe that if you are a male sex worker you must be gay. I know a lot of straight-identified male sex workers who will sleep with men (this is often called "gay for pay"). Some do it out of basic survival needs, others to get money for drugs, and others just to pay the rent. Some simply do it because it pays more than their mainstream jobs ever could and gives them more freedom to spend their time as they would like.

Some of my straight male friends who like to drink sometimes find themselves short of cash at the end of the month. Because they can't afford to buy drinks on their own, they'll come with me to the gay bar to flirt and tease the men there. Oftentimes, the gay guys are quite eager and happy to buy them drinks, and the situation works out well for both parties: the gay guy gets to hang out with a superhot straight boy for the night, and the straight boy gets all the drinks he needs to keep him happy. Some male sex workers will similarly barter in this way, as trading companionship for a necessary or desired item is often an easy exchange.

For many straight-identified male sex workers, the threat of being found out by their non-sex-working peers or of being labelled bisexual or gay is a significant concern. It pains me to think about all of the men who work under these homophobic pressures and the difficulty it causes them. Ultimately, I think that people should be able to act however they want without fear of reprisal. Yet many people find this difficult to do. For instance, when I was working in porn, a lot of gay performers made disparaging comments about the performers who engaged in gay sex in front of the camera yet insisted on identifying themselves as "straight" afterward. A lot of these performers were happily married with wives or girlfriends and had families. Sex work was work for them, and they were acting in porn for the cash, pure and simple. If you believe that such performances are real, it just means that the performers are good at their job. Further, I know many straight guys who like to have their asses played with by their female partners; to deny this reality is to be closed-minded and judgmental. If you like what the performers do on set, who cares how they identify or what they call themselves afterward?

I have been hired by and have had sex with several women in my life, yet most people who meet me would never label me as straight. Usually, once people start talking to me, they figure out that I'm gay pretty quickly. I am not hyper-effeminate, but I cannot pass for straight, nor do I have any desire to do so. This can impact the types of client I attract and the way that the client and I interact. The majority of the time, it is a non-issue since I'm cute and good at what I do. However, it can raise issues for some clients who have internalized homophobia and masculine gender issues, as I tend to be a top in the bedroom. Often, these clients are uncomfortable having "gay sex" to begin with and can find that sex with a gay man triggers their issues and fears. This situation doesn't make for a good fit for either of us, and I'm happy that there are other guys out there with whom these men can pair up.

Conclusion

Despite all the myths and misconceptions, the reality is that sex work has been a great choice for me, and I defend it passionately. It has its share of pressures and issues like any other occupation. However, for me, it has been a great experience, and my life has been deeply enriched by it. At the end of the day, it's my body, my life (which I enjoy very much), and my choice to do what I do. I hope that one day society will learn to accept the realities of sex work and to see it for what it really is – a lot more complex and diverse than most people think. This occupation is all about knowing and believing in who you are and being able to set strong boundaries. What makes the job difficult is not the work itself but the crap that society throws at people who engage in it. Sucking cock for cash is easy; it's the moralistic judgments for doing so that create problems and can be harmful to sex workers. Personally, I've never understood why sex work is such a big deal, but clearly my life adventures make other people uncomfortable. If people challenged their stereotypes and dropped their assumptions, phobias, judgments, and biases, it would create more space for male (and female) sex workers to exist with respect. Ultimately, I think that we would all be a lot freer, healthier, happier with ourselves, and generally on our way to having much more fun and better sex!

Note

This chapter is an updated revision of a previous publication: Redwood, R. (2013). Myths and realities of male sex work: A personal perspective. In E. van der Meulen, E.M. Durisin, and V. Love (Eds.), *Selling sex: Experience, advocacy, and research on sex work in Canada* (pp. 45–57). Vancouver, BC: UBC Press.

References

Barry, K. (1979). *Female sexual slavery*. Upper Saddle River, NJ: Prentice Hall.

Dworkin, A. (1981). *Pornography: Men possessing women*. London, UK: Women's Press.

Farley, M., & Barkan, H. (1998). Prostitution, violence, and posttraumatic stress disorder. *Women and Health, 27*(3), 37–49. https://doi.org/10.1300/J013v27n03_03

Global Commission on HIV and the Law. (2012). *Risks, rights and health*. New York, NY: United Nations Development Program.

Hoigard, C., & Finstad, L. (1992). *Backstreets: Prostitution, money, and love*. University Park, PA: Pennsylvania State University Press.

Jeffreys, S. (2004). Prostitution as harmful cultural practice. In C. Stark & R. Whisnant (Eds.), *Not for sale: Feminists resisting prostitution and pornography* (pp. 386–99). North Melbourne, Australia: Spinifex.

Joint United Nations Program on HIV/AIDS. (2012). *UNAIDS guidance note on sex work and HIV*. Geneva, Switzerland: World Health Organization. Retrieved from http://www.unaids.org/en/resources/documents/2012/20120402_UNAIDS-guidance-note-HIV-sex-work

Law, T. (2013). Transitioning out of sex work: Exploring sex workers' experiences and perspectives. In E. van der Meulen, E.M. Durisin, & V. Love (Eds.), *Selling sex: Experience, advocacy, and research on sex work in Canada* (pp. 101–10). Vancouver, BC: UBC Press.

MacKinnon, C. (2005). Pornography as trafficking. *Michigan Journal of International Law, 26*(4), 993–1012.

Rodger, A., Bruun, T., Cambiano, V., Vernazza, P., Estrada, V., Van Lunzen, J., ... Lundgren, J. (2014). HIV transmission risk through condomless sex if HIV+ partner on suppressive ART: PARTNER Study. Paper presented at the 21st Conference on Retroviruses and Opportunistic Infections, Boston, March 3–6.

Sanders, T. (2005). 'It's just acting': Sex workers' strategies for capitalizing on sexuality. *Gender, Work and Organization, 12*(4), 319–42. https://doi.org/10.1111/j.1468-0432.2005.00276.x

Vosko, L.F. (Ed.). (2006). *Precarious employment: Understanding labour market insecurity in Canada*. Montreal and Kingston: McGill-Queen's University Press.

Worker's Action Center. (2007). *Working on the edge*. Toronto, ON: Worker's Action Center.

Legislation

Bill C-36, *Protection of Communities and Exploited Persons Act*, SC 2014, c. 25.

13

Champagne, Strawberries, and Truck-Stop Motels
———— On Subjectivity and Sex Work
VICTORIA LOVE

I grew up in a small farming community in rural Ontario, and not unlike many teenagers in rural communities, I remember feeling trapped by my life in the country. My father suffered from severe alcoholism, and I felt ashamed of my family. He was an immigrant to Canada, part of the last generation of industrial workers with well-paying jobs. As is the case for many children of working-class immigrants, I was strongly encouraged in academics and also took dance and piano lessons for several years. Although painfully shy, I loved to perform. I watched the movie *Fame* obsessively, found inspiration in the glossy pages of dance and fashion magazines, and dreamed of a much more interesting and exciting life far away from the one I found myself inhabiting.

I was about fourteen years old when Madam Alex, the infamous Los Angeles madam, was in the news. I came across a magazine article profiling her and some of her "call girls." I was intrigued. I studied the article closely, paying attention to how the women dressed, what lingerie they wore, and how they did their makeup. For me, the women espoused a beauty and glamour that I could only dream of. I didn't completely understand what it meant to be a call girl, but I knew it involved sex, something I had only a vague understanding of. What I did know was that the women were beautiful and that I wanted to be like them.

Looking back over the twenty years since I first did sex work, I see that it has been an unclassifiable mixture of good times, excitement, shame, and challenges. Time and time again, the allure of intrigue and glamour drew me back to the strip club, the parlour, or the agency. As a young woman discovering the cultural mystique of the call girl, I had a powerful desire to embody a subjectivity other than the shame and lack of sophistication that marked my childhood. In this chapter, I discuss some of my experiences working in the sex industry, during the course of which I shifted from a working-class to a middle-class subjectivity. I also describe how feminist theories that conceptualize sex work as exploitation and violence have negatively impacted my understanding of my work and of myself.

Beginnings: Sex Work as a Young Woman

My family situation became increasingly difficult for me to deal with, and I left home when I was fifteen years old. People who hear my story often try to impose a narrative of familial abuse that caused me to enter prostitution – which is much too simplistic. My response to difficulties at home also reflected my own needs and motivations – including a thirst for adventure and a desire to live my life on my own terms – in the context of limited options and dysfunction. I grew up in a patriarchal nuclear family where my father's economic and gender privilege insolated him from being held to account for his actions. I knew when I was twelve that I was going to leave home as soon as I could; I didn't want the situation for myself that my mom had endured for so many years. For me, starting to do sex work was a way to meet a critical need for the money that would enable me to gain a degree of independence. It was also a way of saying "fuck you" to the family structure that had hurt me.

By the time I was seventeen, I was living in an apartment with a friend of mine in a working-class city in Ontario. Although I had always excelled in academics, I had lost interest in high school and did not return after Grade 11. Instead, I started working at a coffee shop down the street from my apartment. My roommate was trying to finish high school and was on welfare; together, we plastered our apartment with images from *Vogue* magazine and dreamed about being fashion designers. In reality, however, we were young, poor, and uneducated.

I wanted more for myself than life's circumstances at that time could offer. Still holding on to that image of the glamorous and successful call girl from years earlier, I picked up the local newspaper, looked through the adult listings, and called an escort agency named Mercedes because it sounded "classy." I was inexperienced and did not know it was wrong for the agency owner to "interview" me by having sex with me. Women often experience sexual assault in the context of work or are compelled to exchange sex for support or resources from men; I understand now that my experience was not exceptional. At the time, however, I was just discovering my sexuality and was flattered by the novelty of a man desiring me in a sexual way.

My first client was an older man. I wasn't sure what to do, except for some vague directions given to me by the agency owner. Uncertain, I gave him a blow job. The experience was neither good nor bad. Having that much money in my hands was the wonderful part. Then, as now, there was an erotic charge attached to the exchange of sex for money. In one hour, I made as much money as I would have made in a couple of days of pouring coffee. What I didn't like, however, was the agency owner. He started to act as though I owed him something, expected to have sex with me for free, and pressured me to work much more than I wanted.

After a few months, I left the agency for another one that turned out to be much better. I was still seventeen, and the new agency wanted to see my identification; I used my friend's driver's licence and pretended I was twenty-two. I had never had access to so much money before, and I was suddenly able to pay my bills, buy food for my roommate and myself, and purchase clothing and perfume that made me feel beautiful and sophisticated. All of these things made me feel quite powerful in the context of my life. I felt like I was "somebody" for the first time, and my self-confidence started to grow.

Although I held on to the image of the intriguing and glamorous call girl, during my early years in the business, it mostly was not like that. I had many fun times, and I remember with fondness the women I worked with back then, but there were lots of moments that were decidedly unglamorous as well. I'm sure I have spent more time in truck-stop motels than any of Madam Alex's girls ever did! I remember late-night calls to budget hotels in order to see drunk clients, and "dead" calls at 4:00 in the morning in the middle of winter.[1] I don't remember much about the clients, but the majority of my encounters passed without any problems. Sometimes, I got to go where the "rich people" lived, and I saw homes, met people, and was exposed to lifestyles unlike anything I had ever seen in my life. This experience gave me a host of new things to dream about. After seeing the "good life" that some of my clients had, I set my sights on going to university.

Shifting Identity: Middle-Class Subjectivity and Anti–Sex Work Sentiment

Seeking to transition out of escort work, I saved my money, invested in breast-implant surgery, and started to work as an exotic dancer. Around this time, I became involved with a man I had met as a client; he became my first boyfriend and the first person I ever loved. He bought a condo that I lived in as I finished high school while continuing to dance. It was around this time that negative values surrounding sex work started to affect my feelings about my occupation. My feminist consciousness was developing, and I searched the shelves of my local public library for information about prostitution.[2] I started to feel that what I was doing was *very* wrong. I wondered whether I was being exploited and whether I was doing something bad for women; I began to experience deep and crushing shame. To cope with the embarrassment and judgment, I adopted a negative perspective on the sex industry and my place within it. I broke up with my boyfriend, applied for welfare, and passed on the judgment that I felt to other women I knew in the industry. I questioned why they couldn't get their lives together like I had. I finally started university intent on becoming a lawyer and "helping" all the women who just weren't as lucky as I was certain that I was.

My change of perspective about sex work was an attempt to cope with profound shame and also marked the start of my transition to a bourgeois, feminine subject position – one that understands the self to be an ethical subject who seeks to save "Others" (see Heron, 2007). In retrospect, I understand that this was less about sex work than it was about my own identity as a white, working-class woman embodying a middle-class subjectivity and about my desire to be read as a "good" woman. During this time, the only way I could speak of my involvement in sex work was as a "reformed" prostitute. When I see former sex workers adopting anti-prostitution perspectives, as I once did, I am reminded of the power of dominant discourses of feminine respectability and the desire that many of us have to position ourselves in relation to them.

Because I was affected by the stigma that society places upon women who work in the sex industry, my initial foray into feminist theorizing on prostitution caused me to loathe parts of my own history and experience, wresting from me an appreciation of my own resilience. My encounter with anti-prostitution feminism while I was finishing high school and starting university helped to produce a painful rupture in my "self" and reified a division between my "prostitute" self and my "straight" self. The realization of how bad it was to be a prostitute made me feel disgusted. While finishing my undergraduate degree, I was exposed to sex-radical theory (Rubin, 1984), sex-positive feminism (Chapkis, 1997), and the third wave of the women's movement (Baumgardner and Richards, 2000). I began to rethink my own history and started to feel the first stirrings of pride in my experiences rather than shame. It was only when I stumbled upon other ways of understanding prostitution – initially through a history of sex work written by a sex worker (Roberts, 1993) and later through meeting other sex workers – that I was able to reject the anti-prostitution, feminist narrative, strip bare the regulatory function of the whore stigma, and reclaim my history.

Take Two: My Return to the Sex Industry

My initial involvement in sex work took place when I was a youth with limited options for supporting myself financially, whereas my return to sex work occurred at a time when I enjoyed not only race privilege but also a newly acquired, albeit relative, class privilege (see also James, this collection). Despite my burgeoning middle-class subjectivity and my new educational capital, I was still, economically speaking, working-class. In short, my material circumstances had changed, but the fact remained that I had limited options for funding my graduate education.

During my final year of undergraduate studies, I started to work at an escort agency in Toronto on weekends. Similar to my experience nearly ten years earlier, I initially felt excited and empowered by the work. Only this time, I was embracing the part of me that I had tried so hard to disavow and to distance myself from in an effort to live up to my narrowly defined feminist ideals. In a number of ways, this was a very affirming experience; it was like saying a big "fuck you" to those anti-prostitution activists who had caused me to feel so much incapacitating shame that sometimes it made me want to die.

I worked at the agency for a number of years before moving to a massage parlour and then transitioning to independent escort work. For me, working as an independent was a wholly different experience. When I worked at agencies, I saw regulars with whom I had ongoing relationships, but never did I cultivate the sort of intimate and enduring relationships that I've developed with my clients as an independent. I have clients I've been seeing for over a decade; some celebrate my birthday with me, and others will email me to see whether I've returned home safely from a trip. On rare occasions, someone I meet as a client enters fully into my personal life, becoming a friend or lover.

For the most part, my relationships with clients are neither fully personal nor fully commercial, existing in a space that we lack adequate language to describe. Although my personal feelings for clients are not the same as for lovers or partners, I have watched my clients' children grow up and have provided support during the death of family members; these are not disinterested relationships but in fact very human ones. There have also been times when my own feelings of sexual desire or affection for clients have not been reciprocated. During times in my life when I am unattached, clients may offer the only form of intimacy to which I have access, imperfect as it may sometimes be.

The "Girlfriend Experience":[3] Emotional Labour and Intimacy in Sex Work

Although I try to maintain a degree of distance between myself and my clients, I do not have a firm boundary between my work life and my personal life, and my interactions with clients are simultaneously genuine and performative. I bring what I understand as my "authentic self" to interactions with clients, but what they see are strategically woven together aspects of my personality that produce a particular affect, or the persona I seek to create. In other words, as much as I present genuine variations of who I am, the pieces are purposefully stitched together to present a confident and entertaining companion positioned within the upper echelons of the indoor sex industry.

There are moments when I find relationships with clients to be positive and affirming, but at other times the labour involved is exceptionally draining. Often, clients relate to me as they would a girlfriend, largely because there are few other frameworks through which to understand our relationship. As a result, I find myself trying to manage boundaries and to maintain balance when my clients – perhaps unwittingly – take too much of my time and energy. I often resent the privilege that permits them to be oblivious to the work involved in producing our encounters. It's also not uncommon for my clients to want to know what I enjoy sexually, how I feel about them, and, importantly, how they can make me have an orgasm – one of the questions I find annoying and intrusive, along with queries such as "how did a nice girl like you start doing *this*?" Managing clients' feelings and their desire for access to my personal life is the part of my job I find the most difficult; I have different levels of disclosure that give me control over how much I let anyone know me.

When I reflect on my experiences, I can see that I have been able to use my work in the sex industry to achieve a comfortable level of material and financial stability while still maintaining control over my time in a way that most workers are not able to. Indeed, if not for my work in the sex industry, it is unlikely that I would have been able to pursue graduate education or have access to the advantages of a middle-class lifestyle. The irony of my situation is perhaps that the education I pursued with the initial understanding that it would lead to a job outside the sex industry has permitted me success within it.

How my sexual labour is commoditized in the sex industry is very much related to how I am positioned as a white, bourgeois, feminine subject. My rural, working-class background, my family's immigrant status, and the marginalization I experienced as a youth all become hidden from view. The subject position of the call girl, of which Madam Alex's working women are but one example, is one that I identified with at a young age and one that I have enacted in many moments of my life. This image and the ideas associated with it are one component of what I sell to clients; I sell neither my "self" nor my body.

Sometimes, my clients tell me that they call me rather than other escorts because I'm "educated"[4] or because they want to see someone they consider sophisticated. To me, what clients are saying speaks to the ways that bodies are located in the hierarchy of the sex industry. Because of my race and class privilege, I have been able to position myself in the most comfortable spheres of the sex industry and in conditions that do not reflect those of many other sex workers. Moreover, my gendered, raced, and classed labour reproduces my clients' bourgeois subjectivity – the feelings they have about themselves as middle-class men and the meanings attached to that status. This process is not unique to the sex industry; the production of identity through consumption is a feature of capitalist society (Langman, 2003).

Conclusion

Reflecting on my thoughts and experiences over the years since I first worked in the sex industry, I have come to understand that the way sex work is conceptualized is still far too limiting. Sex work is about emotionally complex relationships that involve genuine feelings of intimacy, it's about relationships of power, it's about the complex layers of meaning we attach to our lives and activities, and it's about using those options available to us to make a living. I have at times been very happy in sex work, and I have gained much wisdom from the many intelligent, strong-willed sex workers who have mentored and taught me.

I resolutely theorize sex work as work, yet at nearly forty years of age and with a lengthy career in sex work behind me, I do not always want to continue in the occupation. I am fatigued by the limitations and problems with sex work: the stigma, the lack of status, the secrecy, and the endless worry about law enforcement. The problem is not the work itself. The problem is that sex work is permitted to exist in our society only in certain conditions and, too often, in very difficult ones. As the economy systemically devalues women's labour and offers unsatisfactory options for paid work, even to those of us who are highly educated, sex work remains for me the best option. Unsurprisingly, although I'm not a happy hooker, I remain an unrepentant whore.

Notes

This chapter is an updated revision of a previous publication: Love, V. (2013). Champagne, strawberries, and truck-stop motels: On subjectivity and sex work. In E. van der Meulen, E.M. Durisin, and V. Love (Eds.), *Selling sex: Experience, advocacy, and research on sex work in Canada* (pp. 58–64). Vancouver, BC: UBC Press.

1 A "dead" call refers to a client arranging a meeting with an escort without the intention of following through with the encounter. Commonly, when the escort arrives at his home or hotel, he does not answer the door or otherwise respond.
2 I had not heard of the term "sex work" at the time.
3 A girlfriend experience, or GFE, typically refers to an affectionate and amicable encounter involving kissing, oral sex, and penetrative sex.
4 I note that I am "well educated" in my advertisements, and I formerly included information about my educational background on my work website. This approach is not uncommon in the sector where I work.

References

Baumgardner, J., & Richards, A. (2000). *Manifesta: Young women, feminism, and the future*. New York, NY: Farrar, Straus and Giroux.

Chapkis, W. (1997). *Live sex acts: Women performing erotic labor*. New York, NY: Routledge.

Heron, B. (2007). *Desire for development: Whiteness, gender, and the helping imperative*. Waterloo, ON: Wilfrid Laurier University Press.

Langman, L. (2003). Culture, identity and hegemony: The body in a global age. *Current Sociology, 51*(3–4), 223–47. https://doi.org/10.1177/0011392103051003005

Roberts, N. (1993). *Whores in history: Prostitution in Western history*. London, UK: Grafton.

Rubin, G. (1984). Thinking sex: Notes for a radical theory of the politics of sexuality. In C. Vance (Ed.), *Pleasure and danger: Exploring female sexuality* (pp. 267–319). Boston, MA: Routledge and Kegan Paul.

14

"The Paradox?!"
Racialized and Indigenous Sex Workers' Encounters within a Capitalist Market

MENAKA RAGUPARAN

The adult commercial sex industry has evolved with the emergence of the Internet and has been shaped by the globalization of the consumer-driven, service-based economy (Bernstein, 2007; Brents and Hausbeck, 2010; Gall, 2006). The evolution of the sex industry is so significant that Brents and Hausbeck (2010) argue that the mainstream culture and the adult commercial sex industry are converging in many important ways. Gall (2006) claims that this move toward the normalizing and mainstreaming of the sex industry is detrimental to women, as it relies on and reproduces a narrow and dehumanizing conception of womanhood and femininity. In Canada the sex industry is criticized for excluding women of colour and Indigenous women from the "upscale" parts of the industry by confining them to the street, where they are subjected to violence (Razack, 1998).

In this chapter, I draw from the experiences of forty racialized and Indigenous sex workers and grapple with the tensions of the sex industry and its impacts on this group of women. My objective is to deconstruct narratives that fix sex workers' identities and relations within the homogenous notion of victimhood. By deconstructing grand narratives, I am engaging in the process of producing the roadmaps of the not yet fully understood identities and lived experiences of racialized and Indigenous women who work within the indoor sectors of the contemporary sex industry. A deconstructive analytical approach also allows me to capture and explore the perpetual mobility of identity categories, including gender, race, and class. From this perspective, we can consider how racialized and Indigenous women negotiate and navigate their identity, power relations, and labour practices to compete for economic rewards in the neoliberal marketplace.

Here, I show that racialized and Indigenous women's labour practices in the indoor sectors of the sex industry do not, as Gall (2006) claims, narrow or dehumanize conceptions of femininity and womanhood. Neither, however, do I argue that women's participation in the sex industry will bring them closer to realizing gender or racial equality. Indeed, it is this tension that positions me to unpack the ways that sex workers engage in transforming their "human capital" in pursuit of happiness.[1] In othe words, I contend that to increase income-earning capacity and to realize an improved quality of life, sex workers engage in entrepreneurial activities that both enable and constrain their expressions of self-identity and their self-representation in ways that are uniquely raced, gendered, and classed.

My analysis highlights the inherent instability and permeability of identity categories such as race, class, and gender. By conceptualizing multiple and shifting identities, I demonstrate how racialized and Indigenous sex workers' identities are intertwined, mutually constitutive, and how they vary across time and space (Carastathis, 2008; Puar, 2005; Taylor, 2009). By conceptualizing racialized and Indigenous sex workers' experiences within capitalist structures, I also shed light on the way that institutions and entities under capitalism are both powerful and paradoxical (Allen, 2011; Kennedy, Zapasnik, McCann, and Bruce, 2013). Conceptualizing power and power relations in this way allows me to disrupt predetermined class categories – such as rich, poor, and middle-class – as well as to focus on the ambiguity of these categories (DeLanda, 2006) and to foreground the ways that racialized and Indigenous sex workers' multiple marginalizations interact with their partial privilege (see also James, this collection).

Method and Participants

Forty sex workers were interviewed for this study. Thirty-eight individuals self-identified as women, and two who worked as women in the sex industry self-identified as gender nonbinary.[2] With the exception of one participant who held a student visa, all participants were Canadian citizens or permanent residents. Participants self-identified as belonging to the following racial/ethnic groups: Arab (2), East Asian (4),[3] Indigenous (3), South Asian (6),[4] Black (13), and mixed-race (12).[5] Two women had transitioned out of sex work, whereas the remaining thirty-eight were engaged in the indoor sex industry working as webcam performers or for escort agencies, massage parlours, strip clubs, or independent in-call and out-call services. Participants' tenure in the sex industry ranged from two months to over twenty-five years. Research participants from seven different cities across Canada responded to recruitment texts circulated through email, Facebook, and Twitter. Purposive snowball sampling was also used; ultimately, most research participants learned about this study through word of mouth. Transcripts from all forty interviews were uploaded into NVivo 10 for analysis. Three stages of inductive coding were used to organize and separate the different themes that arose throughout the interviews. Descriptive coding was used to obtain a broad sense of the primary themes of the interviews. Following this analysis, two levels of subcodes were used to narrow down the broad descriptive codes. The final phase of coding involved reorganizing the codes into main themes for discussion.

Why the Sex Industry?

Unanimously, the sex workers in this study reported that they had made an informed, rational choice to work in the sex industry.[6] Although the need to earn a living wage was a strong motivator for all of the participants, they also all pointed out that their decision to enter indoor sectors was based on a cost-benefit calculation. That is, operating in a society that is hierarchically structured by race, gender, and class, racialized and Indigenous women in my study had to choose from among the economic options available to them; in many cases, this came down to minimum-wage work, social assistance, or sex work. Oxfam has reported that, in Canada, 60 percent of minimum-wage workers are women whose inability to earn a living wage entrenches them in poverty, regardless of how hard they work (Ravon and Stefov, 2016). Women in this study, wanting to avoid being part of this statistic, sought access to economic rewards that ensured a higher standard of living. The indoor sectors of the sex industry afforded these women the opportunity to compete in the market and to increase their wage-earning capacity. Absent this opportunity, many of them would have been part of the working poor:

> I worked a lot of fast-food places and stuff like that, as a cashier in places, grocery stores. Places like McDonald's and Tim Horton's and stuff. Not really anything that I can make a career or money off of ... I was sort of

stuck. I knew people at my work that have been working there for three
years or four years and still making eleven bucks an hour ... I was tired of
working two jobs for minimum wage, and I saw the opportunity ... My best
friend, her roommate, used to do this and make a lot of money doing it, so I
thought, "Why not give it a try?" And it just worked for me. I enjoy it. (Iona,
independent escort)

In addition to the ability to earn a living wage, racialized and Indigenous
women in this study were motivated by their desire for independence,
mobility, flexibility, and job security.[7] These important factors profoundly
affected the lives of the workers I interviewed. All research participants
identified themselves as self-employed, although a handful reported a long
tenure in one establishment; notably, even these women were not exclusive to any one workplace or sector. Whereas some women worked full-time
in the sex industry, others preferred to work part-time while attending to
their domestic responsibilities, furthering their education, or pursuing
another career. Independent in-call and out-call service providers[8] – women
who do not work for a third party – enjoyed the most independence and
flexibility, as they had a greater choice regarding the numbers of hours and
days they worked, the types of clients they saw, and the amount they charged:

One of the reasons why I chose to be independent [is] so that I have agency.
I have my will and my wants, and I don't see anyone I don't want to see. I
work when I want to work, and I work around my schedule of being a parent and being an activist. And I work, and I get paid as much as I work, and
it creates a level of independence that is not present in the corporate world.
(Violet, independent escort)

More importantly, many of the respondents in this study moved between different sectors of the sex industry and transitioned in and out of sex work to
manage other life events and demands. As is the case for many sex workers,
some women even worked simultaneously in multiple sectors. In short, racialized and Indigenous sex workers identified with a broad range of sex work
employment histories (see also James, this collection; Love, this collection).
    Some of the women's lengthy and complex tenures in the sex industry
also included travelling to other cities and internationally for sex work (see
also Hannem, this collection). Similar to other groups of sex workers, many
racialized and Indigenous women crossed spatial borders for adequate

remuneration. That is, to increase their demand, these sex workers reported travelling to different geographical locations where there were not many women of colour or Indigenous women, allowing them to increase their earning capacity. Phoebe and Priyanka explained the intersection of space, demand, and desirability:

Sometimes it [i.e., being racialized] does and sometimes it doesn't [help]. And I find, especially in Vancouver, it can be a big disadvantage as well – huge. Like if I were to work maybe in Calgary or a predominant – like Saskatchewan or something – a predominantly white community, I think that would be a definite asset. I've even gone out to – oh, I have worked independent ... I went with a friend. We went to Kamloops, and it's predominantly white ... And we did one night or two nights or something. I did very well, just because there were no Asian girls. (Phoebe, independent escort/masseuse)

Yeah, so in Alberta. I think I am very exotic in Alberta. It's mostly Caucasian women, and there's not a lot of Asian women ... So in Vancouver I can work a full day; I can put in twelve hours, and the likelihood of me making any money that day is probably 50 percent. But in Calgary, or most cities in Alberta ... I am at least looking at $500 to $1,000 a day. That's a huge difference, and it kind of goes to show that my niche is more liked there than here, so I will often go there. (Priyanka, independent escort)

As we see, sex workers' decisions to engage in sex work and continue to work in this form of labour highlight the intersections of race, class, and space (see also Love, this collection). That is, sex workers interviewed for this study overwhelmingly reported that the Canadian sex industry had provided them with economic opportunities to which they may not otherwise have had access in a society structured hierarchically by race, gender, and class. In addition to affording racialized and Indigenous women the opportunity to earn a living wage, sex work offered them the privileges of independence, flexibility, and mobility, placing them in a social and economic position that could not be realized through minimum-wage and precarious work. These findings suggest that, through sex work, racialized and Indigenous women, regardless of socio-economic background, can experience a degree of power, happiness, social and political gains, social mobility, and an improved quality of life.

Technologies to Transform the Limits of Human Capital: Aesthetics and Stylization

Mainstream, Eurocentric, idealized representations of feminine beauty can be understood to be white beauty – epitomized by the pale, thin, tall woman with flowing, straight, blond hair and blue eyes. Racialized and Indigenous sex workers with whom I spoke pointed out that within the sex industry this idealized image of femininity and beauty is linked to earning potential. That is, women who conform to this Eurocentric, Western "ideal type" can demand the highest fees, whereas the prices for services decrease the more that one deviates from this image of feminine beauty. For instance, Black women with natural hair charge significantly less than white women.[9] White-passing Indigenous and mixed-race women charge rates comparable to white women:

> Oh yeah, I play white, yeah [laughing]. That's what sells, right? So I mean blond-haired, light-skinned. Very much so, exactly. That's what they want. That's what they want, blond hair. I mean if I could, you know, get rid of the brown eyes, I am sure I would have tried. If I could stand putting my finger [in my eyes] to put a contact on, I would have gone blue at some point. Yeah, but that's what sells, right! Blond hair, big boobs. (Nisha, independent escort)

The intersection between beauty and labour market positionality is not unique to the sex industry. Hamermesh (2011) notes that in many, if not all, labour markets, workers' beauty is an economic issue and can directly influence economic behaviour. The influence is so profound that in many markets good looks are rewarded with premium pay and bad looks are subjected to pay penalties (ibid.). Under these circumstances, how do women of colour and Indigenous women compete for economic success in the sex industry? I suggest that their entrepreneurial strategies not only involve careful calculation of when, where, and which sector they should work in but also entail styling practices that conform to, and resist, idealized Eurocentric feminine beauty.

As part of their styling practices, many workers talked about the types of clothes they wore, the ways that they styled their hair, how they maintained their body size and image, and their self-presentation at work. For instance, all research participants pointed out that the manner in which they behaved toward, interacted with, and presented themselves to clients involved

conscious calculations. Workers noted that they usually started by researching the location and dressing accordingly and that their clothing choices had
a profound impact on their identity and work experiences. Depending on
the occasion and location, women also had to be conscious not to reify any
racial or sex work stereotypes. Often, women had to dress elegantly and
perform high-class rituals, such as knowing when to use which fork during
a multicourse meal, sipping their wine slowly, and so on: "So I just, I know
how to put on that middle-class privileged face like, 'Ah, I am so happy, I am
going to whatever' ... like I know how to play the roles" (Niran, independent
escort). Geena, who worked for an escort agency, explicitly drew on racist
and classist tropes to distinguish her presentation of self as "classy": "Like I
don't talk, excuse me, with a, with a like ghetto accent, I don't use swear
words or curse words or slang, you know ... You wouldn't catch me dead
doing it, at all, no." As Geena pointed out, performing class not only involves
enacting hyper-femininity and the ability to have a "good" conversation on a
range of topics but also requires women to be conscious of specific gestures
and behaviours that are read as cultural markers of race and class. In addition, for women to make a profit and establish healthy working relationships, not only do they have to convince clients that their money is well
spent, but they also have to make the relationships look organic rather than
transactional. Therefore, many women in this study invested time and
money in improving their communication skills and their ability to dress
appropriately for the occasion.

Racialized and Indigenous sex workers pointed out that performing a
middle-class or high-class identity by investing in their style of dress and by
improving how they behaved was relatively easy, compared to, for instance,
transforming their hair or body size. Like non-racialized sex workers, the
women with whom I spoke found that working in the sex industry made
them more conscious about healthy lifestyles, which included a balance
between healthy eating and exercise. Many women talked about a regular
workout regime and about limiting dining out to when they were working.[10]
Although healthy eating and regular exercise regimes are in general good
practices, they are also habits that symbolize Eurocentric and middle-
class or upper-middle-class consciousness. Studies on body image and
body size show that Black men and women express a preference for and
tolerance of larger female silhouettes and that Black girls' ideal bodies are
proportioned differently from those embraced by white girls (Cachelin,
Rebeck, Chung, and Pelayo, 2002; Chin Evans and McConnell, 2003;
Kelch-Oliver and Ancis, 2011). In my study, some women who had a thin

silhouette noted that although their body size allowed them to compete in the neoliberal marketplace, their parents and extended family members often expressed dissatisfaction with their very thin figure. Workers also pointed out that their parents associated their slim body with not having enough to eat and often invited them to come and live at home so that the parents could care for their needs. In this sense, racialized and Indigenous sex workers had to negotiate the tensions around body size and image on a regular basis. That is, the Eurocentric ideal of thinness, which not only represents ideal femininity but also symbolizes higher social strata, runs counter to the ideals of many ethnic cultures, which associate a thin silhouette with starvation and lower social strata.

The women in this study spoke at length about their hairstyling practices to overcome the natural tendencies of their hair (e.g., curly). In this respect, it appears that mixed-race women and Indigenous women who had the capacity to pass as white, with minimum time and effort required to transform their hair, had an advantage over other racialized women in competing to gain economic rewards and to increase their revenues. Women who were included in the roster of workers in indoor sectors owned or managed by a third party were sometimes encouraged to adopt a self-presentation that obscured their racial identity. This practice was more prevalent for mixed-raced women who had a lighter skin tone. For example, Beckie, an independent and agency escort with a Black father and white mother, had a lighter skin tone but had her father's hair. She was asked to wear a wig to hide her hair and "pass" (see Raguparan, 2017):

When I first started working, I was twenty-three, and I was a stripper for a month ... And I worked by the airport, and [the agency] specifically told me that I was not to identify myself as Black, that I, in fact, had to wear this like ... like a Spanish wig. Because of my light colour, there's possible for people to see me as Spanish. You know, that Black women were not [who the clients] wanted to see, you know. They didn't give me a specific reason. They just basically insinuated, and I had a girl working with me ... that had worked there long, and she also strongly encouraged me to not wear my hair like this, you know.

Beckie noted that she could easily alter her hair by straightening it with a flat iron or by wearing a wig. Transforming her hair allowed Beckie not only to keep her race/ethnicity a secret from her clients but also to keep her identity as a sex worker hidden from her family and friends. That is, Beckie was photographed while wearing a wig in her profile pictures on the agency's website. Because of the wig, family members or friends who might visit the website would not recognize her. More importantly, Beckie's thoughtful strategy to keep her racial identity and sex worker identity closeted allowed her to manage the stigma associated with Black women in sex work and to increase her wage-earning capacity (see Raguparan, 2017). Similarly, some Indigenous women who can pass as white colour their hair blond and identify as mixed-race or as French Canadian to increase their capacity to earn income. These women's hairstyling practices can also be linked to their efforts to avoid stigma: "I actually had blond hair [laughing] ... It used to be short and blond. When I had my blond hair, it was like ... you know, people didn't know who, what kinda background I had, so like, yeah whatever, and I can play this up and whatever make money" (Kylie, independent escort).

Whereas the mixed-race and Indigenous women in this study could easily transform their hair by colouring and styling it to conform to the idealized image of feminine beauty and to compete for economic rewards, the Black women found that transforming their hair was a challenge. Many women discussed the associated costs and lamented the time and effort it took to maintain permed or relaxed hair:

The thing with the hair, where my hair is more processed, it's chemically processed, and it's more straight, which is more of ... work-related, compared to my hair, [which] was more natural and kinky and coarse, like afro thing, which is the big trend in the Black community to go natural hair. But natural hair for me won't make me any money ... So I am in between where I would love to have dreads one day, but dreads aren't exactly considered sexually attractive. It's the silky, long, flowing hair that's attractive, which costs me a lot of money to make my hair that way. Where it feels like when I am working, all I am doing is paying for ads and getting my hair done ... All my money goes to my hair and ads and everything else to keep my image attractive to make money. (Quinn, independent escort)

When I first started, I had like, I didn't wear wigs, but I had like hair that was like fairly long and straightened, like chemically straightened. And that was like a huge issue for me, right, because I could never get wet if I am showering. And it took so much preparation ... I think that's like one of the big issues for me is always having to have this like very white-friendly appearance, and it's also like very like fem appearance ... I would be like

spending like hours like doing my nails, doing my hair, doing my makeup,
putting on perfume. (Sonya, independent and agency escort)

Quinn and Sonya echoed the challenges that many Black workers mentioned. Banks (2000) notes that "hair shapes black women's ideas about
race, gender, class, sexuality, images of beauty, and power" (p. 3). Black sex
workers in this study pointed out that their hair styles were political in
that these styles had conditioned their perceptions about the "appropriate" picture of professionalism and femininity. Some Black women went to
great lengths to straighten or relax their hair and perform whiteness.
According to these women, hair in a relaxed style related to looking professional (Banks, 2000) or "dignified and appropriately feminine" (Craig,
2002, p. 122).

Some Black women decided to maintain a natural look, wearing an
afro, or braids, or cornrows. These women's hairstyles, which affirmed
their Blackness, were part of a political statement to resist Eurocentric
ideas of beauty and femininity. Banks (2000) points out that with skin and
hair being the most important physical attributes for racial classification,
Eurocentric images of beauty and hair not only intersect along the lines of
race and gender for Black women but often also relate to devaluing tightly
coiled black hair. To resist this devaluation, these women framed their
"culturally appropriate" hairstyling practices (e.g. afros, braids, and cornrows) to represent exoticness and consciously subjected themselves to the
category of "other" to make a profit. As previously mentioned, customers
who seek the services of Black women often desire the authenticity of
Blackness; accordingly, these workers' cost-benefit calculation operated in
relation to market supply and demand. In this sense, even though these
workers did not transform their human capital, they still used their initial
investment to compete for economic success in the process of becoming
an entrepreneur.[11]

The need for racialized and Indigenous women to avoid the stigma of
racial inferiority and compete for economic rewards was so profound that
some women resorted to plastic surgery in order to overcome some of the
"limits" of their human capital.[12] Dena's story is unique at the same time as
it speaks to the anxieties and stigmas that all participants in this study
experienced. Dena, a mixed-race woman with Indigenous and white ancestry who worked as a masseuse, pointed out that she had her father's
Indigenous features but her mother's light skin colour and blue eyes. She
comfortably passed as white and experienced the privileges of being white

during everyday, mundane social interactions. According to Dena, her nose was the only thing that cast doubt on an otherwise very successful white performance:

> I dye my hair lighter. It's sort of medium-brown naturally, and I used to have this big, honking nose that was my father's completely, but I got a nose job. I never liked my – it was a weird love-hate relationship with my nose. It's kinda, I felt like, it was my one possible Native marker. It was the one thing that people would squint at me and be like, "Oh maybe, maybe I kinda see it there." So when I got it done, there was this weird fight between like I knew I didn't like the way my nose looked, but it also felt like giving up part of my identity there and that's something ... the weird feelings, regret, and loss that you get sometimes when you, overall you are happy with the end result. There's some weird stuff that comes up, so there's that, too.

The sex workers I interviewed reported that their efforts to transform their bodies in order to become successful economic subjects sometimes resulted in alienation. For example, Black sex workers reported that hair-styling practices that conformed to white femininity (i.e., relaxed, flowing, long hair) alienated them from the Black community, and Dena felt that by getting a nose job, she had abandoned her ancestry. She also noted that after she had transformed her nose, people in her Indigenous community did not recognize her; when she visited her community for cultural events, she was perceived to be a white visitor who was accompanying her sister. Although South Asian and Arab women did not report any transformation of their bodies, they too talked about experiencing a disconnection from their families and communities. Whereas Dena did not intentionally separate herself from her extended community, South Asian women often distanced themselves from their communities to succeed as entrepreneurs within the sex industry. Their decision to do so was based on the demands of their job and on their capacity to effectively manage their different identities.

Conclusion

Entrepreneurial activities and work experiences in the sex industry under capitalism reveal that the identities of racialized and Indigenous women are unstable and highly permeable. The uniquely raced, gendered, and classed ways that the women in this study transformed their identities to increase their capacities to compete for economic rewards both enabled and constrained them. Furthermore, racialized and Indigenous women's participation in the indoor and "upper" echelons of the Canadian sex industry contradicts anti-capitalistic rhetoric, as this participation not only problematizes the exclusion of marginalized populations from legitimately and fully participating in the capitalist enterprise but also challenges the capitalist principles that work to exclude marginalized populations from the means of production. Given these tensions and paradoxes inherent in capitalist structures and labour practices, any habitual characterization of race, gender, and class as fixed and powerful becomes noncoherent and nonsensical. In other words, identity categories and power relations are always fluid and relational and vary in relation to context, time, and space.

Notes

1 The notion of human capital within a neoliberal paradigm is used by Foucault (2008) to indicate that one's body, brains, genetic materials, race, class, and so on are utilized within capitalist economic processes.
2 I acknowledge that the term "woman" does not refer to a static category, nor does it have an internal homogeneity. To refer to all forty participants of this study, I use the term "women" as an everyday term available to us.
3 These were women with ancestry in China, Korea, the Philippines, or Vietnam.
4 These were women with ancestry in India, Pakistan, or Sri Lanka.
5 Mixed-race women had parents who were of two or more races, such as Black and white, Black and East Asian, East Asian and white, or South Asian and white.
6 See Chapkis (1997) for the distinctions between rational choice and free choice.
7 In cohorts of sex workers in Australia (Maher, Pickering, and Gerard, 2013) and the United Kingdom (Sanders, 2005), researchers point to similar themes of self-interest and similar motivations for women to enter the sex industry.
8 In-call workers provide services from a fixed location, such as their home or an apartment kept for this purpose, and out-call workers provide services in the client's home or at a hotel. Independent sex workers can provide both in-call and out-call services.
9 Although women of colour charged less than white women, their rates were significantly higher than any of the provincial minimum wages in Canada. The hourly rate that racialized and Indigenous women charged ranged from $40 to $120.
10 Many sex workers pointed out that they frequently had to accompany their clients on dinner dates.
11 See Deleuze and Guattari (1987) on the process of becoming.
12 See Foucault (2008) for a discussion of how plastic surgery is one of the tools for transforming human capital.

References

Allen, J. (2011). Powerful assemblages? *Area, 43*(2), 154–57. https://doi.org/10.1111/j.1475-4762.2011.01005.x

Banks, I. (2000). *Hair matters: Beauty, power, and black women's consciousness.* New York, NY: New York University Press.

Bernstein, E. (2007). Sex work for the middle classes. *Sexualities, 10*(4), 473–88. https://doi.org/10.1177/1363460707080984

Brents, B.G., & Hausbeck, K. (2010). Sex work now: What the bluring of boundaries around the sex industry means for sex work, research, and activism. In M.H. Ditmore, A. Levy, & A. Willman (Eds.), *Sex work matters: Exploring money, power, and intimacy in the sex industry* (pp. 9–22). New York, NY: Zed Books.

Cachelin, F.M., Rebeck, R.M., Chung, G.H., & Pelayo, E. (2002). Does ethnicity influence body-size preference? A comparison of body image and body size. *Obesity Research, 10*(3), 158–66. https://doi.org/10.1038/oby.2002.25

Carastathis, A. (2008). The invisibility of privilege: A critique of intersectional models of identity. *Les Ateliers de l'Éthique, 3*(2), 23–38.

Chapkis, W. (1997). *Live sex acts: Women performing erotic labor.* New York, NY: Routledge.

Chin Evans, P., & McConnell, A.R. (2003). Do racial minorities respond in the same way to mainstream beauty standards? Social comparison processes in Asian, Black, and white women. *Self and Identity, 2*(2), 153–67. https://doi.org/10.1080/15298860309030

Craig, M.L. (2002). *Ain't I a beauty queen? Black women, beauty, and the politics of race.* New York, NY: Oxford University Press. https://doi.org/10.1093/acprof:oso/9780195152623.001.0001

DeLanda, M. (2006). *A new philosophy of society: Assemblage theory and social complexity.* London, UK: Continuum.

Deleuze, G., & Guattari, F. (1987). *A thousand plateaus: Capitalism and schizophrenia.* (B. Massumi, Trans.). Minneapolis, MN: University of Minnesota Press.

Foucault, M. (2008). *The birth of biopolitics: Lectures at the Collège de France, 1978–1979.* (G. Burchell, Trans.). New York, NY: Palgrave Macmillan.

Gall, G. (2006). *Sex worker union organising: An international study.* New York, NY: Palgrave Macmillan. https://doi.org/10.1057/9780230502482

Hamermesh, D.S. (2011). *Beauty pays: Why attractive people are more successful.* Princeton, NJ: Princeton University Press.

Kelch-Oliver, K., & Ancis, J.R. (2011). Black women's body image: An analysis of culture-specific influences. *Women and Therapy, 34*(4), 345–58. https://doi.org/10.1080/02703149.2011.592065

Kennedy, R., Zapasnik, J., McCann, H., & Bruce, M. (2013). All those little machines: Assemblage as transformative theory. *Australian Humanities Review, 55*, 45–66.

Maher, J., Pickering, S., & Gerard, A. (2013). *Sex work: Labour, mobility and sexual services.* New York, NY: Routledge.

Puar, J.K. (2005). Queer times, queer assemblages. *Social Text, 23*(3–4), 121–39. https://doi.org/10.1215/01642472-23-3-4_84-85-121

Raguparan, M. (2017). 'If I'm gonna hack capitalism': Racialized and Indigenous Canadian sex workers' experiences within the neo-liberal market economy. *Women's Studies International Forum, 60,* 69–76. https://doi.org/10.1016/j.wsif.2016.12.003

Ravon, L., & Stefov, D. (2016, October 17). Shortchanged: Make work paid, equal, and valued for women. *Oxfam Briefing Note.* Retrieved from https://www.oxfam.ca/shortchanged-report

Razack, S. (1998). Race, space, and prostitution: The making of the bourgeois subject. *Canadian Journal of Women and the Law, 10*(2), 338–76.

Sanders, T. (2005). *Sex work: A risky business.* Devon, UK: Willan.

Taylor, Y. (2009). Complexities and complications: Intersections of class and sexuality. *Journal of Lesbian Studies, 13*(2), 189–203. https://doi.org/10.1080/10894160802695361

15

Double Punishment

Immigration Penality and Migrant Trans Women Who Sell Sex

NORA BUTLER BURKE

Collaboration between criminal and immigration law enforcement agencies has long been a mainstay in the policing of migrant sex workers in Canada. In recent years, human trafficking has emerged as a central legal paradigm that drives the state's regulation and removal of migrant sex workers. As workplace raids and deportation have become increasingly commonplace, there has been an important resurgence of critical analysis, community organizing, and cross-movement alliance building at the intersections of immigration and criminal law. One area deserving greater attention is the particular impact of everyday immigration and criminal law enforcement on migrant trans women sex workers.

It is well known that trans women who sell and trade sex – particularly street- and bar-based workers – are regular targets of police surveillance, arrest, and prosecution and are often charged with prostitution-related offences, as well as for drug possession, assault, and theft (Butler Burke, 2016; Namaste, 2000). As a consequence, trans women sex workers are frequently incarcerated, primarily in provincial men's jails, and often live in otherwise precarious conditions marked by unstable housing, limited access to healthcare and education, and inconsistent sources of income (Gobeil, 2011; Namaste, 2005). One factor that commonly sets migrant trans women's experiences apart from those of other trans women sex workers is the ongoing punitive role that both criminal *and* immigration law enforcement plays in governing their lives (see also Lam and Gallant, this collection). As criminalized subjects, these women are submitted to additional punitive measures within the immigration system – ranging from probationary-like measures that greatly restrict social life and survival to detention and deportation.

This chapter situates immigration penality (Pratt, 2012) within the daily, and nightly, lives of migrant trans women. This writing draws on a larger ethnographic project that emerged from my experience as an outreach worker with migrant trans women in Montreal. Building on interviews with seven migrant trans women in 2016,[1] as well as on legal archives,[2] this study analyzed the relationship of the women with the institutions and laws that govern their lives. Taking everyday life as the point of departure, this chapter examines the distinct ways that criminal and immigration law shapes the lives of migrant trans women sex workers in Montreal and broadens the analysis of how immigration law is employed to regulate and control migrant sex workers.

Defining Immigration Penality

Canada's colonial borders have historically been governed according to an ever-evolving array of exclusionary immigration laws, policies, and practices. Pratt (2012) suggests that we understand border control and the governance of migration as a distinct form of penality – immigration penality. She describes immigration penality as being "made up of diverse and intersecting state and non-state authorities, technologies, forms of knowledge, and regimes of rule," which together comprise a system that, she claims, "controls borders; polices non-citizens; identifies those who are dangerous, diseased, deceitful or destitute; and refuses them entry or casts them out" (ibid., p. 276). Pratt (2006) identifies detention and deportation as "the most extreme and bodily sanctions of immigration penality" (p. 1), while pointing to a vast array of mechanisms through which immigration penality manifests in the everyday lives of criminalized migrants.

Whereas earlier iterations of immigration law and border control relied on overtly racialized categories of exclusion and inclusion, more recent manifestations of Canadian immigration law have been articulated through liberal logics of national security, public safety, and risk management. Under contemporary immigration law, criminality has been a central category through which immigration penality is organized and enacted. With the introduction of the Immigration and Refugee Protection Act (IRPA) in 2001, "serious criminality" was established as the grounds upon which non-citizens could be declared inadmissible to Canada and, as such, stripped of or denied immigration status (e.g., permanent residency, asylum) and deported. "Serious criminality" for a permanent resident includes a conviction for a criminal charge that, within Canada, is punishable by a maximum of at least ten years in prison or a conviction for a criminal charge that results in a prison sentence of six months or more (IRPA, 2001, s. 36). Similarly, criminal convictions from outside Canada are assessed according to their equivalency under the Criminal Code and can also be the basis for an inadmissibility ruling and potential deportation.

Once an individual is under investigation by the Canadian Border Services Agency (i.e., the federal agency that enforces immigration law) for "serious criminality," multiple processes may be triggered. Detention and deportation are commonly understood as the primary mechanisms of immigration penalty, yet it frequently manifests in a multiplicity of other ways, including immigration-admissibility hearings, fines and probationary-like conditions, and removal of immigration or protected (e.g., refugee) status. Although immigration penalty poses substantial harms for many migrants, including women who sell and trade sex, migrant trans women face distinctive mechanisms and impacts of immigration penalty that make their experiences worthy of focused attention. In the remainder of the chapter, I briefly present the context within which immigration penalty has taken shape for migrant trans women sex workers in Montreal, highlight mechanisms at play, and examine their consequences.

Encounters with the Criminal Justice System

Montreal has long been home to migrant trans women – predominantly racialized women, many of whom have made refugee claims in Canada. Although some migrant trans women have been granted "protected" status by Immigration, Refugees and Citizenship Canada, this does little to spare them from a complex matrix of social exclusion, state and interpersonal violence, and legal, administrative, and economic marginalization. Income opportunities are rarely viable for these women, partly due to the barriers to obtaining gender-congruent identity documents for non-citizens in Quebec, and social assistance programs introduce increased levels of surveillance into migrant lives. Although many trans migrants access income through state-subsidized French-language programs, the programs' staff are commonly cited as hostile toward and unwelcoming of trans women. In this context, selling sex has proven a more consistent source of both income and community for many migrant trans women, who have consequently figured prominently in street- and bar-based prostitution in Montreal. Bars and cabarets such as Citi Bar and Café Cléopâtre have served as vital spaces for meeting clients, performing on stage, and building friendship and support among trans women. These spaces have commonly played an important role in facilitating access to hormones, sharing tips on how to spot under-cover officers, and providing emotional support and care long after the bars close for the night.

In recent years, however, bar closures have followed in the wake of inten-sified policing and the gentrification of working-class neighbourhoods, par-ticularly the Centre Sud and the historic red light district (on this topic, see also Ross, this collection; Page, this collection).[3] As a result, trans women – particularly migrant trans women – have been increasingly pushed from their collective workplaces and their homes alike, which has forced them to live and work in greater isolation. Understanding this shift is absolutely critical for addressing the current context of migrant trans women who sell sex. In this chapter, I focus on the period leading up to these acts of displacement and dispersal.

Selling sex, although a fundamental means of survival for many migrant trans women in Montreal, is a heavily policed and thus highly precarious source of income. Understanding the role of law enforcement in policing migrant trans sex workers' lives is key to untangling the workings of immi-gration penality. For several decades, the Moralité, alcool et stupéfiants (MAS) section of the Service de Police de la Ville de Montréal (SPVM) has played a central role in the policing of trans sex work in Montreal (Namaste, 2005). Many of the women I interviewed described being arrested by under-cover MAS agents posing as clients as among their first encounters with the SPVM. In particular, women spoke of their panic and terror, as they initially feared that they were being either kidnapped or detained by immigration authorities before realizing that they were being arrested. During these encounters, it was not uncommon for police to make racist, xenophobic, and otherwise violent statements that threatened the safety and bodily integrity of the women interviewed. Gloria,[4] a forty-five-year-old woman, recalled police making statements such as, "Why do you live here if you don't speak French?!" They also told her that she had no rights and threat-ened her with deportation – waving at her and taunting, "Bye-bye Canada." Sasha, twenty-eight, described the years that she spent living in what could be considered a fugitive state, during which she experienced nearly constant police surveillance and was perpetually at risk of arrest whenever she went out in the daytime. In one memorable instance, a police officer promised to make her life unlivable: "Until you die, you will never have a happy day."

The vast majority of migrant trans sex workers' encounters with the police occurred on the job – on the street and in bars – with the most frequently recurring charges being solicitation, as well as charges for violating the administration of justice (e.g., breach of conditions, not appearing for court).[5] Such violations included failing to abide by strict zoning restrictions that prohibit people – commonly sex workers, drug users, and homeless people – from being in designated areas (e.g., specific streets, bars) and neighbourhoods. These zones of exclusion frequently covered the areas where women worked, lived, and accessed social services and healthcare. Being found within a designated zone could itself result in arrest and further charges, fines, and conviction. The range of charges arising from policing trans sex workers extended to a number of other municipal-bylaw violations commonly associated with the policing of public space. As Sasha explained, "Oh my god, I went through the whole book! I got charged with *flânage* [loitering], for spitting on the ground ... They charged me with everything, and I went into prison so many times."

For many, policing also extended well beyond the realm of their work lives. A number of women had been charged with assault for acts of self-defence. Liliana, thirty-two, described how she and her group of friends – all Latina trans women – had been violently removed from a gay nightclub by private security. When one of the security personnel refused to return her friend's purse, the friend pounded on the club's window with her high heel, breaking the glass: "We didn't even have a knife or anything like that. It was a high heel, but yes, we were charged with armed assault [laughing], against a window no less!"[6] This occurred within a broader context of the social cleansing of a gentrified neighbourhood and corresponding efforts on the part of club management to expel Latina trans women presumed to sell sex, despite their long history as customers and performers at the venue.

In other instances, women faced criminal charges after defending themselves at home against abusive partners and violent building staff. The tone of police conduct varied in these encounters but often turned aggressive, if not outright violent, when a woman's transsexual status was disclosed or otherwise revealed during the encounter. Fatima, twenty-nine, recalled her boyfriend kicking her out of their shared home. Police arrived while she was gathering her belongings and were initially sympathetic, offering to detain her boyfriend and to direct her to a domestic violence resource for women. When she declined the offer and informed the officers that she was transsexual, they drastically changed their demeanour: "Once I said 'transsexual,' oh Lord Jesus ... All I remember is the two guys took me ... and just literally put the handcuffs on me. They put me in the car, and they put me in the back with the windows all closed, and I couldn't breathe." Panicked and suffocating, she kicked out the police car window. She was charged with mischief and served a fifty-two-day jail sentence. During another arrest at home, Jessica, fifty-four, overheard an arresting officer exclaim, "Oh, they're faggots!" as he noticed a photo of her and her boyfriend embracing. Threats followed: "The police told me that they were going to take me to the woods and kill me."[7]

More often than not, women I spoke with lacked a strong legal defence in court and were generally advised to plead guilty, with the understanding that if they paid their fine and served their sentence, they would not be subject to any further repercussions. In some cases, this was offered as a strategic manoeuvre to avoid the risk of lengthy sentences in men's prison facilities: "The lawyer visited us in prison and told us we had to plead guilty. 'That way, you will all get out right away, [or else] you will remain in this men's prison much longer.'" And what did we want? To get out of prison right away! So we pled guilty, even though we weren't" (Liliana).[8]

Unbeknownst to the women I interviewed, these guilty pleas would have harmful consequences for their immigration status. Although a conviction for solicitation was unlikely on its own to constitute a "serious" crime, charges related to armed assault, as well as drug trafficking, fraud, and mischief, constituted potential grounds for a ruling of criminal inadmissibility by immigration authorities. Although access to adequate legal counsel would not have eliminated the structural violence inherent to the criminal justice system, it may have helped to minimize the punishment that would eventually be imposed by the immigration system.

Immigration Penality in the Everyday

With little to no prior understanding that a criminal record could have any substantial consequences for their immigration status, it came as a shock to many of the women to find themselves suddenly under the scrutiny of immigration authorities on the grounds of their potential criminal inadmissibility to Canada. For some, it was when applying for immigration status – making a refugee claim or applying for permanent residency or citizenship – that they were informed that they would be subject to an investigation that could result in their eventual deportation. For others, it was upon release from prison or police custody that they were instructed to report to immigration authorities for questioning, only to be served with a deportation order. Those who had previously presumed a certain degree of stability in Canada were suddenly cast into doubt. For all of the women I spoke with, fears of deportation loomed prominently.

In some instances, institutional records revealed surveillance and collaboration with other law enforcement agencies, particularly when the Canadian Border Services Agency was unable to locate an individual. In one case, the agency's notes clearly attest to information being obtained from a neighbourhood police department: "SPVM confirms that the subject is a male prostitute who dresses in women's clothing. Best time to find him [sic] is after midnight on the following streets."[9] When an arrest warrant was eventually issued, she was aggressively apprehended while eating at a neighbourhood diner, taken into police custody, and transferred to immigration authorities for questioning.

Several women were called to an inadmissibility hearing in front of the Immigration Division of the Immigration and Refugee Board. For Liliana, the recent murder of her friend, a young Mexican trans woman who had been deported from Canada and subsequently shot outside her home, haunted her in the days leading up to her hearing. At the hearing's conclusion, the immigration commissioner put a stay on her deportation and ordered her to conform to a set of probationary-like conditions for the following two years, after which her admissibility would be reassessed. Conditions included ceasing to sell sex and finding "legal" employment, returning to French school (no longer eligible for subsidies, she would be charged $600 per month), and avoiding any future criminal charges. When she attempted to comply, she was unable to secure mainstream employment, partly as a consequence of provincial legal barriers that prohibit non-citizens from modifying their legal sex and name on identity documents. Worried that she would be unable to pay her rent and school tuition, she gradually returned to sex work, despite knowing that she risked being reported to immigration if she was arrested.

Many women, as a consequence of their hearings and investigations, were denied or stripped of permanent immigration status and thrust into states of greater precarity and uncertainty. Deportation remained a constant source of stress and worry. Fatima, who had lived in Canada since she was a child, elaborated on her fears: "I get nightmares sometime because I dream about ... walking down the streets, that one day I will be deported, whoosh, just like that, for no reason." Although several of the women had received removal or deportation orders, for complex administrative reasons, they were never actually enforced. Nonetheless, immigration authorities went to great lengths to draw out their conditions of punishment – including lengthy periods of detention, additional fines or bail fees, costly and demanding rehabilitation procedures, and numerous other laborious probationary-like conditions.

The consequences of immigration penalty experienced by the trans women I interviewed were at times subtle, perhaps less apparent than the obvious violence of deportation faced by many other migrant sex workers. Several women were ordered to undergo rehabilitative measures in order to demonstrate their ability to reform and be productive, law-abiding citizens. In one case, fifty-nine-year-old Carmen had to pay Immigration, Refugees and Citizenship Canada a $1,000 fee and attest that she posed no risk of reoffending based on a twenty-year-old criminal conviction in another country. Some women experienced intensified isolation from their community, as they were instructed to dissociate from people with criminal records or from people who sold sex or used drugs. For others, these circumstances further augmented their reticence to rely on the police for protection from interpersonal violence and abuse.

Several women experienced greater instability as a consequence, including losing housing after being released from immigration detention, as well as living in men's homeless shelters and on the streets, despite being ordered to maintain a permanent address. Multiple interviewees discussed struggling for years to navigate immigration bureaucracies in order to regain their immigration status, without which they could not access healthcare, social assistance, subsidized housing, or other basic services. Jessica described living undocumented with relative comfort for a decade before police arrested her for solicitation and discovered that she was being sought by immigration authorities, who promptly detained her for many months and nearly deported her. Following a lengthy legal battle, after which her deportation order was annulled and she was reissued protected status, she left detention in a state of deep despair and loss. For the next ten years, she struggled to rebuild her life, to find housing, and to sustain a living, yet she was never able to acquire the practical and financial support needed to apply for immigration status. As she explained, "I was abandoned. Nobody knew what to do. It's more difficult today than before. I was better when I was illegal than today now that I'm legal."[10] Her experience reverberates in the stories of many other migrant trans women who have been subjected to an endless struggle against a state of uncertainty and insecurity driven by immigration penalty.

Conclusion

Migrant trans women are among the thousands of migrant sex workers in Canada whose lives are precariously bound up within regimes of border control and criminal law enforcement. Undoubtedly, migrant trans women who sell sex commonly bear the weight of heavy state surveillance, violence, and confinement, and they are often deeply entangled in an unending cycle of criminalization. Policing practices extend beyond traditional jurisdictional bounds to incorporate elements of border control – with threats of deportation, inquiries into immigration status, and occasional collaboration with immigration authorities. At the same time, "criminality" has become a central mode through which immigration is governed in Canada, generating a new form of probationary status through which the "dangerous, diseased, deceitful or destitute" are managed (Pratt, 2012). Immigration penality offers an important lens through which to better understand the various institutions, authorities, and systems of knowledge that govern the everyday lives of migrant trans women sex workers, and it offers insight to strengthen our analysis of the regulation of migration and sex work in Canada.

Notes

1 Research participants were invited to take part in a semi-structured interview and to share access to personal legal records. Interviews focused on themes related to encounters with the criminal law, everyday life, and the impacts of their immigration status. A thematic analysis of the interviews that drew out themes highlighted in this chapter was conducted. A thematic analysis of legal archives, totalling over 5,000 pages, allowed me to situate the interviews and to better understand the broader social and institutional context.
2 Legal archives from municipal and provincial courts, the Canadian Border Services Agency, the Immigration and Refugee Board, and Immigration, Refugees and Citizenship Canada included internal records (e.g., database entries), correspondence with other institutions, case notes, rulings, and transcripts of hearings. These archives were accessed via Access to Information and Privacy Act requests with the consent of participants.
3 The heart of the red light district was at the intersection of Rue Sainte-Catherine and Boulevard Saint-Laurent. It has undergone massive redevelopment in the past decade and has been renamed the Quartier des Spectacles. For more, see Crago and Clamen (2013), Michaud O'Grady (2015), and Namaste (2015).
4 All names have been changed to protect confidentiality.
5 Solicitation charges dated from before the introduction of Bill C-36, the Protection of Communities and Exploited Persons Act, in 2014.
6 Author's translation from French.

7 Author's translation from French.
8 Author's translation from French.
9 Author's translation from French.
10 Author's translation from French.

References

Butler Burke, N. (2016). *Double punishment: Immigration penality in the daily lives of migrant trans women.* (Unpublished MA thesis). Concordia University, Montreal, Quebec.

Crago, A., & Clamen, J. (2013). Né dans le Redlight: The sex workers' movement in Montreal. In E. van der Meulen, E.M. Durisin, & V. Love (Eds.), *Selling sex: Experience, advocacy, and research on sex work in Canada* (pp. 147–64). Vancouver, BC: UBC Press.

Gobeil, D. (2011). Pourquoi je suis devenue militante, 1999. In M.N. Mensah, L. Toupin, & C. Thiboutot (Eds.), *Luttes XXX: Inspirations du mouvement des travailleuses du sexe* (pp. 251–59). Montreal, QC: Éditions du remue-ménage.

Michaud O'Grady, L. (2015). '*La répression, ça finit par donner des résultats': The displacement and erasure of street culture in downtown Montréal 1995–2010.* (Unpublished MA thesis). Concordia University, Montreal, Quebec.

Namaste, V. (2000). *Invisible lives: The erasure of transsexual and transgendered people.* Chicago, IL: University of Chicago Press.

Namaste, V. (2005). *C'était du spectacle! L'histoire des artistes transsexuelles à Montréal, 1955–1985.* Montreal and Kingston: McGill-Queen's University Press.

Namaste, V. (2015). *Oversight: Critical reflections on feminist research and politics.* Toronto, ON: Women's Press.

Pratt, A. (2006). *Securing borders: Detention and deportation in Canada.* Vancouver, BC: UBC Press.

Pratt, A. (2012). Immigration penality and the crime-security nexus: The case of Tran Trong Nghi Nguyen. In K.N. Varma, K. Ismaili, & J.B. Sprott (Eds.), *Canadian criminal justice policy: Contemporary perspectives* (pp. 273–97). Don Mills, ON: Oxford University Press.

Legislation

Bill C-36, *Protection of Communities and Exploited Persons Act,* SC 2014, c. 25.

Immigration and Refugee Protection Act, SC 2001, c. 27.

16

"Harassing the Clients Is Exactly the Same as Harassing the Workers"
Street-Based Sex Workers in Vancouver

ANDREA KRÜSI, BRENDA BELAK, AND SEX WORKERS
UNITED AGAINST VIOLENCE

There is a well-established body of global epidemiological and social science research demonstrating the negative impact that legislation and policies criminalizing sex work has on the health and safety of sex workers (Lowman, 2000; Shannon and Csete, 2010; van der Meulen and Durisin, 2008). Prohibitive sex work legislation and restrictive policing strategies have consistently been linked to negative effects on the working conditions of sex workers because they reduce the ability of sex workers to screen clients and displace them to isolated and dark areas where there is little chance for escape or help in case of violence (Deering et al., 2013; Lowman, 2000; Simić and Rhodes, 2009). Despite this, a number of higher-income countries have attempted to eradicate prostitution by criminalizing the purchase, but not the selling, of sexual services. This approach to regulating sex work, known as the Swedish model, has been implemented in a number of European countries, including Sweden, Norway, Iceland, and Northern Ireland, despite a lack of evidence supporting this legal framework (Oppenheim, 2014). First employed in Sweden in 1999, the primary objective of the approach is to eradicate prostitution by eliminating demand. However, evidence from Sweden and Norway indicates that the law has been unsuccessful in meeting this objective (Amnesty International, 2016; Goodyear and Weitzer, 2011). Instead, many sex workers remain subject to a high level of police attention and are being targeted and penalized by police in multiple, intersecting ways, such as through police stops, identity and immigration checks, deportation, evictions, and area restrictions. The continued high level of policing and criminalization of sex workers constitutes a clear human rights violation and negatively shapes the working conditions and safety of sex workers (Amnesty International, 2016; Global Commission on HIV and the Law, 2012; Scoular, 2004).

Following the Supreme Court of Canada's decision in *Canada (Attorney General) v. Bedford* (2013), which declared core provisions of Canada's prostitution laws unconstitutional, the former Conservative government implemented Bill C-36, the Protection of Communities and Exploited Persons Act (PCEPA), in 2014 (see also Belak, this collection). A key feature of the new legislation is that it criminalized the purchase of sexual services for the first time in Canadian history. PCEPA was implemented despite a lack of evidence that it would address the harms associated with the previous sex work laws in Canada. However, in January 2013 the Vancouver Police Department had already adopted new Sex Work Enforcement Guidelines that shifted the focus away from charging sex workers and toward those who purchase sexual services. Vancouver thus became a de facto Swedish model environment in 2013 prior to the implementation of PCEPA in December 2014, providing a unique opportunity to evaluate how laws and policies that criminalize clients shape sex work transactions for street-based sex workers.

This chapter draws upon research that includes ethnographic fieldwork and qualitative interviews with street-involved sex workers about their working conditions, interactions with police, and negotiations of health and safety with clients in Vancouver from January through November 2013 following the implementation of the Sex Work Enforcement Guidelines by the Vancouver Police Department. Herein, we document how an enforcement strategy that targeted clients but not sex workers shaped sex workers' interactions with police and clients and resulted in the reproduction of harms created by the criminalization of sex workers. Owing to increased policing of clients, sex workers in our study had to work for longer periods of time and were compelled to accept less desirable clients in order to earn their needed level of income, compromising their health and safety. Policing strategies surrounding the criminalization of clients severely undermined sex workers' safety strategies and ability to negotiate transactions with clients (see also Khan, this collection). Our analysis provides strong empirical evidence that the continued criminalization and policing of clients negatively impacts sex workers' working conditions and their health and safety while reinforcing mistrust of police.

The AESHA Research Project in Vancouver

The research project discussed in this chapter was built on partnerships established in 2004 with sex worker, community, policy, and health stakeholders, and it ran alongside a sister project, An Evaluation of Sex Workers' Health Access (AESHA). AESHA is a community-based longitudinal study of over 800 sex workers that is focused on evaluating the physical, social, and policy environments shaping their health and safety (Shannon et al., 2007). Interview participants for the project on which this chapter is based were recruited through purposive sampling from the sex workers involved in the larger AESHA study in order to reflect variations in demographics (e.g., age, ethnicity, and gender) and in work environments (e.g., geographic neighbourhoods). Thirty-one sex workers (twenty-six cisgender and five transgender women) participated in qualitative interviews. The average age of participants was thirty-eight years (with a range of twenty-four to fifty-three); twenty-one identified as white, eight as Indigenous, and two as members of other visible minorities. The study focused on experiences of street-involved sex workers, a segment of the sex industry that is disproportionately the target of criminalization and enforcement (Lewis, Maticka-Tyndale, Shaver, and Schramm, 2005; Lowman, 2000; Shannon et al., 2008).

Semi-structured interviews were conducted using an interview guide designed to encourage discussion of working conditions, police interactions, and the negotiation of health and safety in transactions with clients.[1] Interview transcripts and ethnographic data were analyzed using thematic analyses. All textual data (i.e., transcripts and ethnographic data) were analyzed using an inductive and iterative process facilitated by the qualitative-analysis software ATLAS.TI. The initial coding framework was based on key themes reflected in the interview guide, participants' accounts, and field notes. Additional, conceptually driven substantive codes (e.g., trust in police and control over sex work transactions) were then applied. Included alongside the qualitative analyses were longitudinal quantitative data from the AESHA study on physical and sexual workplace violence among sex workers in the eight months prior to and following implementation of the Sex Work Enforcement Guidelines (i.e., May–December 2012 and January–August 2013). Analysis was conducted using the statistical software SAS and was restricted to sex workers in the AESHA study who solicited and/or serviced clients on the street. Descriptive frequencies and bivariate analyses were used to test for statistical significance by time period of the implementation (i.e., the eight months before vs. the eight months after implementation) and were reported using odds ratios (OR), 95 percent confidence intervals (CIs), and *p*-values. Finally, we also drew upon official police statistics on prostitution-related Criminal Code charges in Vancouver (VPD, 2014).

Sex Workers' Experiences with the Sex Work Enforcement Guidelines in Vancouver

The Sex Work Enforcement Guidelines emerged after two decades of tremendous violence and murder of street-based sex workers in Vancouver. They were the result of strong pressure from sex worker and other community organizations, legal experts, and academics calling for reforms to local policing practices (Oppal, 2012). The Sex Work Enforcement Guidelines set out a strategy for "open communication" with sex workers in order to prevent violence by prioritizing their safety over enforcement measures (VPD, 2013b). However, the guidelines did not change enforcement practices with clients. In fact, on its website the Vancouver Police Department confirmed that it continued to "target both pimps and customers" (VPD, 2013a).[2] Sex workers' narratives and researchers' ethnographic observations indicated that although police maintained a high level of visibility, they eased up on charging or arresting sex workers and showed increased concern for their safety. Most sex workers in our study reported that they experienced a gradual transformation in policing over a number of years rather than an abrupt change in policing practice with the publication of the Sex Work Enforcement Guidelines in January 2013. The vast majority of street-based sex workers, regardless of gender, ethnicity, and the neighbourhoods where they worked, reported that their interactions with police when soliciting clients were more positive and were generally focused on their safety. Some felt that they were interacting less with police, provided that they solicited clients in two areas of the city that functioned as de facto zones of sex work tolerance, where police generally refrained from enforcing sex work laws: "There's more [police] presence. There's not very many more interactions. Before, the interactions were always there. They'd come and pull you right out of [a] car and, like, push you over. They'd get away with it back then, you know. But now it's like they don't interact" (Anna,[3] transgender woman).

Sex workers indicated that although police permitted sex work–related activities in the tolerance zones, clients continued to be at risk of police scrutiny. According to official statistics of the Vancouver Police Department, charges for sex work–related Criminal Code offences rose by almost 30 percent,[4] from twenty-nine in 2012 to thirty-seven in 2013, after the implementation of the Sex Work Enforcement Guidelines (VPD, 2014). Unfortunately, no statistics are available regarding the proportion of sex workers versus clients who were charged. However, participants' accounts suggest that the rise in prostitution-related offences likely reflected an increase in enforcement efforts targeting clients: "[Clients] do get stopped. A couple of my regulars, they've been chased off the street. They're not allowed to come downtown anymore. Down here, they're bad for that. I guess it's more so not the girls they go after – it's the guys" (Maria, cisgender woman).

Criminalization of Clients Does Not Deter Sex Work

Even when police targeted clients, the participants in this study, many of whom were living in poverty and marginalized due to illicit substance use, reported that they continued to work for the obvious reason that they needed an income. Ethnographic observations and sex workers' narratives indicated that police targeting clients did not deter street-based sex work. For many participants, enforcement that was focused on clients forced them to spend longer hours on the street to earn an income. Thus, contrary to the objectives of criminalizing clients, impeding sex workers' ability to connect with potential clients did not result in these women doing less street-based sex work. Instead, having access to fewer clients made it harder to earn an income. This situation obliged sex workers to accept clients or to provide services (e.g., sex without a condom) that they would otherwise reject due to safety concerns, thereby directly increasing their risks of physical and sexual violence and poor health:

> While they're going around chasing johns away from pulling up beside you, I have to stay out for longer ... whereas if we weren't harassed, we would be able to be more choosy as to where we get in, who we get in with, you know what I mean? Because of being so cold and being harassed, I got into a car where I normally wouldn't have. The guy didn't look at my face right away. And I just hopped in 'cause I was cold and tired of standing out there. And you know, he put something to my throat. And I had to do it for nothing, whereas I would have made sure he looked at me if I hadn't been waiting out there so long. (Violet, cisgender woman)

Criminalization of Clients Severely Limits Sex Workers' Safety Strategies

Our study found that policing strategies targeting clients reproduce the harms created by the broader criminalization of sex work. Analyses of the prevalence of workplace physical and sexual violence against street-based sex workers in Vancouver indicated that the shift in policing policy did not increase sex workers' safety. Specifically, in the eight months before the Sex Work Enforcement Guidelines were brought in, 23.7 percent of sex workers interviewed as part of the AESHA study reported work-related physical and sexual violence (19.3 percent reported physical abuse, and 15.6 percent reported rape). In the eight months following the guidelines' implementation, 24.6 percent experienced work-related physical and sexual violence (22 percent reported physical abuse, and 14 percent reported rape). Thus there was no significant change in sex workers' experiences of physical and sexual violence in the eight months following the guidelines' implementation (OR = 1.05; 95 percent CI = 0.70–1.58; p = 0.804).

Qualitative analysis of the sex workers' narratives reveals three key mechanisms by which criminalization and police targeting of clients severely impact sex workers' ability to negotiate their working conditions and transactions with clients. First, we found that sex workers are unable to adequately screen clients and negotiate the terms of sexual transactions. Sex workers emphasized that when clients are targeted by police, it is in both the client's and sex worker's interests not to get pulled over by police: "Well, usually, I try to hop in the car right away, right? 'Cause I don't want to get seen talking, in case a cop drives by or something ... I'll hop in and then we can like negotiate and talk, you know? First, I like to make sure that nobody's around or following or anything" (Maria, cisgender woman). The policing of clients directly undermines sex workers' ability to screen potential clients, including checking "bad date" sheets for past violent perpetrators and detecting possible weapons or intoxication, and it undermines their ability to negotiate the terms of the sexual transactions before entering a vehicle, including where the date will take place, the fee and types of sexual services, and the use of condoms. These practices have been well documented as critical to sex workers' ability to control their health and safety, including protections from violence, abuse, and HIV or other sexually transmitted infections (Krüsi et al., 2012; Shannon et al., 2009; van der Meulen and Durisin, 2008).

Sex workers further indicated that many clients insist on engaging in sex work transactions away from known sex work areas where there is heightened police presence. Participants reported that being alone with clients in unknown, secluded, industrial areas where there is little chance for help puts sex workers at increased risk of violence and rape and reduces their ability to negotiate the transaction on their own terms, elevating the risk of client condom refusal:

> Clients are worried about police. To avoid police, they wanna move to a different area. I don't want to go out of my zone, right ... Once you get out there, like you know their turf, so it's harder for me 'cause it's their comfort zone or, so they act differently, you know what I mean? Yeah, it never ends up good. (Sandra, cisgender woman)

Lastly, sex workers said they were unable to access police protection. The main objective of the Sex Work Enforcement Guidelines is to foster more trusting relationships between sex workers and police and to prioritize the safety of sex workers. A striking feature of many sex workers' accounts was that they perceived police inquiring about their safety as a nuisance at best and as a form of police harassment at worst. In a context where clients are police enforcement targets, sex workers indicated that it is difficult for police to fulfil their stated objective of prioritizing sex worker safety. Even conversations between sex workers and police can have a destabilizing effect, as any police interactions may scare away clients and raise suspicions that a sex worker might be an undercover police officer:

> It's a drag, you know? I'm out there to make money, not waste twenty minutes talking to them [police]. And then I'm talking to them, and half the dates that see me talking to them now think maybe I'm a cop, so they don't wanna stop. Now they know the cops are around, they don't wanna stop, or they wonder what I've done to attract the cops, so they don't wanna stop, like it's just a hassle, you know? (Charlene, cisgender woman)

Similarly, an important aspect of sex workers' safety is the ability to report theft, violence, and sexual harassment to police (Lewis et al., 2005; van der Meulen and Durisin, 2008). However, the majority of sex workers voiced reservations about reporting such incidents to police. Many sex workers, drawing on historic discrimination and maltreatment by police, doubted that police would take their complaints seriously. They also reported that continued criminalization of clients constituted a significant barrier to reporting violence to police, as any information about where they worked could be used to refine enforcement strategies:

> No, I would never go to the cops [to report violence]. Because it makes it look like we shouldn't be out there, like we can't take care of ourselves. I feel like if I went and reported some of these things, that it might do more harm to the working profession than do good. So I don't do that. Basically, we have to fend for ourselves. They don't really like us to begin with. (Rose, cisgender woman)

Targeting Clients Reproduces the Harms of Criminalization

Our research suggests that criminalization and policing strategies that target clients reproduce the harms created by the criminalization of sex workers, particularly the risks of violence and abuse. This approach has little to no effect on preventing street-based sex work and does not reduce the prevalence of sex work–related violence. Street-involved sex workers living in poverty, Indigenous sex workers, and transgender sex workers have historically been exposed most directly to the negative effects of restrictive policing and criminalized sex work laws (Lewis et al., 2005; Lyons et al., 2017; Shannon et al., 2009). Evidence from Sweden indicates that although all sex workers are negatively affected by the criminalization of clients, marginalized sex workers are most negatively impacted, as they lack the resources to use online advertising and to communicate with clients by phone in order to reduce police scrutiny (Scoular, 2004).

Although rhetorically powerful and politically appealing to some, policies and laws that criminalize clients and purport to prioritize the safety of sex workers are characterized by a fundamental conceptual inconsistency. Our findings suggest that, in practice, policies that criminalize clients cannot be reconciled with policies that aim to prioritize the safety of sex workers. As we have seen, police efforts to prioritize sex worker safety notwithstanding, when clients remain enforcement targets, sex workers continue to be at increased risk of physical and sexual violence and perceive police concern for their safety as a form of nuisance and harassment.

The very existence of specific laws to regulate sex work speaks to the stigma associated with sex work and to the link between sex work legislation and morality (Bruckert and Hannem, 2013). In Canada, as in most settings globally, there are already laws in place that target various forms of violence and exploitation that may arise in the context of sex work, including assault, sexual assault, trafficking in persons, criminal harassment, extortion, and kidnapping. Given the negative impact of prohibitive sex work laws and enforcement practices, our findings lend further support to calls for the full decriminalization of sex work in Canada and for the repeal of PCEPA in order to ensure the health, safety, and human rights of sex workers.

Notes

This chapter is a revised version of two previous publications. The first is Krüsi, A., Pacey, K., Bird, L., Taylor, C., Chettiar, J., Allan, S., Bennett, D., Montaner, J.S., Kerr, T., & Shannon, K. (2014). Criminalisation of clients: Reproducing vulnerabilities for violence and poor health among street-based sex workers in Canada – a qualitative study. *British Medical Journal Open*, *4*(6), 1–10. https://doi.org/10.1136/bmjopen-2014-005191. The second is Sex Workers United Against Violence, Allan, S., Bennett, D., Chettiar, J., Jackson, G., Krüsi, A., Pacey, K., Porth, K., Price, M., Shannon, K., & Taylor, C. (2014). *'My work should not cost me my life': The case against criminalizing the purchase of sex in Canada*. Vancouver, BC: Pivot Legal Society, Sex Workers United Against Violence, and Gender and Sexual Health Initiative. Retrieved from http://www.pivotlegal.org/my_work.

1 All participants provided informed consent and were remunerated with a $30 honorarium for their time, expertise, and travel. The study holds ethical approval by the Providence Healthcare/University of British Columbia Research Ethics Board.
2 As of November 2016, this statement has been removed from the Counter Exploitation Unit website of the Vancouver Police Department.
3 All names used are pseudonyms.
4 Official statistics of the Vancouver Police Department retrieved in January 2014 indicated a 51 percent increase in sex work–related Criminal Code offences between 2012 and 2013. However, these statisitcs were revised down to a 28 percent rise by the Vancouver Police Department on August 12, 2014.

References

Amnesty International. (2016). *The human cost of 'crushing' the market: Criminalization of sex work in Norway*. London, UK: Amnesty International.
Bruckert, C., & Hannem, S. (2013). Rethinking the prostitution debates: Transcending structural stigma in systemic responses to sex work. *Canadian Journal of Law and Society*, *28*(1), 43–63. https://doi.org/10.1017/cls.2012.2
Deering, K.N., Lyons, T., Feng, C.X., Nosyk, B., Strathdee, S.A., Montaner, J.S., & Shannon, K. (2013). Client demands for unsafe sex: The socioeconomic risk environment for HIV among street and off-street sex workers. *JAIDS: Journal of Acquired Immune Deficiency Syndrome*, *63*(4), 522–31. https://doi.org/10.1097/QAI.0b013e3182968d39

Global Commission on HIV and the Law. (2012). *HIV and the law: Risks, rights and health*. New York, NY: United Nations Development Program.

Goodyear, M., & Weitzer, R. (2011). International trends in the control of sexual services. In S. Dewey & P. Kelley (Eds.), *Policing pleasure: Sex work, policy and the state in global perspective* (pp. 16–30). New York, NY: New York University Press. https://doi.org/10.18574/nyu/9780814785089.003.0002

Krüsi, A., Chettiar, J., Ridgway, A., Abbott, J., Strathdee, S.A., & Shannon, K. (2012). Negotiating safety and sexual risk reduction with clients in unsanctioned safer indoor sex work environments: A qualitative study. *American Journal of Public Health, 102*(6), 1154–59. https://doi.org/10.2105/AJPH.2011.300638

Lewis, J., Maticka-Tyndale, E., Shaver, F.M., & Schramm, H. (2005). Managing risk and safety on the job: The experiences of Canadian sex workers. *Journal of Psychology and Human Sexuality, 17*(1–2), 147–67. https://doi.org/10.1300/J056v17n01_09

Lowman, J. (2000). Violence and the outlaw status of (street) prostitution in Canada. *Violence Against Women, 6*(9), 987–1011. https://doi.org/10.1177/10778010022 182245

Lyons, T., Krüsi, A., Pierre, L., Kerr, T., Small, W., & Shannon, K. (2017). Negotiating violence in the context of transphobia and criminalization: The experiences of trans sex workers in Vancouver, Canada. *Qualitative Health Research, 27*(2), 182–90. https://doi.org/10.1177/1049732315613311

Oppal, W.T. (2012). *Forsaken: The report of the Missing Women Commission of Inquiry*. Retrieved from http://www.missingwomeninquiry.ca/obtain-report/

Oppenheim, M. (2014, February 26). MEPs vote to criminalise buying sex. *The Guardian* (London). Retrieved from https://www.theguardian.com/global-development/2014/feb/26/meps-vote-criminalise-buying-sex-european-parliament

Scoular, J. (2004). Criminalising 'punters': Evaluating the Swedish position on prostitution. *Journal of Social Welfare and Family Law, 26*(2), 195–210. https://doi.org/10.1080/014180304200023114

Shannon, K., Bright, V., Allinott, S., Alexson, D., Gibson, K., & Tyndall, M.W. (2007). Community-based HIV prevention research among substance-using women in survival sex work: The Maka Project Partnership. *Harm Reduction Journal, 4*(1), 20–26. https://doi.org/10.1186/1477-7517-4-20

Shannon, K., & Csete, J. (2010). Violence, condom negotiation, and HIV/STI risk among sex workers. *Journal of the American Medical Association, 304*(5), 573–74. https://doi.org/10.1001/jama.2010.1090

Shannon, K., Kerr, T., Allinott, S., Chettiar, J., Shoveller, J., & Tyndall, M.W. (2008). Social and structural violence and power relations in mitigating HIV risk of drug-using women in survival sex work. *Social Science and Medicine, 66*(4), 911–21. https://doi.org/10.1016/j.socscimed.2007.11.008

Shannon, K., Kerr, T., Strathdee, S.A., Shoveller, J., Montaner, J.S., & Tyndall, M.W. (2009). Prevalence and structural correlates of gender based violence among a prospective cohort of female sex workers. *British Medical Journal, 339*, b2939. https://doi.org/10.1136/bmj.b2939

Simić, M., & Rhodes, T. (2009). Violence, dignity and HIV vulnerability: Street sex work in Serbia. *Sociology of Health and Illness, 31*(1), 1–16. https://doi.org/10.1111/j.1467-9566.2008.01112.x

van der Meulen, E., & Durisin, E.M. (2008). Why decriminalize? How Canada's municipal and federal regulations increase sex workers' vulnerability. *Canadian Journal of Women and the Law, 20*(2), 289–311.

VPD (Vancouver Police Department). (2013a). *Counter Explotation Unit.* Retrieved from http://vancouver.ca/police/organization/investigation/investigative-services/special-investigation/vice.html

VPD (Vancouver Police Department). (2013b). *Sex work enforcement guidelines.* Retrieved from http://vancouver.ca/police/assets/pdf/reports-policies/sex-enforcement-guidelines.pdf

VPD (Vancouver Police Department). (2014). *Statistical reports by district and city totals: Year end comparison between 2012–2013.* Retrieved from http://vancouver.ca/police/organization/planning-research-audit/district-statistics.html

Cases

Canada (Attorney General) v. Bedford, 2013 SCC 72, [2013] 3 SCR 1101.

Legislation

Bill C-36, *Protection of Communities and Exploited Persons Act,* SC 2014, c. 25.

17

Everybody Knows Everybody
———— Sex Work in Rural and Small Communities

STACEY HANNEM

The majority of research on sex work in North America has been conducted in large urban centres. Although smaller cities have sometimes been included in analyses (see Benoit et al., 2014; Jeffrey and MacDonald, 2006), little attention has been paid to the particular dynamics of doing sex work in small cities and rural areas and to how these dynamics may differ from those of urban contexts. Based on semi-structured interviews with people involved in the sex industry in Brantford, Ontario, and the surrounding rural counties, this chapter examines the impact of rural and semi-rural location on how sex workers work.

The city of Brantford is located in southern Ontario, southwest of Hamilton in Brant County. With a population of approximately 95,000, Brantford is the only city located in Brant County and the two adjacent counties, Haldimand and Norfolk (BHN);[1] the remainder of the Brant County population comprises about 30,000 people. Once a bustling centre of manufacturing and trade, Brantford and the surrounding counties were hard hit by the recession of the 1980s and resulting economic and social decline, including the closure of factories and large employers and the mass exodus of small businesses from the downtown core, from which the community has yet to fully recover (Groarke, 2009). Adjacent to BHN is Six Nations of the Grand River, the largest First Nations reserve in Canada, with a population of just under 13,000. In this largely working-class region, the sex industry reflects the everyday realities of these communities.[2] Urban and rural sex workers share a number of common experiences, and many similarities between these groups emerged in the research. However, for the purposes of this chapter, the analysis focuses on experiences and issues that are unique to rural and small-city sex work in order to better understand the diversity of sex workers' experiences in Canada.

Researching Sex Work in BHN

This research draws on thirty semi-structured, in-depth interviews with individuals who were or had been involved in the sex industry in BHN, comprising twenty-four women and six men (all cisgender). The research was conducted in partnership with the local advocacy group REAL (Resources, Education, Advocacy for Local Sex Work); participants self-selected by responding to posters or local newspaper articles describing the research.[3] They were given a $40 honorarium for their time, ranging from 45 minutes to 3.5 hours. The interviews were transcribed and coded using a process of thematic and analytical coding that attended to sensitizing concepts arising from previous sex work research in Canada. The research paid particular attention to those themes and experiences that appeared to be distinctly relevant to the rural and semi-rural context.

Nineteen participants were actively involved in the industry at the time of the interview (eighteen sex workers and one manager). Eleven participants were inactive or in the process of moving toward mainstream employment; however, all but one of these had worked in the previous year. Of the six men in the sample, four were sex workers (three serving female clients), and two identified as managers of female escorts (one active and one inactive). The participants had experience in different types of sex work,[4] including as street-based sex workers (9), in-call and out-call sex workers (17),[5] massage parlour attendants (3), erotic dancers (4), and managers (5).[6] Ages ranged from 19 to 53, with an average age of 32 years, and experience in the industry varied from 1 year to more than 20 years, with an average of 7.5 years. The majority of the participants were white; four identified as Indigenous and three as Black.

Although this sample represents workers labouring in various sectors of the sex industry, it is also quite homogenous, reflecting the broader economic and social realities of a largely working-class region. There is a small sector of travelling workers in this area whose approach to their work is characterized by a more urban sensibility and an understanding of the political dimensions of sex work, but the majority of individuals who participated in this research were working-class people who happened to be involved in sexual labour. These "everyday sex workers" (Sterling, 2015) do not have a political agenda, are not actively engaged in fighting for their right to work, and may in fact not even know the laws that surround sex work in Canada. They do not have great privilege, but neither are they the most marginal, and the nature of their work does not necessarily distinguish their lives from those of other working-class people. They face the same struggles that many working-class people in Canada confront. They view their sex work as a pragmatic, income-generating activity, and their realities are often lost in the normative discourses of "high-class call girls" and "exploited victims" (see also James, this collection; Love, this collection). This chapter attempts to briefly examine some of the key features of the experiences of everyday sex workers in a semi-rural, working-class community.

Travel for Work

One feature of rural and small-city sex work is the commonality of transient work, or travel for the purposes of work. Travel out of and into rural areas takes on a variety of forms and may be motivated by a range of concerns. In some cases, sex workers in rural areas and small cities are, in fact, urban or transient escorts. By travelling from town to town and periodically spending short amounts of time in the region, these escorts are able to capitalize on the commodity of newness. Working out of local hotels and advertising their services as available for a "limited time only," they attract clients who are seeking variety in their sexual experiences (see also Raguparan, this collection). This is a significant market in BHN; analysis of local online ads and interviews with travelling escorts found that they were able to command a higher price for their services than local workers. Because they are travelling into a smaller market, with less choice, travelling escorts find that they are able to serve a larger number of clients in less time. They attribute this to a lack of competition, particularly in very rural areas. As Lucy (twenty-three, escort) described,

> [In the city] you're competing, and if there's somebody that doesn't wanna pay your price, then they're just gonna find someone for free or someone younger who doesn't know what the hell's going on. So me being out of town, it's kinda like, "You don't have an option buddy. Unless you're gonna drive for three hours to someone else, all you got is me over here."

Conversely, some sex workers from small cities or rural areas travel to larger urban centres to work so that they can access a greater number of potential clients and can charge more for their services. Molly (twenty-five, escort) described travel for work as one means of augmenting her income:

> Like, I can go to Niagara or Hamilton or Toronto and get a room for the weekend and just make way more than I could here. And I can charge more too. Like, here I can make 120 for an hour. But in the city I can charge 200, or even more if I can splurge on a nice hotel. I put up an ad on Backpage, and I'm the new girl in town, and I'll just get tons of calls. So if business is slow and I need the money, sometimes I just go.

Sometimes, rural sex workers travel not because of market demands or opportunities but due to a desire to separate their private and professional worlds and to preserve anonymity. Maggie (thirty-five, escort and former street-based sex worker) travelled out of town on weekends to work at least once a month; she similarly found that the larger market was quite lucrative. Although she provided a small number of regular clients with in-call services at her home, she explained that she did most of her work out of town in order to avoid being outed as a sex worker to her neighbours:

> I have a friend who is a guy, and he'll take me up there [to the city]. He'll rent the place for me. He gets a motel for me. He rents that ... and then the calls keep coming and coming, and he'll put an ad in the paper. Probably, it's $6,000 worth in a weekend, so it's pretty good out there ... It's easy to get away from here, you know what I mean? So I don't let too many guys know that I work here though because I got neighbours. I don't want people to get that impression. But when I go out of town with him, it's fine.

Anna (thirty-one, escort) similarly described working out of town as a means of avoiding stigma. When asked whether she had ever experienced any judgment in the community due to her work, she replied, "No, because nobody knows. Nobody else. That's why you do out-of-town clients."

Although the choice to engage in transient work or to travel for work is a pragmatic one with respect to increasing access to markets and avoiding stigma, it also poses other potential complications for sex workers. A significant factor in the dynamics of transient work is the fact that, like Maggie above, many workers rely on third parties to assist with their travel. In most cases, the choice to work with a third party is one means of accessing the capital or credit necessary to facilitate travel and cover the costs involved; workers may not have their own means of transportation or a credit card for hotel bookings. Jade (twenty-eight, escort) explained that her friend's boyfriend would help them to travel from their small town to a larger centre:

> Like, you pay the rooms out of your own money, so they're just renting them for you because they have the Visa cards and all that stuff you need, right? So anyways, we went to Niagara Falls ... I think I was only paying, like, 30 percent. So a half an hour was 100 dollars ... so I would give them like 40 or 30 bucks out of a 100.

Another escort, Amanda (thirty-three), often did out-calls to rural areas, but she did not have a driver's licence. She explained: "My husband drives, so, yeah, he'll take me there. What I need goes, so it's basically – last night I pulled him out of bed at one o'clock in the morning, and then he had to get up at six a.m. to go to work." Laughing, Amanda noted, "He wasn't too happy!"

The dynamics of travel and its intersections with third parties in the sex industry are significant given the current state of heightened societal and media attention to the possibility of sex trafficking (see Lepp, 2013). It is important to carefully look at the markers that distinguish transient work or travel for work from human trafficking. Under the law, for an activity to be defined as "human trafficking," there must be an element of coercion or deception that compels the individual to provide sexual or other forms of labour, and the individual must be someone who does not have control over her own movements (*Criminal Code*, 1985, s. 279.01–279.04). Merely travelling from one place to another to do sex work does not constitute human trafficking any more than does the daily commute of hundreds of thousands of workers in Canada. However, the offence prohibiting "material benefit from sexual services" (*Criminal Code*, 1985, s. 286.2) contains a reverse-onus provision, which means that in order to avoid conviction, third parties and the sex workers who work with them would have to prove that any third-party involvement is not coercive and is proportionally beneficial to the sex worker. Many of the participants in this research were or had been involved with third parties, and their experiences varied widely from mutual partnerships and employee-employer arrangements to outright coercion and abuse (for more detailed analyses of the dynamics of third-party management in sex work, see Bruckert and Law, 2013; see also Gillies and Bruckert, this collection). However, the participants themselves clearly distinguished between the kinds of mutually beneficial arrangements that facilitated their travel for work and coercive experiences with third parties.

Stigma and Small Towns

Travel for work is one means of managing stigma (Goffman, 1963) by attempting to minimize the likelihood of being outed as a sex worker and subsequently encountering negative reactions in the community. In small towns and cities, sex workers who desire to remain anonymous may face difficulties in compartmentalizing their occupation from their social lives given the realities of small communities, where it often seems that "everybody knows everybody" (see also Winters and MacDonald, this collection). Although street work is relatively less common in small cities, there is a small street-based market in Brantford; working on this stroll opens workers up to possible violence and harassment:

> People would start knowing [me] from the street. Like people just driving by. Or people having a normal day. So if I was working on [the street], there's bars and stuff there too. So they would kind of see the same girls walking around, which is fine. But then they would start calling us whores and sluts and pigs and all sorts of different names ... There was comments always coming out of vehicles or from other people. (Nancy, forty-three, former street-based sex worker)

Indoor work is often seen as more anonymous and less risky than street-based work in terms of identity management. Certainly, working behind closed doors affords many sex workers the ability to "pass" as non-sex-working. However, in a small city or town with fluid social channels, even indoor work can pose a significant risk to identity. Maggie did the majority of her work out of town and attempted to keep her work discreet, but she still encountered outing and negative treatment in the community: "I'll hear people say, 'Look at that fucking whore over there,' or something if I'm sitting in a bar or something like that, you know? And you hear things and you're just, like, 'Whatever.'"

Some participants identified their online advertisements as a possible site of outing. Sandy (twenty-five, escort) was concerned about a lack of anonymity in small towns: "I work everywhere. I don't like coming back to small places like this 'cause I can't go on the street and walk because everybody knows my face. It's like everyone sees Backpage, like people will read Backpage like the news is how it seems."

The very social networks that are assumed to make small communities safer pose significant risks of stigma and hostility to sex workers when "everybody knows everybody" (Jade, twenty-eight, former escort). As a result, many sex workers go to great lengths to be discreet about their occupation, and the rural industry is much less visible, although relatively no less active, than the urban industry. Many members of the BHN community were surprised to learn that there is a significant sex industry in the region; stereotypes of street-based sex work and the greater routinization of Internet-based advertising and indoor services permit sex workers in small communities to avoid being identified and stigmatized. However, the very stereotypes of street-based sex workers that insulate small-town workers from being identified and outed also contribute to their marginalization when sex work intersects with drug use.

Intersections of Sex Work and Drug Use

The sex industry in BHN, as in any region, is a reflection of the broader community; the prevalence of current or former drug users among the participants in this research speaks to habitual drug use as a key issue in this region. Research on sex work often identifies high levels of drug use among street-based workers (see Bruckert and Chabot, 2010; Krüsi et al., 2014); however, this study found an equally high prevalence of habitual or heavy drug use among indoor workers. Formal sex work to pay for a pre-existing drug habit or informally trading sex for drugs are key features of the sex industry in BHN.

Contrary to dominant social constructions that paint drug use or addiction as invalidating individual agency and negating sex work as a form of labour, participants in this research who engaged in sex work to pay for substance use did not see themselves as victims of addiction. Rather, they viewed their sex work as a viable means of maintaining a pattern of drug use that they were unable or unwilling to end. Relatedly, although many individuals in the health or social service professions assume that when individuals stop using drugs they will also stop selling sex, there is not necessarily a clear-cut relationship between ending drug use and ending sex work. Three individuals in this research had stopped using substances but continued to do sex work, one of whom was Maggie: "Drugs, yeah. I needed drug money and stuff like that. I'm sober now but, so the money still comes, but it stays ... Yeah, no. It's not about the drugs anymore. Chasing money, and that's it." Other participants talked about how much better off they would be financially if they could stop their drug use and continue sex work: "I wish I wasn't smoking [crack], and I wish I could just save my money because, I'm telling you, in one month I think I'd have $15,000" (Rose, thirty-two, escort).

The communities of BHN have identified substance use as a significant issue and have invested resources in services for harm reduction. Notably, Brantford has five methadone clinics, and these services are also available in small villages in the counties, such as the town of Simcoe in Norfolk County, which has two methadone clinics serving a population of approximately 15,000 and surrounding rural areas. The number of indoor workers in this research who habitually used drugs is reflective of the prevalence of functioning users in the broader community, many of whom are engaged in service or blue-collar work. This observation directs us to consider and challenge classist and moralistic assumptions about the relationship between substance use and labour; the use of money earned via sex work to pay for drugs does not invalidate sex work as labour and reduce sex workers to victims any more than spending money on drugs invalidates factory work as labour. There is a tendency to exercise judgment about how individuals spend their money and which circumstances render decisions about sex work "legitimate"; sex work for food, for rent, or to pay bills is "understandable," whereas sex work for drugs is not. Ironically, even some sex workers internalize these kinds of moral judgments about the legitimacy of their work:

> I wish I was [using sex work to pay rent] because that would be more dignifying. But I'm not feeding my kids; I'm not paying my rent. I don't have kids. I commend people who do it to feed their kids or pay their rent or pay their mortgage or bills. I'm doing it just for dope, which makes me feel like a piece of shit. But that's the life of an addict. (Wade, thirty, male escort)

Whereas community service professionals are apt to commend habitual substance users who are able to hold down employment, sex workers who use drugs are given no such credit for their ability to be self-employed and to keep a roof, however precarious, over their head. In a community with such a high prevalence of drug use, this moralism is made visible in the differential treatment of drug-using sex workers, who are routinely encouraged to stop using and "find another job." Although drug use may affect the conditions of sex workers and make their labour more dangerous (see also Bruckert and Chabot, 2010; Hannem, 2016),[7] sex workers in BHN who are also substance users are qualitatively no different from other blue-collar and low-income users in the community.

Conclusion

In many ways, the concerns of sex workers in rural communities mirror those working in urban areas. However, this chapter has provided a brief overview of some of the significant differences and unique aspects of sex work in the counties of Brant, Haldimand, and Norfolk. What is clear is that both researchers and community service agencies should pay more attention to sex work in rural spaces and to how the particular dynamics of rural sex work challenge social assumptions about the nature of sex work in Canada.

Notes

1 Collectively, the region is often referred to as "Brant, Haldimand, Norfolk," which I abbreviate to BHN.
2 See Hannem (2016) for a complete overview of the research findings.
3 See Hannem and Tigchelaar (2016) for a complete description of participant recruitment and the method.
4 Some participants had been involved in more than one type of sex work, so the numbers total more than 30.
5 In-calls involve clients coming to the worker's hotel room or home or to another work location, whereas out-calls entail the worker coming to the client's hotel room or home or to another location.
6 In addition to the two male managers, three women had been involved in managing other workers, as well as engaging in sex work themselves.
7 Arguably, other types of labour, such as factory work or construction work, are also made more dangerous when the worker is under the influence of drugs or alcohol.

References

Benoit, C., Atchison, C., Casey, L., Jansson, M., McCarthy, B., Phillips, R., ... Shaver, F.M. (2014). *A 'working paper' prepared as background to Building on the Evidence: An International Symposium on the Sex Industry in Canada.* Retrieved from http://www.nswp.org/resource/gender-violence-and-health-contexts-vulnerability-resiliencies-and-care-among-people-the

Bruckert, C., & Chabot, F. (2010). *Challenges: Ottawa area sex workers speak out.* Report prepared in collaboration with POWER (Prostitutes of Ottawa-Gatineau Work, Educate, Resist). Retrieved from www.nswp.org/sites/nswp.org/files/POWER_Report_Challenges.pdf

Bruckert, C., & Law, T. (2013). *Beyond pimps, procurers and parasites: Mapping third parties in the incall/outcall sex industry.* Retrieved from http://www.nswp.org/resource/beyond-pimps-procurers-and-parasites-mapping-third-parties-the-incalloutcall-sex-industry

Goffman, E. (1963). *Stigma: Notes on the management of spoiled identity.* Englewood Cliffs, NJ: Prentice-Hall.

Groarke, L. (2009). *Reinventing Brantford: A university comes downtown.* Toronto, ON: Natural Heritage Books.

Hannem, S. (2016). *Let's talk about sex work: Report of the REAL working group for Brantford, Brant, Haldimand, and Norfolk, assessing the needs of sex workers in our community.* Retrieved from http://www.sexworkisrealwork.com/about

Hannem, S., & Tigchelaar, A. (2016). Doing it in public: Dilemmas of images, voice, and constructing publics in public sociology on sex work. *Symbolic Interaction, 39*(4), 634–53. https://doi.org/10.1002/symb.260

Jeffrey, L.A., & MacDonald, G. (2006). *Sex workers in the Maritimes talk back.* Vancouver, BC: UBC Press.

Krüsi, A., Pacey, K., Bird, L., Taylor, C., Chettier, J., Allan, S., ... Shannon, K. (2014). Criminalisation of clients: Reproducing vulnerabilities for violence and poor health among street-based sex workers in Canada – a qualitative study. *British Medical Journal Open, 4*(6), 1–10. http://dx.doi.org/10.1136/bmjopen-2014-005191

Lepp, A. (2013). Repeat performance? Human trafficking and the 2010 Winter Olympic Games. In E. van der Meulen, E.M. Durisin, & V. Love (Eds.), *Selling sex: Experience, advocacy, and research on sex work in Canada* (pp. 251–68). Vancouver, BC: UBC Press.

Sterling, A. (2015). *The 'everyday' escort in the shadow of the law: An examination of legal consciousness and the effects of Bill C-36 on independent escorts.* (Unpublished MA major research paper). University of Ottawa, Ottawa, Ontario.

Legislation

Criminal Code, RSC 1985, c. C-46.

18

Hypocrisy in "Sin City"

────── Space, Place, and Sex Work Stigma in St. John's

LAURA WINTERS AND GAYLE MACDONALD

In comparison to the rest of the country, including the three other provinces that comprise Atlantic Canada, Newfoundland and Labrador is a place unto itself. The island nation joined Canada in 1949, but a fierce spirit of separateness remains on "The Rock."[1] Newfoundlanders have a strong sense of attachment to place, a distinctive cultural identity, and provincial cultural nationalism (Statistics Canada, 2015). Cultural specificity is reflected in the dialect of the province, colourful language, resilient family attachments, and pride in knowing one's neighbours. Unique to St. John's as a capital city is its small population size, which is only 55 percent of Halifax's population (Statistics Canada, 2016). The context of social and spatial proximity in Newfoundland produces unique experiences of sex work. What can sex workers in Newfoundland teach us about selling sex in environments where everyone knows your name? And your business?

This chapter draws on thirty-two interviews that Laura Winters conducted in 2013 with women and men sex workers in and around St. John's.[2] Participants engaged in a wide variety of sex work, including street-based, massage, escorting independently or through agencies, dancing, and webcam performance.[3] Many stated that they were happy with their jobs, whereas some expressed the desire to change their situation or status. Two women self-identified as survivors of child sexual exploitation and reported experiencing exploitation and/or trafficking as youth. Other participants had significant economic privilege and left high-paying jobs to engage in sex work.

To access people working in many types of sex work, diverse sampling methods were used, including posters placed in the washrooms of community organizations and other public spaces, as well as in two massage parlours and an erotic dance club's dressing room. Information about the research project was posted on three websites where workers advertise sexual services, and some participants were referred by community organizations. Other participants learned about the project through word of mouth. The interviews were qualitative, open-ended, and participant-driven; they framed sex workers as the experts of their own lives. The interview transcripts were analyzed using Miller's (2000) method of discourse analysis, which examines routine talk as a "claims making enterprise," and were coded thematically for markers of stigma, resistance, and subjectivity. The research process was presented both as an opportunity for sex workers to "talk back" (Jeffrey and MacDonald, 2006) to the ideas and perceptions that others hold about them and their lives and as a platform for sex workers to articulate their understanding of the world around them and their place in it.

With regard to judgment of sex work, the "whore stigma" is well documented (Pheterson, 1996) and positions the sex worker "outside" of the normative boundaries of "proper" sexual behaviour. Stigma is an attribute that is deeply discrediting and usually attached to norm infractions, resulting in the devaluation of the person (Goffman, 1963). In what follows, we outline some of the factors identified by research participants that contribute to the stigmatization of sex work in St. John's and reflect on their experiences of that stigma. Interestingly, sex workers felt that the general public held the seemingly conflicting belief that sex work did not happen in Newfoundland, while still passing judgment on and stigmatizing those who engage in it. This binary of wilful blindness and moral intolerance is a theme throughout this chapter that, according to participants, is rooted in religion.

"Open Your Eyes": Perceived Public Ignorance of the Sex Industry

> I can guarantee you, someone who lives on either side of you has either paid for it or done it themselves. People are just ignorant to it.
>
> (PARTICIPANT #25, FEMALE, STREET-BASED SEX WORKER)

Research in other parts of Atlantic Canada has found that people who do sex work perceive the public to hold negative attitudes toward both them and their work (Jeffrey and MacDonald, 2006). This was certainly the case in Newfoundland; however, interestingly, the sex workers interviewed also felt that much of the general public considers sex work to be something that happens only on "the mainland" (i.e., the rest of Canada) or in "big cities" like Toronto, Montreal, or even Halifax:

> It's not a very open-minded city. You can't compare it to Toronto or Montreal; it's been embedded there for years. They [sex workers in those places] have their own communities; it's still on the QT [quiet] here. It's slow in catching up and opening up, right? That'll come in time. (Participant #7, male, independent indoor sex worker)

Many participants expressed that "if people just opened their eyes," they would see that there is a thriving sex industry in the city:

> There's lots of shit going on in this city that the majority of people don't know or don't care to know. They don't want to know. They don't want to know because if you wanted to know and wanted to get involved in your community, all you gotta do is open your eyes. (Participant #5, female, independent escort)

The wilful blindness of the public to sex workers is reflected in the refusal of governmental agencies to acknowledge sex work in the province. In 2011 the provincial government commissioned a community agency to do a study on youth identified as sexually exploited (Community Youth Network–St. John's and CASEY, 2011) only to subsequently refuse to release it and to prevent community members involved from speaking publicly about the issue (*CBC News*, 2013). A request via the Access to Information Act resulted in the release of a redacted version of the report four years later (*CBC News*, 2015). By suppressing these findings, the government appears to be stating that "this doesn't happen here," reinforcing the wilful blindness around the sex industry in the province.

Although the consensus opinion was that the residents of St. John's were naive about the realities of the sex industry, this finding certainly did not mean that stigma was not an issue or that people were unconcerned about the ramifications of being outed in their communities. These preoccupations were compounded by the cultural specificities of St. John's as well as the size of the city. In what follows, participants speak at length about what St. John's small size means for them and their work.

"Who's Your Father?" The Impact of Social and Spatial Proximity

> So it was this girl, Amy, [who got me involved in sex work], and another
> girl, Linda. And Linda was from the same place I was from. And Amy, I
> knew Amy's two brothers ... I said, "Amy, you better not tell nobody, man."
> She said, "Will ya do it?" I said, "Fuck yes!"
>
> (PARTICIPANT #9, MALE, STREET-BASED SEX WORKER)

The quotation above highlights the interconnectedness of social circles in St. John's. Having grown up in small-island cultures ourselves (i.e., Newfoundland and Cape Breton, respectively), the authors know that when meeting individuals of similar age, it is common to realize that you have shared acquaintances. Some of the participants jokingly asked the researcher, "Who's your father?" It is a common question in small Newfoundland communities, as people often identify shared relatives or acquaintances. These intimate interpersonal webs can pose problems for sex workers (see also Hannem, this collection). The men and women in this research reported that they felt vulnerable to being outed to friends and family, especially when working outdoors. The same man quoted above was outed as a sex worker to his community and subsequently discovered the identity of the individual who shared the information:

> I was down sellin' myself, and someone from the same place where I live
> saw me get in a car and followed us down by the fuckin' lake. And saw
> buddy giving me head and passing me money. And it took a long time
> for me to figure out how this person knew. Bastard wouldn't come right
> out and say it to me, he was tellin' people, and it was coming back to
> me second-hand news. And I finally found out who it was, and he lived
> in the same community as me. (Participant #9, male, street-based sex
> worker)

Several women spoke about being outed to friends, family, and others who know them. One woman noted that her mother became aware of her work from someone in the community:

> My mom's a social worker, and she asked me about it one day. So somehow
> it got to her. Nothing ever came out openly through me, but somehow it got
> to her that that was something I was doing, and she asked me about it. And
> I was like, "That's bullshit, that's people. Because I'm a junkie, they're sayin'

I'm at that." I flipped out, basically, denying it. (Participant #16, female, street-based sex worker)

The level of familiarity and closeness of the community also increased the likelihood that participants would "run into" clients outside of work:

Go to Walmart or wherever, you'd always run into the guy and his wife. I would just look at him and half smile and go on. You know? ... Make sure the wife didn't see! (Participant #5, female, independent escort)

A woman who was working online doing webcam shows noted that clients were trying to find her in her "real life" based on the fact that she was from St. John's; she subsequently took steps to protect her identity:

I made the mistake when I first joined [the webcam website] to say I was from St. John's. So I started getting people, like within the first week of me joining, asking, "Do you go to MUN? Do you go to CONA?"[4] All those kinds of questions. I instantly changed it to, "Oh I live in Eastern Canada," and when I'm talking about the time zone of when my usual show times are, I used just Eastern Standard Time. (Participant #18, female, webcam worker)

Another male sex worker was so concerned about confidentiality that he agreed to participate in the interview only after being assured that it would be transcribed and the data erased immediately afterward. Despite the need for discretion and problems posed by familiarity, he also spoke of security advantages of the small-city context:

St. John's is a small town, so there's ways to research the person you're going to see. And you know, there's a way to just basically investigate a little bit before I sort of jump into any situation ... I have to be comfortable, and my security and safety is number one. (Participant #19, male, independent escort)

Although the size of St. John's offers those engaged in sex work some security advantages, it also imposes a lack of anonymity that can lead to stigma, discrimination, and violence (WHO et al., 2013). Sex workers' experiences of stigma are explored in the following section, where participants discuss its perceived religious roots.

"Holier Than Thou": Sex Work Stigma, Family, and Religiosity

As is the case with sex workers in the rest of Canada, the Newfoundlanders in this research project spoke extensively about the stigma associated with the sex industry (Bruckert, 2012; Lazarus et al., 2012). A woman engaged in street-based sex work spent much of her interview talking about her family, which was her principal source of support, and about the impact of stigma:

> Well, I come from a good family. My father and mother were very mad; they don't want to see me down around there [on the stroll] like that ... People, of course, they sees me around, and that's even worse, 'cause now it's like you're labelled, you're named ... They know who you are basically ... I lost a lot of friends, and Mom and Dad are so mad; they hates letting me in [their house] because they don't want me down around here whatsoever. (Participant #14, female, street-based sex worker)

Family ties are strong in Newfoundland, and being ostracized by family would be devastating for many research participants. For some, it would mean being cut off from their only means of financial, emotional, and social support; for others, it could result in homelessness and alienation from their community. One of the sex workers who was working independently indoors recounted that her father joked about being labelled as a client when seen in public with her – although, in her words, he was "only half joking":

> I was giving him [Dad] a kiss and a hug gettin' out [of his car], and he was like, "Jesus! Don't let anybody see you hug me! They'll take my picture, and I'll be on the front page of the *Evening Telegram* ... They'll have me labelled as a john!" (Participant #15, female, independent indoor sex worker)

A number of participants expressed that they would be open about their work if not for the impact of stigma on their families, often noting that they kept their work hidden not to protect themselves but to protect family members. In discussions of stigma, a theme emerged around the impact of religion on public perceptions of sex work. Laura, as both a researcher and a resident of St. John's, can attest that the effects of religion are felt in Newfoundland in ways that they may not be in other cities in Canada. For example, until secular public schools were established in 1997, the Catholic Church had a full monopoly over the school system (Rollmann, 1999).

Participants spoke about the lingering influences, especially in relation to family and "Catholic guilt":

> I feel there's a lot of guilt, too, around my grandmother. I was born and raised Catholic, and she's Catholic ... And I always think, like every day, "What if my grandmother could see me now?" I can't see my grandmother ever, like, not talking to me or disowning me, but just knowing, she would be disappointed in me, you know? (Participant #4, male, independent indoor sex worker)

Other research participants noted similar experiences:

> St. John's, it's Sin City, I'm sorry, stuff happens ... My mom is Catholic, and if she found out ... I would be kicked out of the family. "Nope, don't have a son, sorry." So when I do get a client, I kinda screen them so it's, "I don't know you, you don't know me, perfect" ... This is the whole Catholic thing ... I think that's half the reason we have such high STI rates too ... Catholics don't need condoms! [laughs] Right? And the Catholic Brothers don't have any problems! (Participant #1, male, independent indoor sex worker)

Although the perceived judgment that the Catholic mother (and presumably other Catholics) would level at sex workers is noted, the quotation above also "talks back" to the general public and the Catholic Church. "Sin City" is a common nickname for St. John's that nods to the hypocrisy of people who would judge sex workers based on religious convictions but also engage in "illicit" sexual activities themselves. This reference to "Sin City" brings us back to the twin pillars of wilful blindness and moral judgment by highlighting the tensions between two versions of St. John's: the quaint, family-friendly place depicted in tourism ads; and the reality of St. John's as a city where "immoral" activities are part of the fabric of life.

The reference to the "Catholic Brothers" evokes the scandal of the Mount Cashell Orphanage, a foster home that for decades was the site of physical and sexual abuse perpetrated by the Christian Brothers against the boys who were entrusted to their care (Harris, 1991). Several participants referred to this scandal while describing religious judgment and the perceived hypocritical stance of the church toward sex, implying that Catholics should not judge sex workers given the lengthy history of abuse in the local churches. At the time of the scandal, the wilful blindness of St. John's residents was coupled with rampant religious morality and superiority. In employing references to local religious scandal as parlance for the hypocrisy of sexual stigma, sex workers were resisting not only the beliefs of the church regarding sex but also the right of anyone to judge them based on those beliefs. Such nuances highlight the cultural specificity embedded in sex work research and the importance of researchers' ability to interpret what is said within the context of shared cultural knowledge.

Conclusion

Although it may seem that the sex workers involved in this research were hiding in the shadows, invisibilized by the denial that sex work happens in Newfoundland, many of them used the space of the interview to communicate that they are valuable members of society who deserve to be acknowledged and heard. The research participants' narratives mirrored those of sex workers across Canada (Benoit and Shaver, 2006; Lewis, Shaver, and Maticka-Tyndale, 2013; O'Doherty, 2007) in their resistance to stigma and judgment, whether grounded in religion or otherwise (Winters, 2016), and in their desire to have meaningful conversations about themselves and their work, the very thing that stigma prevented them from doing:

> It makes me want to educate them. It makes me what to tell them my life, who I was and where I came from, so that they'd be better educated and have a better understanding of it. Then they could tell someone else, someone else, and someone else, and before you know it, the whole world got a better understanding of it. (Participant #16, female, independent indoor worker)

Sex workers interviewed in Newfoundland expressed their desire to use their experience to make change and to challenge moralistic views of sex work. The Safe Harbour Outreach Project (SHOP), a local sex worker support, advocacy, and outreach service that formed after the completion of the interviews, has been fighting to create a space for sex workers to engage in that desired public resistance. On International Sex Worker Rights Day in March 2016, SHOP and the City of St. John's partnered to create an exhibition showcasing sex workers' voices entitled *Sex Workers Speak Out: Coast to Coast Perspectives about Canada's Harmful Laws* (Bradbury, 2017; Crocker, 2017). The exhibit provided sex workers an opportunity to take control of the narrative around sex work in their city and to publicly "talk back" to stigma. This drastic shift from the situation only three years earlier, where the provincial government refused to publicly acknowledge that sex work happens in Newfoundland, demonstrates the value of having an advocacy organization for sex workers and the power of the collective voices of sex workers in creating social change (see also Beer, this collection).

Notes

1 Newfoundland is nicknamed "The Rock" because most of the island's terrain is rock rather than soil.
2 The majority of interviews took place in St. John's and a smaller number in the neighbouring cities of Mount Pearl and the Goulds. The project received ethical approval from the University of New Brunswick in June 2013.
3 Webcam performance entails online sex shows on hosting websites.
4 MUN refers to Memorial University of Newfoundland, and CONA refers to College of the North Atlantic, which is Newfoundland and Labrador's public college.

References

Benoit, C., & Shaver, F.M. (2006). Critical issues and new directions in sex work research. *Canadian Review of Sociology, 43*(3), 243–52. https://doi.org/10.1111/j.1755-618X.2006.tb02222.x

Bradbury, T. (2017, February 27). Sex workers speak out in new exhibit. *The Telegram.* Retrieved from http://www.thetelegram.com/news/local/sex-workers-speak-out-in-new-exhibit-128835/

Bruckert, C. (2012). The mark of 'disreputable' labour: Workin' it: Sex workers negotiate stigma. In S. Hannem & C. Bruckert (Eds.), *Stigma revisited: Implications of the mark* (pp. 55–78). Ottawa, ON: University of Ottawa Press.

CBC News. (2013, October 22). Sex exploitation report deemed too 'harmful' to release. Retrieved from http://www.cbc.ca/news/canada/newfoundland-labrador/sex-exploitation-report-deemed-too-harmful-to-release-1.2129162

CBC News. (2015, October 9). Not releasing sex trade report earlier 'a bit of a tragedy', advocate says. Retrieved from http://www.cbc.ca/news/canada/newfoundland-labrador/not-releasing-sex-trade-report-earlier-a-bit-of-a-tragedy-advocate-says-1.3264182

Community Youth Network–St. John's & CASEY. (2011). *It's nobody's mandate and everyone's responsibility: Sexual exploitation and the sex trade in Newfoundland and Labrador.* Retrieved from http://www.exec.gov.nl.ca/exec/wpo/publications/STR.pdf

Crocker, E. (2017, February 28). St. John's city hall and SHOP celebrating international sex workers rights day. *The Overcast.* Retrieved from https://theovercast.ca/st-johns-city-hall-and-shop-celebrating-international-sex-workers-rights-day/

Goffman, E. (1963). *Stigma: Notes on the management of spoiled identity*. Englewood Cliffs, NJ: Prentice-Hall.

Harris, M. (1991). *Unholy orders*. Toronto, ON: Penguin Books.

Jeffrey, L., & MacDonald, G. (2006). *Sex workers in the Maritimes talk back*. Vancouver, BC: UBC Press.

Lazarus, L., Deering, K., Nabess, R., Gibson, K., Tyndall, M., & Shannon, K. (2012). Occupational stigma as a primary barrier to health care for street-based sex workers in Canada. *Culture, Health and Sexuality, 14*(2), 139–50. https://doi.org/10.1080/13691058.2011.628411

Lewis, J., Shaver, F.M., & Maticka-Tyndale, E. (2013). Going 'round again: The persistence of prostitution-related stigma. In E. van der Meulen, E.M. Durisin, & V. Love (Eds.), *Selling sex: Experience, advocacy, and research on sex work in Canada* (pp. 198–209). Vancouver, BC: UBC Press.

Miller, L. (2000). The poverty of truth-seeking: Postmodernism, discourse analysis and critical feminism. *Theory and Psychology, 10*(3), 313–52. https://doi.org/10.1177/0959354300103002

O'Doherty, T. (2007). *Off-street commercial sex: An exploratory study*. (Unpublished MA thesis). Simon Fraser University, Vancouver, British Columbia.

Pheterson, G. (1996). *The prostitution prism*. Amsterdam, NL: Amsterdam University Press.

Rollmann, H. (1999). Religion in Newfoundland and Labrador. *Heritage Newfoundland and Labrador*. Retrieved from http://www.heritage.nf.ca/articles/society/religion.php

Statistics Canada. (2015). *Sense of belonging to Canada, the province of residence and the local community*. Retrieved from http://www.statcan.gc.ca/pub/89-652-x/89-652-x2015004-eng.htm

Statistics Canada. (2016). *Population of census metropolitan areas*. Retrieved from http://www.statcan.gc.ca/tables-tableaux/sum-som/l01/cst01/demo05a-eng.htm

WHO, UNFPA, UNAIDS, NSWP, World Bank, & UNDP. (2013). *Implementing comprehensive HIV/STI programmes with sex workers: Practical approaches from collaborative interventions*. Retrieved from http://www.who.int/hiv/pub/sti/sex_worker_implementation/en/

Winters, L. (2016). Everything about them, without them: Sex work and the harms of misrecognition. In C. Smith & Z. Marshall (Eds.), *Critical approaches to harm reduction: Conflict, institutionalization, (de-)politicization, and direct action* (pp. 137–69). New York, NY: Nova Science.

PART 3

SEX WORKERS' RESISTANCE

Building Alliances and Subverting Narratives

19

Canadian Feminism and Sex Work Law
————— A Cautionary Tale

MARIANA VALVERDE

Many Canadian feminists have published legal and policy analyses and made recommendations in the area of sex work law, but feminist movement activity has not been systematically documented. Given the lack of literature, I draw on my own experiences of the 1980s, when I was active as a public intellectual in the feminist "sex wars," and also on more recent activities related to sex work law reform. To try to counteract personal bias, however, I conducted twelve interviews, informal conversations, or email exchanges in the winter of 2014–15. The two key conclusions of this chapter are that focusing energies on constitutional challenges can lead to a dangerous neglect of the legislative arena and that small groups of feminists who try to shape public policy in the absence of a strong and coordinated women's movement cannot have a real impact, even if some feminist language is borrowed by either courts or legislatures.

Sex Work and the Law in Canada: A One-Year Revolution

In December 2013 sex workers and their allies were thrilled to see the Supreme Court of Canada strike down Canada's three main prostitution-related laws in *Canada (Attorney General) v. Bedford* (2013), with "safety" and "security" the keywords of the decision (see also Belak this collection; Porth this collection). By contrast, freedom of speech and gender equality – two other constitutionally protected rights – were muted in the arguments presented at trial and were completely sidelined in the Supreme Court's judgment. Stressing sex workers' vulnerability was legally useful but politically very risky given the transnational dissemination of new laws paternalistically labelling all prostitution as inherently exploitative.

Taking advantage of this global trend, and forced by the Supreme Court to write a new law, the Conservative majority government then in power cherry-picked a few feminist-sounding phrases about prostitution being inherently exploitative to decorate a new law, Bill C-36, the Protection of Communities and Exploited Persons Act, which came in to effect in December 2014 and is far more draconian and anti-feminist than the Sweden-style laws (e.g., there is a ban on advertising that does not exist in other countries' legislation). Even noted American prohibitionist Kathleen Barry responded to the new law by noting, "The press release [about the new law] from Canadian MPs has twisted a new, very regressive law to look like a gain for women ... This is a correction to the misleading press release which announces the law as a feminist gain."[1] But perhaps to avert an "I told you so" reaction, Barry emailed me in February 2015 to say that overall the law is still a gain for feminism, even though it is out of keeping with the Swedish approach because some street-based work is recriminalized.

A similar reluctance to openly criticize the new law is found among Canadian feminists sharing Barry's prohibitionist views, who have remained largely silent since the law's passing. The Native Women's Association of Canada (NWAC), a very significant feminist organization that supports criminalizing clients, does not mention the new law on the main pages of its website. Under several layers of hyperlinks, one can find a June 2014 press release by a pro-criminalization women's coalition that gives very lukewarm support to the new law, entitled "New Law Begins to Recognize the Harm in Prostitution." That press release quotes an NWAC spokesperson, but NWAC's own posted press releases and documents avoid saying that the new law is helpful to Indigenous or any other women.

Similarly, the Canadian Association of Elizabeth Fry Societies, a venerable feminist organization representing women in conflict with the law, had also vocally supported criminalizing customers during the constitutional challenge, but it has remained publicly silent since the law's passing. Its 2015 annual report makes no mention of the law, and its 2013–14 annual report mentions only its own intervention in the *Bedford* case, not the new law. Perhaps most significantly, the major feminist law reform organization in the country, Women's Legal Education and Action Fund (LEAF), remained consistently silent during the *Bedford* litigation, reportedly due to internal differences, and has remained silent since. Thus, although many feminists, and all sex worker organizations with any public profile, openly denounced the new law, pro-criminalization feminists maintain what one can only call a studied public silence. The new Liberal majority government, elected in October 2015, has not made any moves in regard to sex work law reform. But when it does, it may be helpful for Canadian feminists to reflect on past experiences, recent and not so recent – which is the aim of this chapter.

Interventions in the Legal Arena: A Tale of Feminist Failure

Before turning to the feminist organizations that sought intervener status in the successful *Bedford* litigation, it will be helpful to compare the political context of the Toronto challenge (the one that went forward) with that prevailing in Vancouver, where a separate challenge had also been in the works (see also Beer, this collection). The challenge that reached the Supreme Court was conducted primarily by a libertarian law professor from Osgoode Hall Law School, Alan Young, who made some effort in 2006 to reach out to the main Toronto sex workers' advocacy and social service organization, Maggie's: Toronto Sex Workers Action Project, but then immediately sent Maggie's a memo outlining his strategy. The case was thus conducted without accountability to that major local organization and seemed also disconnected from the work already undertaken in Vancouver.

Young's positioning of himself as a heroic lawyer opposed to Big Brother stood in sharp contrast to the situation in Vancouver. Well before the nationwide outcry about police disrespect for murdered sex workers that helped to trigger the current National Inquiry into Missing and Murdered Indigenous Women and Girls, Vancouver's progressives were unusually well prepared for constitutional litigation by a remarkable local poverty-law organization, PIVOT Legal Society. PIVOT had worked with sex worker groups, including Sex Workers United Against Violence (SWUAV), to launch a constitutional challenge in the early 2000s. But the PIVOT-led challenge was halted by a judge's technical ruling on the question of standing (i.e., the right to challenge the law).

If it had gone forward first, the Vancouver challenge would have been accountable to the only semi-organized street-based sex workers' community in the country – and would have proceeded on different legal grounds. At a panel in Toronto in February 2014, Katrina Pacey, then the organization's litigation director and now its executive director, emphasized that although the Supreme Court's *Bedford* decision was a victory, the court's choice to follow Young's sole focus on preventing harm to sex workers – rather than promoting sex worker dignity and autonomy – was problematic. If PIVOT had taken the lead, I believe that its legal strategy would have acknowledged the gendering of sexuality and sex work without reproducing the gender binary; its arguments would have established that it is possible for prostitution law reform to recognize gendered power while avoiding gender essentialism and victimism.

Thus a Vancouver judge's negative ruling on standing (later reversed but only when the Toronto challenge was already further up the ladder) had the effect of marginalizing, legally, the only group in the country with the legal and political wherewithal to conduct a constitutional challenge with accountability to the sex worker community. Subsequently, PIVOT and SWUAV had to squeeze their arguments into a short intervener brief.

But PIVOT is not an organization representing women at large. An explicitly feminist standpoint could best have been claimed by the leading legal-feminist organization in the country, LEAF. In its heyday, when a federal Court Challenges program funded equality-seeking groups that wanted authoritative interpretations of the then new Canadian Charter of Rights and Freedoms, LEAF was a major player in both the women's movement and the Canadian legal scene. That is not the case today, but despite its far lower visibility, LEAF remains active. Given its history of Supreme Court briefs, if LEAF had intervened its position would have been received respectfully, but it did not even seek intervener status. If LEAF had acted to support the PIVOT approach, court decisions may or may not have been substantially different, but subsequent discussions about legislation would certainly have been influenced by the views of a key feminist legal voice.

By contrast with LEAF, whose work is familiar to judges across the country, the two main self-described legal voices of Canadian women that sought to intervene had no prior existence and thus far less credibility. The main one called itself the Women's Coalition, which, I was told, was put together by Lee Lakeman, a Vancouver feminist known for her anti-trans views. The official spokesperson was University of British Columbia law professor Janine Benedet, long known for claiming that no woman can seriously consent to engaging in sex work. The Women's Coalition brief lists a number of members, starting with the Canadian Association of Sexual Assault Centres. But in fact many local sexual assault and anti-violence organizations supported the opposite, decriminalization group: the Feminist Coalition, discussed below.

The support of NWAC was important, indeed key, to the credibility of the Women's Coalition in feminist circles. But this support was counterbalanced by the vocal Indigenous street workers allied with PIVOT in Vancouver, who appeared repeatedly in the media, both during the litigation and as the law was passed, vehemently supporting decriminalization. Nationally, it was not NWAC but the executive director of the Canadian Association of Elizabeth Fry Societies, Kim Pate, who most strongly defended criminalizing male customers. At a panel at the University of Toronto on the *Bedford* decision in February 2014, Pate faced direct protests by about a dozen sex workers, who stood up in the audience and turned their backs on her as she began her remarks.

The prohibitionist Women's Coalition (2011) presented an intervener brief, written by lawyers Fay Faraday and Janine Benedet, which refers to all sex workers as "prostituted women" (para. 9) and states that sex workers' own accounts are not necessarily reliable since women may not know that they are being pimped (para. 16). In the end, however, the brief did not appear to have much, if any, effect on the Ontario Court of Appeal decision and even less at the Supreme Court level (see Belak, this collection). However unrepresentative the Women's Coalition might have been, the group accumulated some legal capital. Legal capital was in remarkably short supply, by comparison, for the Feminist Coalition, quickly put together for the purpose of countering the Women's Coalition. The Feminist Coalition drew up a document seeking intervener status at the Supreme Court level on the basis that it represented twenty-three organizations whose views were only partially covered by the Women's Coalition; the court did not grant it standing to intervene.

Although powerless in the court process, the Feminist Coalition did make an impression in the women's movement. Feminists learned that a large number of organizations that do frontline work on violence against women felt that the victimist Women's Coalition did not represent their views, and they instead supported feminist liberty and dignity arguments. That a wide range of anti-violence, largely radical feminist organizations, including a number of sexual assault centres, would support decriminalization is significant since it challenges the usual association between radical feminist theories and pro-criminalization strategies.

It is not clear that a less fragmented and better organized feminist movement could have had an impact on Parliament and its lawmaking since it, too, would likely have had little influence on the courts; the Harper government ignored not only social movements but even much mainstream opinion, especially in its later years. But apart from the might-have-beens, it is useful for Canadian feminists to put our experience of sex work law reform in a broader context by revisiting related events from the 1980s that are not widely known.

The 1980s: A National Policy Exercise Evokes a Relatively United Feminist Policy on Sex Work Law

A Special Committee on Pornography and Prostitution, commonly called the Fraser Committee for its chairperson Paul Fraser, was convened in 1983 by the Liberal government of the day (Brock, 1998). Much feminist energy was being devoted to opposing pornography in the early and mid-1980s, when "objectification of women" was a new and exciting idea. By contrast, the issue of prostitution was reduced to street soliciting and its impact on respectable neighbourhoods – with sex work being thus strangely degendered (in sharp contrast to today, when sex work is hyper-gendered). The Fraser Committee – a notable group of experts – was thus given a hybrid mandate, only one part of which (i.e., pornography) was then thought of as involving feminist stakeholders. Since, in relation to sex work, only street-based work was politically visible, the committee largely ignored the infamous bawdy-house laws and focused primarily on street soliciting.

The committee's highly publicized and amply funded cross-country hearings prompted feminist groups to pay attention to an issue that few people, other than sex workers themselves, had previously regarded as central to feminism. The two sex worker organizations that testified, the Vancouver-based Alliance for the Safety of Prostitutes and the Toronto-based Coalition for the Rights of Prostitutes, advocated decriminalization. But a mainstream group with close ties to the ruling Liberals, the Canadian Advisory Council on the Status of Women, made an odd presentation to the committee to the effect that all street soliciting, for any purpose, should be criminalized (Department of Justice, 1985, pp. 5–6).

A lone feminist law professor, Constance Backhouse, then at Western University, currently at the University of Ottawa, presented an early version of the Swedish approach. Her recommendation to criminalize all purchases of sex was met with total incredulity. The Fraser Committee, basking in the glow of the then new Charter, could not imagine punishing private consensual interactions, even if only male customers were charged. "Society would need a repressive form of morals police to enforce such a broadly based prescription," the committee politely objected (Department of Justice, 1985, p. 521).

The country's main voice of women, the 600-group coalition known as the National Action Committee on the Status of Women (NAC), was too diverse in composition to have a predictable view on what was then not a central feminist issue. I was one of a group of left-wing activists who attended NAC's 1983 national convention in Ottawa. Partly through microphone-control tactics learned from the union movement, we took advantage of the feminist political vacuum on this issue to ensure that NAC took a position in favour of decriminalization. I remember thinking after the vote that the delegates of NAC, who belonged to the organization through their local YWCA or the United Church, were undoubtedly unhappy with NAC's now official position. But once the position had been taken, NAC was bound to present it to the Fraser Committee. The final report of the Fraser Committee quotes at length from NAC's submission and gives it much weight, perhaps because it was a sophisticated and detailed legal policy document, in contrast to what many other groups presented.

NAC first asked for the repeal of the soliciting law but carefully added that, "in the alternative," Parliament ought to refrain from strengthening it. NAC then called for repealing the bawdy-house law and stated that if not repealed, that section of the Criminal Code should be amended so that a few sex workers could legally work together indoors. NAC also recommended that the nuisances associated with soliciting be dealt with by means of "legal remedies other than criminal sanctions," such as municipal bylaws (Department of Justice, 1985, p. 359).

In line with NAC, the Fraser Committee's report recommended allowing one or two sex workers to legally operate indoors. This was not then a radical view. When the Fraser Committee was struck, Justice Minister Mark MacGuigan stated that "there was strong sentiment in some Western provinces to completely legalize prostitution" (Sallot, 1983, n.p.) The municipal-regulation approach advocated by MacGuigan died, however, with the Liberal government that created the Fraser Committee. What sex workers (and municipalities) got instead was wholly contrary to the NAC and Fraser recommendations, namely a draconian criminal law banning all communication in a public place for the purpose of prostitution, a 1985 statute that was one of the three struck down by the Supreme Court in 2013.

During the Fraser Committee process, then, a large, inclusive feminist coalition – NAC – supported a combination of legalization and decriminalization, whereas what later became famous as the Swedish or Nordic approach was supported only by one law professor. In retrospect, it is interesting that Backhouse's suggestion was dismissed out of hand as incompatible with basic liberal legality. By contrast with the arched eyebrows with which the Fraser Committee met the asymmetrical criminalization views of Backhouse, NAC's decriminalization recommendations, although novel for a mainstream feminist organization, do not seem to have been far from what the Liberal government would have done if it had won the 1984 election.

In 2014 the situation was completely different. The Swedish approach, with its radical rejection of any private sphere for sex workers and their customers, had been gaining ground steadily in Canada, as in Europe, since 1999, when Sweden first voted to criminalize the purchase of sexual services but not the sale. Also, the Harper government had successfully passed a wide range of law-and-order measures despite the fact that such measures did not necessarily enjoy wide support. These factors combined to frustrate feminist (and sex worker) efforts to shape the legislative process.

Conclusion

The historical combination of government policy inaction and buck-passing to the courts, which has been the dominant feature of the wars over sex and the law in Canada since the passing of the Charter in 1982, still existed in 2013–14. At the time of the 2013 *Bedford* decision, none of the three main political parties – Liberal, Conservative, and New Democrat – had a publicly available policy on sex work. Among progressive feminists, too, the focus was on the constitutional challenge, not on policy. Significantly, the persistent issues surrounding municipal regulation of sexually oriented businesses never gained traction for feminists at large. In this atmosphere, in which the only publicly visible activity was the *Bedford* constitutional challenge, the ruling Conservatives managed to turn their defeat in the courts into a political victory, one that many of the feminist groups that had advocated the Swedish approach hesitated to denounce despite its clear law-and-order, anti–sex worker slant.

At this writing, we do not know when sex work law reform will return to the foreground of the political agenda. But it is doubtful that when that happens, Canadian feminists will have managed to come together in a diverse national coalition that is treated seriously by governments, one that does not stifle internal dissent but at least prevents anti-women statutes and policies.

Note

1 Comment posted June 5, 2014, to Women's Studies Listserv (WMST-L), University of Maryland.

References

Brock, D. (1998). *Making work, making trouble: Prostitution as a social problem.* Toronto, ON: University of Toronto Press. https://doi.org/10.3138/97814426 76930

Department of Justice. (1985). *Pornography and prostitution in Canada: Report of the Special Committee on Pornography and Prostitution.* (Vol. 2). Ottawa, ON: Communications and Public Affairs Canada.

Sallot, J. (1983, June 24). Criminal Code amendments: Prostitutes' clients may be charged. *Globe and Mail.*

Women's Coalition (2011). Factum for the Intervener Women's Coalition. Court of Appeal for Ontario, Between Terri Jean Bedford, Amy Lebovitch, Valerie Scott, and Attorney General of Ontario and Attorney General of Ontario. Court Files Nos. C52799 and C52814.

Cases

Canada (Attorney General) v. Bedford, 2013 SCC 72, [2013] 3 SCR 1101.

Legislation

Bill C-36, *Protection of Communities and Exploited Persons Act,* SC 2014, c. 25.

Canadian Charter of Rights and Freedoms, Part I of the *Constitution Act, 1982,* being Schedule B to the *Canada Act 1982* (UK), 1982, c. 11.

20

Whorganizers and Gay Activists

———————— Histories of Convergence, Contemporary Currents of Divergence, and the Promise of Non-Normative Futures

BECKI L. ROSS

In the late 1960s, social movements forged by activist gay men and activist sex workers converged, only to later diverge, in urban centres across Canada.[1] In the early 1970s, the promise of allegiance between gay liberationists and sex work organizers emerged from shared histories of stigmatization, criminalization, and marginalization. However, by the late 1980s, economic, legal, and social shifts had made sustained, productive solidarity between these subaltern sexual renegades less and less likely. In this chapter, I start by addressing points of convergence, underscoring how gay men and female sex workers – logical allies – made the case for sexual freedom through the power of nonmonogamous sex unencumbered by shame, inhibition, or the fear of arrest. I then turn to exploring points of divergence, which include white, middle-class gay men's increasing emphasis on privacy, domesticity, and consumption; the intransigence of the whore stigma; and the interlocking of "gay rights" with Canadian, white-settler colonialism in the context of deepening neoliberalism. I uncover how subjugation as sexual outlaws became insufficient grounds for gay activists and "whorganizers" to forge meaningful solidarity.[2]

Medico-Moral and Legal Proximities

Western histories of homosexuality and prostitution reveal overlapped legacies of criminalization and persecution. For more than a century across

Canada and the United States, homosexuality and prostitution were administered by medico-moral authorities as sources of maladjustment, degeneration, and threats to the health of the white-settler nation. Homosexuals were routinely punished as criminal, sinful, and pathologically disordered perverts (Foucault, 1980; Kinsman, 1996; Terry, 1999). Prostitutes were similarly scorned as disreputable vectors of disease, homewreckers, and sexual degenerates (McMaster, 2008; Poutanen, 2015; Valverde, 2008). For much of the nineteenth and twentieth centuries, "queers" and "fallen women" were defined in legal and moral discourses as responsible for moral, physical, and cultural contagion; immigration statutes prohibited their entry to Canada. Anti-vice squads, religious leaders, politicians, and medical experts dedicated entire careers to stamping out the "sex crimes" of "sex criminals," who were widely believed to endanger the sanctity of white, patriarchal, monogamous, respectable, and procreative marriage (Francis, 2006; Freund, 2002). Moral repugnance was routinely directed at both groups of "sex offenders," with particular opprobrium reserved for interracial and cross-class intimacies wherein favours and/or money were exchanged (Shah, 2011).

In Canada the long history of state-sponsored homophobia, biphobia, and transphobia dates back to the colonization of Indigenous peoples and repressive measures against two-spirit traditions (Cannon, 1998; Egale, 2016; Hunt, 2016). In the late nineteenth century, federal laws criminalized same-sex sexual activity in public places such as streets, parks, hotels, nightclubs, apartments, vehicles, laneways, and bathhouses (Kinsman, 1996). Laws against "gross indecency" put men who sought sex with men at risk of arrest and imprisonment, including hustlers who were gay or bisexual (Churchill, 2004; Higgins, 1999; Maynard, 1997). Men who frequented bathhouses in Montreal and Toronto, cruising grounds in Vancouver's West End, the "hill" near the Legislature in Winnipeg (watched over by the Golden Boy statue), and Ottawa's Major's Hill Park were routinely subjected to police entrapment, harassment, and surveillance (Ingram, 1997; Korinek, 2012; Warner, 2002). In the late 1950s, it was the policy of the Government of Canada to search for "alleged" and "confirmed" homosexuals, interrogate them, extract confessions, press them to incriminate others, and fire them. Thousands lost their jobs in the civil service, military, and Department of National Defence, with some killing themselves (Kinsman and Gentile, 2010).

Alongside the violent treatment of homosexuals, especially men who sought sex with men, the targeting of female sex workers has been a long-standing staple of anti-vice forces (Pheterson, 1996; St. James, 1987).

In Vancouver, for example, prison records from 1897 to 1907 reveal street-walkers, madams, and brothel employees sentenced to months of "hard labour" at the jail in New Westminster (Nilsen, 1980). Racialized women marked as prostitutes, especially those who were Indigenous or Chinese, were subjected to forms of violence and terror that were not only sanctioned by the colonial state but also enabled through law itself (Mawani, 2009).

Affective Proximities

In the 1970s and early 1980s, social movements forged by Canadian gay male liberationists and sex work activists initially converged around a shared desire for sexual sovereignty, as well as freedom from state sexual regulation and oppressive policing (Bearchell, 1984a, 1984b; S. Bell, 1995; Smith, 2014). As sexual renegades, gay men, lesbians, and prostitutes challenged the normative sex/gender system of patriarchal, heterosexual marriage by engaging in nonmonogamous and nonreproductive sexual acts. For many gay men, sexual experimentation and promiscuity, or "tricking" – a staple activity of sex workers – became a celebrated component of gay culture (Bronski, 1998; Persky, 1989; Rubin, 1984). In large urban settings across Canada and the United States, gay men often signalled sexual availability through an erotic semiotics of codes and uniforms, including coloured handkerchiefs and bunches of keys, just as sex workers invented flamboyant "hooker fashion" that emphasized glamour, sexual openness, and erotic allure (Hamilton, 2008; Raigen, personal communication, July 28, 2008). Within the two communities, a democratic sexual ethos involved consensual, often interracial, cross-class, and intergenerational sexual liaisons. For decades, activist gay men and sex workers openly repudiated the idealization of monogamy as exemplary of adult sexual maturity.

In the 1970s and 1980s, activist gay men (and lesbians) strove to throw off the shackles of homophobia and heterosexism (Ross, 1995; Smith, 1999; Warner, 2002), just as activist prostitutes, or whorganizers, strove to liberate themselves from the whore stigma that scapegoated sellers of sex as spreaders of venereal disease and disorder (see Alliance for the Safety of Prostitutes, 1984; L. Bell, 1987; S. Bell, 1994; Chateauvert, 2013; Hartley, 1997; Nagle, 1997; Queen, 1997; see also Beer, this collection). Gay men and sex workers navigated oppressive forces within institutional apparatuses of the law, organized religion, families, politics, mass media, medicine, and education. In the mid-1980s a new moral panic – AIDS – targeted "hookers" and "faggots" as sexually spoiled and fatally promiscuous. The pain and shame of imposed and internalized stigma necessitated subcultural formations as bulwarks against hate and violence. Such formations included numerous gay-liberationist political and cultural groups across the country,[3] as well as sex worker rights groups, albeit on a significantly smaller scale.[4]

Notwithstanding significant points of intersection and histories of persecution shared by activist queers and sex workers in the 1970s and 1980s, coordinated allegiance never materialized in urban centres across Canada. The voices of working-class, white cisgender women, women of colour, transgender women, and male hustlers in the sex industry have been largely absent from gay, lesbian, and feminist political forums and action plans (Gilmore, 2010; Namaste, 2005; Ross and Sullivan, 2012). Although a minority of grassroots activists in Vancouver, Toronto, Winnipeg, Halifax, and Montreal at the time voiced support for decriminalization of prostitution, sex work activists were not able to curry the favour of gay, lesbian, feminist, labour, or political leaders locally or nationally (Arrington, 1987). Indeed, a number of white, upwardly mobile gay men who organized against the "nuisance" of prostitution consistently put their own needs above those of "hos and hustlers" in shared neighbourhoods (Ross and Sullivan, 2012; see also Page, this collection).

In Vancouver in the early 1980s, the visibility of street-level prostitution in the West End – a largely white, middle-class enclave and emergent "gaybourhood" – directly conflicted with city boosters' fantasy of hosting Expo 86 (Bishop, 2013; Chan, 1983). Punitive bylaws in Vancouver, Calgary, and Toronto zeroed in on street-level solicitation as a strategy to eliminate on-street sex work (Brock, 2009; Larsen, 1992; Lowman, 1986). Gay and straight residents and business owners complained bitterly about the surge of on-street prostitutes as responsible for noise, loitering, drug use, needles, a high volume of traffic, and declining property values (Wiseman, 1983). The hoisting of white gay men ever higher up the respectability ladder impeded solidarity with otherwise logical allies – street-involved sex workers – who were unable to marshal the resources necessary to thwart the juggernaut of anti-prostitution forces.

Sex worker rights, including the right to public solicitation, never emerged as a priority for the majority of gay activists, who became increasingly absorbed in equality-seeking rights struggles in the mid to late 1980s. In 1982 gay (and lesbian) activists became emboldened by a new Canadian Charter of Rights and Freedoms that did not explicitly name sex workers or trans folks (see Ross and Sullivan, 2012). After the bathhouse raids in Toronto in 1981, the Right to Privacy Committee affirmed a campaign to protect gay sex from entrapment and arrest (Kinsman, 1996). Although some activist, white gay men made bargains with police in numerous Canadian cities to "tone down" public sex and cruising, sex workers, especially cis and trans women of colour, faced new and more punitive legislation, along with intensified police intimidation (see also Butler Burke, this collection). In 1984 in Vancouver's West End, the once vibrant, racially diverse, and pimp-free "outdoor brothel culture" was demolished following a legal injunction from the BC Supreme Court that prohibited prostitutes from living and working in that neighbourhood (McEachern, 1985; Ross, 2010). A year later, anti-prostitution laws were stiffened by the ruling federal Conservative government, which made any communication for the purpose of prostitution in a public place illegal, including the inside of a motor vehicle (see Brock, 2009).

The Rise of Whitened, Neoliberal Homonormativity

From the mid-1980s onward, influential, white, middle-class gay leaders in Vancouver, Toronto, Winnipeg, Ottawa, Montreal, and Halifax secured wide-ranging reforms, from access to "pink market" consumption to homo-familial equality provisions for relationships, marriage, and queer families (see Peñaloza, 1996; Vaid, 1995; Walcott, 2015). Indeed, the enfoldment of same-sex marriage into the preservation of monogamous marriage, and by extension white Western civilization, underscores how some gay activists worked to achieve what Walcott (2015) terms "homo-rights" and "homosexual arrival benefits" (pp. vii, viii).

For the past six decades, gay-led initiatives have productively penetrated the law, the labour force, schools, social services, the military, organized religion, sports, and popular culture. Numerous gains have been registered, including decriminalization of homosexuality, anti-discrimination bills, gay-straight alliances in schools, gay and lesbian caucuses in labour unions, gay and lesbian refugee claims, Pride marches, sports leagues, lesbian and gay military service, LGBTQ community centres, Pride House in Vancouver at the 2010 Winter Olympics, and more. In addition, we have witnessed an increase of out politicians, entertainers, and athletes, alongside a proliferation of LGBTQ media, including films, music, radio, television, and social media.

In June 2016 Toronto's chief of police, Mark Saunders, publicly expressed regret for the police-led bathhouse raids and arrests of 300 men in Toronto in 1981 and for the raid on queer women's night at the Pussy Palace in 2000 (see Winsa and Powell, 2016). Also in 2016, a resurgence of outrage from the We Demand an Apology Network ramped up the pressure on the Canadian government to apologize for the hundreds of gays and lesbians fired or demoted from their civil service jobs in the 1950s and 1960s (Ibbitson, 2016; Kinsman and Gentile, 2010). In 2017, Canadian prime minister Justin Trudeau delivered a federal apology to LGBTQ2 folks for the country's past discriminatory treatment, with promises to expunge the records of those convicted under homophobic laws and to provide financial compensation for victims (Broverman, 2016; Catungal, 2017).

By contrast, unlike the substantive victories achieved by LGBTQ activists across Canada, sex workers have made significantly fewer gains in medical, legal, socio-political, and affective arenas. Unlike organizers in gay-liberation groups, unions, reproductive rights, environmental organizing, civil rights, and anti-war movements, whorganizers have struggled to radicalize, politicize, or mobilize constituencies in order to combat stigmatization and criminalization (see also Clamen and Gillies, this collection). The December 2013 Supreme Court ruling that struck down sex work–related laws as harmful to sex workers' safety and security, and thus unconstitutional (*Canada (Attorney General) v. Bedford*, 2013) stood as a colossal victory and a harbinger of hope for justice for close to a year (Pivot Legal Society, 2013). However, in December 2014 the federal Conservative government passed Bill C-36, the Protection of Communities and Exploited Persons Act (PCEPA), which defines all commercial sex as exploitation and aims to punish buyers of sex, those who carry advertising for sexual services, and those who gain material benefit from sex work (see Canadian Alliance for Sex Work Law Reform, 2016; Wingrove, 2014). Sex workers and allies have loudly condemned PCEPA for violating sex worker rights of freedom of expression and association, security of the person, and equal treatment under the law (Canadian Alliance for Sex Work Law Reform, 2016). For Hele, Sayers, and Hunt (2015), the new law will further dehumanize and recriminalize Indigenous sex workers, while renewing the white-saviour rhetoric of rescue.

Whorephobia and violence persist for sex workers, with pernicious and often lethal effects (Lowman, 2000; Pratt, 2005). The most marginalized sex workers – trans, poor, queer, and racialized – contend with cis-sexism, homophobia, transphobia, poverty, and racism (Namaste, 2005, 2015; Ross, 2012). Sex workers' daily lives are compromised by economic and social precarity compounded by banishment from Indigenous and peer networks, the fear of having children apprehended, and the ever-present threat of violence, incarceration, and murder (Hunt, 2013). Cast out as disposable and marked for death, sex workers remain among those most vulnerable to the necropolitics of state power, which has the capacity to dictate who may live and who must die (Mbembe, 2003; Snorton and Haritaworn, 2013).

Today, in spite of the rising tide of sex worker rights organizations, disagreement about sex work hobbles solidarity in the context of progressive social movements. Vocal prohibitionists who insist on women's victimization in the sex industry have renewed their emphasis on the global phenomenon of "sex trafficking" (Farley, 2004; Jeffreys, 2011). In opposition, supporters of the rights of sex workers agree that an anti-criminalization approach is a necessary first step toward workers' health and safety (Abel, 2014; Lowman, 2013; Zangger, 2015). In Vancouver alone, more than sixty-five women – two-thirds Indigenous – have been murdered or have disappeared since the late 1970s (Dean, 2015). At the same time, sex work activism has expanded to generate awareness of sex worker rights, to coordinate training for police and judges, and to provide frontline services. Still, sex workers have never been invited to lead Vancouver's Pride Parades, International Women's Day, or SlutWalk protests; their foundational roles in Vancouver's early gay liberation, gaybourhood formation, and the advancement of women's right to sexual sovereignty have tended to be ignored or forgotten (Ross and Hamilton, 2016).

Critics persuasively argue that a focus on LGBTQ equality rights is linked to a preoccupation with free markets, individualism, and tropes of white, Western moral superiority (Puar, 2007). "Homonormativity," a term coined by Duggan (1992), is grounded in a rights-based LGBT framework that has afforded some elites the privileges of homocitizenship and the approximation of what Berlant (2011) terms "good-life fantasies" (p. 7). Sexual exceptionalism or the normative narrative of Canada as a safe "gay haven" for family-friendly queer subject-citizens erases LBGTQ complicities in white-settler colonialism (Awaad, 2015; Dhoot, 2015; Morgensen, 2011). And mainstream gay and lesbian "success stories" obfuscate the exclusion of sex workers, especially street-involved, trans, nonbinary, and two-spirit folks of colour – racialized, gendered, and sexual renegades – from full, substantive inclusion.

Unapologetic and unrepentant, activist sex workers signify the *queerest of the queer* not because they possess an authentic queer identity (although some do) but because they *do* sexual practices, labour, and kinship queerly and in ways not easily recuperated within the fold of white, monogamous, and settled homonationalism (Puar, 2007). Unlike LGBTQ folks who do not publicly sell sexual services, sex workers remain vulnerable to state-governed violence, police intimidation, and extermination (Ferris, 2015). A singular rights-based LGBTQ framework focused on sexuality or gender is exclusionary. As chapters of Black Lives Matter across Canada and the United States have made clear, LGBTQ communities are heterogeneous, comprising people with differential access to privilege and resources, as well as different histories with colonial policing, white-settler state policies, and border imperialism (Khan, 2016; Trevenen and Degagne, 2015). At the same time, racialized sex workers are among those most overpoliced and under-protected in cities across Canada – another reminder that "protection" is unevenly apportioned and never guaranteed (see Jiwani, 2002).

Conclusion

On June 11, 2016, a lone gunman massacred forty-nine and wounded fifty others at Pulse, a gay nightclub in Orlando, Florida. On "Latin Night," the majority murdered were queer men of Puerto Rican and Cuban heritage (Alvarez and Madigan, 2016). A heinous tragedy, with unspeakable losses for families and loved ones, the event took place amid new anti-gay laws launched under the guise of freedom of religion (Bociurkiw, 2016). At the same time, postmassacre media reports did not mention the long history of informal sex exchanged for money (and favours) in gay clubs or how hustlers were most likely among those killed at Pulse. Similarly, the murders of more than twenty-five trans women of colour over the past three years in Canada and the United States – most of whom sold sex – have largely failed to attract the attention of white queer commentators and activists (Cifredo, 2016). Progressive political parties at the local, provincial, and federal levels have long curried the favour of queer voters, yet they have refused to make a priority of solidarity with sex workers, particularly around the decriminalization of consensual, adult sexual commerce. Canadian feminist legal organizations such as Women's Legal Education and Action Fund (LEAF) have not demonstrated consistent leadership. And anti-violence feminist groups such as Rape Relief continue to advance anti-trans and anti–sex work agendas (Elliot, 2010).

After six decades of struggle, activist sex workers continue their work, in spite of uneven or absent allegiance with activist LGBTQ folks. Small victories have been registered, although losses persist. Within the past five years, police forces and city councils in Vancouver, Victoria, Saskatoon, and Toronto have adopted guidelines to promote the health and well-being of sex workers. Yet industry workers still face formidable barriers to dignity, safety, and security, and crimes against them tend not to be taken seriously by police. Independent sex workers' organizations persevere (see Porth, this collection), and although state funding for some of these advocacy groups has enabled longevity and stability, the efficacy of others has been weakened by the lack of core funding (Beer and Tremblay, 2014; see also Beer, this collection). Cultural production has begun to flourish, with the *Hooker Monologues* play, burlesque troupes such as Operation Snatch and Virago Nation, novels and poetry by Amber Dawn, blog posts by Annie Temple, Jamie Lee Hamilton, and Velvet Steele, a TED Talk by Valerie Scott, documentary films, and Canada's first and only commemorative installation, the West End Sex Workers Memorial in Vancouver (Hamilton and Ross, 2014, 2016; Newton, 2016a, 2016b; Ross and Hamilton, 2016).[5] At the same time, mainstream news media rarely profile stories that foreground the lives of sex workers on their own terms, and sex workers' organizations struggle to unpack their white privilege and leadership (Jiwani and Young, 2006; Panichelli, Wahab, Saunders, and Capous-Desyllas, 2015; see also Lam and Gallant, this collection).

In the end, as the late José Esteban Muñoz (2009) insisted, "we must dream and enact new and better pleasures, other ways of being in the world, and ultimately new worlds" (p. 1). Working to manifest these new worlds requires movements integrated across the fields of racial justice, sex workers' sovereignty, Indigenous justice, opposition to police brutality, reproductive justice, anti-poverty work, and justice for LGBTQ, nonbinary, and two-spirit folks. This work will entail unsettling all cis-normative constructions of desire, intimacy, and fantasies of belonging to white-settler colonialism. Sex workers who laid the groundwork for urban gaybourhoods from New York to San Francisco to Vancouver's West End deserve at least that much. Rather than having "arrived," homos, whores, and hustlers – in all of their entwined histories and layered complexities – are just getting started.

Notes

1 My focus is on activist, white gay men in the context of emergent gay liberation across Canada and the United States.
2 The term "whorganizer" was the name of the newsletter published and circulated in Vancouver by the Alliance for the Safety of Prostitutes, formed in 1982.
3 For gay liberationists, political and cultural groups included Gays and Lesbians Together (St. John's), Gay Liberation of Moncton, the Atlantic Gay Alliance, the Judy Garland Memorial Bowling League (Toronto), AIDS Action Now (Toronto),

the Gay Association of Sudbury, L'Association gaie de l'ouest québécois (Gatineau-Hull), the Gay Montreal Association, Gays of Ottawa, Gay Information and Resources Calgary, Lesbian and Gay Saskatchewan, Gays for Equality (Winnipeg), and the Gay Alliance Toward Equality (GATE) (Vancouver).

4 Sex workers' groups that emerged in the 1970s and 1980s included Call Off Your Old Tired Ethics (COYOTE) in San Francisco, the Alliance for Safety of Prostitutes (ASP) in Vancouver and Calgary, and the Canadian Organization for the Rights of Prostitutes (CORP) in Toronto. Trans sex workers assumed leadership roles in Vancouver's Dogwood Monarchist Society, which was incorporated in 1976 and still operates as a drag-focused "imperial court," charitable organization, and support network.

5 In November 2008 trans, Indigenous sex worker Jamie Lee Hamilton and I co-founded the West End Sex Workers Memorial Committee. Eight long years later, in September 2016, we realized our shared dream of a memorial lamp post and bronzed inscription at the corner of Jervis and Pendrell Streets in Vancouver's West End, on the doorstep of St. Paul's Anglican Church.

References

Abel, G. (2014). A decade of decriminalization: Sex work 'down under' but not underground. *Criminology and Criminal Justice, 14*(5), 580–92. https://doi.org/10.1177/1748895814523024

Alliance for the Safety of Prostitutes. (1984). Prostitution, a brief presented to the Fraser Committee. Rare Books and Special Collections, University of British Columbia, Service, Office, and Retails Workers Union of Canada (SORWUC), Box 1, File 1-13.

Alvarez, L., & Madigan, N. (2016, June 14). The dead in Orlando, Puerto Ricans hear a roll call of their kin. *New York Times*. Retrieved from https://www.nytimes.com/2016/06/15/us/in-orlando-victims-puerto-ricans-hear-a-roll-call-of-their-kin.html?_r=0

Arrington, M. (1987). Community organizing. In L. Bell (Ed.), *Good girls/bad girls: Sex workers and feminists face to face* (pp. 104–8). Toronto, ON: Women's Press.

Awaad, J. (2015). Queer regulation and the homonational rhetoric of Canadian exceptionalism. In O. H. Dryden & S. Lenon (Eds.), *Disrupting queer inclusion: Canadian homonationalisms and the politics of belonging* (pp. 19–34). Vancouver, BC: UBC Press.

Bearchell, C. (1984a). Cold shoulder for a hot issue. *Body Politic,* (108), 14. Retrieved from https://walnet.org/97_walnut/chris_bearchell/cb_writing.html

Bearchell, C. (1984b). Pornography, prostitution and moral panic. *Body Politic,* (101), 7. Retrieved from https://walnet.org/97_walnut/chris_bearchell/cb_writing.html

Beer, S., & Tremblay, F. (2014). Sex workers rights organizations and government funding in Canada. In C. Showden & S. Majic (Eds.), *Negotiating sex work: Unintended consequences of policy and activism* (pp. 287–310). Minneapolis, MN: University of Minnesota Press.

Bell, L. (1987). Introduction. In L. Bell (Ed.), *Good girls/bad girls: Sex workers and feminists face to face* (pp. 1–15). Toronto, ON: Women's Press.

Bell, S. (1994). *Reading, writing, and rewriting the prostitute body.* Bloomington, IN: Indiana University Press.

Bell, S. (1995). *Whore carnival.* New York, NY: Autonomedia.

Berlant, L. (2011). *Cruel optimism.* Durham, NC: Duke University Press. https://doi.org/10.1215/9780822394716

Bishop, S. (2013). *'Livability is the victim of street prostitution': The politics of the neighbourhood and the rightward turn in Vancouver's West End, 1981–1985.* (Unpublished MA thesis). Simon Fraser University, Vancouver, British Columbia. Retrieved from http://summit.sfu.ca/item/13511

Bociurkiw, M. (2016, June 15). Old homophobia is rising again in the United States: Orlando carnage occurred amid a terrifying new wave of anti-gay laws passed under the guise of freedom of religion. *Now.* Retrieved from https://nowtoronto.com/news/in-the-us-old-homophobia-is-rising-again/

Brock, D. (2009). *Making work, making trouble: The social regulation of sexual labour.* (2nd ed.). Toronto, ON: University of Toronto Press.

Bronski, M. (1998). *Pleasure principle: Sex, backlash, and the struggle for gay freedom.* New York, NY: St. Martin's Press.

Broverman, N. (2016, August 12). Canada is apologizing to its gay citizens – will America follow suit? *The Advocate.* Retrieved from https://www.advocate.com/world/2016/8/12/canada-apologizing-its-gay-citizens-should-america-follow-suit

Canadian Alliance for Sex Work Law Reform. (2016, September 20). Under anti-prostitution laws, sex workers face constrained choices. *Ricochet.* Retrieved from https://ricochet.media/en/1410/under-anti-prostitution-laws-sex-workers-face-constrained-choices

Cannon, M. (1998). The regulation of First Nations sexuality. *Canadian Journal of Native Studies, 18*(1), 280–94.

Catungal, J.P. (2017, November 28). "Trudeau's LGBTQ apology a good start, but it's not enough." *Maclean's Magazine.* Retrieved from http://www.macleans.ca/politics/trudeaus-lgbtq-apology-is-a-good-start-but-its-not-enough/

Chan, M. (1983, June 12). In this corner: ASP counters CROWE. *West Ender,* 9–10.

Chateauvert, M. (2013). *Sex workers unite: A history of the movement from Stonewall to SlutWalk.* Boston, MA: Beacon.

Churchill, D. (2004). Mother Goose's map: Tabloid geographies and gay male experience in 1950. *Journal of Urban History, 30*(6), 826–52. https://doi.org/10.1177/0096144204266743

Cifredo, J. (2016, November 19). Why are so many trans women of color murdered every year? *The Advocate.* Retrieved from https://www.advocate.com/commentary/2016/11/19/why-are-so-many-trans-women-color-murdered-every-year

Dean, A. (2015). *Remembering Vancouver's disappeared women: Settler colonialism and the difficulty of inheritance.* Vancouver, BC: UBC Press.

Dhoot, S. (2015). Pink games on stolen land: Pride House and (un)queer reterritorializations. In O.H. Dryden & S. Lenon (Eds.), *Disrupting queer inclusion: Canadian homonationalisms and the politics of belonging* (pp. 49–65). Vancouver, BC: UBC Press.

Duggan, L. (1992). The new homonormativity: The sexual politics of neoliberalism. In R. Castronova & D. Nelson (Eds.), *Materializing democracy: Toward a revitalized cultural politics* (pp. 175–94). Durham, NC: Duke University Press.

Egale. 2016. *Grossly indecent: Confronting the legacy of state-sponsored discrimination against Canada's LGBTQ2SI communities.* Retrieved from https://egale.ca/wp-content/uploads/2016/06/FINAL_REPORT_EGALE.pdf

Elliot, P. (2010). *Debates in transgender, queer, and feminist theory: Contested sites.* Surrey, BC: Ashford.

Farley, M. (2004). 'Bad for the body, bad for the heart': Prostitution harms women even if legalized or decriminalized. *Violence Against Women, 10*(10), 1087–25. https://doi.org/10.1177/1077801204268607

Ferris, S. (2015). *Street sex work and Canadian cities: Resisting a dangerous order.* Edmonton, AB: University of Alberta Press.

Foucault, M. (1980). *The history of sexuality.* (Vol. 1). New York, NY: Vintage.

Francis, D. (2006). *Red light neon: A history of prostitution in Vancouver.* Vancouver, BC: Subway.

Freund, M. (2002). The politics of naming: Constructing prostitutes and regulating women in Vancouver, 1939–1945. In J. McLaren, R. Menzies, & D. Chun (Eds.), *Regulating lives: Historical essays on the state, society, the individual, and the law* (pp. 231–58). Vancouver, BC: UBC Press.

Gilmore, S. (2010). Strange bedfellows: Building feminist coalitions around sex work in the 1970s. In N. Hewitt (Ed.), *No permanent waves* (pp. 342–94). New Brunswick, NJ: Rutgers University Press.

Hamilton, J.L. (2008). Interview with Becki L. Ross, Vancouver, British Columbia, February 12.

Hamilton, J.L., & Ross, B.L. (2014, July 2). Opinion: Sex workers seek apology, redress. *Vancouver Sun.* Retrieved from http://www.vancouversun.com/life/Opinion+workers+seek+apology+reparations/9990825/story.html

Hamilton, J.L., & Ross, B.L. (2016, October 14). Why some objections to sex workers memorial smack of moralism and sex shame: Whorephobia lives – the second coming of CROWE 2.0. *Daily Xtra.* Retrieved from https://www.dailyxtra.com/vancouver/news-and-ideas/opinion/objections-sex-workers-memorial-smack-moralism-and-sex-shame-208319?m=privacy-policy

Hartley, N. (1997). In the flesh: A porn star's journey. In J. Nagle (Ed.), *Whores and other feminists* (pp. 57–65). New York, NY: Routledge.

Hele, C., Sayers, N., & Hunt, S. (2015, September 14). What's missing from the conversation on missing and murdered Indigenous women and girls. *The Toast.* Retrieved from http://the-toast.net/2015/09/14/whats-missing-from-the-conversation-on-missing-and-murdered-indigenous-women/

Higgins, R. (1999). *De la clandestiné a l'affirmation: Pour une histoire de la communauté gaie montréalaise.* Montreal, QC: Comeau and Nadeau.

Hunt, S. (2013). Decolonizing sex work: Developing an intersectional Indigenous approach. In E. van der Meulen, E.M. Durisin, & V. Love (Eds.), *Selling sex: Experience, advocacy, and research on sex work in Canada* (pp. 82–100). Vancouver, BC: UBC Press.

Hunt, S. (2016). *An introduction to the health of two-spirit people: Historical, contemporary, and emergent issues.* Prince George, BC: National Collaborating Centre for Aboriginal Health.

Ibbitson, J. (2016, August 11). Trudeau to apologize for historical persecution of gay Canadians. *Globe and Mail.* Retrieved from https://www.theglobeandmail.com/news/politics/justin-trudeau-to-apologize-for-historic-persecution-of-gay-canadians/article31376155/

Ingram, G.B. (1997). 'Open space' as strategic queer sites. In G.B. Ingram, A.M. Bouthillette, & Y. Retter (Eds.), *Queers in space: Communities, public places, sites of resistance* (pp. 95–126). Seattle, WA: Bay.

Jeffreys, S. (2011). Live pornography: Strip clubs in the international political economy of prostitution. In M.T. Reist & A. Bray (Eds.), *Big porn inc.: Exposing the harms of the global pornography industry* (pp. 136–43). North Melbourne, Australia: Spinifex.

Jiwani, J. (2002). The criminalization of 'race' and the racialization of crime. In W. Chan & K. Mirchandani (Eds.), *Crimes of colour: Racialization and the criminal justice system in Canada* (pp. 67–86). Peterborough, ON: Broadview.

Jiwani, J., & Young, M.L. (2006). Missing and murdered women: Reproducing marginality in news discourse. *Canadian Journal of Communication, 31*(4), 895–917. https://doi.org/10.22230/cjc.2006v31n4a1825

Khan, J. (2016, July 6). Exclusive: Black Lives Matter Toronto co-founder responds to Pride action criticism. *Now.* Retrieved from https://nowtoronto.com/news/exclusive-black-lives-matter-pride-action-criticism/

Kinsman, G. (1996). *The regulation of desire: Homo and hetero sexualities.* Montreal, QC: Black Rose Books.

Kinsman, G., & Gentile, P. (2010). *The Canadian war on queers: National security as sexual regulation.* Vancouver, BC: UBC Press.

Korinek, V. (2012). 'We're the girls of the pansy parade': Historicizing Winnipeg's queer subcultures, 1930s–1970. *Social History/Histoire sociale, 45*(89), 117–55. https://doi.org/10.1353/his.2012.0002

Larsen, N. (1992). The politics of prostitution control: Interest group politics in four Canadian cities. *International Journal of Urban and Regional Research, 16*(2), 169–89. https://doi.org/10.1111/j.1468-2427.1992.tb00167.x

Lowman, J. (1986). Prostitution in Vancouver: Some notes on the genesis of a social problem. *Canadian Journal of Criminology, 28*(1), 1–16.

Lowman, J. (2000). Violence and the outlaw status of (street) prostitution in Canada. *Violence Against Women, 6*(9), 987–1011. https://doi.org/10.1177/10778010022182245

Lowman, J. (2013). Crown expert-witness testimony in *Bedford v. Canada:* Evidence-based argument or victim-paradigm hyperbole? In E. van der Meulen, E.M. Durisin, & V. Love (Eds.), *Selling sex: Experience, advocacy, and research on sex Work in Canada* (pp. 230–50). Vancouver, BC: UBC Press.

Mawani, R. (2009). *Colonial proximities: Cross-racial encounters and juridical truths in British Columbia, 1871–1921.* Vancouver, BC: UBC Press.

Maynard, S. (1997). Through a hole in the lavatory wall: Homosexual subcultures, police surveillance, and the dialectics of discovery, Toronto 1890–1930. In J. Parr

& M. Rosenfeld (Eds.), *Gender and history in Canada* (pp. 165–84). Toronto, ON: Copp-Clark.

Mbembe, A. (2003). Necropolitics. *Public Culture, 15*(1), 11–40. https://doi. org/10.1215/08992363-15-1-11

McEachern, A. (1985). *Attorney General of British Columbia v. Couillard et al.* (Judgment, July 4, 1984). In *British Columbia Law Reports* (Vol. 59, Part 1, pp. 102–12). Calgary, AB: Carswell Legal Publications.

McMaster, L. (2008). *Working girls in the West: Representations of wage-earning women.* Vancouver, BC: UBC Press.

Morgensen, S.L. (2011). *Spaces between us: Queer settler colonialism and Indigenous decolonization.* Minneapolis, MN: University of Minnesota Press. https://doi. org/10.5749/minnesota/9780816656325.001.0001

Muñoz, J.E. (2009). *Cruising utopia: The then and there of queer utopia.* New York, NY: New York University Press.

Nagle, J. (1997). Introduction. In J. Nagle (Ed.), *Whores and other feminists* (pp. 1–15). New York, NY: Routledge.

Namaste, V. (2005). *Sex change, social change: Reflections on identity, institutions, and imperialism.* Toronto, ON: Women's Press.

Namaste, V. (2015). *Oversight: Critical reflections on feminist research and politics.* Toronto, ON: Women's Press.

Newton, R. (2016a, September 13). Sex workers to be honoured with West End monument. *Daily Xtra.* Retrieved from https://www.dailyxtra.com/vancouver/news -and-ideas/news/sex-workers-honoured-with-west-end-monument-206261

Newton, R. (2016b, September 16). Police apologize for kicking sex workers out of West End: New memorial honours sex workers for the first time in Vancouver. *Daily Xtra.* Retrieved from https://www.dailyxtra.com/vancouver/news-and -ideas/news/police-apologize-kicking-sex-workers-west-end-206453

Nilsen, D. (1980). The 'social evil': Prostitution in Vancouver, 1900–1920. In B. Latham & C. Kess (Eds.), *In her own right* (pp. 205–28). Victoria, BC: Camosun College.

Panichelli, M., Wahab, S., Saunders, P., & Capous-Desyllas, M. (2015). Queering whiteness: Unpacking privilege within the US sex worker rights movement. In M. Laing, K. Pilcher, & N. Smith (Eds.), *Queer sex work* (pp. 234–44). New York, NY: Routledge.

Peñaloza, L. (1996). We're here, we're queer, and we're going shopping! A critical perspective on the accommodation of gays and lesbians in the U.S. marketplace. *Journal of Homosexuality, 31*(1–2), 9–41. https://doi.org/10.1300/ J082v31n01_02

Persky, S. (1989). *Buddies: Meditations on desire.* Vancouver, BC: New Star Books.

Pheterson, G. (1996). *The prostitution prism.* Amsterdam, NL: Amsterdam University Press.

Pivot Legal Society. (2013). *Supreme Court rules in favour of sex workers!* Retrieved from http://www.pivotlegal.org/canada_v_bedford_a_synopsis_of_the_supreme_ court_of_canada_ruling

Poutanen, M.A. (2015). *Beyond brutal passions: Prostitution in early nineteenth-century Montreal.* Montreal and Kingston: McGill-Queen's University Press.

Pratt, G. (2005). Abandoned women and the spaces of exception. *Antipode, 37*(5), 1052–78. https://doi.org/10.1111/j.0066-4812.2005.00556.x

Puar, J. (2007). *Terrorist assemblages: Homonationalism in queer times*. Durham, NC: Duke University Press. https://doi.org/10.1215/9780822390442

Queen, C. (1997). Sex radical politics, sex-positive feminist thought, and whore stigma. In J. Nagle (Ed.), *Whores and other feminists* (pp. 125–35). New York, NY: Routledge.

Ross, B.L. (1995). *The house that Jill built: A lesbian nation in formation*. Toronto, ON: University of Toronto Press.

Ross, B.L. (2010). Sex and (evacuation from) the city: The moral and legal regulation of sex workers in Vancouver's West End, 1975–1985. *Sexualities, 13*(2), 197–218. https://doi.org/10.1177/1363460709359232

Ross, B.L. (2012). Outdoor brothel culture: The un/making of a transsexual stroll in Vancouver's West End, 1975–1984. *Journal of Historical Sociology, 25*(1), 126–50. https://doi.org/10.1111/j.1467-6443.2011.01411.x

Ross, B.L., & Hamilton, J.L. (2016). West End Sex Workers Memorial: Redress and reconciliation, 2016. *Think Sociology!* 2(7), 4–5. Retrieved from http://soci.sites. olt.ubc.ca/files/2017/03/Fall-2016.pdf

Ross, B.L., & Sullivan, R. (2012). Tracing lines of horizontal hostility: How sex workers and gay activists battled for space, voice, and belonging in Vancouver, 1975–1985. *Sexualities, 15*(5–6), 604–21. https://doi.org/10.1177/1363460712446121

Rubin, G. (1984). Thinking sex: Notes for a radical theory of the politics of sexuality. In C. Vance (Ed.), *Pleasure and danger: Exploring female sexuality* (pp. 276–319). New York, NY: Routledge.

Shah, N. (2011). *Stranger intimacy: Contesting race, sexuality, and the law in the North American West*. Los Angeles, CA: University of California Press.

Smith, M. (1999). *Lesbian and gay rights in Canada: Social movements and equality-seeking, 1971–1995*. Toronto, ON: University of Toronto Press. https://doi.org/10.3138/9781442676633

Smith, M. (2014). Interview with Chris Bearchell, Lasqueti Island, 1996. *Journal of Canadian Studies, 48*(1), 252–75. https://doi.org/10.3138/jcs.48.1.252

Snorton, C.R., & Haritaworn, J. (2013). Trans necropolitics: A transnational reflection on violence, death and the trans of color afterlife. In S. Stryker & A.Z. Aizura (Eds.), *The transgender reader 2* (pp. 66–75). New York, NY: Routledge.

St. James, M. (1987). The reclamation of whores. In L. Bell (Ed.), *Good girls/bad girls: Sex workers and feminists face to face* (pp. 81–87). Toronto, ON: Women's Press.

Terry, J. (1999). *An American obsession: Science, medicine, and homosexuality in modern society*. Chicago, IL: University of Chicago Press. https://doi.org/10.7208/chicago/9780226793689.001.0001

Trevenen, K., & Degagne, A. (2015). Homonationalism at the border and in the streets: Organizing against exclusion and incorporation. In O.H. Dryden & S. Lenon (Eds.), *Disrupting queer inclusion: Canadian homonationalisms and the politics of belonging* (pp. 100–15). Vancouver, BC: UBC Press.

Vaid, U. (1995). *Virtual equality: The mainstreaming of gay and lesbian liberation*. New York, NY: Anchor Books.

Valverde, M. (2008). *The age of light, soap, and water: Moral reform in English Canada, 1885–1925.* (2nd ed.). Toronto, ON: McClelland and Stewart.

Walcott, R. (2015). Foreword. In O.H. Dryden & S. Lenon (Eds.), *Disrupting queer inclusion: Canadian homonationalisms and the politics of belonging* (pp. vii–ix). Vancouver, BC: UBC Press.

Warner, T. (2002). *Never going back: A history of queer activism in Canada.* Toronto, ON: University of Toronto Press.

Wingrove, J. (2014, July 15). Canada's new prostitution laws: Everything you need to know. *Globe and Mail.* Retrieved from https://www.theglobeandmail.com/news/politics/canadas-new-prostitution-laws-everything-you-need-to-know/article19610318/

Winsa, P., & Powell, B. (2016, June 21). Toronto Police to apologize for 1981 bathhouse raids. *Toronto Star.* Retrieved from https://www.thestar.com/news/insight/2016/06/21/toronto-police-to-apologize-for-1981-bathhouse-raids.html

Wiseman, L. (1983, July). The end. *Vancouver Magazine, 30*–35, 73.

Zangger, C. (2015). *For better or worse? Decriminalisation, work conditions, and indoor sex work in Auckland, New Zealand/Aotearoa.* (Unpublished doctoral dissertation). University of British Columbia, Vancouver, British Columbia. Retrieved from http://www.sexworklaw.co.nz/pdfs/Zangger_(2016)_PhD_Thesis.pdf

Cases

Canada (Attorney General) v. Bedford, 2013 SCC 72, [2013] 3 SCR 1101.

Legislation

Bill C-36, *Protection of Communities and Exploited Persons Act,* SC 2014, c. 25.

21

Fighting for Homewood

Gentrification and the History of
Violent Struggle over Trans Sex
Workers' Strolls in Canada

MORGAN M. PAGE

> They're trying to find ways to get us off of our territory, off of our comfort
> zone.
>
> – SIMONA BLACK, TRANS SEX WORKER AT HOMEWOOD AND MAITLAND (2009)

In the summer of 2008, tensions between homeowners and trans sex workers erupted in the heart of Toronto's historically gay Church and Wellesley Village, resulting in a series of violent attacks, harassment, protests, counter-protests, and increased policing in the neighbourhood. Caught in the cross-fire between angry local residents, LGBTQ community workers, municipal politicians, and sex work activists from around the city, trans sex workers on the stroll watched as their entire economy was decimated, never to recover. But how did we get here? In this chapter, I position this clash in relation to the long history of similar struggles between trans sex workers and gay neighbourhood residents across Canada that began in the late 1970s and continues today. The decriminalization of homosexuality, anti–sex work legislation, and the rise of gay-gentrification efforts all play key roles in understanding the history of violent struggle over trans sex workers' right to occupy public space in Canada. After examining the historical and political antecedents, I discuss the building of resistance against gentrification's deleterious effects on trans sex workers through the words of activists, residents, and sex workers, supplemented with my own recollections as a central member of the Take Back Homewood and Maitland organizing committee.

We've Been Here Before

The clash at the intersection of Toronto's Homewood Avenue and Maitland Place in 2008 was not the first instance of violent struggle between gay residents and trans sex workers in Canada. Two earlier cases, in Vancouver and Montreal, illustrate the painful divides and disparities within the LGBTQ community that have grown since the decriminalization of homosexuality in 1969 (Ross and Sullivan, 2012; see also Ross, this collection). When Prime Minister Pierre Trudeau amended the Criminal Code to remove provisions against adult homosexual sex and uttered his famous phrase "there's no place for the state in the bedrooms of the nation" (*CBC Television News*, 1967), a process of upward mobility began that saw the formation of gay villages and openly gay businesses across the country.

In the late 1970s, Vancouver's West End saw a sudden increase in street-based sex work following police raids on supper clubs frequented by sex workers, and since the Supreme Court of Canada ruled in *Hutt v. The Queen* (1978) that solicitation must be "pressing or persistent" to warrant criminal charges, many were able to engage in street-based work with little police interference (Ross, 2012). The stroll in the West End clustered around Davie Street – the centre of Vancouver's gay village (Ross and Sullivan, 2012), which had been recently emboldened by the decriminalization of homosexuality. Gay men in the neighbourhood began rapidly organizing for improved rights, leading to various conflicts with local law enforcement. In 1975 the Gay/Police Liaison Committee was formed to "mediate disputes between the gay community and the Vancouver Police Department" (ibid., p. 607). The committee's decision that "cruising and public sex had to be toned down" (ibid.) indicated a strong turn toward a politics of respectability.

The move toward respectability proved successful for the influx of largely white gay men who had been pouring into the Davie Street area during this period. By the early 1980s, however, aspirations of respectability had begun to clash with the vibrant street culture and, in particular, with the highly visible group of (largely Indigenous) trans sex workers who worked there. In 1980 growing anti-prostitution sentiments spurred a group of middle-class, white residents to form Concerned Residents of the West End (CROWE) – an anti–sex worker group headed by two gay men, Gordon Price and a man identified only as George. CROWE, along with "its vigilante posse" (Ross and Sullivan, 2012, p. 608) Shame the Johns, began waging an all-out war on sex workers in the West End; they organized street patrols and ad campaigns, recorded and published information on sex workers' clients, and even protested outside the homes of some clients – tactics that, as we will see shortly, were later taken up in Toronto. Meanwhile, CROWE success-fully lobbied politicians, gaining crucial support from Conservative mem-ber of Parliament Pat Carney. CROWE's campaign was so successful that in 1983 British Columbia's attorney general stated in no uncertain terms, "We are going to declare war on these people and drive them from the streets" (ibid., p. 609). As captured in the documentary *Hookers on Davie*, sex work-ers and their allies – including some gay residents – pushed back against CROWE through demonstrations organized by Vancouver's first sex work group, the Alliance for the Safety of Prostitutes (Dale and Cole, 1984).

In 1984, however, CROWE would deliver its victory blow with the help of the British Columbia Supreme Court's chief justice, Allan McEachern, who banned "blatant, aggressive, disorderly prostitutes" from the West End through an "unprecedented" legal injunction (Ross and Sullivan, 2012, p. 613). This effort to gentrify the physical space of the so-called gaybourhood (motivated by concerns over property values) was also an effort to clean up the image of homosexuality in Canada. It allowed white, upwardly mobile gay men to form alliances with their straight neighbours and politicians in the face of a common enemy: the hookers and transsexuals who were the queens of Davie Street at night.

Efforts to gain respectability did not stop in Vancouver. In the 1990s an eerily similar, although less well-documented, struggle unfolded in Mont-real's gay village. Located just east of the red light district – subsequently rebranded as the Quartier des Spectacles – this area in the 1980s and 1990s also had an active and vibrant street culture of trans sex workers and male hustlers (Namaste, 2000). Residents of the Centre-Sud gay village estab-lished a community group in the summer of 1993 to organize against the presence of transsexual sex workers and intravenous drug users. Although the group of "right wing extremists" (ibid., p. 298) was formed by residents of the gay neighbourhood, the sexual demographics of the group members remain unclear, as they also engaged in various homophobic activities. As Namaste writes, "groups of citizens harassed and assaulted sex workers in the area, intimidated their clients, and vandalized an apartment known to be a *piquerie,* or shooting gallery," for injection drug use (ibid., p. 154). Although officially the group distanced itself from such vigilante actions, Namaste recalls one meeting she attended in which a man openly discussed his plan to expel two Haitian trans sex workers from the neighbourhood by attacking them with a baseball bat (ibid., p. 154). She also notes that when the group demonstrated, its members used chants such as "dehors les putes" (whores out), "dehors les gauchistes" (leftists out), and "plus de tapettes dans notre quartier" (no more fags in our neighbourhood) (ibid., p. 298). These battles over public space and respectability played out on the bodies of racialized, trans women sex workers (see also Butler Burke, this collection). A thread of political violence is thus drawn from 1980s Vancouver to 1990s Montreal that takes us all the way to 2000s Toronto and the fight for Homewood.

The History of Homewood

To understand what happened that summer at Homewood, it is important to first take a brief look at the neighbourhood and its history. The corner of Homewood Avenue and Maitland Place is a pocket of quiet residential housing in the middle of downtown Toronto. A block or two in any direction are central arteries of the city. On the northwest corner is the field behind Jarvis Collegiate Institute, the second-oldest high school in Canada. To the northeast is a high-rise apartment, and to the south are a series of houses, another apartment building, and several public housing residences. This land was the original territory of the Mississaugas of the New Credit First Nation and is currently part of Toronto's historic gay village.

The sex workers and residents with whom I have spoken over the years have given conflicting accounts of the specific boundaries of the Homewood-Maitland stroll and when it came into existence. Most agree that the "tranny stroll" was originally on Church Street, the main thoroughfare in the heart of the gay village, and that trans sex workers were pushed farther east by business owners sometime in the 1980s. For a brief period, the stroll was at the corner of Jarvis and Maitland, before establishing itself at the corner of Homewood and Maitland at some point before the 1990s. Further oral history research would be needed to pinpoint an exact timeline, but this specific corner was a known sex work stroll for at least a decade and a half before the 2008 clashes. Its rough and permeable boundaries formed a square of streets with Wellesley at the north, Jarvis at the west, Sherbourne at the east, and Carleton at the south.

On May 21, 1996, Marcello Palma shot and murdered two trans sex workers – Deanna Wilkinson and Shawn Jr. Keegan – on Homewood Avenue, after murdering cisgender sex worker Brenda Ludgate in Parkdale, a different Toronto neighbourhood (Kealy, 1996). The tragic event sparked public outcry from all sides, with the newspapers blaming sex workers, gay residents blaming trans people, sex work activists blaming gays, and community workers blaming the lack of public services. Eventually, the out-cry led to the creation of Meal Trans, Canada's first multiservice trans pro-gram at the 519 Church Street Community Centre; it also planted the seeds for a movement to eradicate the "tranny stroll."

Resistance on Homewood

On the night of August 15, 2008, I received a series of text messages from my friend and fellow activist Rebecca Hammond, asking me to meet her at the corner of Homewood and Maitland. I was twenty-one years old and had had a long day working one of several minimum-wage jobs that I had taken on after "exiting" sex work. She urged me to come to a protest in support of trans sex workers. Although I knew nothing about the situation, I felt suffi-cient solidarity to attend the 11:00 p.m. event. When I arrived, there were approximately eighty sex worker rights activists gathered on the corner (Syms, 2008). Listening to Hammond and local sex worker activist Wendy Babcock speak on a megaphone, I learned that a group of residents from the Church and Wellesley area had formed the Homewood Maitland Safety Association (HMSA) and had been harassing and, according to some accounts, assaulting trans sex workers and their clients. Some of the sex workers who worked the stroll spoke directly about the harassment they had faced in recent months. Across the street huddled a group of about twenty HMSA members.

The night erupted within minutes, as the HMSA members, who were primarily white gay men, began screaming at us – a mixed-race and mixed-gender group of sex workers, queers, and other residents. The two groups converged, aggressively shouting at each other while the local LGBT media outlet *Daily Xtra* snapped pictures. Babcock moved back and forth between the groups, trying to reason with HMSA and delivering political sermons to the growing crowd of supporters and media. This continued until the HMSA members finally retired to their homes sometime after 2:00 a.m.

That night kicked off six weeks of counterprotests, largely organized by Babcock and myself. Every Friday and Saturday night between 11:00 p.m. and 4:00 a.m., Babcock and I would physically place our bodies between increasingly irate HMSA members and trans sex workers who were just trying to earn a living. Assisted by a small number of occasional helpers, we attempted to engage HMSA members in discussions about their harm-ful tactics. We also talked with sex-working residents about how best to support trans workers and their clients. We spoke regularly with the

police – whom HMSA called on a weekly basis – and with reporters cover-
ing the clashes for all of Toronto's major media outlets.

HMSA, led by Paul Hyde and Michel Bencini, was largely composed of
white, middle-class gay men who had recently purchased homes in the
neighbourhood (Syms, 2008). Hyde and his partner were the owners of Ban-
ting House, a gay bed and breakfast on Homewood (Houston, 2011). The
members of HMSA claimed that the neighbourhood's pre-existing, active
street economy (into which they had moved) caused a number of problems
for them – including "bringing noise, bumper-to-bumper traffic and fights
at all hours" (Syms, 2008, n.p.). They also claimed that trans sex workers had
attacked at least one member of their group (*Daily Xtra*, 2009); surprisingly,
the pro-police HMSA does not appear to have brought charges against the
accused (and unnamed) worker. They further claimed that the presence of
trans sex workers drove down property values – the same low property values that had enabled them to buy homes in the heart of downtown Toronto
in the first place. The group argued that sex workers should be moved to a
red light district that did not yet exist, claiming that the neighbourhood's
transformation was already underway: "We can't turn back the clock – this
area has become gentrified. It's just a sociological fact. The kind of upper-
middle-class person who buys here has a very low tolerance for illegal activity" (Bencini, quoted in Syms, 2008, n.p.).

Interestingly, HMSA relied on a number of tactics pioneered by CROWE
and Shame the Johns two decades earlier in Vancouver, as well as on tactics
employed over ten years before in Montreal. In addition to organizing street
patrols to physically intimidate trans sex workers with placards displaying
anti–sex work slogans and with what one worker described to me as "large
flashlights" used to assault workers, HMSA members recorded licence
plates of clients and posted them on the Internet. They also actively lobbied
local government, beginning with City Councillor Kyle Rae, followed years
later by City Councillor Kristyn Wong-Tam. Rae, to his credit, refused their
impossible call to "move the hookers": "I can't move them. And I'm not
going to move them" (quoted in Baute, 2008, n.p.). Instead, Rae tried to
mediate between workers and HMSA members through the 519 Church
Street Community Centre.

HMSA attempted to draw support from other residents by printing
anti–sex worker flyers and distributing them in mailboxes up and down the
street. Not all residents, however, were supportive of their efforts. For
example, Claude Mercure, who lived in the same building as Hyde and Bencini, told a reporter, "If they [trans sex workers] were pushy or unpleasant,

or if there were many of them, I might object to their presence. But I've lived here nine years, and it has never bothered me" (quoted in Syms, 2008, n.p.). In addition to distributing flyers, HMSA carried out a targeted campaign of harassment in the "blogosphere" (ibid.) against me, Babcock, and other supporters of the sex workers, although it denied responsibility for the most violent forms of intimidation, which included threatening to "come after" me if I did not stop going to Homewood. Beyond threats, its members delighted in shouting misogynist obscenities at me and Babcock, most memorably telling Babcock to "get the sand out of your vagina, Wendy!"

Babcock and I prioritized building relationships with sex workers on the stroll. The women and drag queens we talked with were primarily Indigenous, some living with HIV, and many had worked the stroll for a decade or longer. They told us that HMSA members had physically attacked some of them. One trans woman, Alicia, reported that they had swarmed her one night when she had tried to enter a friend's car. "Everybody in the city is entitled to use of that street and everyone who is [a] Canadian citizen is entitled to use of that street," she said at the time (quoted in Baute, 2008, n.p.).

After six weeks of clashes, Babcock and I were exhausted – as were HMSA members, many of whom had stopped coming outside, partly due to the change in weather. After consulting with sex workers, who had seen a dramatic drop in clientele over the past few months of harassment, we ceased our counterpatrols. Although tensions settled for the winter, HMSA sprang back into action the following spring. At the 519 Church Street Community Centre in early 2009, I attended a community mediation where City Councillor Kyle Rae and community worker Kyle Scanlon attempted to defuse the friction between HMSA and sex workers. The meeting quickly devolved into a shouting match, as HMSA members denounced Rae and Scanlon for not taking their side. The group continued sporadic activities over the next several years (Houston, 2011), regaining momentum after Wong-Tam took Rae's spot on Toronto City Council in 2010. Wong-Tam, more amenable to the displacement of sex workers than was Rae, consulted with HMSA on a proposed vehicle-turning restriction that would prevent clients from being able to drive down Homewood after dark – an approach that even the police admitted would be largely ineffective (ibid.).

But by this time, the street-based sex work economy on Homewood had already been devastated by HMSA's actions. In 2010 I began working as the coordinator of trans community services at the 519 Church Street Community Centre, providing, alongside a peer worker, weekly street outreach on Homewood and in surrounding areas. Between 2010 and 2014, we saw the once vibrant and active stroll dissipate into a shadow of its former self. Although Homewood still draws a small number of trans sex workers, most have been displaced to adjacent neighbourhoods that are farther from the lively crowds of the gay village without groupings of queer and trans community members that provide safety and security; or they have decided to move their business online.

Conclusion

The battle for Homewood is only one recent example in the ongoing struggle between upwardly mobile, white gay men and racialized and other trans sex workers over public spaces in Canada (see also Ross, this collection). These violent conflicts highlight the pronounced economic and political disparity within Canada's LGBTQ community, which cuts along race, class, and gender lines. Although the street culture of trans sex workers – a source of sisterhood and strength for many of them (Ross, 2012) – has never fully recovered in Vancouver, Montreal, and Toronto, this somewhat forgotten history of sex workers pushing back against gentrification can provide us with the seeds of inspiration for future resistance.

References

Baute, N. (2008, September 6). Take a walk on someone else's wild side. *Toronto Star*. Retrieved from https://www.thestar.com/news/2008/09/06/take_a_walk_on_someone_elses_wild_side.html

CBC Television News. (1967, December 21). Trudeau: 'There's no place for the state in the bedrooms of the nation.' Retrieved from http://www.cbc.ca/archives/entry/omnibus-bill-theres-no-place-for-the-state-in-the-bedrooms-of-the-nation

Daily Xtra. (2009, October 2). Checking out Toronto's tranny sex worker stroll. Retrieved from https://www.youtube.com/watch?v=vce7AWAa4R8

Dale, H., & Cole, J. (1984). *Hookers on Davie*. (Documentary). Spectrum Films.

Houston, A. (2011, November 2). Homewood Stroll battle heats up. *Daily Xtra*. Retrieved from https://www.dailyxtra.com/toronto/news-and-ideas/news/homewood-stroll-battle-heats-4631

Kealy, M. (1996, June 6). Gays isolate hookers, activist says. *Daily Xtra*. Retrieved from http://www.walnet.org/csis/news/toronto_96/xtra-960606.html

Namaste, V. (2000). *Invisible lives: The erasure of transsexual and transgendered people*. Chicago, IL: University of Chicago Press.

Ross, B.L. (2012). Outdoor brothel culture: The un/making of a transsexual stroll in Vancouver's West End, 1975–1984. *Journal of Historical Sociology, 25*(1), 126–50. https://doi.org/10.1111/j.1467-6443.2011.01411.x

Ross, B.L., & Sullivan, R. (2012). Tracing lines of horizontal hostility: How sex workers and gay activists battled for space, voice, and belonging in Vancouver, 1975–1985. *Sexualities, 15*(5–6), 604–21. https://doi.org/10.1177/1363460712446121

Syms, S. (2008, September 11). On the stroll: Sex work and fireworks at Homewood and Maitland. *Daily Xtra*. Retrieved from https://www.dailyxtra.com/on-the-stroll-37756

Legislation

Hutt v. The Queen [1978] 2 SCR 476.

22

Do Black Sex Workers' Lives Matter?
Whitewashed Anti-Slavery, Racial Justice, and Abolition

ROBYN MAYNARD

Claiming to be a modern anti-slavery ambassador has social cachet. On billboards, in commercials, and online, highly visible anti-prostitution campaigns pledging to "abolish sexual slavery" abound – often premised on saving or freeing sex workers and eradicating the sex industry by criminalizing clients and third parties. This messaging has become a familiar part of the Canadian and American landscape and beyond. At the same time, with far less visibility and funding, another revitalized abolition movement has been steadfastly mobilizing for the abolition of prisons and punitive regimes. Incarcerated political prisoners, radical Black activists and scholars, and writers from diverse backgrounds have organized for the abolition of carceral punishment systems on the premise that "prison is the modern day manifestation of the plantation" (James, 2005, p. xxiii).[1] Perhaps the most recognizable face of this movement is Angela Davis, a former political prisoner and modern-day icon of the Black anti-incarceration struggle. What, then, are we to do in a context where two movements – anti-prostitution and prison abolitionism – lay claim to the same historical legacy, with anti-prostitution advocates linking their contemporary struggle to that of those who fought to end chattel slavery in the Americas?

Slavery's legacy is not a politically neutral metaphor. The transatlantic slave trade was one of the world's most violent acts of genocide and dispossession, and invoking chattel slavery to lend moral support to one's political cause should not be undertaken lightly. Scholar of Black art history and slavery studies Charmaine Nelson (2016), paraphrasing novelist Toni Morrison, states that transatlantic slavery "'broke the world in half,' spanning more than four hundred years and causing cataclysmic ruptures of the social, political, cultural, and psychic contexts of vast populations" (p. 1). In a historical moment when merely stating that "Black lives matter" is controversial, if not dangerous, invoking notions of slavery remains ethically, emotionally, and historically loaded, as Black men and women are still living and dying in slavery's wake. In what many are calling the Age of Ferguson, when police killings of Black people regularly go unpunished, it is perhaps more urgent than ever to look critically at movements that use the call to end slavery in order to push for the criminalization of the exchange of sexual services. Just as it is often overlooked that the violence of slavery was gendered – enslaved Black women were not only forced to perform labour similar to that of men, in addition to the burden of domestic duties, but were also subject to rape and other forms of sexual violence (Cooper, 2006; Davis, 2005) – overlooked, too, is slavery's living legacy for Black women today. Endemic state violence against Black cis and transgender women is ongoing yet largely invisible (Crenshaw and Ritchie, 2015; Maynard, 2017; Tanovich, 2011). As Black, feminist anti-carceral activism reaches new heights, it is now more than ever essential to intervene in any invocations of abolition that participate in the resubjugation of Black people, particularly of Black women.

Given this context, I approach this chapter on the uses and abuses of abolition from a Black, intersectional, feminist framework, focusing on historical and contemporary abolition movements as they have impacted, and been impacted by, Black women's lives and organizing. In so doing, I argue that the (ab)use of the term "abolition" by anti-prostitution crusaders appropriates Black suffering, exacerbating the harms toward Black women in general and toward those with perceived or real involvement in the sex industry in particular. Moreover, I argue that this whitewashed abolition has undermined liberation struggles led by Black women (both cis and trans) to end racially targeted punishment.

A Brief History of Two Abolitions: Historical Movements to Address "Neoslavery"

The term "abolition" evokes the history of multiple struggles to end the transatlantic slave trade and the practice of enslaving Africans as chattel. Although a detailed history of these movements and those that followed is beyond the scope of this chapter, it is worth noting that, within the Americas, "abolition" often refers more specifically to the liberation movement led by formerly enslaved Black persons in the United States and, to a lesser extent, Canada, such as Hariett Tubman, Frederick Douglas, Mary Ann Shadd, and Sojourner Truth, as well as to white allied individuals and organizations that fought the economy of enslavement. And although, as James (2005) reminds us, abolitionism has never been an ideologically uniform movement – indeed, abolitionists held varied ideas surrounding racial justice and state violence – and although not all were anti-racist, for the purposes of this chapter, I argue that abolition at least *should* have a relationship to the emancipatory visions of Black freedom fought for by formerly enslaved persons, not to the often flawed visions of their white supporters.

Slavery formally ended in Canada in 1834 and in the United States in 1865. But looking toward the late nineteenth and early twentieth centuries, we see that both anti-prostitution and racial justice organizers saw themselves as taking up slavery's legacy by working toward the abolition of what slavery left in its wake. In 1904 civil rights activist W.E.B. Du Bois published an edited collection entitled *Some Notes on Negro Crime, Particularly in Georgia,* which situated post-emancipation slavery in the surge in arrests and forced, unpaid prisoner labour of largely Black inmates. Since then, many Black scholars, including Angela Davis (2003), Joy James (2005), and Sarah Haley (2016), have continued to identify imprisonment and forced labour of Black persons after emancipation as the direct lineage of slavery. James (2005) has an expansive understanding of neoslavery that includes the state-sanctioned racial violence and terror that have been, and continue to be, inflicted on racialized bodies, including lynching in the late nineteenth and twentieth centuries. In Canada, despite the absence of practices such as chain gangs and convict leasing, slavery-era tropes continued to haunt formally emancipated Black men and women. We see this situation in, for example, the high rates of arrest and deportation of Black persons throughout the time period (Maynard, 2017; Walker, 2010; see also Mathieu, 2010). This underacknowledged reality renders evident the legacy of "managing" Blackness through punitive state policy and Black captivity in the wake of slavery's abolition.

It follows, then, that abolition, after slavery's end, involved challenging the prevailing anti-Blackness that continued to structure social institutions. Individuals like Ida B. Wells who fought convict leasing and lynchings throughout the nineteenth and twentieth centuries is an example of post-emancipation abolitionism (James, 2005, p. xxxiii). Highly critical, too, of the criminalization of Black women and men, she mobilized against both racist and gendered state violence (Hobson, 2016). In Canada Black women also organized against other forms of state-mandated discrimination that conscripted Black lives to deprivation, poverty, and social death.[2]

Although the politics of Wells and others included a critique of Black criminalization and dehumanization, another so-called abolitionist movement emerged at the same time, which created, rather than challenged, racial injustice. Unlike Black activists, anti-prostitution campaigners of the same era did not acknowledge slavery's legacy of incarceration, lynchings, and other forms of state violence but focused on prostitution and called for the protection of white women from racialized men. In doing so, they forwarded a whitewashed notion of slavery voided of its relationship to Black dehumanization. In Canada in the late nineteenth and early twentieth centuries, the National Committee for the Suppression of the White Slave Traffic, supported by the National Council of Women and the Women's Christian Temperance Union, identified Chinese and Japanese men as the purported leading perpetrators of the white slave trade – that is, the traffic in white women's bodies. This moral panic was used to drum up support for the restriction of nonwhite immigration to Canada (Mawani, 2009; Valverde, 1991).

The so-called new slavery was also implicated in asserting state control over Black women's bodies and sexuality. Slavery-era tropes denigrating Black women as deviant and hypersexual were originally crafted to "deflec[t] attention from racialized sexual violence inflicted by white men" (James, 1996, p. 142). After emancipation, these same tropes were used to punish and regulate Black women. In Canada, for example, popular and state representations of Black women as degraded and immoral "Jezebels" affected all Black women, including those working as domestics, who were subject to deportation throughout the twentieth century for suspected sexual immorality and prostitution (Calliste, 1993–94). We see, too, that Canadian anti-prostitution laws had a significant impact on Black women, who were disproportionately arrested for prostitution offences in cities across the country (Maynard, 2017; Mosher, 1998; Walker, 2010). At the same time, the Women's Christian Temperance Union in the southern United States represented Black women as sexual deviants who needed to be quarantined from society and kept under the watchful eye of middle-class, white women (Haley, 2016). In contrast to the racial justice abolitionist work by Black men and women, anti-prostitution abolitionists mobilized the emotive racist narratives of the transatlantic slave trade in their anti-Black political projects, which enabled the surveillance, arrest, confinement, and deportation of Black women and other racialized populations in the wake of emancipation.

(Neo)slavery and Abolitionist Strategies Today

Black emancipation has remained elusive despite formal equality through national policies such as the Charter of Rights and Freedoms. State-sanctioned violence and neglect continue to mark definitively the Black experience in both Canada and the United States and, indeed, in the entire African diaspora. This situation can be seen in the ongoing hyper-surveillance of Black men and women, the largely unpunished deaths of Black persons at the hands of police, and the many Black people who waste away behind bars across North America. These are all part of what African American scholar Saidiya Hartman (2007) refers to as slavery's "afterlives" (p. 6) – the multi-faceted forms of unfreedom that are institutionalized in the treatment of Blackness. James (2005) likewise names the war on drugs, penal sites, immigration detention centres, and police stations as contemporary "dead zones" of democracy and as the locations of (neo)slavery (p. xxxi). In particular, Black women remain one of Canada's poorest demographics and one of the fastest-rising prison populations in the country (Sapers, 2015). Black women have their children taken away by child welfare agencies at appalling rates and have been disproportionately arrested for drug trafficking and other poverty offences (Lawrence and Williams, 2006; United Nations, 2016).

It stands to reason that if early feminists like Wells were turn-of-the-century abolitionists, those fighting state violence against Black lives today are the rightful inheritors of contemporary abolitionist struggle. Indeed, Black and racialized feminists deliberately assume this legacy. Activist groups such as BYP100, Black Lives Matter, and INCITE! Women of Color Against Violence locate the state as the primary source of harm against racialized persons and consciously address the legacies of slavery by taking aim at state violence and the criminalization of Black, brown, and poor people, with a particular focus on women, trans persons, and gender nonconformists (e.g., see INCITE! Women of Color Against Violence, 2006). Due to the work of Black and racialized feminists like Angela Davis, Andrea Ritchie, and Beth Richie, as well as innumerable activists who are less well known, there are vibrant contemporary movements with the explicit goal of ending state and gender-based violence against women of colour, *without* the use of the criminal justice system.

Despite significant differences, like their turn-of-the-century counter-parts, anti-prostitution organizations continue to forward an anti-slavery narrative that is too often devoid of solidarity with Black lives and politics. Slavery remains, here, decontextualized from Black struggle and is instead repurposed to describe the multiplicity of workplaces where sexual services are exchanged for remuneration: brothels, dance clubs, massage parlours, and the street. This anti-prostitution abolition, like its historical predeces-sor, perpetuates rather than combats carceral practices that negatively impact Black women's lives and exacerbate state violence.

Hundreds of millions of dollars globally have been allocated to cam-paigns aimed at eradicating prostitution by means of criminalization (GAATW, 2014). This is frequently done using highly emotive anti-slavery narratives and discourses as a moral backdrop. For example, the Coalition Against Trafficking in Women, a prominent US-based anti-prostitution group, frequently lobbies for the criminalization of the sex industry, casually referred to as contemporary slavery (CATW, 2001). In Canada former Con-servative member of Parliament Joy Smith repeatedly evoked the imperative to "rescue the victims of Modern Day Slavery" in order to justify legislation criminalizing sex work (see Smith, n.d.) and explicitly assumed a direct lin-eage with those who fought and opposed the transatlantic slave trade (Smith, 2015). The rape crisis centre located in Vancouver, called Rape Relief, simi-larly links its efforts to criminalize all forms of prostitution to the anti-slavery movements of the eighteenth century in the West Indies, the United States, and Canada. It further positions itself as a modern anti-slavery ambassador in "a new international abolitionist movement [that] has recently emerged" (Lakeman, 2008, n.p.). Although invoking slavery pro-vides important emotional weight to those who wish to criminalize prosti-tution, its association with slavery results in an empirically inaccurate description of the sex industry as a whole. In Canada a national study inves-tigating the topic found that most women working in the sex trade do not consider themselves victims, nor could they be considered slaves by any legal categorization (Benoit et al., 2014). Despite invoking slavery and its abolition, there remains little acknowledgment in the anti-prostitution movement of the legacies of brutality against Black persons that have fol-lowed in the wake of Black enslavement or of the ongoing harms posed by the criminal justice system in Black communities.

Troublingly, not only is Black suffering appropriated and evacuated from this so-called new abolitionist movement, but it is also invoked to champion measures that will clearly harm marginalized women who sell or trade sex.

In Canada contemporary advocates of sex work abolition support "end-demand" intiatives, known as the Swedish model. Although this approach is purportedly aimed at decriminalizing the activities of people who sell sex, always assumed to be victimized women, it has actually resulted in arrests of street-based sex workers,[3] and it still leaves the state the power to criminalize sex workers who work in groups or with third parties for safety. End-demand policy and policing approaches put in place by the Vancouver Police Department even prior to the recent modifications to the Criminal Code, which purport to protect sex workers by criminalizing clients, left street-based sex workers isolated, displaced, and vulnerable to violence (Krüsi et al., 2014; see also Krüsi, Belack, and Sex Workers United Against Violence, this collection). As in many unregulated and criminalized industries, working conditions in the sex sector can be far from ideal, and indeed some may experience coercion and violence, particularly racialized, Indigenous, Black, and migrant street-based workers. Yet these conditions are exacerbated, not improved, by criminalizing aspects of the commercial exchange of sexual services. Criminalizing prostitution, then, is hardly analogous to anti-slavery since anti-prostitution laws are demonstrably counterproductive in addressing or abolishing forced labour and coercion (Maynard, 2015; UNAIDS, 2009).

Criminalizing and demonizing sex work places Black women in danger since popular associations of cis and transgender Black women with "deviant sexuality" and prostitution continue to inform policing practices and state violence against Black women. Although there have been no large-scale contemporary Canadian studies on Black women and sex work specifically (although see Raguparan, this collection) – or even on Black women in the criminal justice system – the Ontario Human Rights Commission has found that Black women reported being profiled as prostitutes by police when they were in a car with a white man, assumed to be their customer (Ontario Human Rights Commission, 2003). The police identified suspected prostitution as among the reasons that a Jamaican tourist, Audrey Smith, was stripped naked at a busy intersection in Toronto in 1993 (Lawson, 2002; Maynard, 2017). Presumed prostitution was, as well, the reason given by law enforcement officers for stopping Stacy Bonds on a street in Ottawa, before she was violently physically and sexually assaulted in police custody in 2008 (Maynard, 2017; Tanovich, 2011). In both cases, the allegations of prostitution turned out to be false. In Montreal Black and racialized cis and transgender women, particularly trans migrant women involved in street-based sex work, have been subjected to profiling and police violence (Butler Burke,

2016; Maynard, 2017; see also Butler Burke, this collection). American data confirm similar forms of abuse.[4] As has been the case historically, the relationship between Black women and police, existing within a larger context of anti-Blackness in the criminal and immigration enforcement agencies, has been hostile. Regardless of intent, increasing the policing and criminalization of sex work renders Black and other racialized women more, not less, vulnerable to state violence.

Measured against the harms that their end-demand framework and tactics have imposed on Black women, anti-prostitution campaigners cannot, ethically speaking, be called abolitionists. I am neither arguing that all anti-prostitution advocates are racist nor denying the valuable and important services that some groups provide. Nonetheless, under the banner of abolition, movements to criminalize sex work co-opt the horrors of slavery to justify racist state practices and create conditions that keep Black women in general and Black sex workers in particular vulnerable to harassment, profiling, arrest, and violence. Just as importantly, the appropriation of the term "abolition" by anti-prostitution advocates undermines the organizing of current Black feminist movements against state and carceral violence; that is, it undermines the prison-abolition organizing of populations most directly impacted by incarceration.

Conclusion

The legacy of the abolition of slavery rightly belongs to those who are still living (and dying) in its wake. More than 100 years after Ida B. Wells documented the racist lynching practices of the United States and following decades of organizing by Black and other racialized women across Canada and the United States, the issue of police and state violence against Black women is finally beginning to be identified and addressed outside of small community and activist circles (see Crenshaw and Ritchie, 2015). Regardless of intention, the harms created by an overreliance on the criminal justice system as the "front-line approach toward ending violence against women of colour" (CR10 Publications Collective, 2008, p. 21) are clear, and grassroots movements are taking heed. The Movement for Black Lives has insisted that those most marginalized, including Black sex workers and trans women, must be moved from "the margins into the center" (Charlene Carruthers, quoted in Sankofa, 2016; see also Black Lives Matter, 2016). When we centre the experiences of Black women with real or perceived involvement in the sex trade, it becomes clear that the criminalization of prostitution is a source of harm to Black women and that the decriminalization of sex work is indeed a racial justice issue.

Yet the decriminalization of sex work should also be part of a larger movement for prison abolition, as Indigenous, Black, and migrant sex workers, particularly those who are transgender, face enormous legal barriers beyond prostitution law, including state surveillance and the overpolicing of their very existence. Even with the decriminalization of sex work, they would quite likely remain targeted by oppressive state policies and practices like racialized drug, child welfare, and immigration enforcement. A sex worker rights movement grounded in racial justice and abolition must go beyond decriminalizing sex work to address all forms of harms experienced by all sex workers, particularly the most marginalized (see also Lam and Gallant, this collection). Although decriminalizing sex work is crucial for gender and racial justice, so too is decriminalizing drugs. Indeed, the decriminalization of both sex work and drugs is necessarily part of a larger political decarceration movement advocating for disinvestment from punitive institutions such as prisons and border regulation and for investment in health, education, and work (Davis, 2003; Black Lives Matter, 2016). Black feminist praxis is rooted in the notion that freedom is "the necessary universal outcome for all if those at the bottom of society attain theirs" (Hobson, 2016, p. 6). It is only in allying ourselves to end the state's war on Black women, including trans Black women and Black sex-working women, that we can truly deign to call ourselves abolitionists.

Notes

This chapter is based on a previously published blog posting: Maynard, R. (2015, September 9). #Blacksexworkerslivesmatter: White-washed 'anti-slavery' and the appropriation of Black suffering. Retrieved from http://www.thefeministwire.com/2015/09/blacksexworkerslivesmatter-white-washed-anti-slavery-and-the-appropriation-of-black-suffering/

1 There is a long history, too, of penal abolition in the Quaker movement dating back to the 1700s, which is ongoing to the present day.
2 For a brilliant historical anthology on Black Canadian women fighting state-sanctioned racism, assembled by Black feminist historians, see *'We're Rooted Here and They Can't Pull Us Up': Essays in African Canadian Women's History* (Bristow et al., 1999).
3 In fact, the law has been used to arrest street-based sex workers. For example, an article published in the *St. Catharines Standard* shows a woman in handcuffs and quotes a police officer, Staff Sergeant Jim Leigh, as saying, "We arrest them, and they are offered a diversion program" (Sawchuk, 2016).

4 Ritchie and Mogul (2007) found that racialized cis and trans sex workers in the United States experience high rates of sexual assault at the hands of police. Another American report found that that nearly 40 percent of Black and Black-multiracial transgender persons who traded or sold sexual services had been subjected to pervasive harassment, violence, and arrest (Fitzgerald, Patterson, and Hickey, 2015).

References

Benoit, C., Atchison, C., Casey, L., Jansson, M., McCarthy, B., Phillips, R., & Shaver, F.M. (2014). *A 'working paper' prepared as background to Building on the Evidence: An International Symposium on the Sex Industry in Canada.* Retrieved from http://www.nswp.org/resource/gender-violence-and-health-contexts -vulnerability-resiliencies-and-care-among-people-the

Black Lives Matter. (2016). *A vision for black lives.* Retrieved from https://policy. m4bl.org/

Bristow, P., Brand, D., Carty, L., Cooper, A.P., Hamilton, S., & Shadd, A. (1999). *'We're rooted here and they can't pull us up': Essays in African Canadian women's history.* Toronto, ON: University of Toronto Press.

Butler Burke, N. (2016). Connecting the dots: National security, the crime-migration nexus and trans women's survival. In T. Martínez-San Miguel & S. Tobias (Eds.), *Trans studies: The challenge to hetero/homo normativities* (pp. 113–21). New Brunswick, NJ: Rutgers University Press.

Calliste, A. (1993–94). Race, gender and Canadian immigration policy: Blacks from the Caribbean, 1900–1932. *Journal of Canadian Studies, 28*(4), 131–48. https:// doi.org/10.3138/jcs.28.4.131

CATW (Coalition Against Trafficking in Women). (2001, April 27). *Written statement to the United Nations Commission on Human Rights 57th Session.* Retrieved from http://catwinternational.org/Home/Article/53-written-statement-to-the-united-nations-commission-on-human-rights-57th-session

Cooper, A. (2006). *The hanging of Angélique: The untold story of Canadian slavery and the burning of old Montreal.* Toronto, ON: HarperCollins.

Crenshaw, K.W., & Ritchie, A.J. (2015). *Say her name: Resisting police brutality against black women.* Retrieved from http://static1.squarespace.com/static/ 53f20d90e4b0b80451158d8c/t/560c068ee4b0af26f72741df/1443628686535/ AAPF_SMN_Brief_Full_singles-min.pdf

CR10 Publications Collective. (2008). *Abolition now! Ten years of strategy and struggle against the prison industrial complex.* Oakland, CA: AK Press.

Davis, A.Y. (2003). *Are prisons obsolete?* New York, NY: Seven Stories Press.

Davis, A.Y. (2005). Reflections on the black woman's role in the community of slaves (abridged). In J. James (Ed.), *The new abolitionists: (Neo)slave narratives and contemporary prison writings* (pp. 101–12). Albany, NY: State University of New York Press.

Du Bois, W.E.B. (Ed.). (1904). *Some notes on Negro crime, particularly in Georgia.* Atlanta, GA: Atlanta University Press.

Fitzgerald, E., Patterson, S.E., & Hickey, D. (2015). *Meaningful work: Transgender experiences in the sex trade.* Retrieved from http://www.transequality.org/sites/default/files/Meaningful%20Work-Full%20Report_FINAL_3.pdf

GAATW (Global Alliance Against Traffic in Women). (2014). Following the money: Spending on anti-trafficking. *Anti-Trafficking Review,* (3), 1–175. Retrieved from http://gaatw.org/ATR/AntiTraffickingReview_Issue3.2014.Following_the_Money.pdf

Haley, S. 2016. *No mercy here: Gender, punishment, and the making of Jim Crow modernity.* Chapel Hill, NC: University of North Carolina Press.

Hartman, S. (2007). *Lose your mother: A journey along the Atlantic slave route.* New York, NY: Farrar, Straus and Giroux.

Hobson, J. (2016). Introduction. In J. Hobson (Ed.), *Are all the women still white? Rethinking race, expanding feminisms* (pp. 1–18). Albany, NY: State University of New York Press.

INCITE! Women of Color Against Violence (Ed.). (2006). *Color of violence: The INCITE! anthology.* Cambridge, MA: South End.

James, J. (1996). *Resisting state violence: Radicalism, gender, and race in U.S. culture.* Minneapolis, MN: University of Minnesota Press.

James, J. (2005). Introduction: Democracy and captivity. In J. James (Ed.), *The new abolitionists: (Neo)slave narratives and contemporary prison writings* (pp. xxi–xlii). Albany, NY: State University of New York Press.

Krüsi, A., Pacey, K., Bird, L., Taylor, C., Chettier, J., Allan, S., ... Shannon, K. (2014). Criminalisation of clients: Reproducing vulnerabilities for violence and poor health among street-based sex workers in Canada – a qualitative study. *British Medical Journal Open,* 4(6), 1–10. http://dx.doi.org/10.1136/bmjopen-2014-005191.

Lakeman, L. (2008). *Abolition of prostitution: A feminist definition of abolition.* Retrieved from http://www.rapereliefshelter.bc.ca/campaigns/abolition-prostitution/abolition-prostitution

Lawrence, S.N., & Williams, T. (2006). Swallowed up: Drug couriers at the borders of Canadian sentencing. *University of Toronto Law Journal,* 56(4), 285–332. https://doi.org/10.1353/tlj.2006.0015

Lawson, E. (2002). Images in Black: Black women, media and the mythology of an orderly society. In N.N. Wane, K. Deliovsky, & E. Lawson (Eds.), *Back to the drawing board: African-Canadian feminisms* (pp. 199–223). Toronto, ON: Sumach.

Mathieu, S.J. (2010). *North of the color line: Migration and black resistance in Canada, 1870–1955.* Chapel Hill, NC: University of North Carolina Press.

Mawani, R. (2009). *Colonial proximities: Crossracial encounters and juridical truths in British Columbia, 1871–1921.* Vancouver, BC: UBC Press.

Maynard, R. (2015). Fighting wrongs with wrongs? How Canadian anti-trafficking crusades have failed sex workers, migrants, and Indigenous communities. *Atlantis: Critical Studies in Gender, Culture, and Social Justice,* 37(2), 40–56.

Maynard, R. (2017). *Policing black lives: State violence in Canada from slavery to the present.* Black Point, NS: Fernwood.

Mosher, C.J. (1998), *Discrimination and denial: Systemic racism in Ontario's legal and criminal justice system, 1892–1961.* Toronto, ON: University of Toronto Press.

Nelson, C. 2016. *Slavery, geography and empire in nineteenth-century marine landscapes of Montreal and Jamaica.* New York, NY: Routledge.

Ontario Human Rights Commission. (2003). *Paying the price: The human cost of racial profiling.* Retrieved from http://www.ohrc.on.ca/en/paying-price-human-cost-racial-profiling

Ritchie, A.J., & Mogul, J. (2007). *In the shadows of the War on Terror: Persistent police brutality and abuse of people of color in the United States.* Retrieved from http://www2.ohchr.org/english/bodies/cerd/docs/ngos/usa/USHRN15.pdf

Sankofa, J. (2016, December 12). From margin to center: Sex work decriminalization is a racial justice issue. *Amnesty International - Human Rights Now Blog.* Retrieved from http://blog.amnestyusa.org/us/from-margin-to-center-sex-work-decriminalization-is-a-racial-justice-issue/

Sapers, H. (2015). *Annual report of the Office of the Correctional Investigator 2014–2015.* Retrieved from http://www.oci-bec.gc.ca/cnt/rpt/pdf/annrpt/annrpt 20142015-eng.pdf

Sawchuk, B. (2016, July 20). Undercover cops take aim at sex trade. *St. Catharines Standard.* Retrieved from http://www.stcatharinesstandard.ca/2016/07/20/undercover-cops-take-aim-at-sex-trade

Smith, J. (n.d.). *Joy Smith bio.* Retrieved from http://www.joysmithfoundation.com/main.aspx?CategoryCode=71C5B41B-2BE9-45BB-BE76-B808B9C1C779&pageCode=7997F659-0AEC-4876-B3D1-1175D68560C2

Smith, J. (2015). *Joy Smith on International Day of Remembrance of the Victims of Slavery and the Transatlantic Slave Trade.* Retrieved from https://openparliament.ca/debates/2015/3/31/joy-smith-1/only/

Tanovich, D.M. (2011). Gendered and racialized violence, strip searches, sexual assault and abuse of prosecutorial power. *Criminal Reports, 79*(6), 132–50.

UNAIDS. (2009). *UNAIDS guidance note on HIV and sex work.* Retrieved from http://www.unaids.org/sites/default/files/sub_landing/JC2306_UNAIDS-guidance-note-HIV-sex-work_en.pdf

United Nations. (2016). *Statement to the media by the United Nations' Working Group of Experts on People of African Descent, on the conclusion of its official visit to Canada, 17–21 October 2016.* Retrieved from http://www.ohchr.org/EN/NewsEvents/Pages/DisplayNews.aspx?NewsID=20732

Valverde, M. (1991). *The age of light, soap, and water: Moral reform in English Canada, 1885–1925.* Toronto, ON: University of Toronto Press.

Walker, B. (2010). *Race on trial: Black defendants in Ontario's criminal courts, 1858–1958.* Toronto, ON: University of Toronto Press.

23

Migrant Sex Workers' Justice

————— Building Alliances across Movements

ELENE LAM AND CHANELLE GALLANT

In recent decades, the sex worker rights movement has been successful in changing the discourse around sex work; increasingly, people recognize sex work as a form of work, understand that workers deserve rights, and appreciate that sex workers' agency should be acknowledged. Sex workers have been pushing hard to have their voices heard in the media, in the academy, and in community spaces. They have insisted that their perspectives be included in policy debates and have built alliances with community groups, healthcare providers, and legal organizations, as well as in academic and research contexts. However, because of isolation, racism, language differences, and anti-immigrant xenophobia, migrant sex workers' voices are still missing from these conversations – both within broader society and within the sex worker rights movement itself. This absence is exploited by anti–sex work prohibitionists who advocate for anti-trafficking measures that often work against the rights of sex workers and migrants.[1] Anti-trafficking measures rely on fears about sex work and about the cross-border movement of working-class women from the Global South, so one of the most effective ways that migrants and sex workers can protect their rights is to ensure that migrant sex workers' voices are included and centred as authorities about migration and sex work issues.

In this chapter, we begin by briefly clarifying some of the realities around migrant sex work in Canada, who migrant sex workers are, the kinds of work they do, and the struggles they can face both within and outside of the sex trade. We then turn to an examination of how xenophobic aspects of the sex worker rights movement have excluded migrant sex workers. Finally, we discuss how we can work to build alliances across social justice movements by drawing on our experiences establishing the Migrant Sex Worker Project, North America's first grassroots organization of sex workers, migrants, and allies.[2]

The Colonial Government and Migration

To understand the experiences of migrant sex workers and what we can do to create meaningful, lasting change, we need to begin with an understanding of the root of the problem. The oppression of migrant sex workers connects with the power of the Canadian government to create and enforce laws, define borders, and control migration. We all live on Indigenous lands, and together we wrote this on the territory of the Mississaugas of the New Credit, the Haudensaunee, and the Huron/Wendat Confederacy. Yet these nations are not recognized as having the authority to determine laws and borders, as this power resides only with the different levels of white-settler government. This is where we centre our analysis. Few people know that Canadian law explicitly criminalized prostitution-related activities in the Indian Act of 1876 (see Sayers, 2014; see also van der Meulen and Durisin, this collection). When we challenge Canadian laws about migration and sex work, we must also question the legitimacy of the Canadian government to be the sole authority on laws and borders.

In the past two decades, the Canadian government has introduced numerous policies that remove the rights of migrants, making it harder and harder to access residency, citizenship, public services, and good jobs. At the same time, migrant justice advocacy has gained momentum, resulting in increased pressure for policy changes and concrete improvements to labour conditions. Recently, migrant justice activists in over fifteen Canadian cities organized protests against the "4 and 4 rule," which requires migrant workers to leave after four years of cumulative employment and bans them from returning for another four years, uprooting tens of thousands of migrant workers and causing mass deportations (Coalition for Migrant Worker Rights Canada, 2016). Historically, however, although migrant justice advocates have been vocal about many injustices to migrant communities, they have not engaged with migrants in the sex trade or with the specific labour issues they confront. For example, since the Canadian government explicitly bars migrants who are not permanent residents from engaging in sex work – including in those parts of the industry that are legal, such as massage parlours and strip clubs – many migrant sex workers are left with no option but to work in illegal and clandestine ways.[3] Permanent residents are still vulnerable, however, as they may lose their status and be deported if they are convicted of a serious crime, including sex work–related offences (Stella, 2016). Police engage in workplace raids that target the migrant sex industry's businesses, detain women without citizenship status, and frequently deport them (Butterfly, 2016; Hempstead, 2015). As a direct consequence of their systemic marginalization and criminalization, some migrant sex workers experience appalling levels of violence (POWER, 2015). In spite of this situation, the sex worker rights and migrant justice movements have rarely worked together in Canada – a reality we hope to change.[4]

Sex Work and Migration 101

Who are we talking about when we refer to migrant sex workers? There are many stereotypes, but simply put, a migrant sex worker is anyone who has left where they live to go to another place (through formal or informal channels) and who works in the sex industry. People migrate for many reasons. Some have been pushed out of their home countries by poverty and discrimination, whereas others have been forced off their lands by developers or because their lands no longer sustain them as a result of climate change. Some are seeking a better future for themselves and their families, whereas others are looking for adventure and travel (Agustín, 2007). All of these motivations are also found among migrant sex workers.

Migrant sex workers are of all genders, but they are more likely to be women, both cisgender and transgender. Although they immigrate to Canada from around the world, many are racialized, poor, and working-class women who confront xenophobic and racist discrimination in society and throughout the immigration process. Once in Canada, migrants engage in a variety of sex industry jobs. They might work in strip clubs, see customers in condos, massage parlours, and dungeons, or solicit on the streets and on the Internet.

Migrant sex workers' labour experiences and working conditions differ substantially according to their gender, age, race, class, and immigration status. However, these differences do not mean, as is often assumed, that migrant women who are working-class and racialized have less agency than other women and enter into the sex industry only because they have been duped, tricked, or forced. If migrants cannot access work through regular channels, they may need to seek employment in underground economies such as sex work, construction, or restaurants and get paid "under the table." In this context, working-class, racialized women from the Global South are still making decisions for themselves, and for some, sex work is their best economic option as it can offer better working conditions, higher pay, and greater flexibility than other work available to them (e.g., live-in caregiving) (Agustín, 2006; Migrant Sex Workers Project, 2015). We honour that people who migrate are capable of consenting to sex work – and that their consent is relevant. All too often, non-Western, Third World women are seen as "ignorant, poor, uneducated, tradition bound, domestic, family-oriented, victims, etc." (Kempadoo, 1998, p. 11). This view is not only paternalistic but also actively harmful to migrant sex workers, whose agency is decreased by measures apparently intended to "protect" them.

As we see throughout this collection, many sex workers struggle with gaining access to stable housing, health services, and labour protections – struggles that are made much worse by the criminalization and stigma surrounding sex work. Many migrants are also unable to access these supports because of their immigration status, societal racism, and the criminalization of sex work (see also Butler Burke, this collection). In our experiences working with migrant sex workers, the fear of arrest and deportation can intensify already existing health conditions, and the risk of domestic violence further excludes migrant sex workers from governmental support systems (Lam, 2016). All of these factors increase vulnerability to violence and exploitation, as well as numerous human rights abuses.

Until 2012, for example, migrants were able to legally work in the erotic dance industry through an exemption in the Temporary Foreign Worker Program (Diaz, 2007; Durisin and Heynen, 2015). The Canadian government justified closing down this program by citing the risk of exploitation in the sex industry, yet no evidence of human trafficking among migrants in Canada's strip clubs was provided (Durisin and Heynen, 2015). The ideological underpinnings of this move become even more apparent when we consider that although migrant workers entering Canada under the Temporary Foreign Worker Program in other industries face notoriously high risks of exploitation, this situation has not led to calls by the government to restrict all foreign workers (Canadian Council for Refugees, 2013).

Since migrant sex workers are no longer eligible for temporary work permits, many who need or want to leave their homes for Canada are being forced to seek underground methods of migrating, relying on potentially exploitative third parties. Restricting the pathways of migration, then, pushes sex workers into the hands of third parties, or "smugglers," who will help them travel through informal channels. At times, these voyages can be exploitative or violent, yet migrant sex workers frequently have few other options. Increasing the options for people to migrate keeps power in the hands of migrants themselves and can effectively reduce harmful migration experiences. This is one of the reasons it is so important to support migrant sex workers; for years, human rights organizations have been reporting that many migrant women face abuse in the name of anti-trafficking measures designed to "rescue" them (GAATW, 2007; ICRSE, 2016; see also O'Doherty et al., this collection).

Sex Workers, Migrants, and the Fight for Rights

The sexist, racist, and xenophobic tropes that exist outside of the sex industry also exist within it. When nonmigrant sex workers complain about the lower rates that migrants charge, they are blaming them for the fact that migrants have been pushed into lower-paying parts of the industry, something that is not the fault of the migrants. Sex workers are voicing the same xenophobic sentiment that we see elsewhere in Canadian society – the story that "immigrants are stealing our jobs." In reality, we are all forced into competition with each other by the elites who control increasing amounts of wealth (Lambert and McInturff, 2016). Both the sex worker rights movement and the migrant justice movement are weakened when we think that the most marginalized are the enemy rather than recognizing that the problem is those who wield real political and economic power.

In our experience, we have witnessed some sex workers and others express their racism in patronizing pity. They believe that migrant women – especially Asian women – lack the ingenuity or "guts" to choose sex work because they are more passive and docile than other women. They believe that Asian women are either trafficked and exploited, or are more likely to be. Anyone with less political power and money is, of course, more vulnerable to being exploited, but that has nothing to do with being a woman of colour; the solution to systemic vulnerability is more power, not pity.

We have also witnessed some white sex workers avoid alliance building with communities of colour because they believe these communities to be more "conservative" about sex and gender. This racial stereotyping fails to acknowledge that white people using racist frameworks are the ones who have determined anti–sex work policies in this country. It also ignores the very real pressures that migrants of colour in Canada face and their need to protect their right to be here, to guard against the constant pressure to assimilate, and to defend against ongoing threats to their cultures. Finally, it overlooks the unique strengths of communities of colour, including the strong sense of community and resilience that comes from surviving racism. Rather than stereotyping people of colour, we ask you to seek out opportunities to understand issues, listen to people, engage with a wide range of racialized people, and meet people where they are at – literally, where they hang out.

When it comes to activism, discrimination can look like white-centrism in the political priorities and leadership of sex work organizations if and when groups fail to build solidarity with migrant justice organizations and/ or do not consider migrant justice issues to be fundamental sex work issues. Further, some sex work activism depends heavily on being publicly out as a sex worker (see Sayers, this collection; Porth, this collection), which has dramatically different implications for migrants who are barred from working in the sex industry or who may not have legal status in the country. For many reasons, the sex worker rights movement has not effectively collaborated with migrants in the sex trade, nor has it sufficiently challenged issues of white supremacy, border imperialism, and colonialism in its activities. This lack of engagement has had dangerous implications for migrants – and has been exploited by anti–sex work and anti-trafficking movements that increase the stigma surrounding sex work, develop and enforce anti-migrant and anti–sex work policy, and attack sex worker rights (GAATW, 2007; ICRSE, 2016). Indeed, the anti-trafficking movement is only too happy to exploit the gaps in the sex worker rights movement.[5] Instead, we argue that it is important for the sex worker rights movement to shift frameworks and centre the voice of migrants in the sex industry, which was the key impetus behind our co-founding of a grassroots organization of sex workers, migrants, and allies: the Migrant Sex Worker Project (MSWP).

Building Bridges and Lessons Learned

The MSWP is a grassroots group of migrants, sex workers, and allies who demand safety and dignity for all sex workers, regardless of immigration status. It was formed in 2014 when three long-time grassroots activists – Elene Lam, Chanelle Gallant, and Tings Chak – came together to address problems facing migrants in the sex trade. MSWP uses a justice-based framework that places sex worker rights on equal footing with racism, settler colonialism, and border imperialism. We create tools that migrant sex workers can use to protect themselves against human rights violations, educate the public about the dangers of anti-trafficking, and advocate to change policies that hurt and exploit migrants in the sex trade.

> ELENE: After moving to Canada from Hong Kong, where I had been involved in the sex worker rights movement for over a decade, I founded Butterfly (Asian and Migrant Sex Workers Support Network) to support and organize migrant sex workers in Toronto. At the time, Chanelle was working at Canada's oldest sex worker–run organization, Maggie's: Toronto Sex Workers Action Project, and recognized the necessity of adopting an intersectional perspective in the sex worker rights movement. She saw the importance of providing direct support to migrant sex workers through Butterfly. As an activist, Chanelle realized that she could contribute to and support the movement by leveraging her privilege, resources, and networks. Instead of imposing her assumptions, she kept asking me: "What do you need?" This was so important in understanding my concerns and needs. Sometimes, the help I needed was connecting to people and volunteers with particular knowledge and skills (e.g., translating or building a website) or just securing space to have meetings.

> CHANELLE: I was excited to organize with Elene because of her experience and skills in sex work activism in Asia as well as her different perspective on cross-movement organizing in Canada. Sex work is deeply connected to many issues, and justice for sex workers requires addressing those connected issues. All too often, however, sex work activism is disconnected from other political movements because of white-centrism.

Not only was it important to educate other sex workers about why it is essential to include migrant sex workers in the movement, but it was also necessary to reach out and build alliances with migrant communities. To this end, we connected with Tings Chak of No One Is Illegal, an organization that has a long history of advocating for migrant rights. Together, we formed MSWP after a few meetings and discussions about the issue of migrant sex workers.

Currently, MSWP mobilizes volunteers and organizations to support the ongoing work of Butterfly, and it engages in advocacy activities like community forums, educational events, performances, and art exhibits. We have also produced a publication to address the harms of anti-trafficking investigations (Butterfly, 2016), and we identify strategies to support migrant sex worker rights in Toronto and across the country. Below, we present a series of suggestions and discuss our lessons learned to help others who want to develop similar alliances across social movements or who may want to engage more meaningfully with migrant sex workers.

Make Building the Movement Your First Priority

Are you part of a sex work organization or are you an ally? Either way, you have a role to play as an organizer in an important social justice movement. The priority for an organizer is not to develop the most perfect critique of oppression but to build the power of the people in your movement. As an organizer, you should see yourself as a catalyst and influencer; use your resources and power to bring people in. For example, Butterfly is now a member of the Migrant Workers Alliance for Change, which is a national coalition of migrant worker groups and allies, and Butterfly also works closely with the Workers' Action Centre, which is a Toronto-based organization fighting for fair and dignified work, especially for people in low-wage and unstable employment. Through these relationships, Butterfly has access to space, photocopying, and solidarity. These relationships were built over time. As an organizer, you are responsible for helping people with great ideas to get in the door and for facilitating access to other organizations and funding.

Build Relationships with Migrants in the Sex Trade

The most important thing is to create space in your heart for others. That is what is different about being an organizer: you not only talk about your issue but also care about other people's well-being, whether it directly affects you or not. This work can include supporting migrants in the broader community when they need help or studying the issues affecting migrants so that you can be a better ally and provide meaningful support. Use whatever privilege or leverage you have to get migrants into leadership positions in the sex worker rights movement and beyond, and then support them like hell once they are there! When marginalized people take up leadership roles, they face additional barriers, risks, and discrimination that people with privilege do not. Set people up for success by giving them support throughout, make sure you understand the issues, and build people up. Remember your priority is support, not critique!

Support Nonmigrants to Understand the Issues and
Reduce Barriers to Migrants

Supporting migrants means dealing directly with racism among sex workers and allies and addressing the ways that racism plays out in relationships. At an organizational level, it might mean, for example, speaking out against discriminatory bylaw and licensing policies. In many instances, migrants are not allowed to apply for body rub or strip club licences and are readily suspected of being trafficking victims, which can lead to questioning from municipal enforcement officers, police, and/or the Canada Border Services Agency. Understanding the complex and multilevelled issues that migrants face means that you can be a better ally in your advocacy efforts, especially those that aim to reduce the barriers people face.

Support Migrant Justice Politically and Personally
Supporting migrant justice means speaking up and showing up for migrants in your personal relationships. This includes down-to-earth, meaningful work on relationships with people in other social and political movements. Sometimes, people in other movements are open but not yet ready to work together. Gradually, lay the groundwork so that you can connect with different movements in the future, such as labour, migrant, and anti-racism movements. Learn about the real-life issues they are facing, such as racism, problems with law enforcement, and discrimination, so that you can offer practical support.

Questions to Ask Yourself as You Begin Migrant Sex Work Activism

- How are my ideas excluding other people? For example, when I think of migrant sex workers, do I also acknowledge Black and African migrants? It is important to recognize the diversity and intersectionality within migrant sex workers' communities.
- What can I do as an ally? Am I asking migrant sex workers, "How can I help?" Remember that no contribution is too small! For example, you can offer to drive people to an event, or offer your expertise, or volunteer your time. Mobilizing resources and creating space for others are important and valuable aspects of being an ally.
- Who is excluded in the spaces I create, and how can I bring these individuals in? What can I do to include more people? Don't stop at critique; you may not bring in everyone, but you can always widen the circle. Consider the ways that you might be excluding people so that you can be more inclusive.
- How is my organizing language and culture excluding people? A lot of communities, especially marginalized ones, cannot join the sex workers' movement because of how it is organized. For example, it is very reliant on having regular Internet access and an understanding of academic discourse, and it is dominated by people who speak only English (or

French) and who share the same politics, skills, background, and understandings. How can you reduce language and class barriers?
- Now ask: Am I ready to do migrant sex work justice work?

Conclusion

The migrant sex workers' movement is still in its early stages, and there are many opportunities for solidarity that may change both migrant and sex work organizing in ways that make us stronger and more inclusive. We are excited about these opportunities! Our strategy here is twofold: to include sex workers from a range of movements on the left of the political spectrum and to develop durable relationships that are the foundation for our work together. At the same time, we are working to address migrant exclusion in the sex worker rights movement, to build an understanding of migrant issues, and to value migrant leadership, particularly that of working-class, racialized migrants. We know that this work can be messy, but that is okay as long as you act in ways that are principled and others can feel what is in your heart.

Notes

1 For example, migrant women who are not in the sex trade are sometimes racially profiled as suspected trafficking victims based on stereotypes about East Asian women and are refused entry to Canada.
2 This chapter comes out of knowledge that we developed while in communities among sex workers and migrants over the course of decades and spanning a number of countries. Where we include references, we have made the intentional and political choice to give credit to community-based activists for their intellectual labour.
3 The Canadian government's Immigration and Refugee Protection Regulations state that all temporary residents of Canada must "not enter into an employment agreement ... with an employer who, on a regular basis, offers striptease, erotic dance, escort services or erotic massages" (Government of Canada, 2017, s. 183(1)(b.1)).
4 For a discussion of migrant sex workers' organizing in Toronto, see Brock, Gillies, Oliver, and Sutdhibhasilp (2000).
5 For an excellent analysis of this situation, see Maynard (2015).

References

Agustín, L.M. (2006). The disappearing of a migration category: Migrants who sell sex. *Journal of Ethnic and Migration Studies, 32*(1), 29–47. https://doi.org/10.1080/13691830500335325

Agustín, L.M. (2007). *Sex at the margins: Migration, labour markets and the rescue industry.* New York, NY: Zed Books.

Brock, D., Gillies, K., Oliver, C., & Sutdhibhasilp, M. (2000). Migrant sex work: A roundtable analysis. *Canadian Women's Studies, 20*(2), 84–91.

Butterfly (Asian and Migrant Sex Workers Support Network). (2016). *Stop the harm from anti-trafficking policies and campaigns: Support sex workers' rights, justice, and dignity.* Retrieved from https://www.butterflysw.org/harm-of-anti-trafficking-campaign-

Canadian Council for Refugees. (2013, May). *Migrant workers provincial and federal report cards.* Retrieved from http://ccrweb.ca/sites/ccrweb.ca/files/migrant-worker-report-cards.pdf

Coalition for Migrant Worker Rights Canada. (2016, December 14). *We won! 4-and-4 repealed! Lets win status for all.* Retrieved from http://migrantrights.ca/en/we-won-4-and-4-repealed-lets-win-status-for-all/

Diaz, G.P.B. (2007). Dancing here, 'living' there: Transnational lives and working conditions of Latina migrant exotic dancers. In S. Krishnamurti & L. Goldring (Eds.), *Organizing the transnational: Labour, politics, and social change* (pp. 145–56). Vancouver, BC: UBC Press.

Durisin, E.M., & Heynen, R. (2015). Producing the 'trafficked woman': Canadian newspaper reporting on Eastern European exotic dancers during the 1990s. *Atlantis: Critical Studies in Gender, Culture, and Social Justice, 37*(2), 8–24. Retrieved from http://journals.msvu.ca/index.php/atlantis/article/view/3907

GAATW (Global Alliance Against Traffic in Women). (2007). *Collateral damage: The impact of anti-trafficking measures on human rights around the world.* Retrieved from http://www.gaatw.org/Collateral%20Damage_Final/singlefile_CollateralDamagefinal.pdf

Government of Canada. (2017, December 18). *Immigration and refugee protection regulations (SOR/2002–227).* Retrieved from http://laws-lois.justice.gc.ca/eng/regulations/SOR-2002-227/section-183.html?term=183

Hempstead, D. (2015, May 11). 11 massage workers face deportation. *Ottawa Sun.* Retrieved from http://ottawasun.com/2015/05/11/11-massage-workers-deporte d?token=1f990241431e5820a8ccf598eac20455

ICRSE (International Committee on the Rights of Sex Workers in Europe). (2016). *Surveilled. Exploited. Deported: Rights violations against migrant sex workers in Europe and Central Asia.* Retrieved from http://www.nswp.org/resource/surveilled -exploited-deported-rights-violations-against-migrant-sex-workers-europe-and

Kempadoo, K. (1998). Introduction: Globalizing sex workers' rights. In K. Kempadoo & J. Doezema (Eds.), *Global sex workers: Rights, resistance, and redefinition* (pp. 1–28). New York, NY: Routledge.

Lam, E. (Ed.). (2016). *Journey of Butterflies 2016.* Toronto, ON: Butterfly (Asian and Migrant Sex Workers Support Network). Retrieved from https://www.butterflysw.org/legal-information-for-services-prov

Lambert, B., & McInturff, K. (2016). *Making women count: The unequal economics of women's work.* Ottawa, ON: Canadian Centre for Policy Alternatives and Oxfam Canada. Retrieved from https://www.policyalternatives.ca/sites/default/files/uploads/publications/National%20Office/2016/03/Making_Women_Count2016.pdf

Maynard, R. (2015). Fighting wrongs with wrongs? How Canadian anti-trafficking crusades have failed sex workers, migrants, and Indigenous communities. *Atlantis: Critical Studies in Gender, Culture, and Social Justice, 37*(2), 40–56.

Migrant Sex Workers Project. (2015). *Migrant sex workers rights are human rights!* Retrieved from http://www.migrantsexworkers.com/about.html

POWER (Prostitutes of Ottawa-Gatineau Work Educate and Resist). (2015, May 11). *Sex worker rights groups condemn the raids on massage parlours that led to the deportation of eleven women.* Retrieved from https://www.ohscanada.com/eleven-women-face-deportation-following-human-trafficking-investigation-in-ottawa/

Sayers, N. (2014, March 27). Prostitution laws: Protecting Canada's crackers since 1867. *Tits and Sass.* Retrieved from http://titsandsass.com/prostitution-laws-protecting-canadas-crackers-since-1867/

Stella. (2016). *Immigration status and sex work.* Retrieved from http://chezstella.org/wp-content/uploads/2015/12/Immigration-Status-and-Sex-Work.pdf

24

Will the Real Supporters of Workers' Rights Please Stand Up?
Union Engagement with Sex Work in Canada

JENN CLAMEN AND KARA GILLIES

Canada's prostitution laws have undergone significant review and revision since 2007 when one current and two former sex workers launched a constitutional challenge of several key criminal laws governing sex work (see Belak, this collection). In 2014, less than a year after the Supreme Court struck down the impugned laws, the then Conservative government introduced Bill C-36, the Protection of Communities and Exploited Persons Act, which reframed sex work as a form of exploitation, positioned sex workers as inherently victims, and replicated the harms of the repealed provisions (e.g., see Krüsi, Belak, and Sex Workers United Against Violence, this collection). The extended court challenge and subsequent government consultations and parliamentary committee hearings that preceded the implementation of the new legislation provided multiple opportunities for rights groups to take a stand in favour of decriminalization and sex worker rights. In addition to civil liberties organizations, groups promoting LGBT, HIV/AIDS, women's, and Indigenous rights spoke up in support of total decriminalization. At the same time, sex workers and allies organized in opposition to the new oppressive legal regime, working in support of decriminalization and attempting to shift the popular discourse, in part, to a labour framework for advancing sex worker rights (see Beer, this collection).

Where were Canada's labour unions during these pivotal times? This chapter poses this question and explores the importance and potential impacts of organized labour's involvement in sex worker rights. We examine what has been achieved to date and consider both the barriers to, and strategies for, moving forward.

Unions are exceptionally well placed to support sex worker rights. At the broadest level, organized labour in Canada has a solid and proud history of advancing a social justice agenda and supporting the rights of communities and individuals facing multiple oppressions. Indeed, unions "have pushed for social and legal change for equity-seeking groups such as racial minorities, women, persons with disabilities, and gays and lesbians. Over the past sixty years, unions have often provided critical support to these disadvantaged groups in achieving, securing, and protecting important gains" (Champ, 2014, p. 114). One early effort to advance the well-being of sex workers occurred in 2002, when the Canadian Labour Congress (CLC), concerned about sex workers' safety and lack of formal protections, passed a resolution to "consult within labour and the community to develop policies that provide supportive measures for sex trade workers" (CLC Solidarity and Pride Working Group and CLC Women's Committee, 2005, p. 1). This was significant; as an umbrella organization for multiple international, national, and local unions/councils, the Canadian Labour Congress represents over 3 million workers, and resolutions serve to develop and define its official position on an issue.

Often, union actions that advance the rights of marginalized communities result from efforts to support union members who belong to these (and intersecting) communities. An example of this occurred in the early 2000s when the Canadian Labour Congress organized a series of consultations to enhance union representation of its trans members. The discussions revealed "the importance of unions being accountable not only to their workers but to those trans people who were unable to secure employment, let alone unionized employment, because of transphobia or the criminalization of sex work" (Clamen, Gillies, and Salah, 2013, p. 116). Trans and cisgender sex workers' issues thus became part of the dialogue. This draws our attention to the possibility that sex workers who are also employed at unionized social service agencies in "peer" positions such as support or outreach work could provide an organic point of entry for unions to champion sex worker rights issues.

More vitally, unions should be engaged with sex workers' issues as a specific form of workers' rights. Too frequently, sex work is cast as a social or personal pathology and disconnected from concepts of labour. However, regardless of political and moral positioning on sex work, exchanging labour – in this case, sexual labour – for money is indeed work. Sex workers in Canada and around the globe have long fought for their work to be recognized as legitimate labour and for their work activities, worksites, and work relations to be governed and protected as such (Bruckert and Parent, 2014; Clamen et al., 2013; Gall, 2012, 2016; van der Meulen, 2012). Union involvement and acknowledgment of sex work as labour reinforces this effort and reality. Such union recognition is especially critical in Canada's new legislative context, which frames sex work as a form of exploitation in need of elimination. Union perspectives could assist in differentiating the genuine labour exploitation that occurs in the sex trade from the ideological construct of prostitution as sexual exploitation.

Beyond identifying occurrences of exploitation in the sex trade as labour exploitation, unions have a central role to play in mitigating such exploitation and advancing sex workers' labour rights, health, and safety. Integral to this is the fight for the decriminalization of all elements of, and parties to, sex work. Ironically, the laws that purport to help people in the sex trade actually expose them to harm and exclude sex workers from even the most basic labour protections. The criminal provisions against procuring and receiving a material benefit from another party's sex work effectively illegalize the employer-worker relationship, thus barring sex workers from entitlements or redress under provincial and territorial laws respecting employment, labour, occupational health and safety, and human rights (Gillies, 2013; see also Gillies and Bruckert, this collection). These are essential mechanisms for advancing the labour rights and well-being of workers in any industry. The same is true of unionization and collective bargaining, which are, of course, equally unachievable when employers are criminalized.

Over the years, a number of unions and labour organizations have acknowledged the harms of criminalization on sex workers (e.g., CLC Solidarity and Pride Working Group and CLC Women's Committee, 2005; OPSEU, 2014, 2015). A couple have done one better and called for the decriminalization of sex work in Canada. The Canadian Union of Public Employees (CUPE), the country's largest union, which represents approximately 640,000 public sector workers nationally, was a leader on this front, moving in 2001 that "CUPE adopt a convention resolution calling for the decriminalization of sex work in Canada" (CUPE, 2001, n.p.). Disappointingly, the national union failed to follow up with any significant actions in this regard (Clamen et al., 2013). However, when the new prostitution laws of Bill C-36 were under debate in 2014, the president of CUPE

Ontario wrote an opinion piece that appeared in the *National Post*, stating in part,

> The criminalization of any part of sex work prevents sex workers from negotiating and enforcing workplace health and safety standards. It also prevents redress from labour abuses and discrimination ... CUPE Ontario has always fought for workers' rights in the workplace and in our communities. Trade unions must support the health and safety of everyone, especially those working in precarious industries. We therefore stand in solidarity with sex workers and all organizations that are committed to defeating this regressive and dangerous legislation. We call on the federal government to reject Bill C-36, and implement a policy of full decriminalization of all forms of sex work. (Hahn, 2014, n.p.)

The Ontario Public Service Employees Union (OPSEU) represents about 130,000 workers in the Ontario public and broader public sectors. Like other unions, it has various committees that attend to specific issues or member interests. In recent years, its Provincial Women's Committee (PWC) has taken a bold and public stand in favour of total decriminalization, with a particular focus on the negative impacts of the colonial criminal laws on Indigenous women in the sex trade (Provincial Women's Committee of OPSEU, 2015a, 2015b). The PWC's early work led to an OPSEU resolution in 2014 that recognized the rights of sex workers to equality, workplace safety, and labour protections while calling for full decriminalization, including that of sex work clients and third parties (OPSEU, 2014). On December 4, 2015, the PWC penned an open letter to the federal minister of justice, saying,

> We stand with organizations like Amnesty International, the World Health Organization, the International Labour Organization and the Global Network of Sex Work projects in calling for the immediate decriminalization of sex work. We believe firmly that the criminalization of sex work has never protected women from violence. In fact, in Indigenous communities, the evidence is clear that the opposite is true. (Provincial Women's Committee of OPSEU, 2015a, n.p.)

The PWC followed up this letter with an announcement commemorating the International Day to End Violence against Sex Workers:

> The PWC also calls for the federal government to fully decriminalize sex work to ensure dignity and security of all sex workers, and to recognize that

enforcement disproportionately targets black, indigenous, migrant and trans women, and street-based sex workers ... The PWC stands in solidarity with sex workers in calling for:

- the repeal of Bill C-36 and the full decriminalization of sex work in Canada
- legal and labour rights for sex workers
- provincial and municipal non-enforcement of Bill C-36
- the de-stigmatization of sex work
- the recognition of the dignity and value of sex workers. (Provincial Women's Committee of OPSEU, 2015b, n.p.)

After the new anti–sex work legislation came into effect, OPSEU (2015) passed a follow-up resolution denouncing the laws and calling for their non-enforcement in Ontario.

It is heartening to witness these forms of union support for sex worker rights and for decriminalization in particular. On the whole, however, it is too little, too late, and from too few within organized labour. Where were the unions when *Bedford v. Canada* (2010) was making its way through the various courts? The constitutional challenge took nearly seven years to travel through not one, not two, but three levels of court, and there were plenty of opportunities for unions to participate or intervene. There were also opportunities to engage directly with the policy process during the committee hearings on Bill C-36 held in both the House of Commons and the Senate (see Porth, this collection). And there has been no union participation in ongoing local and national law reform initiatives driven by sex workers and their allies, such as the lobbying undertaken by over thirty groups united under the banner of the Canadian Alliance for Sex Work Law Reform. Overall, the labour movement in Canada has failed to vigorously and meaningfully engage with legal and social reforms for the advancement of sex workers' basic rights, including labour rights.

Reflecting on this failure, we have identified several barriers to effective union advancement of sex worker rights in Canada. The first, and arguably the largest, is conceptual and is based on whether sex work is accepted as labour or whether it is misrepresented as a form of exploitation and violence against women. The National Executive Board of the Canadian Auto Workers – a large private-sector union representing workers in auto, rail, mining, and other industries – grappled with this question back in 2005, noting, "The philosophies underlying various approaches (sex work as violence against women, sex work as simply a service, sex work as work like all other dangerous work) are controversial in themselves. We need to understand these philosophies clearly and think through their implications" (CAW/ TCA, 2005, n.p.). They went on to say, "We need answers to the question, 'Does decriminalization and/or legalization increase or decrease harm to sex workers, overall?'" (ibid., n.p.).

In reality, we have answers to these questions, as demonstrated by the positive labour, health, and social outcomes in jurisdictions with decriminalized regimes (Abel et al., 2010, 2014). However, active lobbying by the small but vocal numbers of anti–sex work (i.e., prohibitionist) feminists who take the stance that sex work is violence has sowed doubt and confusion in the minds of otherwise clear-thinking people, both within and outside the labour movement. As with climate change deniers, evidence-based research has been cast aside by anti–sex work feminists in favour of ideological positions. When this biased positioning is presented as fact, it is understandable that people within labour and other social justice movements fear taking positions or actions that they have been told will perpetuate violence against women. This influence was at least partially responsible for the derailment of CUPE's potential actions on its 2001 decriminalization resolution, noted above (Clamen et al., 2013).

In some cases, the anti–sex work feminist perspective is the only one considered and upheld by a union. In 2013, for example, the Quebec union Confédération des syndicat nationaux (CSN) made its prohibitionist position public in the report *La prostitution: Une exploitation à dénoncer et une pratique à combattre!* (CSN, 2013). Founded in 1921, CSN is the most politically active union in Quebec and has a decentralized structure whereby local unions are organized into federations; CSN comprises almost 2,000 unions across the province. Since the release of its report, it has continued a steady stream of actions to publicly denounce sex worker rights. These actions include its involvement and leadership in campaigns such as Buying Sex Is Not a Sport that encourage the heightened presence of police and other law enforcement in the lives of sex workers through arrests, raids, and detentions (CSN, 2016). Interestingly, because unions themselves are divided from within on sex work issues, incoherent messages, some supportive, may emerge from within the same union. On December 17, 2016, one union housed within CSN – the Syndicat des travailleuses et travailleurs en intervention communautaire, which provides outreach and frontline services to drug users, sex workers, people living with or at risk of homelessness, and other marginalized communities – publicly announced its support for total decriminalization of sex work (STTIC, 2016). Similarly, the Public Service Alliance of Canada (PSAC), which holds a staunchly anti–sex work perspective (PSAC, 2016), was met with resistance from Ontario members through its Greater Toronto Area Pride Committee, which passed a resolution[1] at an Ontario Regional Convention committing PSAC to developing and implementing "regional and national awareness campaigns ... to promote the rights of sex workers" (Ontario Regional Office, PSAC, 2016, n.p.). The plan is to bring the resolution to the May 2018 PSAC national convention for possible debate and adoption.

Union structure and a lack of cohesive means to develop political policy across unions housed within the same organization may explain why unions do not stand up in favour of sex worker rights. Other barriers to effective union engagement with sex worker rights are structural or logistical. The bureaucracy, administration, and processes of unions, especially those that have large memberships, impede progress and present multiple points at which motions and actions can be challenged, diluted, or eliminated. The stigma and criminalization of sex work often result in workers not identifying as sex workers either to themselves or to others, avoiding involvement in sex-work initiatives, and/or frequently changing work locations and identities, all of which hinder alliance building. The occasional or transient nature of the work for some people is a barrier, as are other systemic and structural inequities in people's lives, such as gender, race, poverty, and immigration status (see Lam and Gallant, this collection). Finally, there are many social service and law enforcement sectors represented by unions and involved in the direct or indirect administration of sex work criminalization and its consequences, thus creating a potential conflict of opinion or even interest (Clamen et al., 2013).

Despite these and other challenges, there are actions that unions have taken and many more that they could take to promote the rights of sex workers and to establish sex work as a legitimate labour concern. Recently, some unions and labour organizations have established internal and external education campaigns. For example, OPSEU runs workshops for its members on how to be an ally to sex workers; LabourStart, an online news service for the international trade union movement, included a session on sex work and labour organizing as part of its 2016 Global Solidarity Conference in Toronto; and the Ontario Regional Office of the Public Service Alliance of Canada passed a 2016 resolution that committed it to developing and implementing "a social media campaign to educate members – and the public by extension – about the systemic inequalities and risks" faced by sex workers (Ontario Regional Office, PSAC, 2016, n.p.). Indeed, both social and traditional media are excellent platforms for organized labour and individual union members to dispel myths and demonstrate support for sex worker rights, as are simple day-to-day conversations within workplaces, communities, and family life.

As documented above, some unions have developed resolutions in support of sex workers. Even if these resolutions do not pass a vote of the local membership, and thus do not become officially endorsed by the union, these initiatives spark discussion and open the possibility for further engagement with sex worker rights within organized labour. Several unions and labour councils have also recognized days commemorating sex worker rights, such as December 17, the International Day to End Violence against Sex Workers. Although some have kept these efforts internal, the Provincial Women's Committee of OPSEU (2014a, 2015b) and the Syndicat des travailleuses et travailleurs en intervention communautaire (STTIC, 2016) have, as noted above, issued public statements of support, as have the Toronto and York Region Labour Council. The Provincial Women's Committee of OPSEU (2014b, 2015c) also included sex worker rights and a call for decriminalization in its 2014 and 2015 statements on the National Day of Remembrance and Action on Violence against Women. Such integration of sex workers' issues into broader social justice issues is another useful strategy for unions to adopt.

When consultations and hearings about sex work are held by any level of government, unions should take the opportunity to leverage their political power and speak out in support of sex workers as workers deserving labour rights and protections. Unions can be a powerful partner in the fight for decriminalization and labour rights. When the federal government revisits the current laws, organized labour should be prepared to work with sex workers to craft a strong union intervention. Indeed, labour organizations that have consulted and collaborated with sex workers and sex workers' groups have been the most successful in their initiatives. Meaningful involvement of sex workers is essential to the integrity and accomplishment of allied efforts.

Even absent a decriminalized environment, unions can support sex workers in informal organizing and lobbying, including with financial and other resources. In its 2016 Action Plan, CUPE Ontario (2016), for example, said that it would "support and [lend] resource[s] [to] sex workers' struggle for human and labour rights, condemn the criminalization of sex workers, support their labour organizations and harm reduction programs and support legal sex workers in accessing their labour rights" (p. 17). In other industries, unions have been vocal and important supporters of labour rights and protections for marginalized workers, especially those who are excluded from formal labour protections. Although not criminalized, Ontario agricultural workers, including migrant workers, have long been omitted from collective bargaining and occupational health and safety legislation. In response, the United Food and Commercial Workers (UFCW) of Canada set up Agricultural Workers Support Centres (Mehta, 2014), which now exist across the country and provide information on topics such as working conditions, health and safety, and labour rights, as well as practical support for accessing labour protections ("UFCW Canada ...," n.d.).

When the federal Parliament repeals the criminal laws on sex work – whether in one year or one hundred – unions and organized labour can support sex workers to navigate provincial labour and employment mechanisms and can negotiate with provincial ministries of labour where necessary. Under decriminalization, unions can organize interested sex workers,[2] potentially through sectoral bargaining[3] if such a model becomes available for the types of small workplaces that are typical of the sex trade in Canada.

To conclude, we want to share the following call to action by CUPE (2004): "We can all help. We can fight the criminalization and stigmatization of sex work as we have fought other forms of discrimination. We can support sex workers by helping them fight for their rights as workers" (p. 4). With this call in mind, we ask the real supporters of workers' rights to please stand up.

Notes

1 A resolution is a written proposition put forward by an individual member or local within a trade union that outlines a problem or concern and that provides clear direction or instruction to the union. It is voted on by members before becoming policy.

2 As is the case for workers in other sectors, sex workers can choose to work independently, collectively, as freelancers, or as employees. Unionization might be a preferred and applicable model for some sex workers and not for others. For a more fulsome discussion of this matter, see Clamen et al. (2013).

3 Sectoral bargaining is a labour relations model that allows unions to organize workers in a specific industry, or sector, across multiple workplaces and employers. This model has been under discussion in both British Columbia and Ontario and is seen by proponents as a way to improve access to collective bargaining for precarious workers and for workers in small businesses or at small business sites. It differs from the current approach across Canada, which generally restricts collective bargaining to employees working for a single employer or at a single worksite.

References

Abel, G. (2014). A decade of decriminalization: Sex work 'down under' but not underground. *Criminology and Criminal Justice, 14*(5), 580–92.

Abel, G., Fitzgerald, L, Healy, C., & Taylor, A. (Eds.). (2010). *Taking the crime out of sex work.* Bristol, UK: Policy Press at the University of Bristol.

Bruckert, C., & Parent, C. (2014). The in-call sex industry: Gender, class, and racialized labour in the margins. In *Criminalizing women: Gender and (in) justice in neoliberal times* (2nd ed., pp. 92–129). Black Point, NS: Fernwood Publishing.

CAW/TCA (Canadian Auto Workers). (2005). *CAW National Executive Board discussion paper on the sex trade.* Retrieved from http://caw.ca/assets/pdf/Sex-TradeDiscussionPaper.pdf

Champ, P. (2014). Advancing human rights for all Canadians. In M. Behrens (Ed.), *Unions matter: Advancing democracy, economic equality, and social justice* (pp. 101–14). Toronto, ON: Between the Lines.

Clamen, J., Gillies, K., & Salah, T. (2013). Working for change: Sex workers in the union struggle. In E. van der Meulen, E.M. Durisin, & V. Love (Eds.), *Selling sex: Experience, advocacy, and research on sex work in Canada* (pp. 113–29). Vancouver, BC: UBC Press.

CLC Solidarity and Pride Working Group & CLC Women's Committee. (2005). Sex trade discussion paper. Paper presented at the CLC Solidarity and Pride Conference, Quebec City, November 6–8.

CSN (Conféderation des syndicats nationaux). (2013). *La prostitution: Une exploitation à dénoncer et une pratique à combattre!* Retrieved from http://tempserv.csn.info/c/document_library/get_file?uuid=8d8d1f1f-a21e-4f91-86a3-52665a391543&groupId=13943

CSN (Confédération des Syndicats Nationaux). (2016). *Commentairessur l'approche d'ONU Femmes concernant le travail sexuel, le commerce sexuel et la prostitution.* Retrieved from https://www.csn.qc.ca/2016-10-14_commentaires_prostitution_csn/

CUPE (Canadian Union of Public Employees). (2001). Proceedings of the Twentieth Biennial CUPE National Convention. Vancouver, British Columbia, November 19–23.

CUPE (Canadian Union of Public Employees). (2004). *Sex work: Why it's a union issue.* Retrieved from http://ibrarian.net/navon/paper/Canadian_Union_of_Public_Employees.pdf?paperid=1720556

CUPE Ontario. (2016). *Action plan 2016: Privatization: Paving the way to poverty.* Retrieved from https://cupe.on.ca/wp-content/uploads/2016/07/2016-06-15-Action-Plan-2016-Final-Version-Ratified-by-members-at-convent-.pdf

Gall, G. (2012). *An agency of their own: Sex worker union organizing.* United Kingdom: Zero Books.

Gall, G. (2016). *Sex worker unionisation: Global developments, challenges and possibilities.* Basingstoke, UK: Palgrave.

Gillies, K. (2013). A wolf in sheep's clothing: Canadian anti-pimping law and how it harms sex workers. In E. van der Meulen, E.M. Durisin, & V. Love (Eds.), *Selling sex: Experience, advocacy, and research on sex work in Canada* (pp. 113–29). Vancouver, BC: UBC Press.

Hahn, F. (2014, July 9). Sex workers deserve the same protections as all other workers. *National Post.* Retrieved from http://nationalpost.com/full-comment/fred-hahn-sex-workers-deserve-the-same-protections-as-all-other-workers

Mehta, N. (2014). A changing union tide hurts vulnerable workers: A case study on migrant workers. In M. Behrens (Ed.), *Unions matter: Advancing democracy, economic equality, and social justice* (pp. 115–21). Toronto, ON: Between the Lines.

Ontario Regional Office, PSAC (Public Service Alliance of Canada). (2016, June 5). Email communication from Janel Coe to Kara Gillies.

OPSEU (Ontario Public Service Employees Union). (2014). *Minutes of Executive Board meeting of June 18–19, 2014.* Retrieved from https://opseu.org/information/minutes-executive-board-meeting-june-18-19-2014

OPSEU (Ontario Public Service Employees Union). (2015). *Minutes of the June 17, 2015 Executive Board meeting.* Retrieved from https://opseu.org/information/minutes-june-17-2015-executive-board-meeting

Provincial Women's Committee of OPSEU. (2014a, December 17). *International Day to End Violence against Sex Workers – December 17, 2014.* Retrieved from https://opseu.org/news/international-day-end-violence-against-sex-workers-december-17-2014

Provincial Women's Committee of OPSEU. (2014b, December 3). *National Day of Remembrance and Action on Violence against Women – December 6.* Retrieved from https://opseu.org/news/national-day-remembrance-and-action-violence-against-women-december-6-2014

Provincial Women's Committee of OPSEU. (2015a, December 4). *Letter to the Minister of Justice to decriminalize sex work.* Retrieved from https://opseu.org/news/letter-minister-justice-decriminalize-sex-work

Provincial Women's Committee of OPSEU. (2015b, December 17). *PWC marks International Day to End Violence against Sex Workers.* Retrieved from https://opseu.org/news/pwc-marks-international-day-end-violence-against-sex-workers

Provincial Women's Committee of OPSEU. (2015c, December 4). *Statement on the National Day of Remembrance and Action on Violence against Women.* Retrieved from https://opseu.org/news/statement-national-day-remembrance-and-action-violence-against-women

PSAC (Public Service Alliance of Canada). 2016. *Prostitution is not decent work: PSAC position paper.* Retrieved from https://gallery.mailchimp.com/53667ba335b8b62f97a2b47de/files/EN_Prostitution_Paper.pdf

STTIC (Syndicat des travailleuses et travailleurs en intervention communautaire). (2016). Letter. Retrieved from http://www.fsss.qc.ca/download/etablissements/STTIC_sex_work_WEB.pdf

UFCW Canada opens third migrant agricultural workers support centre in Simcoe. (n.d.). http://www.ufcw.ca/index.php?option=com_content&view=article&id=449&Itemid=6&lang=en

van der Meulen, E. (2012, Spring). When sex is work: Organizing for labour rights and protections. *Labour/Le Travail, 69,* 147–67.

Cases

Bedford v. Canada, 2010 ONSC 4264.

Legislation

Bill C-36, *Protection of Communities and Exploited Persons Act,* SC 2014, c. 25.

25

Sex, Lies, and Committee Hearings

———— Challenging Prostitution Propaganda

KERRY PORTH

In 2013 sex workers experienced a significant victory at the Supreme Court of Canada in *Canada (Attorney General) v. Bedford*, and along with their supporters from across the country, they literally erupted in cheers of joy (see also Belak, this collection). The highest court in the land had finally listened to what sex workers had been saying for more than forty years: laws that many believed were meant to protect sex workers from harm had instead created environments where they were more vulnerable to violence and exploitation. However, a more sombre mood quickly took hold. Mindful that the issue of prostitution had become extremely polarizing both in Canada and internationally, many were fearful that the federal majority Conservative government would respond by enacting new laws to replace the ones just deemed unconstitutional.

The fears were justified. A mere six months after the Supreme Court decision, Bill C-36, the Protection of Communities and Exploited Persons Act (PCEPA), was introduced. This proposed bill, according to many observers, aimed to essentially refashion the previous laws and would therefore reproduce the same harms (see also Krüsi, Belak, and Sex Workers United Against Violence, this collection).[1] Instead of working with sex workers to craft a legal framework that would improve safety and recognize sex workers' agency, the purpose of the proposed legislation was to abolish prostitution by criminalizing the purchase of sexual services. That PCEPA defined sex work as inherently violent and sex workers uniformly as victims was evident in the Department of Justice's (2014) press release announcing its introduction: "Today, our Government is responding to the Supreme Court of Canada's ruling in *Canada v. Bedford* to ensure that Canada's laws and the criminal justice system continue to address the significant harms that flow from prostitution to those engaged in prostitution and to other vulnerable persons, while protecting Canadian communities" (n.p.). Sex workers in Canada felt like they were being punished for having had the temerity to assert their rights in court. Proponents of the two dominant ideological positions on sex work – prohibitionists, who believe that sex work is violence and must be abolished, and harm reductionists, who favour addressing the legal and social contexts that render sex workers vulnerable to violence – gathered their forces for the coming battle.

In order for PCEPA, or any proposed legislation for that matter, to receive royal assent and be implemented, it first needed to travel through three readings of the House of Commons and another three readings of the Senate. During both of these phases, bills are sent to a committee that is tasked with studying them in detail and hearing from invited witnesses prior to making recommendations for potential changes or modifications. In the summer and fall of 2014, along with a handful of other current or former sex workers, I testified before both the House of Commons Standing Committee on Justice and Human Rights as well as the Senate Standing Committee on Legal and Constitutional Affairs. Drawing from the transcripts of both sets of hearings, I argue that these were transparently partisan exercises orchestrated to ensure smooth passage of the legislation.[2] Well-funded pro-PCEPA witnesses were selected and outnumbered those who opposed the proposed law. Careful consideration of facts and evidence was rejected in favour of dramatic storytelling; morality politics played a large role in the hearings. The few courageous current or former sex workers who testified against PCEPA experienced an incredibly hostile environment that left them disillusioned and frustrated (see also Sayers, this collection).

To begin with, the two sides in this debate were not evenly matched. The prohibitionist position was put forward by conservative religious organizations, radical feminist scholars and activists, some women's anti-violence organizations, and groups that purport to help the victims of trafficking. Although it is extremely unusual to find feminists of any stripe in the same camp as conservative religious groups given their widely divergent positions on the status and rights of women, in this instance they came together and advanced a moral position that prostitution is wrong and harmful (Bernstein, 2010). A prominent voice within the pro-hibitionist camp, and one that receives considerable public and media attention, is that of a small group of women who previously engaged in sex work but who now take a strong stand against it and refer to themselves as "survivors." Drawing on emotive and sensationalist imagery and narra-tives, prohibitionists have been successful at shifting public perception and influencing policy makers. Given the layers of misinformation, myth-ology, and moralizing about the sex industry, as well as the well-funded and socially-legitimated organizations and individuals who oppose it, the prohibitionist witnesses at both sets of hearings represented a formidable foe for the harm-reductionist sex worker rights organizations and allies, who occupy a marginal position within civil society.

In the contemporary context, outing oneself as a current or former sex worker often comes with enormous costs. These costs can be particularly high for marginalized sex workers who are Indigenous or racialized (see also Raguparan, this collection), struggling with issues related to drug depend-ency or mental health, and/or living in situations where selling or trading sex is a basic subsistence strategy. So entrenched is sex work stigma and discrimination that disclosure of one's sex work status can result in the loss of disability or social assistance benefits, housing, and other employment, rejection by family members, and/or the apprehension of children by state actors (Bowen and Bungay, 2016). As a consequence, few sex workers are willing to come forward and out themselves in order to speak to parliament-ary committees. Further complicating this context is the insufficient fund-ing that many sex worker rights organizations receive, making it more difficult for them to advocate for law reform (Clancey, Khushrushahi, and Ham, 2014; Rose, 2015). Nevertheless, a number of individual sex workers and harm reduction allies presented as witnesses at the hearings and advo-cated for sex workers' interests.

In the context of the committee hearings, the position of harm reduc-tionists was marginalized from the onset. After all, the preamble to PCEPA (2014) explicitly reflects the prohibitionist position:

> Whereas the Parliament of Canada has grave concerns about the exploita-tion that is inherent in prostitution and the risks of violence posed to those who engage in it; Whereas the Parliament of Canada recognizes the social harm caused by the objectification of the human body and the commodi-fication of sexual activity; ... Whereas the Parliament of Canada wishes to encourage those who engage in prostitution to report incidents of violence

and to leave prostitution; And whereas the Parliament of Canada is committed to protecting communities from the harms associated with prostitution. (pp. 1–2)

Arguably, PCEPA is steeped in morality politics, which Wagenaar and Altink (2012) define as "a situation where the minimum common ground, that is a condition for engaging in effective collective problem solving, has broken down into irreconcilable conflict over moral positions about what is right or virtuous with regard to the issue at hand" (p. 282). That criminal law increases sex workers' vulnerability to violence is a difficult argument to make when the proposed law at issue defines prostitution as *inherently* violent and exploitative (Bruckert, 2015). Since the preamble to PCEPA asserts that prostitution is *morally* wrong, anyone arguing against the law is then, by definition, immoral. Illustrative of this, those arguing for the decriminalization of sex work have been named by prohibitionists as the "pimp lobby" or the "pro-violation constituency." Indeed, guilt by association has the effect of silencing objectors and shutting down debate by delegitimating those who challenge this moralistic orthodoxy. It is also incredibly galling to those of us who are current or former sex workers and who *have* experienced violence and exploitation to have prohibitionists suggest that we desire such harm to be visited upon others; after all, that is precisely what we are working so hard to prevent.

In this echo chamber where "the victimized prostitute becomes equated with the truth of prostitution, the sex worker who does not speak of victimization may be seen as a fraud" (Rose, 2015, p. 57). Current and former sex workers who testified that the laws increase their vulnerability to violence and exploitation were vilified by committee members from the governing Conservative Party of Canada (CPC) as being unrepresentative, attempting to minimize violence against sex workers, and/or "glossing over" hardships. In the following example, Stella Ambler (Mississauga South, CPC), a member of the House of Commons Standing Committee on Justice and Human Rights, responded to Natasha Potvin, who had recounted having been threatened with the removal of her child by child protection services on the basis of her sex work:

You mentioned that you liked some of your clients, and liked some of them less, but that overall you're proud of your choice and that it's worked for you in your life. The way you tell it, frankly, it sounds like a TV sitcom about happy hookers. I just can't reconcile this with the other things I've heard.

I'm wondering if this bill were enacted, would it put you out of business? (Standing Committee on Justice and Human Rights, 2014e)

Sex workers like Natasha who asserted that they were not victims and that violence is facilitated by criminal law were not only challenged by members of the committee but also confronted by prohibitionist witnesses as being heartless opportunists sacrificing the well-being of marginal sex workers for their own benefit:

Ms. Larissa Crack (Northern Women's Connection): But there comes a point where the able and willing must put their wants and desires to the side – where the majority of those involved in the sex trade are there completely through exploitative means. (Standing Committee on Justice and Human Rights, 2014d)

Ms. Gunilla Ekberg (Lawyer, University of Glasgow): I urge the committee and in turn the government to resist the dramatic promotion of and the resulting normalization of arguments about prostitution as individual choice or legitimate and empowering work, in the Canadian public debate put forward by what is called in international human rights theory the "pro-violation constituency," meaning organizations, individuals, etc., who, when their interests are threatened, lobby for and consent to policies associated with human rights and norms violations. (Standing Committee on Justice and Human Rights, 2014b)

As Phipps (2016) writes, such "selective empathies" (p. 304) to experiential narratives "can *actively* be used as a tool of silencing which works to reinforce the power of the dominant through capitalising upon emotional responses and invisibilising structural dynamics" (p. 306, emphasis in original). Other witnesses were silenced in a more straightforward manner. When Elin Sigurdson, a lawyer for Pivot Legal Society with whom I was co-presenting, deferred a question better answered by someone with sex work experience to me, Conservative committee member Stella Ambler looked me in the eye and said that she did not have enough time to listen to my response (Standing Committee on Justice and Human Rights, 2014a). Indeed, none of the committee members asked me a single question that day.

Another effective tool used by prohibitionists to elicit selective empathy is their focus on the narratives of so-called survivors of prostitution. These powerful stories of abuse and violation are deemed representative of all sex workers' experiences and are the narrative bedrock of prohibitionist claims that exploitation is inherent to sex work. Thus current and former sex worker witnesses who were critical of the proposed legislation, and who supported sex worker rights to safe and fair workplaces, were actively discredited as "not representative." Of course, by responsibilizing shadowy men (e.g., pimps and clients) for all of the harms experienced by sex workers (see Khan, this collection; Gillies and Bruckert, this collection), the state is relieved of its obligation to provide equal protection under the law for its citizens, to craft laws that are consistent with the Canadian Charter of Rights and Freedoms, and to address the systemic inequality and discrimination that leave some with few options but to resort to sex work in dangerous environments.

When morality politics are infused in discourses on sex work and emotionally charged survivor narratives are held as the one and only truth, they tend to distract from everyday experiences and systemic issues (Wagenaar and Altink, 2012). Although both the prohibitionist and the harm-reductionist positions draw on personal narratives to illustrate their perspectives, harm reductionists tell relatively banal and thoughtful tales of bad work conditions, police misconduct, and the denial of social, civic, and labour rights. Conversely, prohibitionists use highly emotive language and dramatic storytelling intended to generate shock and pity (Weitzer, 2005). During both sets of hearings, self-identified sex work survivors told lurid stories and were lauded as heroes for coming forward. The following testimony by Bridget Perrier, a co-founder of Sex Trade 101, is a case in point:

> I was lured and debased into prostitution at the age of 12 from a child welfare-run group home. I remained enslaved for 10 years in prostitution. I was sold to men who felt privileged to steal my innocence and invade my body. I was paraded like cattle in front of men who were able to purchase me, and the acts that I did were something no little girl should ever have to endure here in Canada, the land of the free. (Standing Committee on Justice and Human Rights, 2014c)

These stories fed into the hearings' focus on human trafficking and the sexual exploitation of children and youth – crimes that were never at issue in the *Bedford* case but that have, in recent years, been so successfully conflated with prostitution by prohibitionists that the existence of, and demand for, prostitution is blamed for trafficking and sexual exploitation (Farley, 2004). The flaw in this logic is, or should be, self-evident since, by the same logic, one could argue that labour exploitation and human trafficking in the agricultural and garment industries happen because we eat food and wear clothes. The difference, of course, is that labour exploitation and trafficking are addressed through worker organizing and labour laws, which are precisely what sex workers are asking for, whereas prohibitionists claim that the harms that occur in sex work can be addressed only by abolishing prostitution entirely. This overly simplistic fallacy underpins the "logic" that unless prostitution is abolished by criminalizing the demand for paid sexual services, women will be trapped in "sexist and racist role playing that is often slavery and always a slavery-like practice" (Farley, 2013, p. 370).

In a policy area as contentious as prostitution, there is an expectation that debate on proposed legislation affecting a highly stigmatized and marginalized population should rely on sound research and testimony by experts. The period of time that the Conservative Party held a majority of seats in Parliament, however, was marked by a distinct lack of respect for scientific study and evidence, as demonstrated by cuts to federal funding of research, the muzzling of government scientists, and the implementation of increasingly punitive criminal justice policies (Mann, 2016; Walton-Roberts et al., 2014; Zinger, 2016). Furthermore, we seem to live in an era when what people *believe* to be true means more than what evidence *proves* to be true. For example, divisions between liberal and conservative ideologies on social issues such as prostitution, substance use and misuse, and gender identity have become entrenched since people began spending greater amounts of time in online communities of choice that act as virtual echo chambers in which beliefs and opinions are rarely challenged. When confronted with contrary evidence, people express outrage or disgust rather than engaging in meaningful dialogue. It is very difficult to have a rational debate when feelings matter more than facts!

Both the House of Commons and Senate committee hearings on PCEPA were replete with disdain for evidence. Some of the most rigorous and ethically sound research on sex work has been conducted by Canadian academics – many of whom are indeed contributors to this collection – yet very few were invited to testify. Those who did found themselves treated with disrespect or outright hostility by Conservative Party committee members. This was certainly the experience of Chris Atchison of the University of Victoria, who has conducted ground-breaking research on sex work clients in Canada:

> SENATOR DENISE BATTERS (CPC APPOINTED): Do you follow up with the person they apparently bought the sexual service from to find out if that particular purchaser was telling the truth, if they were or were not violent in that situation? I'm trying to find out how much of a potential methodological problem the self-reporting aspect of this research would be.

> MR. CHRIS ATCHISON: Like I said, no more of a methodological problem around self-reporting than we see with the existing research on sex workers' experiences within the industry. You seem to be asking whether we should have a double standard of the acceptance of the truth of someone's claim just because of their status as a purchaser or seller of sexual services. As [a] researcher, I find that peculiar.

> SENATOR DONALD PLETT (CPC APPOINTED): You have been emphatic here on saying that you haven't been able to find where people actually want to be violent ... And then you sit here and you somehow self-righteously say that we shouldn't be calling those people perverts. (Senate Standing Committee on Legal and Constitutional Affairs, September 11, 2014)

Discredited and vague claims – for example, that the average age of entry into prostitution is twelve to fourteen[3] – were bandied about, and unsubstantiated assertions that "many" and "most" sex workers are street-based and unwilling participants in the sex trade were simply accepted as fact by Conservative Party committee members, even when disproved by witnesses testifying against PCEPA. And why not? Those assertions are in line with committee members' own framing and assumptions about sex work and sex workers.

Partisan bias was clearly evident in the selection of witnesses; although there were more written briefs submitted by those who were critical of PCEPA, more witnesses in favour of it were selected to present to the committees.[4] Indeed, the way that opinion was valued over expertise demonstrates another key feature of morality politics, namely that it is "owned by everyone, while sources of technical authority that might arbitrate conflicts of belief or opinion are either absent or drowned out. Instead, every member of the public ... believes that he has an expert opinion about the issue at hand" (Wagenaar and Altink, 2012, p. 283).

Sex workers can agree that we are not all victims, yet many among us who testified against PCEPA in the summer and fall of 2014 certainly felt victimized by the process. The committee rooms were incredibly intimidating, and on most days the public gallery was packed with prohibitionists who hissed, jeered, and cursed at us. It was not uncommon to hear them shout "shame!" at current and former sex workers who advocated for decriminalization. Transparently partisan, the Conservative committee chairs did nothing to address this behaviour, but when Terri-Jean Bedford, a long-time sex worker and the eponymous applicant of *Bedford v. Canada* (2010), became upset while testifying, she was escorted from the room.

When we asserted our agency, we were told that we were not representative of sex worker experiences. If we spoke about violence, stigma, and our inability to turn to the police when needed, there were no expressions of concern or commendations for our bravery in coming forward – just disdain, disbelief, and negation. Sex workers who put themselves at risk by presenting to the committees were routinely asked questions that were completely unrelated to the proposed legislation, such as whether they were paid for their work at sex work organizations or whether they knew any sex workers under eighteen. All of us acknowledged that violence and exploitation occur in the sex industry, but we were consistently portrayed as attempting to minimize or obscure those abuses. Many of us left feeling hurt, angry, and disillusioned about future engagement in this type of policy process. Perhaps unsurprisingly, although very disappointingly, PCEPA received royal assent less than two months after the Senate committee hearings and came into force on December 6, 2014, almost entirely unmodified from its original proposed form.

At the time of writing, sex workers and allies are once again gearing up to engage with the government and advocate for legal reform, this time with the Liberal Party of Canada, which now comprises a majority federal government. Will there be another pro forma exercise in committee hearings where the outcome has already been determined, or will sex workers finally be heard? Only time will tell.

Notes

1 See, for example, the information sheet *Reckless Endangerment* (Canadian HIV/ AIDS Legal Network, Pivot Legal Society, and Stella, 2014).

2 The author personally participated in two sets of hearings and reviewed the hearings on ParlVu (a service that provides video of House of Commons proceedings and public committees). In addition, the author participated in a

textual analysis. The inductive analysis, inspired by grounded theory, established and refined codes that emerged through the process of review and analysis. Questions were classified and coded around three dimensions: content, tone, and nature (Fuji Johnson, Burns, & Porth, 2017). For this chapter, the author focused on evidence and testimony presented in favour of the government bill that was demonstrably false, exaggerated, and/or intended to elicit shock and outrage, as well as on structural bias in the selection and treatment of witnesses.

3 See Lowman (2013) for an evidence-based critique of this claim.
4 For example, 69 percent of the briefs submitted to the House of Commons committee and 67 percent of the briefs submitted to the Senate committee articulated serious critiques of PCEPA, yet only 33 percent of the House of Commons committee witnesses and 41 percent of the Senate committee witnesses were selected to speak against PCEPA (Fuji Johnson, Burns, and Porth, 2017).

References

Bernstein, E. (2010). Militarized humanitarianism meets carceral feminism: The politics of sex, rights, and freedom in contemporary antitrafficking campaigns. *Signs: Journal of Women in Culture and Society, 36*(1), 45–71. https://doi.org/10.1086/652918

Bowen, R., & Bungay, V. (2016). Taint: An examination of the lived experiences of stigma and its lingering effects for eight sex industry experts. *Culture, Health and Sexuality, 18*(2), 184–97. https://doi.org/10.1080/13691058.2015.1072875

Bruckert, C. (2015). *Protection of Communities and Exploited Persons Act:* Misogynistic law making in action. *Canadian Journal of Law and Society, 30*(1), 1–3.

Canadian HIV/AIDS Legal Network, Pivot Legal Society, & Stella. (2014, June 25). *Reckless endangerment – Q&A on Bill C-36: Protection of Communities and Exploited Persons Act.* Retrieved from http://www.aidslaw.ca/site/reckless-endangerment-qa-on-bill-c-36-protection-of-communities-and-exploited-persons-act/?lang=en

Clancey, A., Khushrushahi, N., and Ham, J. (2014). Do evidence-based approaches alienate Canadian anti-trafficking funders? *Anti-Trafficking Review, (3),* 87–108.

Department of Justice (2014, June 4). *Statement by the Minister of Justice regarding legislation in response to the Supreme Court of Canada ruling in Attorney General of Canada v. Bedford et al.* (News release). Retrieved from https://www.canada.ca/en/news/archive/2014/06/statement-minister-justice-regarding-legislation-response-supreme-court-canada-ruling-attorney-general-canada-v-bedford-al-.html?wbdisable=true

Farley, M. (2004). 'Bad for the body, bad for the heart': Prostitution harms women even if legalized or decriminalized. *Violence against women, 10*(10), 1087–125.

Farley, M. (2013). Prostitution, liberalism, and slavery. *Logos: A Journal of Modern Society and Culture, 12*(3), 370–86.

Fuji Johnson, G., Burns, M., & Porth, K. (2017). A question of respect: A qualitative text analysis of the Canadian parliamentary committee hearings on *The Protection of Communities and Exploited Persons Act. Canadian Journal of Political Science, 50*(4), 921–53. https://doi.org/10.1017/S0008423917000294

Lowman, J. (2013). Evidence-based argument or victim-paradigm hyperbole? In E. van der Meulen, E.M. Durisin, & V. Love (Eds.), *Selling sex: Experience, advocacy, and research on sex work in Canada* (pp. 230–50). Vancouver, BC: UBC Press.

Mann, R.M. (2016). The Harper government's new right neoliberal agenda and the dismantling of Status of Women Canada and the family violence initiative. *International Journal for Crime, Justice and Social Democracy, 5*(2), 50–64. https://doi.org/10.5204/ijcjsd.v5i2.308

Phipps, A. (2016). Whose personal is more political? Experience in contemporary feminist politics. *Feminist Theory, 17*(3), 303–21. https://doi.org/10.1177/1464700116663831

Rose, A. (2015). Punished for strength: Sex worker activism and the anti-trafficking movement. *Atlantis: Critical Studies in Gender, Culture, and Social Justice, 37*(2), 57–64.

Standing Committee on Justice and Human Rights. (2014a, July 8). *Evidence.* (No. 37, 2nd Session, 41st Parliament). Retrieved from http://www.ourcommons.ca/DocumentViewer/en/41-2/JUST/meeting-37/evidence

Standing Committee on Justice and Human Rights. (2014b, July 9). *Evidence.* (No. 38, 2nd Session, 41st Parliament). Retrieved from http://www.ourcommons.ca/DocumentViewer/en/41-2/JUST/meeting-38/evidence

Standing Committee on Justice and Human Rights. (2014c, July 9). *Evidence.* (No. 39, 2nd Session, 41st Parliament). Retrieved from http://www.ourcommons.ca/DocumentViewer/en/41-2/JUST/meeting-39/evidence

Standing Committee on Justice and Human Rights. (2014d, July 9). *Evidence.* (No. 40, 2nd Session, 41st Parliament). Retrieved from http://www.ourcommons.ca/DocumentViewer/en/41-2/JUST/meeting-40/evidence

Standing Committee on Justice and Human Rights. (2014e, July 10). *Evidence.* (No. 42, 2nd Session, 41st Parliament). Retrieved from http://www.ourcommons.ca/DocumentViewer/en/41-2/JUST/meeting-42/evidence

Wagenaar, H., & Altink, S. (2012). Prostitution as morality politics or why it is exceedingly difficult to design and sustain effective prostitution policy. *Sexuality Research and Social Policy, 9*(3), 279–92. https://doi.org/10.1007/s13178-012-0095-0

Walton-Roberts, M., Beaujot, R., Hiebert, D., McDaniel, S., Rose, D., & Wright, R. (2014). Why do we still need a census? Views from the age of 'truthiness' and the 'death of evidence.' *Canadian Geographer, 58*(1), 34–47. https://doi.org/10.1111/cag.12065

Weitzer, R. (2005). Flawed theory and method in studies of prostitution. *Violence Against Women, 11*(7), 934–49. https://doi.org/10.1177/1077801205276986

Zinger, I. (2016). Human rights and federal corrections: A commentary on a decade of tough on crime policies in Canada. *Canadian Journal of Criminology and Criminal Justice, 58*(4), 609–27. https://doi.org/10.3138/cjccj.2016.E06

Cases

Bedford v. Canada, 2010 ONSC 4264.
Canada (Attorney General) v. Bedford, 2013 SCC 72, [2013] 3 SCR 1101.

Legislation

Bill C-36, *Protection of Communities and Exploited Persons Act,* SC 2014, c. 25.

26

Action, Advocacy, and Allies
———— Building a Movement for Sex
Worker Rights

SARAH BEER

The story of the sex worker rights movement in Canada begins in the early
1970s when sex workers in major cities across the country faced increased
repression and began organizing in a sustained way. Sex workers supported
one another with information regarding laws, safety, and working conditions, with a focus on political transformation. The emergent movement
was redirected in the mid-1980s with the onset of the HIV/AIDS epidemic
(Brock, 1998; Jenness, 1993). In partnership with public health agencies, sex
workers and allies mobilized resources and formalized movement organizations. These initiatives helped to legitimize experiential knowledge and to
advance a human rights framework as the best strategy both to fight HIV/
AIDS and to improve health and safety in the sex industry overall. The limited agenda associated with HIV funding, however, narrowed the political
scope of the movement. Activists dealt with this situation by splitting into
two types of organizations, those affiliated with the health sector and service provision and those adhering to an advocacy-based agenda of political
change (Beer, 2010).

Over the past thirty-five years, three different governmental review committees have examined the status of sex work in Canada, and each has recommended legislative change to reduce violence against sex workers
(Canada, 1985, 1998, 2006). However, the status quo has been maintained.
Lack of political motivation to alter the legislative framework, especially in
light of the high-profile cases of murdered and missing women in

Vancouver, alongside numerous other reports of violence against sex workers across the country, was the impetus behind recent constitutional litigation (*Bedford v. Canada*, 2010; *Downtown Eastside Sex Workers United Against Violence Society v. Canada*, 2010). This chapter provides a brief overview of the development of the sex worker rights movement in Canada in the lead-up to legal mobilization, which ultimately resulted in legislative change.

The Emergence of the Sex Worker Rights Movement

Prostitution came under increased public scrutiny in the 1970s. At the time, sex work strolls were most often located in neighbourhoods with a concentration of strip clubs, adult movie houses, cabarets, pornographic bookstores, massage and body rub parlours, and other forms of adult entertainment. "The Main" in central Montreal was a near-legendary red light district, Toronto's Yonge Street was becoming the country's notorious "sin strip," and Vancouver's West End was gaining a reputation as the "prostitution capital of Canada." By the mid-1970s, however, plans were underway for a renewal of commercial development, with municipal politicians anxious to make urban centres more appealing to middle-class shoppers, with police set to re-establish control over prostitution areas, and with major newspapers garnering support for "clean-up" campaigns. The results of these campaigns were the same across many of Canada's major cities; as indoor venues were shut down, more sex workers turned to the streets. City bylaws were implemented to curb street solicitation, although they did little except push workers from one neighbourhood to another. Resident groups organized against street-based sex workers (see also Butler Burke, this collection; Page, this collection), and the media drew attention to what was fast becoming defined as a national concern (Brock, 1998; Lowman, 2011; Ross, 2010; Shaver, 1994).

With mounting economic and police pressure, alongside harassment from resident groups and media outlets, sex workers started to speak out. In 1977, inspired by the American sex worker rights organization COYOTE (Call Off Your Old Tired Ethics), Margaret Spore founded the Toronto-based group BEAVER (Better End All Vicious Erotic Repression). Composed primarily of erotic dancers, the group found it difficult to mobilize other sex workers to get involved. In 1979 the name was changed to CASH (Coalition Against Street Harassment, 1979–80), and members worked to bring attention to the violence and harassment that sex workers experienced on the street due to hostile attitudes and law enforcement practices (Sorfleet, 1995). That same year, the Canadian Association of Burlesque Entertainers (1979–82) formed a local of the Canadian Labour Congress, becoming the first erotic dancers' union in the country. In the face of mounting anti-prostitution campaigns, a small group of sex workers in Vancouver formed the Alliance for the Safety of Prostitutes (1982–86). Since the 1980s, a number autonomous groups have emerged across the country, and although most were short-lived, they highlighted the issue of working conditions and demonstrated that sex workers had a voice that deserved, and needed, to be heard.

The emergent movement for sex worker rights was altered dramatically by the HIV/AIDS epidemic in the early 1980s. Health agencies began to view HIV as a public health concern, and sex workers, alongside gay men, were deemed probable sources of HIV transmission. Many public health departments across the country eventually adopted a harm reduction approach in an effort to reduce HIV transmission, abandoning the existing moralized approach, which sought to eradicate prostitution. Working from a harm reduction perspective, sex workers articulated their ability to instigate safer sex practices and to offer peer education and outreach services to marginalized sex workers; for the first time, they were able to garner government funding in order to support these efforts.

In 1986 members of a small, Toronto-based political group, the Canadian Organization for the Rights of Prostitutes (CORP), applied for and received funding from all levels of government.[1] They founded and incorporated Maggie's: The Toronto Prostitutes' Community Service Project (now Maggie's: Toronto Sex Workers Action Project), named in honour of Margaret Spore, the founder of BEAVER. It was the first charitable organization of its kind in Canada – funded, staffed, and directed by sex workers – and it inspired similar peer-education projects internationally (Shanahan, 2007). Not long afterward in Montreal, community organizers explored the feasibility of an HIV intervention program, and out of these meetings the group Stella, l'amie de Maimie was born. Modelled after Maggie's and its harm reduction framework, Stella was mandated to provide a drop-in space where women working in the sex industry could meet, develop relationships, and build community. Like Maggie's, it received charitable status and government funding to support this work, and in 1995 it opened its doors to local sex workers.

Maggie's and Stella, alongside others, such as PACE Society in Vancouver, are among the most established and well-known groups dedicated to sex worker rights in the country. These organizations foreground experiential knowledge and input, provide alternate or additional employment opportunities, facilitate skill development, offer resources, and generate a sense of community. Actions are focused on outreach provision, peer and public education, and alliance building. Government funding has helped to sustain these organizations, but it is also fraught with additional challenges and concerns.

Funding formalizes organizational structures but tends to bureaucratize mobilization. The outreach services that are provided can be restricted based on funding criteria (e.g., funders might give money only to do street-based, not indoor, outreach). This situation can inadvertently reaffirm misconceptions about the industry and those working within it. Likewise, a significant portion of funding comes from HIV prevention programs, which risks perpetuating notions of sex workers as public health threats. And despite the fact that sex worker organizations and their allies identify criminalization as one of the most serious barriers to health and safety, registered charities are limited in their ability to lobby for legislative and political change. Indeed, to devote more than 10 percent of annual resources to political activity contravenes the Income Tax Act (Canada, 2003). As a consequence, sex workers need to organize on multiple fronts.

Promoting Sex Worker Rights through Political Advocacy

In light of these and other challenges, some sex worker activists have instead opted to form unfunded political advocacy groups in order to move decriminalization forward. In lieu of outreach and service provision, their activism consists of campaigning against local bylaws and federal Criminal Code provisions and enforcement practices, as well as raising public awareness about a range of issues confronting sex workers. These two organizational forms – community-based service providers and political advocacy groups – are not entirely distinct, with membership crossover and collaboration. For example, CORP, founded in 1983 in Toronto, played a central role in launching Maggie's. Renamed Sex Professionals of Canada (SPOC) in 2000, this political organization remains unfunded and politically active, its members central to the constitutional challenge in Ontario. Another exemplary political organization, Prostitutes of Ottawa-Gatineau Work, Educate, and Resist (POWER), founded in 2008, organizes rallies, develops educational and resource materials, undertakes research, engages in community-building activities, and collaborates with allied groups, such as the AIDS Committee of Ottawa, Pivot Legal Society, Families of Sisters in Spirit, and various civil liberties associations across the country. This kind of political work defends the rights of sex workers at the local level and supports litigation efforts at the provincial and federal levels.

Political organizations such as these are typically run by current or former sex workers and select allies, and they are explicit in their efforts to be inclusive and representative of sex workers across the gender spectrum and in all sectors of the industry. They reject funding to avoid bureaucratization and political suppression. In so doing, advocacy groups tend to rely heavily on a small core of unpaid individuals to do the bulk of the work. The challenges of attracting and maintaining leadership are compounded by the fact that affiliation with organizations that are run strictly by and for current and former sex workers requires activists who are willing to face the personal and professional ramifications of being out as sex workers (see also Sayers, this collection; Porth, this collection). Although some political groups endure, many become inactive over time. We also see collaborations between political advocacy and service-based organizations and, increasingly, affiliation with other influential allies (see also Lam and Gallant, this collection).

Legislative Activism and Working with Allies

As seen at the beginning of this collection in Brenda Belak's chapter, *"Bedford v. Canada:* A Breakthrough in the Legal Discourse," with few other avenues available and with governments unwilling to improve the current social, legal, and political conditions, two groups of current and former sex workers brought constitutional challenges to their respective provincial courts in 2007. In Toronto, Ontario, long-time sex worker activists Terri-Jean Bedford, Amy Lebovitch, and Valerie Scott were the three applicants, represented by Alan Young. The applicants in Vancouver, British Columbia, were Sheryl Kiselbach and Sex Workers United Against Violence (SWUAV), represented by Pivot Legal Society.

The entrenchment of the Charter of Rights and Freedoms in the Constitution in 1982 and the adoption of the equal rights provision (s. 15) in 1985 expanded the role of the courts in the Canadian political system. More people gained access to the courts as rules on legal standing and third-party intervention were gradually relaxed, and social movements increasingly turned to the legal system to seek rights, redress, and justice. Social movement and socio-legal scholars have been critical of this shift, given the tendency to overemphasize litigation at the expense of broader political goals. The courts are perceived as inherently conservative, and litigation necessarily relies on credentialed experts, diverting resources to lawyers and legal processes at the expense of grassroots mobilization and other forms of political organizing (Boyd and Young, 2003; Conway, 2004; McCann, 2004; Scheingold, 1974; Sheldrick, 2004; Smith, 2005). For the Canadian sex worker rights movement, however, legal mobilization inspired collective action. Pro bono lawyers, allies, and researchers helped to offset the financial burden of litigation for the two Charter challenges and, alongside movement organizations, helped to legitimize a sex worker rights perspective.

Here, we see how longstanding relationships with influential allies enabled strategic litigation. Collaborations with academic researchers and HIV movement organizations over the past two decades have established a body of empirical knowledge crucial to the court rulings. One such organization, the Canadian HIV/AIDS Legal Network, works with sex workers in conducting research and analysis, while engaging in legal advocacy, public education, and community mobilization (see Canadian HIV/AIDS Legal Network, 2005; Canadian HIV/AIDS Legal Network, Stella, and Maggie's, 2007). Such national HIV organizations have helped to advance a rights-based perspective beyond the reach of sex worker organizations around the country.

In the early 2000s, Pivot Legal Society, an advocacy organization in Vancouver's Downtown Eastside, initiated community meetings to understand the legal needs of women in the neighbourhood. Many women who work and live in the area are extremely marginalized, facing issues related to poverty, mental illness, HIV, hepatitis C, disabilities, and drug use, all greatly compounded by racism and colonialism. At these meetings, the women identified the criminalization of prostitution as a central issue. As the group evolved, it formed the Downtown Eastside Sex Workers United Against Violence Society (SWUAV), registered as a nonprofit, and among other projects, mounted a constitutional challenge. Throughout the litigation process, Pivot Legal Society developed a strong relationship with the broader sex worker rights movement, consulted with sex worker organizations, mobilized at both the grassroots and legal levels, and amplified the experiences of those most affected by the laws (see Pivot Legal Society, 2006; Pivot Legal Society Sex Work Subcommittee, 2004).

Ideally, both constitutional challenges would have proceeded alongside one another, each reflecting different aspects of sex work, with the BC case clearly foregrounding the experiences of street-based sex workers and the Ontario case reflecting the needs of indoor workers (see also Valverde, this collection). The Vancouver challenge was delayed when the BC Supreme Court ruled that an anonymous collective of plaintiffs did not have standing or the legal right to bring constitutional litigation. It was five years before the Supreme Court ruled that the plaintiffs did have public interest standing. In the meantime, the challenge in Ontario moved forward, and there was concern within the broader movement that legislative outcomes in Ontario would, at best, benefit commercial sex in private settings and that the precariousness of street work would be exacerbated. Despite the setback in British Columbia, legal mobilization and working closely with allies proved to be a powerful strategy with regard to sex workers' legislative advocacy. In an unexpected victory in 2010, Justice Susan Himel of the Ontario Superior Court of Justice struck down all of the impugned provisions (see also Belak, this collection).

A year later, the case was heard in the Ontario Court of Appeal, where a large number of organizations participated as interveners. Three groups advocated for continued criminalization on religious and moral grounds, and the Coalition for the Abolition of Prostitution, comprising various women's organizations, argued for the criminalization of clients – but not sex workers – based on a view of prostitution as inherently exploitative. Allies to the sex worker rights movement were found in the interveners who advocated for the decriminalization of prostitution based on civil liberties, health, safety, and human rights. These groups included the Canadian HIV/ AIDS Legal Network, the BC Centre for Excellence in HIV/AIDS, and both the Canadian Civil Liberties Association and the BC Civil Liberties Association. Joint sex worker submissions were also presented by PACE Society, SWUAV, Pivot Legal Society, POWER, and Maggie's (*Canada (Attorney General) v. Bedford*, 2012).

The case proceeded to the Supreme Court, and many of these same groups attempted once again to intervene, alongside additional HIV/AIDS organizations, the Simone De Beauvoir Institute at Concordia University, and Aboriginal Legal Services of Toronto. In the end, in terms of experiential knowledge, the court heard only from sex worker representatives of PACE Society and SWUAV. Two sex worker coalitions were denied intervener status: the POWER-Maggie's-Stella Coalition, which spoke to a broad range of industry sectors from multiple geographic regions; and the International Sex Worker Coalition, made up of three national sex worker organizations from Australia, New Zealand, and Sweden,[2] which would have offered valuable insight regarding the effects of criminalized and decriminalized legislative frameworks. Their exclusions reflect the ongoing failure of the judiciary to recognize sex workers as experts on the sex industry; the opportunity for these sex worker organizations to participate, and to have their views on the public record, was lost.

On December 20, 2013, in a 9–0 decision, the Supreme Court of Canada found all of the impugned laws unconstitutional (*Canada (Attorney General) v. Bedford*, 2013). This was an incredible achievement for a movement forty years in the making. Unfortunately for sex workers, the Supreme Court justices delayed striking down the laws for one year to allow Parliament time to introduce Charter-compliant legislation. At the time, a majority Conservative government was in power, and within months, it reinforced a criminalized regime. The new legislation, the Protection of Communities and Exploited Persons Act, came into effect on December 6, 2014, coinciding with the National Day of Remembrance and Action on Violence Against Women.

The newly elected Liberal government has yet, at the time of writing, to follow through on commitments to address the new legislation (see Porth, this collection). As a consequence, the fight to recognize the rights and dignity of sex workers in Canada continues, this time with a well-established network of activists and alliances that are pursuing various strategies.

Conclusion

From entirely grassroots beginnings in the 1970s, sex workers have developed and articulated a sex worker rights perspective and established a national movement. Over this period, some activists garnered resources and formalized sex work organizations, enabling outreach services and community building. Others focused on socio-legal transformation outside of service provision, forming political advocacy groups. Over the years, both types of organizations selectively collaborated with allies who upheld the perspectives of sex workers. As allied groups came to understand that criminalization was the central obstacle to meeting other organizational goals, like harm reduction, they amplified the voices of decriminalization advocates in social, political, and legal contexts.

Notably, the most marginalized sex workers have not been left behind in the drive for rights. Indeed, despite judicial barriers, those most affected by the laws were at the forefront of legal mobilization in British Columbia. As Ontario plaintiffs moved forward with their case, they did not neglect the most disenfranchised, ensuring that diverse prostitution-related provisions were challenged. The political climate has not been favourable, but the expertise that sex workers have been offering over the past forty years – as activists, educators, service providers, community organizers, researchers, and collaborators – has been legitimized. The next chapter of the sex worker rights movement will continue the work of altering social stigma and criminalization – but now with a firmly entrenched sex worker rights perspective, a network of influential allies, and a sense of possibility.

Notes

1 Funding was received from the Toronto Department of Public Health (municipal), the Ontario Ministry of Health (provincial), and Health Canada (federal), alongside private donations.
2 The national sex worker organizations were Scarlet Alliance (Australia), Rose Alliance (Sweden), and the New Zealand Prostitutes' Collective.

References

Beer, S. (2010). *The sex worker rights movement in Canada: Challenging the 'prostitution laws.'* (Unpublished doctoral dissertation). University of Windsor, Windsor, Ontario.

Boyd, S., & Young, C. (2003). 'From same-sex to no sex?' Trends towards recognition of (same-sex) relationships in Canada. *Seattle Journal for Social Justice, 1*(3), 757–93.

Brock, D. (1998). *Making work, making trouble: Prostitution as a social problem.* Toronto, ON: University of Toronto Press. https://doi.org/10.3138/9781442676930

Canada. (1985). *Pornography and prostitution in Canada: Report of the Special Committee on Pornography and Prostitution.* (2 vols.). Ottawa, ON: Canadian Government Publishing Centre.

Canada (Canada Revenue Agency). (2003). *Policy statement: The difference between political purposes and charitable purposes.* Retrieved from https://www.canada.ca/en/revenue-agency/services/charities-giving/charities/policies-guidance/policy-statement-022-political-activities.html

Canada (Federal/Provincial/Territorial Working Group on Prostitution). (1998). *Report and recommendations in respect of legislation, policy and practices concerning prostitution-related activities.* Retrieved from https://walnet.org/csis/reports/

Canada (House of Commons). (2006). *The challenge of change: A study of Canada's criminal prostitution laws.* Retrieved from http://www.ourcommons.ca/DocumentViewer/en/39-1/JUST/report-6

Canadian HIV/AIDS Legal Network. (2005). *Sex, work, rights: Reforming Canadian criminal laws on prostitution.* Retrieved from http://lib.ohchr.org/HRBodies/UPR/Documents/Session4/CA/CANHIVAIDS_LN_CAN_UPR_S4_2009_anx3_SexWorkRights.pdf

Canadian HIV/AIDS Legal Network, Stella, & Maggie's. (2007). *Not up to the challenge of change: An analysis of the report of the Subcommittee on Solicitation Laws.* Retrieved from http://www.aidslaw.ca/site/not-up-to-the-challenge-of-change -an-analysis-of-the-report-of-the-subcommittee-on-solicitation-laws/?lang=en

Conway, J. (2004). *Identity, place, knowledge: Social movements contesting globalization.* Halifax, NS: Fernwood.

Jenness, V. (1993). *Making it work: The prostitutes' rights movement in perspective.* Hawthorne, NY: Aldine de Gruyter.

Lowman, J. (2011). Deadly inertia: A history of constitutional challenges to Canada's *Criminal Code* sections on prostitution. *Beijing Law Review, 2*(2), 33–54. https:// doi.org/10.4236/blr.2011.22005

McCann, M. (2004). Law and social movements. In A. Sarat (Ed.), *The Blackwell companion to law and society* (pp. 506–22). Malden, MA: Blackwell. https://doi. org/10.1002/9780470693650.ch27

Pivot Legal Society. (2006). *Beyond decriminalization: Sex work, human rights and a new framework for law reform.* Retrieved from http://old.nswp.org/resource/ beyond-decriminalization-sex-work-human-rights-and-new-framework-law -reform

Pivot Legal Society Sex Work Subcommittee. (2004). *Voices for dignity: A call to end the harms caused by Canada's sex trade laws.* Retrieved from http://old.nswp. org/resource/voices-dignity-call-end-the-harms-caused-canadas-sex-trade-laws

Ross, B. (2010). Sex and (evacuation from) the city: The moral and legal regulation of sex workers in Vancouver's West End, 1975–1985. *Sexualities, 13*(2), 197–218. https://doi.org/10.1177/1363460709359232

Scheingold, S. (1974). *The politics of rights: Lawyers, public policy and political change.* New Haven, CT: Yale University Press.

Shanahan, N. (2007, April 27). Chris Bearchell, 53: Activist. *Globe and Mail.* Retrieved from http://www.walnet.org/csis/news/vancouver_2007/gandm -070427.html

Shaver, F.M. (1994). The regulation of prostitution: Avoiding the morality traps. *Canadian Journal of Law and Society, 9*(1), 123–45. https://doi.org/10.1017/ S0829320100003537

Sheldrick, B. (2004). *Perils and possibilities: Social activism and the law.* Halifax, NS: Fernwood.

Smith, M. (2005). Social movements and judicial empowerment: Courts, public policy, and lesbian and gay organizing in Canada. *Politics & Society, 33*(2), 327–53.

Sorfleet, A. (1995). *A brief history of sex worker activism in Toronto.* Retrieved from http://www.walnet.org/csis/groups/swat/torontohistory.html

Cases

Bedford v. Canada, 2010 ONSC 4264.
Canada (Attorney General) v. Bedford, 2012 ONCA 186.
Canada (Attorney General) v. Bedford, 2013 SCC 72, [2013] 3 SCR 1101.

Canada (Attorney General) v. Downtown Eastside Sex Workers United Against Violence Society, 2012 SCC 45, [2012] 2 SCR 524.
Downtown Eastside Sex Workers United Against Violence Society v. Canada (Attorney General), 2010 BCCA 439.

Legislation

Bill C-36, *Protection of Communities and Exploited Persons Act,* SC 2014, c. 25.
Canadian Charter of Rights and Freedoms, Part I of the *Constitution Act, 1982,* being Schedule B to the *Canada Act 1982* (UK), 1982, c. 11.

Afterword

JOHN LOWMAN AND FRANCES M. SHAVER

The editors requested that we write an Afterword to this impressive anthology in order to contextualize the chapters in light of prostitution law and social policy developments over the past four decades. Since neither of us has been involved in the business of sex work, they also asked us to describe the circumstances leading to our conducting sex work research. We thus begin by situating ourselves in the debate over sex work law reform that has unfolded in Canada since 1980.

Lowman's first exposure to prostitution was as an undergraduate student at Sheffield University in England from 1968 to 1972:

> Because I lived in the red light district during part of my stay in Sheffield, and because of my own involvement in the local illicit-drug subculture, I got to know many women who sold sexual services, but I did not know them in that capacity. I knew them as neighbours and friends, someone with whom to share a drink at the local pub, or a reefer at the local Shebheen.

While completing his master's degree in geography at York University in Toronto, Lowman spent six months in prison. As a result of that experience, he started taking courses in criminology. He decided to enrol in the geography doctoral program at the University of British Columbia and conduct his research on the geography of crime. Shortly after arriving at UBC in September 1977, serendipity determined the trajectory of that research:

Prostitution in Vancouver was making front page news. The news focused on two developments. The first was the Penthouse Cabaret trial. The Penthouse, a venue where prostitutes met clients through the 1960s and into the 1970s, was closed in December 1975 after the owners and two employees were charged with procuring and living on the avails of prostitution. The second topic concerned the growth of street prostitution in the West End of Vancouver. When the Penthouse closed, what had been conveniently contained indoor prostitution spilled onto the street. That displacement became the theme tying together the various components of my doctoral thesis, which examined the effect of law and law enforcement on crime patterns.

Lowman started his research on prostitution displacement in the spring of 1978. Coincidently, that research unfolded during a period when a series of Vancouver court decisions rendered the street prostitution law of the day – the "soliciting law" – unenforceable. This became the reason many commentators gave for the spread of the so-called street prostitution problem across Canada. Lowman's analysis suggested a different cause, namely that by enforcing contradictory and often self-defeating prostitution prohibitions, Vancouver police had pushed indoor prostitution onto the street (Lowman, 1986).

By 1983 the "street prostitution problem" had become so severe that the federal government struck the Special Committee on Pornography and Prostitution (the Fraser Committee) to study sex work and the law with an eye to recommending law reforms. Since his doctoral thesis included a section on prostitution in Vancouver, the Department of Justice contracted Lowman to conduct the British Columbia component of the background research (Lowman, 1984). Between 1985 and 2001 the Department of Justice contracted Lowman to conduct six further studies of prostitution and the law in the Lower Mainland of British Columbia, including the British Columbia component of the Justice Department evaluation of the communicating law.

Shaver first met women involved in sex work while holding a position as a community worker for First United Church in Downtown Eastside Vancouver from 1967 to 1969:

Since the city jail was across the street and clearly part of the community, I revised my job description to include jail visits. The police chief was enthusiastic and gave me a pass to visit the women in lock-up. Almost all the women I met were involved in prostitution; it wasn't referred to as the sex industry back then. Very few support networks existed. Those that were available were designed for women in conflict with the law: Elizabeth Fry, the John Howard Society, and the Salvation Army. There were no programs designed for sex workers and no organizations by and for sex workers. My objective during these visits – which were extended to Friday lunch at Oakalla Prison – was to provide an opportunity for "square johns" (like me) and "rounders" (like them) to interact and to share stories. In the process, I hoped we would learn something from each other. In short, my role was simply to be a *witness*.

Skip forward fourteen years, and after completing her master's degree, Shaver was in Ottawa working for the Canadian Advisory Council on the Status of Women (CACSW):

I didn't get to write my own job description this time! I was just a research officer. However, as part of my job – and as a tribute to the women I met in the Downtown Eastside – I agreed to help develop the council's publication *Prostitution in Canada* (CACSW, 1984). It was to be the basis of the council's response to the Special Committee on Pornography and Prostitution. I parted ways with the council when it became clear that it was concerned more about women residents than about women sex workers. Sensing that sex workers needed a voice, I submitted a brief to the Fraser Committee entitled "Prostitution: A Critical Analysis of Three Policy Approaches" (Shaver, 1985). Based on secondary data, it concluded with a recommendation for decriminalization in combination with social policy programs.

It was during the planning of the Department of Justice field studies for the Fraser Committee that, in January 1984, Lowman and Shaver first met.

At the time, there were only a handful of prostitution studies. Indeed, up until 1950, every published research article examined prostitution as a vector of disease (Cavers, 1918; Nelson, 1943; Williams, 1941; Yarros, 1920). During the 1950s and 1960s, there was no research on prostitution. The first work in the period after the Second World War was James Gray's (1971) *Red Lights on the Prairies*, a socio-historical study of brothel prostitution in prairie cities during the period of the Christian temperance campaign between roughly 1890 and 1920. Subsequent writers described social attitudes about "fallen women," the "white slave trade," and the "social evil" of prostitution during that same period (see Bell, 1910; Brookig, 1976; Fingard, 1977).

Rotenberg (1974) and Nilsen (1980) provided the first feminist analyses; still focused on the vice crusades during the first two decades of the twentieth century, they developed a labour market perspective that conceptualized prostitution as a form of work rather than a pathology.

Monique Layton's (1975) *Report on Prostitution in Vancouver* marked the first contemporaneous interview study of sex workers in Canada, followed by Prus and Irini's (1980) *Hookers, Rounders, and Desk Clerks,* an ethnography of hotel-based prostitution in Toronto in the 1960s and 1970s. In 1982 a Simon Fraser University master's student published an interview study with sex workers in Vancouver's West End (Kohlmeyer, 1982).

When the Fraser Committee's work began, we knew little about prostitution in Canada. Indeed, one could not have created an anthology like this one in 1983 since the entire compendium of research and experiential writing available at that time could not have filled it. However, the Fraser Committee marked the point at which the trickle of studies turned into a river of new research, which included empirical studies about sex work from a labour perspective – often involving fieldwork, in-depth interviews, and a community-partnered approach. In addition to highlighting the sex industry's diversity, it brought to light sex workers' vulnerability to assault, substandard and unsafe work conditions, the absence of appropriate health and social services to meet their needs, their marginalization or exclusion from mainstream social and community institutions, and the strategies they use to maximize their own safety, security, and well-being. As a whole, the research provided an in-depth analysis of the shifts in sex work legislation and policy in Canada, it highlighted the diverse and complex experiences of sex workers and their relationships with loved ones, colleagues, and clients, and it acknowledged the rise of sex worker resistance to the prohibitionist agenda. These same themes are reflected in this anthology.

The Fraser Committee also, for the first time, created a space for the voices of sex workers. The Alliance for the Safety of Prostitutes (ASP), founded by Sally de Quadros and Marie Arrington in Vancouver, and the Canadian Organization for the Rights of Prostitutes (CORP), established by Peggy Miller and Valerie Scott in Toronto, appeared before the Fraser Committee. Both organizations argued for decriminalization. Sex worker rights organizations have proliferated since then and expanded their services and political initiatives. In the 1990s sex worker groups in Canada began communicating with similar organizations around the world regarding myriad issues, including fears related to HIV/AIDS, the charter of rights for sex workers, support for the migration of sex workers, education of their communities about sex work–related issues, and initiating strategies for decriminalizing sex work and improving their living and working conditions.

Some things have not changed in the thirty-three years since we met. Sex work and sex workers are still stigmatized, marginalized, and vulnerable. Today, as in the past, policy is still driven more by ideology and morality than by justice, understanding, and empirical evidence. Canadian governments have failed to address the evidence-based arguments for decriminalization.

There are, however, also important advances to celebrate. Thanks in part to contributors in this anthology, there is now a substantial body of systematic and reliable research on sex work and its organization. There are more sex worker rights groups now than ever before, and a larger number and greater range of people comprise these groups and alliances. These shifts have resulted in new opportunities for strategic action, including plans for social policy reform, new funding opportunities, innovative use of the Internet, and an enlightening body of public opinion research on sex work and the law (Lowman and Louie, 2012). Sex worker organizations have also become exceptionally competent – in education, research, health and social support, legal sophistication, communication, and self-governance.

Despite the wealth of research and information about prostitution now at our disposal, and the courts' enlightened evaluation of conflicting research evidence claims in *Bedford*, it was distressing to watch the Conservative government and its supporters rely largely on the evidence that the courts explicitly rejected in order to justify the imposition of demand-side prohibition in Canada in 2014. Outside the courtroom, argument-based evidence trumped evidence-based argument. These developments were hardly surprising in light of the Harper government's attack on science more generally (Linnitt, 2013). Nevertheless, the Supreme Court's affirmation of the Ontario Superior Court of Justice's *Bedford v. Canada* (2010) decision and the maturation of sex workers' advocacy groups give us hope that – in the long run – evidence-based argument can win the day. In *Bedford v. Canada*, Justice Susan Himel pointed to the systemic and broad evidence of the defendant witnesses as an important deciding factor in her decision to reject the Crown's position. At the same time, she identified the legal conditions for acceptable evidence. Our legal system did its job, and in doing so, it affirmed the value of high-quality research. It was the legislative system that failed us by passing laws that ignored this research evidence.

Sex workers' advocacy groups have changed in response to emerging challenges, and the initial resistance to researchers that we used to see in the 1980s and 1990s has significantly diminished – in part because of the work of less biased researchers such as those writing for this anthology and also because sex workers and advocates are now conducting their own research. Advocacy groups' access to a broad range of evidence and their use of it in their advocacy work have given new value to such research and revived our hope in its long-term social impact.

If two of our three main social change agents (i.e., legal and public action) have made effective use of research evidence, we can only hope that the third (i.e., legislative action) will eventually follow suit – even if reluctantly. The analyses and information provided in this anthology are important and welcome additions to that end.

References

Bell, E.A. (Ed.). (1910). *Fighting the traffic in young girls, or, War on the white slave trade: A complete and detailed account of the shameless traffic in young girls.* Chicago: G.S. Ball.

Brookig, L.W. (1976). Prostitution in Toronto, 1911. In R. Cook and W. Mitchinson (Eds.), *The proper sphere: Women's place in Canadian society* (pp. 241–49). Toronto, ON: Oxford University Press.

CACSW (Canadian Advisory Council on the Status of Women). (1984). *Prostitution in Canada.* Ottawa: Canadian Advisory Council on the Status of Women.

Cavers, C.W. (1918). Vice and venereal disease in Montreal. *Public Health Journal, 9*(11), 529–33.

Fingard, J. (1977). *The social evil in Halifax in the mid-nineteenth century.* (Unpublished paper). Department of History, Dalhousie University, Halifax, Nova Scotia.

Gray, J. (1971). *Red lights on the Prairies.* New York, NY: Signet.

Kohlmeyer, K. (1982). *An ethnography of street prostitution in Vancouver.* (Unpublished MA thesis). Simon Fraser University, Burnaby, British Columbia.

Layton, M. (1975). *Report on prostitution in Vancouver: Official and unofficial reports.* (Unpublished report). British Columbia Police Commission, Vancouver, British Columbia.

Linnitt, C. (2013, May). Harper's attack on science: No science, no evidence, no truth, no democracy. *Academic Matters: OCUFA's Journal of Higher Education,* 19–22. Retrieved from https://academicmatters.ca/2013/05/harpers-attack-on-science-no-science-no-evidence-no-truth-no-democracy/

Lowman, J. (1984). *Vancouver field study of prostitution.* (Working Papers on Pornography and Prostitution Report No. 8). Ottawa, ON: Department of Justice.

Lowman, J. (1986). Street prostitution in Vancouver: Notes on the genesis of a social problem. *Canadian Journal of Criminology, 28*(1), 1–16.

Lowman, J., & Louie, C. (2012). Public opinion on prostitution law reform in Canada.

Canadian Journal of Criminology and Criminal Justice, 54(2), 245–60. https://doi.org/10.3138/cjccj.2011.E.34

Nelson, N.A. (1943). 'Prostitution' and genito-infectious disease control. *Canadian Journal of Public Health, 34*(6), 251–60.

Nilsen, D. (1980). The 'social evil': Prostitution in Vancouver, 1900–1920. In B. Latham & C. Kess (Eds.), *In her own right: Selected essays on women's history in B.C.* (pp. 205–28). Victoria, BC: Camosun College.

Prus, R., & Irini, S. (1980). *Hookers, rounders and desk clerks.* Toronto, ON: Gage.

Rotenberg, L. (1974). The wayward worker: Toronto's prostitute at the turn of the century. In J. Acton, P. Goldsmith, & B. Shepherd (Eds.), *Women at work, Ontario 1850–1930* (pp. 33–70). Toronto, ON: Canadian Women's Educational Press.

Shaver, F.M. (1985). Prostitution: A critical analysis of three policy approaches. *Canadian Public Policy, 11*(3), 493–503. https://doi.org/10.2307/3550504

Williams, D.H. (1941). The suppression of commercial prostitution in the City of Vancouver. *Journal of Social Hygiene, 27,* 364–72.

Yarros, R.S. (1920). The prostitute as a health and social problem. *Public Health Journal, 10*(13), 606–12.

Cases

Bedford v. Canada, 2010 ONSC 4264.
Canada (Attorney General) v. Bedford, 2012 ONCA 186.
Canada (Attorney General) v. Bedford, 2013 SCC 72, [2013] 3 SCR.

Appendix

——— Prostitution-Related Criminal Code Provisions

Section 213: Offences in Relation to Offering, Providing or Obtaining Sexual Services for Consideration

213 (1) Everyone is guilty of an offence punishable on summary conviction who, in a public place or in any place open to public view, for the purpose of offering, providing or obtaining sexual services for consideration,

(a) stops or attempts to stop any motor vehicle; or
(b) impedes the free flow of pedestrian or vehicular traffic or ingress to or egress from premises adjacent to that place.

(1.1) Everyone is guilty of an offence punishable on summary conviction who communicates with any person – for the purpose of offering or providing sexual services for consideration – in a public place, or in any place open to public view, that is or is next to a school ground, playground or daycare centre.

Definition of *public place*

(2) In this section, *public place* includes any place to which the public have access as of right or by invitation, express or implied, and any motor vehicle located in a public place or in any place open to public view.

Section 286: Commodification of Sexual Activity

Obtaining sexual services for consideration

286.1 (1) Everyone who, in any place, obtains for consideration, or communicates with anyone for the purpose of obtaining for consideration, the sexual services of a person is guilty of

(a) an indictable offence and liable to imprisonment for a term of not more than five years and a minimum punishment of,
   (i) in the case where the offence is committed in a public place, or in any place open to public view, that is or is next to a park or the grounds of a school or religious institution or that is or is next to any other place where persons under the age of 18 can reasonably be expected to be present,
      • (A) for a first offence, a fine of $2,000, and
      • (B) for each subsequent offence, a fine of $4,000, or
   (ii) in any other case,
      • (A) for a first offence, a fine of $1,000, and
      • (B) for each subsequent offence, a fine of $2,000; or
(b) an offence punishable on summary conviction and liable to imprisonment for a term of not more than 18 months and a minimum punishment of,
   (i) in the case referred to in subparagraph (a)(i),
      • (A) for a first offence, a fine of $1,000, and
      • (B) for each subsequent offence, a fine of $2,000, or
   (ii) in any other case,
      • (A) for a first offence, a fine of $500, and
      • (B) for each subsequent offence, a fine of $1,000.

(2) Everyone who, in any place, obtains for consideration, or communicates with anyone for the purpose of obtaining for consideration, the sexual services of a person under the age of 18 years is guilty of an indictable offence and liable to imprisonment for a term of not more than 10 years and to a minimum punishment of imprisonment for a term of

(a) for a first offence, six months; and
(b) for each subsequent offence, one year.

Material Benefit from Sexual Services

286.2 (1) Everyone who receives a financial or other material benefit, knowing that it is obtained by or derived directly or indirectly from the commission of an offence under subsection 286.1(1), is guilty of an indictable offence and liable to imprisonment for a term of not more than 10 years.

(2) Everyone who receives a financial or other material benefit, knowing that it is obtained by or derived directly or indirectly from the commission of an offence under subsection 286.1(2), is guilty of an indictable offence and liable to imprisonment for a term of not more than 14 years and to a minimum punishment of imprisonment for a term of two years.

(3) For the purposes of subsections (1) and (2), evidence that a person lives with or is habitually in the company of a person who offers or provides sexual services for consideration is, in the absence of evidence to the contrary, proof that the person received a financial or other material benefit from those services.

(4) Subject to subsection (5), subsections (1) and (2) do not apply to a person who receives the benefit

(a) in the context of a legitimate living arrangement with the person from whose sexual services the benefit is derived;

(b) as a result of a legal or moral obligation of the person from whose sexual services the benefit is derived;

(c) in consideration for a service or good that they offer, on the same terms and conditions, to the general public; or

(d) in consideration for a service or good that they do not offer to the general public but that they offered or provided to the person from whose sexual services the benefit is derived, if they did not counsel or encourage that person to provide sexual services and the benefit is proportionate to the value of the service or good.

(5) Subsection (4) does not apply to a person who commits an offence under subsection (1) or (2) if that person

(a) used, threatened to use or attempted to use violence, intimidation or coercion in relation to the person from whose sexual services the benefit is derived;

(b) abused a position of trust, power or authority in relation to the person from whose sexual services the benefit is derived;

(c) provided a drug, alcohol or any other intoxicating substance to the person from whose sexual services the benefit is derived for the purpose of aiding or abetting that person to offer or provide sexual services for consideration;

(d) engaged in conduct, in relation to any person, that would constitute an offence under section 286.3; or

(e) received the benefit in the context of a commercial enterprise that offers sexual services for consideration.

(6) If a person is convicted of an offence under this section, the court that imposes the sentence shall consider as an aggravating factor the fact that that person received the benefit in the context of a commercial enterprise that offers sexual services for consideration.

Procuring

286.3 (1) Everyone who procures a person to offer or provide sexual services for consideration or, for the purpose of facilitating an offence under subsection 286.1(1), recruits, holds, conceals or harbours a person who offers or provides sexual services for consideration, or exercises control, direction or influence over the movements of that person, is guilty of an indictable offence and liable to imprisonment for a term of not more than 14 years.

(2) Everyone who procures a person under the age of 18 years to offer or provide sexual services for consideration or, for the purpose of facilitating an offence under subsection 286.1(2), recruits, holds, conceals or harbours a person under the age of 18 who offers or provides sexual services for consideration, or exercises control, direction or influence over the movements of that person, is guilty of an indictable offence and liable to imprisonment for a term of not more than 14 years and to a minimum punishment of imprisonment for a term of five years.

Advertising Sexual Services

286.4 Everyone who knowingly advertises an offer to provide sexual services for consideration is guilty of

(a) an indictable offence and liable to imprisonment for a term of not more than five years; or

(b) an offence punishable on summary conviction and liable to imprisonment for a term of not more than 18 months.

Immunity – Material Benefit and Advertising

286.5 (1) No person shall be prosecuted for

(a) an offence under section 286.2 if the benefit is derived from the provision of their own sexual services; or

(b) an offence under section 286.4 in relation to the advertisement of their own sexual services.

(2) No person shall be prosecuted for aiding, abetting, conspiring or attempting to commit an offence under any of sections 286.1 to 286.4 or being an accessory after the fact or counselling a person to be a party to such an offence, if the offence relates to the offering or provision of their own sexual services.

Contributors

Sarah Beer is a sociology professor at Dawson College in Montreal. She holds a master's degree in criminology from the University of Ottawa and a doctorate in sociology from the University of Windsor. Her dissertation research was on the sex worker rights movement in Canada leading up to constitutional challenges to Canada's prostitution laws. Sarah has published on the impacts of government funding on sex worker rights organizations and has authored a forthcoming article that details the contemporary movement in Canada.

Brenda Belak is a lawyer in Vancouver. From 2015 to 2017 she led the sex work decriminalization campaign for Pivot Legal Society, a nonprofit organization that uses law reform and strategic litigation to advocate for the rights of marginalized people. Pivot represented Sex Workers United Against Violence (SWUAV) in its own constitutional challenge to Canada's sex work laws and in SWUAV's intervention in the *Bedford* case. Brenda has advocated for the rights of women, Indigenous people, and sex workers in national and international law since 1996. She conducted research for BC's Missing Women Commission of Inquiry, which recommended changes to policing to increase sex workers' safety in the wake of a decade of serial murders. She is currently legal counsel at the BC Supreme Court.

Isabelle Bhola holds a master's degree in public policy and public administration from Concordia University and a graduate certificate in business administration from the John Molson School of Business. Isabelle previously obtained an honours bachelor's degree in health sciences from the University of Ottawa. Drawing on her background in health and legal studies as well as her experience as a policy analyst for the Government of Canada, she is motivated to improve the lives of vulnerable populations by producing quality research that will assist policy makers to draft evidence-based legislation.

Steven Bittle is an associate professor in the Department of Criminology, University of Ottawa, where his main research interests are in the areas of crimes of the powerful, corporate crime, corporate criminal liability, and the sociology of law. He has published previously on state responses to youth involved in sex work, including critical assessments of secure care legislation. His most recent publications focus on the class origins of legislation respecting corporate criminal liability and corporate manslaughter.

Chris Bruckert is a professor in the Department of Criminology at the University of Ottawa. Over the past twenty years she has devoted much of her energy to examining diverse sectors of the sex industry and has undertaken qualitative research on street-based sex work, erotic dance, in-call and out-call sex work, clients, male sex workers, and third parties. She is a co-editor, with Colette Parent, of *Getting Past 'the Pimp': Management in the Sex Industry* (2018).

John Bryans is a theatre artist and graduate student based in Montreal. He holds a bachelor's degree in kinesiology from the University of Manitoba and a theatre arts diploma from George Brown Theatre School in Toronto. John is currently completing his master of arts degree in the Department of Sociology and Anthropology at Concordia University. His current research draws from the fields of critical obesity studies and performance studies and is informed by his experiences as a professional actor and by his previous academic research projects regarding the embodied identities and health practices of men in the performing arts.

Nora Butler Burke is a doctoral student at the Interdisciplinary Centre for Studies on Society and Culture at Concordia University. Her research is focused on documenting the role of immigration penalty in the daily lives of migrant trans women in Canada. Previously, she was the coordinator of Action santé travesti(e)s et transsexuel(le)s du Québec, a project of CACTUS Montréal, working with low-income and sex-working trans women.

Jenn Clamen has been active in the Canadian and global sex worker rights movements since 2000. Her passion and work are centred on mobilizing sex workers into meaningful participation in policies and practices that have an impact on sex workers' lives. She has been an active member of Stella, Montreal's sex worker organization, since 2002. In 2003 she co-founded the Canadian Guild for Erotic Labour. Jenn is also an educator in university and community settings, teaching on issues and realities affecting criminalized and marginalized communities, particularly human rights, public space and poverty, women in conflict with the law, and community organizing.

Alison Clancey holds a master's degree in social work from the University of Victoria. She is the executive director of SWAN Vancouver Society, where she critiques the anti-trafficking industrial complex and its impacts on migrant and immigrant sex workers. Alison's activism centres on police mistreatment of sex workers, and she regularly trains police on sex work–related issues.

Elya M. Durisin holds a PhD in political science from York University, where her research focused on sexualized nationalism in narratives of "sex trafficking" in government discourse. Elya has been involved in the sex worker rights movement locally and internationally, and she is a co-editor, with Emily van der Meulen and Victoria Love, of *Selling Sex: Experience, Advocacy, and Research on Sex Work in Canada* (2013).

Chanelle Gallant is an activist-writer with a focus on sex and justice, as well as a long-time organizer. Her writing has appeared in *MTV News*, the *Rumpus*, the *Establishment*, the *Huffington Post*, the *Walrus*, and more. She has presented to the Canadian government and the National Anti-Trafficking Forum on sex work policy, and she co-founded the Migrant Sex Workers Project. She was a 2017 LGBTQ Lambda Literary Fellow and is currently writing a book on sexual labour. She also answers to the names Fallen Woman, Comrade, and Sister. Find out more at https://www.chanellegallant.com.

Kara Gillies has been active in the sex worker rights movement in Canada for over twenty-five years. She has been especially interested in the impact of criminal law on sex workers' personal, social, and workplace well-being and continues to advocate for sex worker rights in these spheres.

Stacey Hannem is an associate professor in the Department of Criminology at Wilfrid Laurier University. Her research interests revolve around the experience of stigma and marginality, particularly the implications of crime and the criminal justice system for families, as well as sex work legislation and policy. She is a co-editor, with Chris Bruckert, of *Stigma Revisited: Implications of the Mark* (2012). Working with REAL (Resources, Education, Advocacy for Local Sex Work), she recently completed a study on sex work in Brant, Haldimand, and Norfolk Counties funded by the Ontario Trillium Foundation.

Elizabeth James is a status, card-carrying Indian of mixed Ojibwe and Irish descent who was born and raised off of her family's reserve. She is thirty-four years old and has been working indoors as an erotic masseuse and escort for the past eight years. Elizabeth is the youngest of five children and lived in poverty throughout her childhood. Her sisters work in the sex industry, and society's hypersexualized media may have contributed to her own experimentations with prostitution at the ages of twelve and sixteen. It was not until she was twenty-six years old and in university that she chose to make the sex industry her sole source of income. Elizabeth will soon begin studying for her second bachelor's degree.

Ummni Khan is an associate professor in the Department of Law and Legal Studies at Carleton University and is the joint chair in women's studies at Carleton University and the University of Ottawa. Her scholarship analyzes the construction and criminalization of sexual deviancy in relation to gender, racialization, class, and disability, along with other axes of difference. She is the author of *Vicarious Kinks: SM in the Socio-Legal Imaginary* (2014). Her current projects address BDSM, violent music, rape fantasies, and the deviantization of sex trade clients, the latter project being supported by the Social Sciences and Humanities Research Council of Canada.

Andrea Krüsi is a research scientist with the Gender and Sexual Health Initiative and a postdoctoral fellow in the School of Population and Public Health at the University of British Columbia. Andrea's research focuses on how evolving sex work legislation and sex work–related stigma shape experiences of violence and poor health among sex workers. Her work is supported by the Canadian Institutes of Health Research and the Michael Smith Foundation for Health Research.

Elene Lam is the founder and executive director of Butterfly (Asian and Migrant Sex Workers Support Network) and a co-founder of the Migrant Sex Workers Project. She has been involved in movements respecting sex work, migrants, gender, labour, and human rights for more than fifteen years in Asia and Canada. She continued to work on organizing migrant sex workers and advocating for their rights after she came to Canada in 2013. She advocates for the human rights of sex workers, for the decriminalization of sex work, and for reducing the harms of anti-trafficking interventions.

Victoria Love is a sex worker and activist based in Toronto. She first worked in the sex industry as a youth and has experience working in a number of different sectors. She is a frequent guest speaker at community events, conferences, and trainings, as well as in university classrooms. She has also written about her experiences in the sex industry and has conducted numerous interviews both for media and for academic research.

John Lowman is a Professor Emeritus in the School of Criminology at Simon Fraser University where he taught for over 30 years. Since 1977 he has studied prostitution, prostitution law, and prostitution law enforcement in Canada. His research includes the *Vancouver Field Study of Prostitution* (1984), *Street Prostitution, Assessing the Impact of the Law, Vancouver* (1989), *Violence against Persons who Prostitute in British Columbia* (with Laura Fraser, 1996), *Men Who Buy Sex* (with Chris Atchison and Laura Fraser, 1997), and *Beyond Decriminalization* (with Pivot Legal Society, 2006). He has given testimony before various parliamentary committees and public inquiries, and he appeared as an expert witness in *Bedford v. Canada*.

Gayle MacDonald is the associate vice-president of research at Mount Saint Vincent University (MSVU) in Halifax and is a professor of sociology and women's studies. She has conducted research on sex workers in the Maritimes and on people living with AIDS in the Atlantic provinces, and she has published on women's resistance, sex work, intersectionality, and the sociology of law. She currently represents MSVU on a violence-prevention initiative with the community, co-led by the Nova Scotia Advisory Council on the Status of Women.

Kimberly Mackenzie is the former outreach coordinator and a current board member of SWAN Vancouver Society. She has frontline experience providing services to both indoor and outdoor sex workers and has developed an advocacy toolkit in order for service providers and the general public to better understand and meet the needs of immigrant and migrant sex workers. She has a master's degree in public policy from Simon Fraser University and is interested in social justice, intersectional feminism, poverty reduction, and community organizing.

Robyn Maynard is a Black feminist author, activist, and educator. A former outreach and support work at Stella, a Montreal organization run by and for sex workers, she currently coordinates workshops at women's prisons with the Black Indigenous Harm Reduction Alliance. The author of *Policing Black Lives: State Violence in Canada from Slavery to the Present* (2017), Robyn has been involved in community organizing and advocacy against racial profiling, the criminalization of sex work, and police violence for over a decade. Her voice has been featured in local, national, and international media, she is a frequent guest speaker at universities across Canada, and her writing has been published in mainstream and alternative media as well as in scholarly journals.

Hayli Millar is an associate professor in the School of Criminology and Criminal Justice at the University of the Fraser Valley. She has worked internationally as a consultant to the United Nations and as a gender, law, and development specialist for the Asian Development Bank. Her current research and teaching interests focus on politicized crimes like human trafficking, migrant smuggling, and terrorism.

Tamara O'Doherty is a lecturer in the School of Criminology at Simon Fraser University. Her research expertise includes gender, human rights, collaborative research methods, and legal research methods. Tamara's recent publications have focused on victimization in sex work, human trafficking, and the effects of criminalization on vulnerable populations. She has also worked with several sex worker–led NGO's and advocacy groups, such as PACE Society and FIRST, a feminist group in support of sex worker rights and access to justice in Canada.

Morgan M. Page is a trans writer, artist, and sex worker in Montreal. She has worked locally, nationally, and internationally on sex work, trans, and

HIV issues for a variety of organizations over the past ten years. A 2014 Lambda Literary Fellow, her writing has appeared in journals such as *Trans Studies Quarterly* and *Plenitude Magazine* and in antholgies such as the first volume of *Best Sex Writing of the Year* (2015).

Kerry Porth is a former sex worker and now a human rights activist. She is currently a member of the board of directors of Pivot Legal Society and a director of the Triple-X Workers' Solidarity Association of British Columbia. Porth regularly provides public education about sex work in her role as a community developer with Living in Community, and she lectures at colleges and universities about sex work stigma, activism, and prostitution law and its impacts. She was instrumental in founding EASE Canada, an education and advocacy organization for people with disabilities who want to safely explore intimacy and sexuality. She is currently the logistical coordinator of a national research project entitled Building a Partnership in Gender, Work and Health in the Sex Industry.

Menaka Raguparan is a doctoral candidate in the Department of Law and Legal Studies at Carleton University. Her research examines the lived experiences of women of colour and Indigenous women in the indoor sectors of the sex industry in Canada. She is a long-time sex worker ally, advocating for sex workers' recognition and respect as human beings and as legitimate participants in the labour force. Menaka's teaching and research interests are in critical race studies, critical feminist studies, sexuality studies, and sex work.

River Redwood has worked in various aspects of the sex industry, from street-level participation to working for mainstream porn companies. He has a long history of activist work in sexual health and sex worker and LGBTQ rights, and he has been involved with a range of organizations connected to these issues. He co-founded and ran his own alternative porn company and has produced a number of films that have appeared at gay and lesbian film festivals around the globe.

Becki L. Ross holds a cross-appointment in the Department of Sociology and the Institute for Gender, Race, Sexuality, and Social Justice at the University of British Columbia. She is a long-time activist in queer, feminist, and anti-colonial struggles, as well as an ally with sex worker and trans movements for justice and liberation. Her books include *The House That*

Jill Built: A Lesbian Nation in Formation (1995), *Bad Attitude/s on Trial: Pornography, Feminism, and the Butler Decision* (with Shannon Bell, Brenda Cossman, and Lise Gotell, 1997), and *Burlesque West: Showgirls, Sex, and Sin in Postwar Vancouver* (2009). With Jamie Lee Hamilton, Ross is a co-founder of the West End Sex Workers Memorial Committee.

Naomi Sayers is an Anishnaabe-Kwe of the Garden River First Nation with sex work experience across Canada, including northern Ontario. She is a fierce Indigenous feminist, influencer, writer, and educator. As a lawyer, she is passionate about working with Indigenous communities or organizations with an Indigenous focus. With her life experiences, Naomi enjoys inspiring others to make change possible in their world. Naomi is the author of *Kwe Today*, a blog that is regularly cited around the world. Her work is also used by national and international organizations to influence policy and law reform.

Valerie Scott always wanted to be a sex worker and has extensive experience in her chosen profession. She is a founding member and a legal coordinator of Sex Professionals of Canada, a sex worker rights organization. She has been a passionate advocate for her colleagues' human, civil, and legal rights for the past thirty-two years. She has testified before Canada's Senate and several parliamentary committees and has spoken at numerous community meetings, colleges, universities, and conferences about the need for full decriminalization of adult sex work. Valerie was one of the three plaintiffs in *Bedford v. Canada*.

Sex Workers United Against Violence (SWUAV) is a peer-based organization of current and former sex workers in Vancouver's Downtown Eastside that is working toward systemic change, including legal reform, so that all sex workers are treated with respect and dignity. SWUAV has a strong representation of Indigenous women and recognizes the legacy of colonization in the current-day social conditions experienced by Indigenous communities. Central to SWUAV's purpose and structure is the idea that sex workers can feel supported personally and politically in an organization of peers, and the issues most relevant to daily survival are at the forefront of the group's agenda.

Frances M. Shaver, a sociologist at Concordia University, has been conducting research on the sex industry for over thirty years. Since 2011 she has been involved in Contexts of Vulnerabilities, Resiliencies and Care among People in the Sex Industry, a project funded by a Team Grant from the

Canadian Institutes of Health Research. This project's team of researchers and community partners from across Canada and internationally is working collaboratively to identify key factors linked to violence and vulnerabilities. Frances was a witness in *Bedford v. Canada* (2010) and has made presentations to House of Commons subcommittees, the Departments of Justice of Ontario, Quebec, and Canada, and a variety of NGOs.

Andrea Sterling is a doctoral candidate at the Centre for Criminology and Sociolegal Studies at the University of Toronto. She is currently the chair of the board of Maggie's: Toronto Sex Workers Action Project and has been involved with sex worker communities in Montreal and Toronto since 2006. Her research examines sex work, legal knowledges, and modes of regulation and is guided by the lived realities of sex workers in her community.

Mariana Valverde was heavily involved in feminist and other politics in Toronto in the 1980s, especially around the legal regulation of sexuality. She then took these interests into an academic context and has been a university professor since 1988. She is the author of seven books and a co-editor of several anthologies, as well as having published numerous scholarly articles. Occasionally, she also writes op-eds and articles for a broader audience that are published in nonscholarly books and magazines.

Emily van der Meulen is an associate professor in the Department of Criminology at Ryerson University. She conducts community-based and participatory research in the areas of feminist and critical criminology, the criminalization and stigmatization of sex work, gendered surveillance studies, and prison health and harm reduction. Her co-edited books include *Selling Sex: Experience, Research, and Advocacy on Sex Work in Canada* (with Elya M. Durisin and Victoria Love, 2013) and *Expanding the Gaze: Gender and the Politics of Surveillance* (with Robert Heynen, 2016).

Laura Winters is a doctoral candidate in sociology at the University of New Brunswick. She completed her undergraduate studies and her master's degree in sociology at Memorial University of Newfoundland. She lives in her home province of Newfoundland and Labrador, where from 2013 to 2016, she created and ran the Safe Harbour Outreach Project (SHOP), the province's only frontline service that advocates for the human rights of sex workers. She is currently a proud SHOP volunteer and community worker in the sectors of housing and violence against women. Her work is grounded in a belief in harm reduction, social justice, and the prioritization of lived experience.

Index